Louis M. Hartwick

Oceana County Pioneers and Business Men of To-Day

History, biography, statistics and humorous incidents

Louis M. Hartwick

Oceana County Pioneers and Business Men of To-Day
History, biography, statistics and humorous incidents

ISBN/EAN: 9783337318444

Printed in Europe, USA, Canada, Australia, Japan

Cover: Foto ©ninafisch / pixelio.de

More available books at **www.hansebooks.com**

OCEANA COUNTY

PIONEERS AND BUSINESS MEN

OF TO-DAY.

HISTORY, BIOGRAPHY, STATISTICS AND
HUMOROUS INCIDENTS.

BY

L. M. HARTWICK AND W. H. TULLER.

PENTWATER, MICH.:
PENTWATER NEWS STEAM PRINT.
1890.

INTRODUCTORY.

—x—

OCEANA COUNTY, 1890.

Although still in the infancy of its development, Oceana County possesses many advantages and attractions not enjoyed by other counties in this great and growing State. It has passed from the critical lumber stage of its existence, and is now fairly entered upon a period of unsurpassed agricultural and horticultural prosperity. Washed by the waters of Lake Michigan, the heat of summer and the rigors of winter are modified, while the invigorating breezes from this great body of water fan the villages and country, sweeping away the germs of malaria, making a climate at once delightful and healthy.

The surface is high and rolling, the soil rich sand loam, heavy clay loam, and light sand. The change from one soil to another is quite marked, and often in the same section all the different characters of soils are to be found. In some localities gravel and stone is abundant, in others whole sections may be searched in vain for a pebble. There are several extensive lime quarries, from one of which, located at Shelby, lime of a very superior quality but of dark color, is manufactured. There are also several extensive clay beds, from which brick equal in appearance and quality to the celebrated Milwaukee brick, are made, the most notable, perhaps, being located upon the banks of Pentwater Lake, owned and worked by the Middlesex Brick & Tile Co.

The county is divided by a range of hills running from the southwest to the northeast, making two water basins. From the southeastern the White River, fed by numerous small tributaries, takes its way to White Lake, while the two branches of the Pentwater River, North and South, flow through the northern and central portions of the county and empty into Pentwater Lake. These streams have been the lumberman's thoroughfare in the past for transporting millions of feet of logs from Oceana's grand forests to the insatiable maw of the great mills. The tributaries to these main streams usually find their source in springs and consequently furnish waters favorable for the propagation of brook trout, or salmon. The grayling, next to the trout, perhaps, the most highly prized by sportsmen, is native to these waters. In 1878 some enterprising sportsmen purchased and planted in several of these streams 2,000 brook trout. In 1880 9,000 more were planted and in 1881, 75,000. The result of their labors has been astonishing, and at the present time the streams of Oceana County furnish the most delightful fishing waters for sportsmen. Trout weighing from two to four and a half pounds have been caught, and as many as fifty in a day by one person. With the gradual abandonment of the large streams by the lumbermen these fish are finding their way thither, and during certain seasons are found in great numbers. The time is not far distant when these streams will have a national reputation for their fish. There are several small lakes in the county which abound with American pike, or pickerel, black bass, and smaller fish of the same specie. Also muskallonge, bull-head and silver eel. The banks surrounding these lakes are usually high and being thickly studded with beech, maple, pine, hemlock and cedar intermingled, form many romantic and picturesque places. Flocks of wild duck and other water fowl annually visit these lakes.

The game of the county is of late years changing. Bear, deer and fox have fired the ambition of local sportsmen in times past. Stories of success in hunting these animals are often heard. Few deer or bear are now found although the fox is still caught. Mink and muskrat are quite plentiful. Otter and coon are often found. Partridge has always been plentiful, and of late quail and meadow larks are beginning to fill the fields with their music. Squirrels were unknown to our forests until quite recently, but are now becoming a favorite game. Rabbits abound largely in localities.

For agricultural purposes the soil of this county is adapted to the successful cultivation of a great variety of products. Hay, corn, oats, wheat, rye, barley and peas are as successfully raised here as in many of the southern counties of the State. Potatoes and all kinds of vegetables are grown in perfection. Owing to the peculiar character of the soil, potatoes are large, sound, mealy, smooth and clean skinned.

It is perhaps the adaptability of soil and climate for fruit raising that has given this section its greatest reputation. The "Michigan Fruit Belt" is a strip of territory with a shadowy interior boundary, in which peaches are grown with a smaller per centage of failures than elsewhere in the State.—(Michigan and its Resources.) This strip extends along the eastern shore of Lake Michigan from Benzie county on the north to Berrien county on the south, and being from ten to twenty miles in width. By an examination of the map of Michigan it will be seen that Oceana lies about midway between the northern and southern extremes of this belt, and it has the greatest projection into Lake Michigan of any portion of the State.

From the "lay of the land" it has a most perfect atmospheric drainage. These things, together with its strong soil, mark it as a locality peculiarly favored by nature for the successful production of peaches and plums. In the scramble for wealth through the avenues of the lumber trade which marked the early history of this county, the above advantages were scarcely noticed. A few persons, however, planted trees and were surprised to find them after a few years bearing fruit each season and of a very superior quality. The experienced horticulturist would have noted the advantages described above, but the actual settler did not realize them until brought face to face with facts. Year after year told the same story until orchard planting became the order of the day and to-day thousands of acres are covered with thrifty growing trees. For fifteen years in succession peaches have been picked from the same trees by some of those who first planted orchards. During a period of thirty years there has been only one season when peach buds were destroyed by the winter cold. In 1889 the frosts of early spring destroyed the peach buds in that portion of the fruit belt that had for many years been relied upon by the commission men of Chicago and Milwaukee, known as the St. Joseph and South Haven district, but Oceana County and a portion of Mason County escaped this visitation and a heavy crop was gathered which bro't good prices. Many a poor man with a few hundred bearing trees found himself at the close of the season the possessor of a good banking account. Fruit was purchased upon the tree in many instances for from $2 to $3 a tree, and the purchaser realized from 25 to 100 per cent. on his investment.

In regard to health, carefully kept records extending over a period of 48 months indicate this to be one of the healthiest localities in the United States. From tables published elsewhere in this work, showing population and deaths in the county, made from public records and reports by Supervisors required by law, it appears that the rate of mortality for the county is 5.91 per thousand of population. Fever and ague is very rare; scarlet fever, diphtheria and other contagious diseases seldom assume a malignant type. The source of the water supply and the natural drainage of the country undoubtedly contributes largely to the general good health that is here enjoyed.

The population of the county is 17,000. Its assessed valuation as determined by the Board of Supervisors at its October session in 1889 is $3,440,821. It has eighty-six school districts employing teachers, and four Union Schools. The school buildings as a general thing are new, commodious, and furnished with modern appliances. There are twenty church organizations having church edifices.

There is invested in manufacturing enterprises over $500,000 capital. There are four banks, five flouring mills, and six newspapers. The Chicago & West Michigan Railway traverses the county from its southern boundary to Pentwater, its northern terminus. It has one lake harbor located at Pentwater repaired and maintained by Government appropriation. The U. S. also has a Life Saving Station and lighthouse established at this point, and a lighthouse at Petite Pt. Au Sable. It has a fine large Court House building located at Hart, the county seat, and a poor farm in the same township, well improved, under a good state of cultivation and with good, commodious buildings.

Standing upon the threshold of a new era in its development it presents three prominent characteristics that have attracted general attention and which will have great influence upon its future growth and prosperity. We refer to its fish, fruit and health. It has been known in the past principally for its lumber productions, but from this time it will be known as the *center* of Michigan's fruit belt, the healthiest location in the State, and a favorite resort for sportsmen.

HISTORICAL.

---x---

CHAPTER I.—NAME.

March 2, 1831, the Territorial Legislature of Michigan passed an Act defining the boundaries of certain territory lying south of a line between towns 12 and 13 north, and gave to the territory there designated the name Oceana. This is the first public record of the State wherein this name appears, although we find evidence of its being used to designate certain undefined territory of Michigan prior to this Act of the Legislature. Who selected the name, or its signification, can only be conjectured.

It has been generally understood to denote the "watery location" of this territory. Charles R. Brown, in his Government of Michigan published in 1874 (page 30) gives the above as the origin of the name. Page's History of Oceana County, published in 1882, says: "This county received its name 'Oceana' in 1831, when it was laid out by the Territorial Legislature. As the name signifies 'lying alongside the ocean,' it may have been named from its position on the great Ocean of Waters in Lake Michigan." (Page 93.) It also says "that while it included its present limits it was much more extensive." (Page 69.) The above appears to have been the accepted idea of the origin and signification of the name, although we have been unable to find any authority in support of it except the mere fact that old settlers became impressed with the idea and gave it as the explanation. This much we do know, the name preceded to this section any of the pioneers now living in the county. An interesting fact in the study of this subject is the evident delusion that Brown, Page, and even the old settlers labored under as to the locality to which this name applied. All seem to have taken it for granted that it was first used to designate territory including that to which it now applies. By reference to Territorial Acts of 1831, page 872, Sec. 8, it will be seen the name was given to territory lying south of this and including territory that at present forms four towns in Montcalm County, eight towns in Kent, eight in Newaygo, four and a fractional town in Muskegon, but did not include any of the territory now embraced in Oceana County. The territory originally named Oceana embraced 834 square miles with only 17 miles of shore line. The present county has 582 square miles with 35 miles of shore line. The most important point of the former in early times was interior; of the latter, the shore. Hence the reason "watery location" in the light of these facts loses much of its force. Again, while Lake Michigan is one of the largest inland bodies of water in the world, it has never been designated an ocean. There is no place similarly situated on the ocean bearing the same name, to suggest it. There is a small inland village in West Virginia named Oceana, but it has a *post bellum* history, and is more likely to have been named from this county, or from a similar cause.

It is possible that the name has an entirely different origin and signification. Without attempting at this time to settle the question, we will simply give further details with reference to this name, and leave it to the reader to draw his or her own conclusions.

The word Oceana was coined and first used by one James Harrington, a distinguished writer on the philosophy of government, who was born in Rutlandshire, in 1611. He was carefully educated and having completed a course in Trinity College, Oxford, he traveled extensively, returning to England in 1646, when he was named as one of the grooms of the bed-chamber to Charles I, who was at that time being conveyed south from Newcastle as a prisoner of Parliament, Though republican in his ideas, he secured the confidence and respect of the King, who showed strong personal regard for him. On the removal of Charles to the Isle of Wight, Harrington was prevented from accompanying him, and was for a short time put in confinement because he would not swear to refuse assistance to the King should he attempt to escape. His feelings of respect also led him to accompany Charles to the scaffold the following year.—(See Ency. Brit.)

After Charles' death Harrington composed a work upon the theory of state. While this work was of the nature of a romance, it embodied his peculiar ideas of government. In this work he gave to an imaginary country the name of Oceana, and also entitled his book Oceana. His views were well known and pleased neither royalists nor republicans, and Cromwell, who was in the ascendency at that time, learning of the intended publication, caused the manuscript to be seized as it was passing through the press. Harrington, however, managed to secure the favor of the Protector's favorite daughter, Mrs. Claypole, through whose influence the work was returned to him, and which he published in 1656, dedicated to Cromwell.—(Ency. Brit.)

This work "Oceana," and the treatises, papers and pamphlets in support and defense of it, embodied the author's idea of a model commonwealth. The ideas were discussed and criticised. A club for the propagation of them called the "Rota," was formed. This caused Harrington's arrest by order of Charles II, on the charge of conspiracy. He was never brought to trial, however, and was finally removed by his friends to a small island, where in 1677 he died. For ten or more years following the publication of this work it engrossed the attention of statesmen and priests, not only of England but of France, and many of the ideas therein expressed have since been adopted by governments.

It was while the public attention of England and France was engaged in discussing this work that the young Jesuit Missionary, Jaques Marquette, of Laon, France, was preparing for his trip to America to establish missions for the Society of Jesus. As he was about to visit a country that possessed but crude notions of government, and as one of his objects was the civilization of savages and bringing them under the control and protection of law, it would be quite natural for him to take with him such published works on the theory of government as he desired, and it is not improbable that "Oceana" was among his effects. He arrived in Canada in 1666. In 1668 he founded the mission of Sault Ste. Marie, on Lake Superior, followed the Hurons to Mackinaw in 1671, and in 1673 in company with Louis Joliet, a native of Quebec, started on his famous mission of discovery. The history of his trip from St. Ignace to Green Bay, up the Fox River, through Lake Winnebago, thence to Portage, across the watershed to the Wisconsin, from this to the Mississippi, down this to the mouth of the Arkansas, back to the Illinois, up the Chicago, and finally back to Green Bay, is familiar. Also how, in the spring of 1675 he started along the eastern shore of Lake Michigan, suffering in the last stages of consumption, with only two white companions and a company of natives, stopping at places where inland waters connected with Lake Michigan, until finally on the evening of May 19, 1675, he landed and encamped on the banks of the stream just twelve miles north of Pentwater that is now known as the Pere Marquette. Here he died and was buried, after having been only nine years in America. The stream upon the banks of which his remains were interred, 172 years after the event, in commemoration of him was given his name.

Who knows but that the word Oceana, which must have been as familiar to him as any word of his language, and signifying many of the ideas of government he taught his followers, with his name and memory has been transmitted from generation to generation, until finally it is selected to mark a locality intimately associated with the closing hours of his life. If this last supposition should prove true, Oceana means "a model commonwealth."

CHAPTER II.

---x---

EARLY HISTORY.

The history of Oceana County from the earliest period of which we have authentic information to the present time, is the history of toil, privation, hardship and physical suffering peculiar to the development of a new country. In many respects the history of the settlement of one county in Michigan is so similar to that of another that a mere change of names and dates is all that is necessary to have a record of both. Prior to the year 1855, our information concerning the locality now known as Oceana County is of a very meager and unsatisfactory character. There is little doubt but that as early as 1615 Lake Michigan had been visited by French explorers. In 1668 Pere Marquette and Pere Claude Dablon founded a mission at Sault Ste. Marie. In 1671 they established one at St. Ignace. In 1673 Father Marquette explored a stream on the eastern shore of Lake Michigan to which he gave the name St. Joseph. In April, 1675, he with two white companions and some natives left the Illinois River in canoes, and coasted along the eastern shore, stopping at places where the inland waters connected with Lake Michigan, until the 19th of May, when, being greatly enfeebled by the ravages of consumption, he made a landing just twelve miles north of Pentwater and encamped on the banks of the stream known among the natives as the Not-a-pe-ka-gon, meaning "river with heads on sticks." Here he died and was buried, and after many years his remains were removed to St. Ignace, where they now repose. The river thus made historic, was over a century and a half after his death, named the Pere Marquette, by which name it is now known and designated on the maps of the State.

From the death of Pere Marquette until the year 1831 we find but little among public records concerning this territory. The little we do find is of a character tending to delay rather than stimulate development. May 6, 1812, Congress passed an Act requiring that 2,000,000 acres of land should be surveyed in the then Territory of Louisiana, and a like quantity in the Territory of Illinois north of the Illinois River, and the same quantity in the Territory of Michigan, in all 6,000,000 acres, to be set apart for the soldiers of the war with Great Britain. The following is the Surveyor General's report that relates to Michigan:

"The country on the Indian boundary line, from the mouth of the great Auglaize River, and running thence for about fifty miles, is (with some few exceptions) low, wet land, with a very thick growth of underbrush, intermixed with very bad marshes, but generally very heavily timbered with beech, cottonwood, oak, etc.; thence continuing north, and extending from the Indian boundary eastward, the number and extent of the swamps increases, with the addition of numbers of lakes, from twenty chains to two and three miles across. Many of the lakes have extensive marshes adjoining their margins, sometimes thickly covered with a species of pine called 'tamarack,' and other places covered with a coarse, high grass, and uniformly covered from six inches to three feet (and more at times) with water. The margins of these lakes are not the only places where swamps are found, for they are interspersed throughout the whole country, and filled with water, as above stated, and varying in extent. The intermediate space between these swamps and lakes, which is probably near one-half of the country, is with a very few exceptions, a poor, barren, sandy land, on which scarcely any vegetation grows, except very small, scrubby oaks. In many places, that part which may be called dry land is composed of little, short sand-hills, forming a kind of deep basins, the bottoms of many of which are composed of a marsh similar to the above described. The streams are generally narrow, and very deep, compared with their width, the shores and bottoms of which are (with a very few exceptions) swampy beyond description; and it is with the utmost difficulty that a place can be found over which horses can be conveyed in safety.

A circumstance peculiar to that country is exhibited in many of the marshes by their being thinly covered with a sward of grass, by walking on which evinced the existence of water, or a very thin mud immediately under their covering, which sinks from six to eighteen inches from the pressure of the foot at every step, and at the same time rising before and behind the person passing over. The margins of many of the lakes and streams are in a similar situation, and in many places are literally afloat. On approaching the eastern part of the military lands, toward the private claims on the *straights* and lake, the country does not contain so many swamps and lakes, but the extreme sterility and barrenness of the soil continues the same. Taking the country altogether, so far as has been explored, and to all appearances, together with the information received concerning the balance, is so bad there would not be more than one acre out of a hundred, if there would be one out of a thousand that would in any case admit of cultivation."

This report was so unfavorable that the 29th of April, 1816, Congress passed an an act repealing so much of the law of the 6th of May, 1812, as related to Michigan and provided for the taking of 1,500,000 acres in Illinois north of the Illinois River, and 500,000 acres in the Territory of Missouri in lieu of the 2,000,000 acres that could not be found in Michigan.

The effect of this report was such as to retard immigration to Michigan for many years, and to give the Territory a reputation for barrenness, sterility and a malaria infected atmosphere, that to this day remains unchanged in the minds of many residents of the Eastern States. The early western Pioneer shunned Michigan as he would a pestilential country, and after being forced by a combination of circumstances, accidents, etc., some settled in the southern portion of the State, and finding the Surveyor General's report erroneous as regards that portion, in all their conversation and letters back to friends confirmed and strengthened the report as regards the more northern portion of the State. Hence it was that the tide of development moved north but slowly.

The fine forests of timber located near the shore of the great lake first attracted the attention of lumbermen, and prior to 1831 a few white men visited this locality to determine the value of its timber tracts and afterwards, in about the year 1848, due to similar influences, the first attempt to make a permanent settlement was made. In 1831 a person by the name of G. W. Rodebough, now a resident of Jackson, Michigan, under authority of Governor Cass, visited this section for the purpose of taking the census of the Indians. He is probably the only white person living who can trace his visit to this county as far back as 1831.

CHAPTER III.

—x—

BOUNDARIES ESTABLISHED.

As intimated in the preceding chapter, the locality now designated upon the map of Michigan as Oceana County, is not the locality, nor does it embrace any of the territory of Oceana County as originally defined by the Territorial Legislature. By an Act passed March 2, 1831, the boundaries of Oceana were defined as follows: "Beginning at the point where the line between ranges eight and nine west intersects the line between townships eight and nine north; thence west to the line between ranges twelve and thirteen; thence north to the line between townships ten and eleven; thence west to the shore of Lake Michigan; thence north on the shore of said lake to the line between townships twelve and thirteen; thence east to the line between ranges eight and nine; thence south to the place of beginning, be and the same is hereby set off into a separate county by the name of Oceana." In 1838 the Gazeteer of Michigan, published by John T. Blois, and which the Legislature gave the character of an official publication by ordering the purchase of three hundred copies, thus bounds Oceana County: "Bounded on the north by the County of Mackinac; on the east by Montcalm; on the south by the counties of Kent and Ottawa, and west by Ottawa and Lake Michigan." This agrees with the Act of 1831, and at the same time shows that the territory now embraced in Oceana County was at that time included in Mackinac.

It appears that many who came from Milwaukee and other points seeking Oceana County, by chance or direction following the shore pushed through the narrow end and located in Mackinac county, supposing that they were in Oceana. That trouble occurred by reason of this is evident, as we find the Legislature on March 28, 1850, passing an Act as follows: "All that portion of Oceana County not embraced within the limits of White River in said county, and all the County of Mason be and the same is hereby attached to the township of White River." From the wording of the above, it is doubtful if the Legisture at this time understood the situation, as the Act is ineffectual to attach the territory intended to be covered.

Feb. 13, 1855, an Act was passed reading as follows, viz.: "The county of Oceana shall be organized and shall comprise townships thirteen, fourteen, fifteen and sixteen north of each of the ranges numbered fifteen, sixteen, seventeen and eighteen west, and the fractional townships numbered thirteen, fourteen and fifteen north of range nineteen west," thus defining the boundaries of the county as it exists at this time. By the same Act the following appears; "Three townships are hereby erected in the county of Oceana to be called Pentwater, Stony Creek and Claybanks. The township of Pentwater shall comprise all of said county of Oceana lying north of the division line between townships fifteen and sixteen north, and the first township meeting therein shall be held at the house of Edwin R. Cobb; the township of Stony Creek shall comprise so much of the territory of said county as lies south of said township of Pentwater and north of the division line between townships thirteen and fourteen north, also sections one, two, three, four, five and six of township thirteen north of range eighteen west, and the first township meeting therein shall be held at the house of Mr. Wheeler at the Stony Creek mills, so called. The township of Claybanks shall comprise the remaining portion of the territory of said county of Oceana, and the first township meeting therein shall be held at the house of John Barr."

From the time of the organization of the township of Stony Creek the name selected by A. R. Wheeler for the Post Office, i. e., Benona, was used by the people to designate the township, and in Feb., 1857, by Act of the Legislature, the name of the township was changed from Stony Creek to Benona.

1857—Dec. 28, the Board of Supervisors ordered the organization of the town of Greenwood by taking what is now Greenwood from Claybanks and what is now Newfield from Benona. Also that of Elbridge by taking what is now Leavitt, Elbridge, Hart and Golden from Benona.

1860—Feb. Otto was ordered to be organized by taking from Claybanks its present territory, and from Benona what is now Ferry. Weare was at this time ordered organized out of territory that now comprises the towns of Crystal and Colfax, and what is now Golden and Hart was taken from Elbridge and ordered organized as Hart.

1862—Feb. Benona was divided, and that portion now known as Benona was ordered organized as Leroy, and the portion now known as Shelby retained the township organization and name of Benona.

1864—Aug. Golden was ordered organized out of Hart.

1865—July. Crystal was ordered organized, taking from Weare what is now Crystal and Colfax.

1866—March. Newfield was ordered organized, taking the north half of Greenwood territory. The town of Grant was ordered taken from Claybanks, and Leavitt from Elbridge.

1867—March 1. By Act of the Legislature the name of Leroy was changed to Benona, and Benona to Shelby.

1868—Oct. Reed township was ordered taken from Otto, and Colfax from Crystal.

1869—March 16. By Act of the Legislature the name of Reed township was changed to Ferry.

1869—April. Township of Colfax was organized out of the territory of Crystal.

At the session of the Board of Supervisors of Dec. 28, 1858, Jas. Hanlon, Elmer H. Lord, Halvar H. Brady, A. Brady, T. Brady, Carl Schenck, H. Hendrickson, O. E. Gordon, E. Brich, P. Bentson, L. D. Eaton, L. N. Curtis, Jacob Fisher and Martin Tyson petitioned the Board to set off to the town of Claybanks Secs. 1, 2, 3, 4, 5 and 6 of Benona. As this would make Claybanks the full town 13 north of 18 west, the petition appeared reasonable and just, and the members at once voted unanimously to comply with the request. When the Board convened again in the afternoon of the same day, objections to annexing Sec. 6 to Claybanks were quite manifest, Benona not caring to lose so valuable a taxation district, and on motion to reannex it to Benona it carried, Alex. S. Anderson alone voting against the proposition. This closes the record of the establishment of the boundaries of county and townships.

CHAPTER IV.

—x—

1831 TO 1855.

This territory remained an unbroken wilderness seldom visited by a white man, unless in the Government employ, and then his work was to simply scan the country from the deck of a vessel and reporting from the vague impressions thus received. In 1840 by Act of the Legislature this territory was attached to Ottawa for judicial purposes, but it was several years before a white settler located to take advantage of the Act. In 1848 two white men, "Dr. Phillips and Mr. Hanson, took a look at the land along the beach, with a view of locating lands, and they chose the position on the clay-banks, on which their farms are now situated, for four reasons: First, it was on the beach, where all travel was; second, there existed an Indian trail from the head of White Lake into what is now J. D. S. Hanson's farm; then the land was a heavy clay loam and remarkably fertile, and there were old Indian clearings altogether of 200 or 300 acres in extent, in patches from half an acre to two or three acres. Accordingly, in 1849, settlement began, so that at the close of that year there were six families and several single men on the Claybanks, which formed the nucleus of the settlement of Oceana county. Of these the first band were: C. B. Clements and wife, Asa C. Haggerty and wife, Alex. Pelett and wife. These are all dead or removed but the wife of C. B. Clements, now the wife of Thomas Byrne, himself among the earliest settlers, and still living on the old John Barr farm. Mrs. Olive Byrne is therefore the oldest settler, and is considered a truthful and intelligent lady. A. C. Haggerty died in 1874; C. B. Clements went away, and, it is said, was killed in the war. The first settlement was then in April, 1849; next came Dr. Phillips and wife, and his father and mother in June, A. W. Langworthy, in July; Richard E. Cater, in August; James O'Hanlon, in September; Alex. S. Anderson, in November or December, all in 1849. Then followed James Fordham in February, 1850; John Barr, the first Sheriff of the county, in 1851. Of these but few remain. Dr. Phillips, Richard E. Cater and James O'Hanlon still survive. Mr. Cater was but a boy of seventeen when he landed, and reports that small-pox, in 1849, threatened to break up the little settlement. Dr. Phillips had engaged a Frenchman, probably Alex. Pelett, to help him on his farm, but as the son of Gaul had been a nurse in the small-pox hospital, in Detroit, he carried infection in his clothing, and the first to be stricken down was the doctor himself, and soon one after another was attacked, until it ran through nearly all, but thanks to vigorous constitutions and the doctor's care, they all recovered, although some will bear the marks to the grave, Cater among the rest. A. W. Langworthy is now in Traverse Bay, Alex. S. Anderson passed away December 29, 1879, and there were, in 1849, besides those mentioned, two single men, T. Byrne, still surviving, and James Flood, since dead. These all settled along the beach in Claybanks township, between Flower Creek and Whisky Creek.

The getting out of shingle bolts was also an inducement for men to come into this country, and accordingly we find that at various points this was the first thing attempted. About this time a Mr. Graham got out shingle bolts along Stony Lake and on Little Point Au Sable, and his death, in 1850, was the first death in this county. Lorenzo D. Eaton, whose widow now resides on Anderson's farm at Claybanks Postoffice, was one of the very earliest settlers. He came from Wisconsin in 1849, to get out shingle bolts, and to prepare for the settlement of his family. Accordingly we find him back in November, 1850, and after considerable hardships, he got his family into a log house, on what is now J. Gibbs' farm, at Blackberry Ridge, claimed to be the first log house in the county. But before this, in 1849, Dr. Phillips built a frame house, and his father another, used as a store at the mouth of Whisky Creek. R. E. Cater built one on lot No. 1, Section 17. The honor of erecting the first log house may be assigned to A. W. Langworthy, on lot 3, Section 17, and torn down in 1880; and the first frame to Dr. Phillips. Among the very earliest marriages, doubtless the first was that of A. C. Haggerty to Ellen Googins, who had to travel on foot all the way to White River, where 'Squire Hulbert "jined" them in the irrevocable bonds of matrimony. Truly, true love did not run smoothly even then. The Rev. Timothy Brigham, Methodist, preached the first sermon, in Haggerty's house, and on week days attended to the soles of his customers as a working shoemaker, following the example of Paul, the tent-maker, in not being a burden on the young community. The first surveyor who laid out the sections of this county was Mr. Rigdon; the first physician was Dr. Phillips, whose beat lay from Pere Marquette (Ludington) to Muskegon, along the beach—rather an extensive run of practice.

By treaty at Grand Rapids, in 1835, and the establishment of a land office at Ionia, in 1836, the lands north of Grand River were brought in market in 1839.

Then, in 1855, a treaty was made by which the tribes mentioned surrendered their land on Grand River, and agreed to select a reservation to the north, and accordingly in 1857-8 they shipped their shattered bands, seventeen in all, at Grand Haven, on board the steamer Ottawa, and Charles Mears, a large propeller owned by Mr. Mears, came to Pentwater, the young men riding their ponies along the beach, and made their way from Pentwater to their reservation in "Injun" Town. They had selected a region twenty-four miles from north to south, and six miles across, now the four towns of Elbridge and Crystal in Oceana county, and Eden and Custer, in Mason County, being Towns 15-16, 16-16, 17-16, and 18-16. The bands who lived on the Muskegon did not wish to journey far, and so they chose a town up that river, now Holton—Town 12-15.

These towns were high and rolling in many parts, in other portions were broad and deep river valleys; all was fertile, and covered with noble pine, or hardwood. Crystal streams of purest water everywhere penetrated the forests. These were alive with grayling, perch and bass, and besides this they fertilized the land, and afforded pure water to refresh man and beast.

These towns lay within a few miles of the lake, whither the Indian could go down and fish, and exchange his maple sugar to the trader at the mouth of the Pentwater. Here was a happy hunting ground for the peaceful bands of the once powerful "Ottawas," the feeble remnant of the Pottawatamies, and the still weaker Chippewas, who sold out their rights on Grand River.

This reservation—still spoken of as "Indiantown"—was chosen with care and wisdom. It was away from white men for many miles, and it would be, they fondly hoped, many years ere they would be pressed out by the fatal encroachments of the ever-restless palefaces.

Let our readers picture to themselves the life of an Indian in these forest glades that are now beautiful farms with waving fields of grain. The wild beast disputed with him the right of possession. Wolves were so numerous that it is related that one Bourget, the advanced scout of the commissioners in building the State road from Muskegon to Grand Haven, on his journey killed and received bounty money for 100 wolves, which he shot at night while he camped surrounded by a camp-fire; his custom being—famous hunter as he was—to imitate the howling of the wolves, and shoot them when they approached in the darkness, their fierce eyes glaring like twin balls of fire. The earliest records of the county contain accounts on every page for the payment of from $8 to $10 for every wolf scalp brought in. The species of wolf was the large gray kind about as large as a Newfoundland dog. The early settlers tell almost uniformly of hearing them howling and seeing their footprints. Some yet exist in Colfax.

Bears, too, were numerous, being of the common black species, and some remain even yet. We hear of some carrying off hogs in Crystal and Colfax. Bear skin and bear meat were objects of interest to our red men.

Besides wolf and bear there were numerous herds of the red or fallow deer, which found the wilds and brooks of Oceana an earthly paradise. Many are the "deer" stories told by the early settlers in all parts. Scarcely one but has been a mighty hunter, a Nimrod in those days:—Dr. Hawley, of Hesperia, gave over counting his after they numbered fifty, and Giles Townsend, of Newfield, is never tired of fighting his deer battles "o'er and o'er again." Gay, of Crystal, Sayles of Elbridge, and indeed all the white men that first came in, hunted the "merrie" deer. These deer were a source of food supply to the early Indian.

Besides wolf and bear and deer and beaver, were countless numbers of marten, coons, mink, muskrat, otter and fisher and other trapped game. The lynx and wild-cat also prowled in these woods, and, in short, nature presented here a model hunting-ground. The waters were full of choice fish; the air was full of edible birds, and wild duck and pigeon, in their season, darkened the air "from morn till noon and dewey eve;" The forest glades were full of the animals of the chase, and wild berries grew, as they do today, in countless profusion; the soil was easily tilled, and produced in abundance to the simple cultivation of the squaws and the men enfeebled by age, plentiful harvests of potatoes and Indian corn. In fact, Nature seems here to have emptied her cornucopia upon these red sons of the soil.

Such was the land chosen by the Aborigines, and the whites who have nearly supplanted them in their birthright, have reason to feel happy in their selection of a settlement.

It may be interesting to know how the Indians supported themselves in this land. We have told how bountiful Nature was, and as there were but seventeen small bands, not exceeding 1,300 in all, it will be easily understood that there was no surplus population to feed. In summer they peeled hemlock bark,—mainly for Charles Mears, of Pentwater,—picked berries and fished, and in the fall they secured their potatoes and corn, then went to the hunt and to trapping. In early spring they made astonishing quantities of maple sugar, some nearly as white as good coffee sugar, this being chiefly done by squaws and the extremely old men and the children, when the men were off hunting and trapping."—Page's History of Oceana County.

We copy the above as it corresponds very closely with our records covering the same period, and contains an interesting description of the establishment of the Indian Reservation in this county and the relations existing between the early pioneers and Indians. There are some changes from the above quotation, and additional information which will be noticed in the following pages.

The end of the year 1854 marks the close of the first era of development, or settlement, of Oceana County. Those who resided here at that time are all entitled to the honor of first settlers. They all came within a very few years of each other, and alike braved the dangers and hardships of first penetrating the wilderness of an unforbidding aspect, and a country so far as was known at that time, with an unpromising future. Some came as agents of others, who failed wholly to compensate them for their trouble, and even neglected the dear ones left behind in their care. Others came, imbued with the spirit of adventure, to discover and hew out a home for themselves. The central points of location were Stony Creek and Pentwater. The territory was designated by another name. They were without local Government, and to redress their grievances and conflicting interests, or even to get married, were obliged to go before officers of White River township. One of the Justices of the Peace of White River township at this time, whose jurisdiction embraced the territory of this and Mason counties, was James Dexter. He, although not residing in this county, by virtue of his jurisdictional authority, and the further fact that he acted as such officer in cases arising in this territory, entitles him to the honor of being the first Justice of the Peace in the county.

We will close the chapter with as complete a list as we have been able to obtain of those who settled in this county prior to January, 1855:

1849—Chauncey B. Clements, dead, and wife, now Mrs. Olive Byrne, living in county.
" Asa Haggerty and wife, dead.
" Dr. Thomas Phillips and wife, living in the county.
" Thomas Phillips, Sr. and wife, dead.
" Edwin R. Cobb, dead.
" James O'Hanlon, dead.
" Andrew Rector, dead.
" Alex. S. Anderson, dead.
" A. W. Langworthy and wife, removed.
" John Fordham and wife, living in county.
" Thomas Byrne, living in county.
" L. D. Eaton, dead.
" Otis Heycock, dead.
1850—A. Brady and wife, living in county.
" Harvey Tower and wife, living in county.
" Timothy Brigham, 1st preacher, M. E. Church.
" John Barr, 1st Sheriff, dead.
" Mrs. John Barr, living in county.
" Mrs. L. D. Eaton, living in county.
" Alex Pelett and wife, removed in 1853.

"   Lyman Flood, dead.
"   James Cody and wife, removed.
"   John Simmons, living in county.
"   Pat Jordan, removed.
"   Richard E. Cater, living in county.
"   Mrs. Rober, removed in 1854.
1852—Wm. J. Haughey and wife, living in county.
"   Woodruff Chapin, living in Silver Creek, N. Y.
"   Mrs. J. O'Hanlon, dead.
'   Owen Farrell, dead.
"   Mrs. Owen Farrell.
"   A. Huston, dead.
1853—A. R. Wheeler, dead.
——Malcom Campbell, Chas. A. Rosevelt, dead, L. N. Curtis, Warren Wilder, Estes Rich, James McNutt, Jasper Thompson, Henry Harris, Charles Blanck.

FIRST COURT HOUSE IN HART.

On the removal of the county seat from Whisky Creek to Hart, the above building, known as the old Corbin building, was utilized for a Court House until the erection of the commodious building on Court House Square, now used. This old relic of former times has been changed in appearance by the addition of a wing on one side and a shed on the other, and is now used in the business of evaporating fruit. When used as a Court House it had no side door or brick foundation, and there was a stairway at the back.

CHAPTER V.

—x—

THE EVOLUTION OF LOCAL GOVERNMENT AND SOCIETY.

1855 finds us with two principal settlement centers in the couny, one located in Claybanks near the old sawmill built by Doctor Phillips, the other where the village of Pentwater now stands.

The two settlements were sixteen miles apart, with a wilderness between. The road by the beach was the only open way of travel and at times it was very difficult to make the journey by this road on account of severe lake storms, driftwood, etc. The leading spirts of the Stony Creek settlement were Doctor Phillips, A. R. Wheelr, Harvey Tower, Alex. S. Anderson and others, while of the Pentvater settlement it was E. R. Cobb and Andrew Rector. The Claybanks settlement, by reason of its proximity to White River and ivilization, settled more rapidly than its northern rival, and when he time came, June 1, 1855, for the first Board of Supervisors to meet, it required no trick to establish the county seat at Stony Creek which was done.

The following from the pen of Harvey Tower, descriptive of the cenes attending the organization of local government, we give in is own language:

"Just how our county machinery was put in motion, I presume very few ever heard. In February, 1855, the Act to provide for the organization of Oceana, Mason and Manistee Counties was passed by he Legislature, and the first election of our county officers was held at Stony Creek (now Benona) on the first Monday of April following.

The County Convention nominated John Barr for Sheriff, Amos R. Wheeler Treasurer, Harvey Tower County Clerk and Register of Deeds. The remainder of the ticket is not remembered. Charles A. Rosevelt aspired to the office of Sheriff, and Malcom Campbell to that of Clerk and Register, and vigorously pushed their claims in that direction, but after a spirited election the whole of the regular ticket was elected. The Act provided that when, by a certain day therein named, the Clerk and Register and Treasurer-elect should file their oaths of office with each other, the official machinery of the county should begin to move, having a legal existence. On the last day of the time allowed for filing said oaths, the officers-elect, with several prominent citizens, met to consider the question whether, after all, it was not better to remain attached to Ottawa, for judicial purposes, as our taxes then were very light, than to incur the much greater expense of supporting a separate county organization; but as the people had expressed a desire to organize, by electing county officers, it was deemed best to perfect the organization.

How the oath was to be administered was a question that seemed greatly to trouble some of the knowing ones anxious to avoid any error that would vitiate the proceedings, and insisting that 'the officers must be sworn in on the Bible.' But to those upon whom devolved the duty of qualifying, *that day*, there was a matter of greater concern than the manner of administering the oath, the nearest officer qualified to do that residing at White River, full fifteen miles distant, the only road being the sandy beach of Lake Michigan. Before a conclusion was reached, the clock numbered 2 P. M., and it took another hour at least to obtain horses for the journey. About three o'clock, Tower led off mounted on his elegant "Brutus," Wheeler closely following on his less showy, but more plucky "Old Rob." Arriving at White River, after some delay Justice J. D. Stebbins was found, who, going immediately to his office, administered the oath with great dignity. Meantime the horses had rested, and the officers, full fledged (save filing their oaths official) mounted their steeds for home, which they reached about ten minutes before 12,—just time enough to file their papers before the time expired.

To say that the rain fell in torrents, would give but a faint idea of the storm encountered on the 'home stretch' of that romantic ride. I doubt if it ever rained harder since the time of Noah. The clothing of the riders was wet through, and the water ran down, filling their boots and running over in streams. Arriving at Stony Creek, we found 'the fire fair-blazing and the vestment warm,' and the new Treasurer, after his first official act of filing the Clerk's oath, came from an adjoining room with glass and decanter in hand, remarking as he appeared: 'Tower, I don't believe a little good Bourbon would hurt either of us.' What could Tower do but take a little? Ye teetotalers, say, say, ye severest, what would ye have done?"

The Board of Supervisors, composed of E. R. Cobb, Pentwater (there is no record showing the organization of Pentwater and Cobbs' election as Supervisor until the year following), A. S. Anderson, Claybanks, and Warren Wilder, Stony Creek, with Harvey Tower as Clerk, met at the house of Alexander S. Anderson, organized, ordered $300 raised for county purposes, established by resolution the county seat on Sec. 8, Claybanks, known as Whisky Creek, and adjourned.

CLAYBANKS.—This township was organized by authority of the Act of the Legislature of Feb. 13, 1855, and the first election took place on the 2nd day of April, 1855, the following persons being elected: Supervisor, A. S. Anderson; Clerk, Timothy Brigham; Treasurer, Thos. Phillips; Justices, A. S. Anderson, L. D. Eaton, James Smith; Commissioners of Highways, Asa Haggerty, L. D. Eaton and James Smith; Constables, R. E. Cater, John Fordham, A. C. Haggerty, L. N. Curtis; School Inspectors; A. S. Anderson and James Cody.

STONY CREEK.—The first township meeting was held at the house of Amos R. Wheeler, in April, 1855. Harvey Tower was Chairman, Warren Wilder and Estes Rich Inspectors of Election, and Malcom Campbell Clerk. The following officers were elected: Supervisor, Warren Wilder; Clerk, Malcom Campbell; Treasurer, James McNutt; Justices, A. R. Wheeler, Jasper Thompson, Henry Harris and Estes Rich; Highway Commissioners, W. Wilder, H. Tower and James McNutt; School Inspectors, W. Wilder and H. Tower.

PENTWATER.—The first town meeting was held in the house of E. R. Cobb, April 7, 1856, when the township officers were elected, although in the 1855 meeting of the Board of Supervisors Edwin R. Cobb appeared and acted as Supervisor for Pentwater. At the township election above mentioned the following officers were elected: Supervisor, E. R. Cobb; Clerk, James Dexter; Treasurer, Norman Rogers: Highway Commissioners, A. Rector, J. D. Green and N. Rogers; Constables, J. G. Blowers, N. Codner; School Inspector, J. G. Blowers. The Inspectors of Election were E. R. Cobb, A. Rector, N. Rogers. $150 was voted for town expenses.

1856—June 6. The Board of Supervisors met at Campbell & Wheeler's store, Stony Creek, but E. R. Cobb being absent, it adjourned until June 18, then Alex. S. Anderson was absent and the Board could do no business. The members present caused him to be specially summoned, but he refused to attend. The members present considered they had done all that was necessary and proceeded to hold the meeting. At this meeting the offices of Clerk and Register were united. A wagon road from Pentwater River to Colton's sawmill on white River, was ordered surveyed.

This year witnessed the organization of four school districts in Stony Creek. The county increased rapidly this year in population. We now find among the records of Stony Creek the names of H. Hendrickson, J. and Nels Munson, A. Brady, Dr. Ira Jenks, W. Thiele, L. Smith, H. D. Clark, L. Webber, W. H. Anderson, Wm. Gardiner, S. Merrifield, J. A. VanTassel, John Stearns, H. and J. Koster, J. Froderson, Jas. Gibbs, Mrs. J. H. Sammons. In Claybanks, H.

Brady, M. Smith, H. Wheat, M. McGulpin, M. Tyson, Peter Bowman, Chas. McCune. In Pentwater we find, Medard Leraux, Edward Brooker, John Brookshes, James Brooker, Wm. Jennings.

1857—The county now begins to assume the air of a permanent organization. In February by Act of the Legislature the name of Stony Creek was changed to Benona. In November the Board of Supervisors met. E. R. Cobb was absent, but the Board, composed of L. D. Eaton, Benona, and A. S. Anderson, Claybanks, did the county business, equalized valuations, audited accounts, fixed salaries and adjourned until Nov. 24. Cobb was still absent. C. A. Rosevelt had removed and the office of Sheriff became vacant. A special election was ordered for Dec. 29 to fill the vacancy. Also that of Clerk in place of M. Campbell, resigned, and Treasurer in place of A. R. Wheeler, resigned.

1858—April 5. The township of Greenwood was organized. The first meeting was held at the residence of Wm. R. Wilson, and the following officers were elected: Supervisor Oliver Swain; Clerk, Cyrus W. Bullen; Treasurer, C. B. Moe; Justices, O. Swain, Nelson Wright, C. W. Bullen, Amos S. Wright; Directors of the Poor, Benjamin Ish and Samuel C. Wood; Constables, Lachlan McCallum, Lyman Brown and B. Moe. School Inspectors, O. Swain and N. Wright.

On the same day, at the house of S. G. Rollins, the township of Elbridge was organized and the first election held. The territory comprised the four towns Golden, Hart, Elbridge and Leavitt, and the number of votes polled at this meeting was 15. Dr. Ira Jenks and H. H. Fuller were Inspectors of Election, H. H. Fuller and E. G. Farmer, Clerks. The following town officers were elected: Supervisor, S. G. Rollins; Treasurer, Ira Jenks; Clerk, H. H. Fuller; Justices, H. H. Fuller, Ira Jenks, Victory Satterlee and S. G. Rollins; Highway Commissioners, V. Satterlee and Nelson Glover; School Inspectors, Robert McAllister and Ira Jenks; Directors of the Poor, Alex. Black and Ira Jenks; Constables, Caleb Green and Daniel Wentworth.

In May there was a special meeting of the Board of Supervisors and we find the following towns represented: Claybanks, A. S. Anderson; Benona, L. D. Eaton; Pentwater, D. G. Weare; Greenwood, Oliver Swain; Elbridge, S. G. Rollins. The meeting was called to arrange for procuring abstracts from the U. S. Land office, but other business was transacted, among which was the authorizing a ferry at Pentwater across the channel. This was done upon the petition of Henry C. Flagg (the present ferryman) and others. A deed of land from Rosevelt and Anderson for Court House Square and contract to build jail was accepted.

The government-makers of the new county, intent upon getting the machinery of their new organization into working order for the time being, forgot that an important part of that organization was the Judicial Department until the following letter was received, which points out the necessary first steps to be taken in this direction, viz.:

JUDGE F. J. LITTLEJOHN.

ALLEGAN, May 26, 1858.

DEAR SIR:—Enclosed I send you my appointment of terms of Circuit Courts for the Ninth Judicial Circuit; please file and post copy as per note at the bottom. Will you consult with your Sheriff and order a place for holding your September term in case you have no Court House. The place should be at the county seat if practicable. Will you also consult with the Sheriff and Prosecuting Attorney and if you determine it to be necessary, see that Grand and Petit Juries are duly drawn and summoned for that term. At the proper time you will please prepare your Calendar of cases, civil, criminal and in Chancery, as also a proper Journal in blank for daily entries of the Court. I make these suggestions supposing you may have had but little practice in Court as Clerk. My address is "Allegan, Allegan County, Mich." Any information you may desire as to your official duties I will cheerfully give on your application. Trusting that our future personal intercourse may prove mutually agreeable, I am yours, &c.,

F. J. LITTLEJOHN.

County Clerk of Oceana County."

Accordingly Sept. 21, of this year the Hon. Flavius J. Littlejohn, Circuit Judge, accompanied by John H. Standish and W. T. Howell, attorneys of Newaygo, and Wm. H. Parks, attorney from Grand Haven, appeared at Whisky Creek, and the first Circuit Court of Oceana County was formally opened by proclamation of the Judge. Luther L. Alexander appears on the Records as Clerk. The Judge appointed W. T. Howell Prosecuting Attorney, and the first case was then tried. It was an action of assumpsit in which John Bowman was plaintiff and Edwin R. Cobb and Andrew Rector were defendants. It was tried without a jury and judgment for $128.17 and costs was rendered in favor of plaintiff. The first criminal case appearing upon the Calendar was the case of People vs. Richard E. Cater, trespass to personal property and assault and battery. The Prosecuting Attorney was allowed to enter *nolle pros.* Andrew Brady and Henry Hoffman were admitted to citizenship, and on the same day we find the following order made by the Circuit Judge:

"In the matter of providing a jail for Oceana County,

It appearing to the Court that there is no jail or other suitable place in said county for the confinement of persons charged with the commission of crime, and upon application thereof by the Prosecuting Attorney ot said county, it is hereby ordered, and the Court does hereby designate and order that the jail of Ottawa County at Grand Haven be used as the jail of Oceana County, also, until otherwise ordered."

September 29th, Court adjourned.

CHAPTER VI.

——x——

EVOLUTION OF EVENTS CONTINUED.

1859--The county organized with five towns, a Circuit Court, and a rapidly increasing population greets this year. At this time, however, a new element of social prosperity begins to manifest itself. Timothy Brigham, a shoemaker and an Elder in the M. E. Church, had preached to the people in Claybanks, sowing the seed of religious truth, and in 1856 Joseph Elliott, an Indian Baptist preacher, appeared among the people and formed a class of whom James Brooker and wife and C. A. Rosevelt were among the first members. Then in 1858 came a Methodist minister by the name of Naylor, and in 1859 the Rev. Beard, whose Circuit embraced Mason and Oceana counties. He perfected the organizations attempted, and encouraged the pioneer workers by frequent visits and words of cheer.

On the 5th day of April this year, the second term of Circuit Court for this county convened, with Judge Littlejohn upon the bench. In L. G. Rutherford's "Bench and Bar," published in Page's History of Oceana County, we find the following description of this term of Court:

"At this term a Sheriff seems to have been present, and that every man might be provided for, he was allowed two assistants for the term. John H. Standish was appointed Prosecuting Attorney, a position which he held for three terms. Four cases were tried, and a judgment for plaintiff rendered in each. That of Asa C. Haggerty vs. Owen C. Farrell was tried before the first jury of the county, drawn specially for this occasion, consisting of Henry Hendrickson, John Nelson, E. R. Cobb, H. C. Flagg, Allen Baker, Jason Carpenter, Lyman Flood, Elbridge G. Farmer, William Underhill and Richard E. Cater. At the September term of the same year, the first attorney (Thomas M. Brady) was admitted to practice, but it does not appear that he was ever actually engaged in practice, and the writer is not aware of what became of him."

The Board of Supervisors held two sessions this year, the first March 14, and the second December 27. It ordered the purchase of a safe for the use of the county; also the laying out of a public highway from Flower Creek to the north line of the county, near Bass Lake.

1860—The local government is now well organized. The character and mental ability of those instrumental in its formation was such that no misappropriation of public funds, or serious blunders appear at this time to embarrass the new government. It is a remarkable fact that thus far unanimity seems to have marked all the steps and the voice of wisdom to have controlled them. This year adds but little to that of 1859. Immigration increases with each year and consequently increasing advantages of civilization and society become more apparent. One mail a week, however, suffices to connect the new settlements with the outside world. This year the Rev. H. M. Joy, Presiding Elder of the M. E. Church for the Grand Rapids District, came to this county and made a special effort to increase the spread of religious truths by organizing classes at Whisky Creek, Benona and Ferry.

April 5, Squire T. Biggeras, after a two days trial in the Circuit Court by the following jury, viz., Edwin R. Cobb, H. C. Flagg, David Dill, Henry O'Niel, Adam Huston, Jas. T. Calant, Dugal Sivik, Jas. Gibbs, Jr., Henry Hoffman, D. G. Weare, L. N. Curtis, Andrew Rector, upon the charge of forgery, was found guilty. The next day affidavits by Respondent and H. C. Flagg were filed, disclosing irregularities, and a new trial was ordered. It does not appear of record that he was ever tried again.

As far back as 1849 whisky had been sold on Sec. 17, Claybanks, and occasionally at other places since, but only spasmodically and surreptitiously. No regular saloon had been established at this time, and no organized temperance effort made. Wolf scalps bro't $8. Interest on county orders which heretofore had been ten per cent., is now seven per cent. Seven towns are now organized and have representation on the Board of Supervisors. The Treasurer has a salary of $400, the Clerk $300, the Sheriff $54, the Judge of Probate $100. Hiram E. Russell heads a petition to the Board to form the township of Hart, which was granted. John Bean, Jr., headed the application to organize the township of Weare, which was granted.

1861—April 2, the township of Weare was organized at the River House, and Myrtle B. High elected Supervisor, A. D. Boomer Clerk, W. P. Harding, Treasurer.

April 9, the township of Hart was organized and the first election held at the school house, on Sec. 17. Josiah Russell, long since deceased, A. W. Peck, now an inmate of the insane asylum at Traverse City, and Dr. Ira Jenks, at present residing at Shelby and nearly blind, were the Inspectors of Election. Josiah Russell was elected Supervisor; A. W. Peck, Clerk, and C. W. Wilson, Treasurer.

The county now has a population of 1816. Eight organized towns. Pentwater has increased to a settlement of sufficient importance and magnitude to make the "want" of a newspaper apparent, and a gentleman by the name of E. R. Powell furnishing the necessary material and Frederick W. Ratzel the brains, combine and on the 20th day of April, 1861, the Oceana Times appeared, with the following salutatory:

"In assuming the responsibilities of a public journal, it is perhaps unnecessary for the undersigned to say more at this time than that he appears before you as an entire stranger, with a modest unassuming sheet, but that it is his intention to become a permanent reisdent in Oceana county, and grow with its growth, and strengthen with its strength. This is a new enterprise, started at a time when many persons would seem inclined to doubt whether it could be sustained. We have good reason to believe that it will be cordially responded to by the people, and if anything like the support is yielded to it, which should be, there can be no doubt of the entire success of the undertaking.

The *Times* will be republican in politics, and devote a large space in its columns to the local intelligence, and the advancement of the interests of our village and county. To our political opponents we shall never use harsh language, but shall rather prefer to be moderate but firm, in the advocacy of our views, relying upon all, whether political friends or enemies to give us their undivided support, knowing that the entire patronage of every resident of the county, must be given us with a liberal hand to insure us that amount of 'material aid' which will be necessary, to make the paper what it should be—a useful advocate of the true interests of the people of Oceana County. With these few desultory remarks we submit our cause into your hands, relying upon your liberal response to this undertaking for a triumphant career.

F. W. RATZEL."

The village at the time this paper appeared was known as *Middlesex*, the name given by Charles Mears to the plat of land which he recorded, and which land embraces that now lying west of Hancock street. Mears owned a large building near the present ferry shanty, with a general store below and a large Hall and store room above. The printing office was first located in the upper story of this building. E. R. Powell, mentioned above, was a publisher at Ionia, and had secured the printing of the list of lands delinquent for taxes for Oceana, Mason and Manistee counties, and as the publication had to be made in this territory he supplied the material for Mr. Ratzel with the understanding that the property would be his (Ratzel's) after the publication of the list of delinquent tax lands as above mentioned. The paper appeared without an advertisement in it for parties in Oceana County. The advertising patrons of the first issue were all from Ionia, Detroit and Philadelphia. It appeared as a five-column folio, and in general typographical appearance as well as matter, was a very creditable paper. At this time there was one paper published at Muskegon, one at Grand Rapids, one at Newaygo, and one at Traverse City.

1861—May 10, the propeller Mears arrived in Pentwater port, bringing papers from outside as late as May 4th, which occasioned general comment.

INCIDENT.—May 23, one Frank Theis, of Pere Marquette, publicly proclaimed in Lincoln, north of Ludington, that "he wished to see the Southern army under Jeff. Davis whip the North, and hoped that afterwards he would hang every republican and negro who escaped higher than Haman." He gave utterance to many other like treasonable sentiments which were lost amid the yells of the excited populace. Stones, brick-bats and other missiles were brought to bear upon Mr. Theis' cranium, and in less time than it takes to describe it, would have silenced him forever had it not been for the timely interference of one Thos. Wood, who, after much difficulty, quieted the mob by the statement that he was crazy and irresponsible. He was then quietly advised to leave the place within fifteen minutes, or hang. He left, taking it down the shore as fast as his legs could carry him. On the 26th of July we again hear of him creating a sensation. It appears that he went to Hart township and hired out to Calvin Cheney to work upon the farm. That on Sunday, while Mr. Cheney and family were at church, he broke open Mr. Cheney's trunk and taking $278 in gold therefrom, left the country. Deputy Sheriffs Wm. Webb and Wm. Merritt started at once in pursuit and tracked him into Muskegon county where they found him in custody of a Mr. Andrews. They brought him back with the money. He was brought before the Justice E. R. Cobb and committed to jail to await his trial in the Circuit Court. Here he plead guilty to the charge, stated that his name was Chas. Randen instead of Frank Theis, and on the 5th day of Oct., 1861, was sentenced to States prison for two years. This was the first inmate of States prison furnished by Oceana County.

In 1858 the settlers in the vicinity of Whisky Creek celebrated the 4th day of July in an imposing manner, but the first grand celebration of this day which gathered the pioneers from all parts of the county and Mason County took place at Pentwater July 4th,

1861. Great preparation was made for this event, as will be seen by the following list of officers which appeared on the bills:

President, Josiah Russell.

Vice Presidents, H. C. Flagg, Malcom Campbell, N. C. Smith, Elnathan J. Reed, Jas. Scott, Abijah W. Peck, Nelson Green and Seth Robinson.

Marshal, Wm. Webb; Assistant, Wm. Merritt.

Chaplain, John Fletcher.

Reader, D. G. Weare.

Orators, C. W. Deane and H. Tower.

Committee, E. D. Richmond, Wm. Underhill; Chas. Rosevelt, M. B. High, A. C. Randall, S. G. Rollins, Oliver Swain, Alex. S. Anderson, John Bean, Jr., Benjamin Reed.

July 15, a small coaster ran to Pentwater port and anchored in the lake away from the dock. The appearance of this hooker excited the curiosity of the people by its suspicious appearance and the actions of those on board. It was commanded by one Capt. McKenzie. The crew were uniformed with blue jackets and red breeches. Finally curiosity became too great and some daring citizens took a row boat and went aboard. They came back well pleased with what they found, but would say nothing to give others any information. Others went and returned maintaining the same mysterious silence as to what they saw. Boat-load after boat-load visited the craft and yet those who staid ashore remained in ignorance of what great attraction was on board this hooker. It was noticed that some visited it several times and each time they returned were more exuberant in their pleasure than before. Monday morning solved the mystery. A goodly number of Pentwater's citizens were found to be hilariously drunk. This craft had on board a cargo of forty rod whisky which was retailed out to the visitors by the drink, and in jugs, bottles, etc. Many of the citizens were indignant, but before anything could be done the captain hoisted sail and, went north to Pere Marquette, where he succeeded in getting himself arrested. This is probably the first saloon in Pentwater.

July 26, Wm. Harding, of Weare, discovered the appearance of the army worm.

Sept. 24.—An incident illustrative of early justice among the Indians, occurred on this day. The Indians on the Reservation were inclined to adopt civilized methods and manners, and when one Au-she-wou-bou-ge-sick beat a squaw by the name of Kau-tau-bausa-que so that she nearly died, the Indians instead of taking the matter in their own hands and disposing of the case, sent a delegation to the Prosecuting Attorney, C. W. Deane, who repaired at once to the Reservation and caused a warrant to be issued by the Justice, H. S. Sayles, for the arrest of the offender. The warrant was served and the prisoner taken before his Honor. The Indians from all parts of the Reservation gathered at the trial. The prisoner acknowledged his guilt, and the Justice, after consulting with the Prosecuting Attorney and the leading red men present, imposed a fine of $15 and costs. Upon this a general discussion took place among the Indians and they finally voted to approve the judgment of the Court, and all went away impressed with the justice of the decision and a high regard for white man's Court and the law.

Peaches of a very superior quality are exhibited in Pentwater, having been grown upon the River House farm owned by Charles Mears and managed by H. C. Flagg. At this time we also find an an account in the newspaper of a trotter owned by Mr. Flagg named "Nelly," record not given.

Wm. Leach is teacher of the Indian school in the old mission building erected by the U. S. Government on the Reservation near H. S. Sayles' residence, which is illustrated on another page.

Sept. 25.—A grocery store is opened in Pentwater by a Mr. Walradth, in which what was known as "wet goods" were kept for sale "on the sly." It created much excitement and the proprietor being threatened with prosecution, agreed to leave town. This is followed within a few days by a stirring temperance lecture by Alonzo Hyde, which is undoubtedly the first temperance effort made in the county. That it was effectual appears from what follows: The proprietor of the "new store" above mentioned did not leave town as he promised, but continued and did apparently a thriving business, and on the 10th day of October he was arrested and brought before Justice Graham, charged with liquor selling, found guilty and fined $10 and costs. This is the first prosecution and conviction. The temperance effort inaugurated by Hyde continues, and the new store continues. On the 25th of October the proprietor of the store is again brought before the Justice, convicted and fined $20 and costs. Dec. 13 he was arrested for the third time for the same offense. The year closes with the store still in existence, and the temperance advocates vigorously at work to suppress it.

BOARD OF SUPERVISORS, met in February of this year. A. J. Underhill appeared as Supervisor from Pentwater, and offered a resolution to move the county seat to Middlesex, which was tabled. Seventy-six inhabitants of Elbridge petitioned the Board to rescind its action creating the town of Hart, and on motion of Mr. Underhill the vote was rescinded on the ground that "it was unjust and would disfranchise the Indians." The county seat motion was now taken from the table and the vote being taken resulted in a tie, consequently failed to carry. Some doubt being expressed by members of the Board as to the legality of the vote rescinding the resolution ordering the organization of Hart, on motion, the matter was finally left with the Prosecuting Attorney. It seems that he decided the rescinding vote illegal, as the township was organized under the previous resolution.

Nov. 25 was the day set apart by the U. S. Government officials to pay the Indians on the Reservation. The Hon. D. W. C. Leach, Indian Agent, with his Assistant, a Mr. Smith, Came with the necessary funds, the week previous, to Pentwater, from which place he proceeded to the Reservation. His appearance occasioned great activity in all quarters throughout the county. Six or seven wagons were loaded with merchandise and then the procession headed by the Paymaster, started for the Reservation. It resembled a great caravan, or as the Oceana Times speaking of it at the time, says: "It might have been taken for a party of Pike's Peak gold hunters." There were J. Godfroy and Julius Houseman, from Grand Rapids, J. Morton, from Ionia, and about every business man in Oceana County, as well as many others who went out of curiosity, or in the hope of a lucky opportunity presenting itself to enable them to get some of the red man's "gunio." Indian payment was a great event for the Indians, and a greater one for the white settler. Indian payment over with, the country resumed its normal condition.

1862.—In February, Col. John H. Standish, of Newaygo, and one of the members of the first Bar of Oceana County, delivers a lecture upon Spiritualism at Middlesex Hall, Pentwater. This is the first time the doctrine of Spiritualism was taught in the county from the rostrum.

The efforts to suppress the sale of liquor having proved unavailing, on the 24th day of February, 1862, a society called the Washingtonian Total Abstinence Society, was formed with the following officers: S. Graham, President; E. B. Burrington and L. D. Grove, Vice Presidents; F. W. Ratzel, Secretary; E. R. Cobb, Treasurer.

An attempt is made this year to organize an Agricultural Society for Mason and Oceana counties, to hold meetings at Pentwater. The preliminary meeting was held and committee appointed, but before the time for the committee to report a majority enlisted and went to the war. The Agricultural Society failed because there was no committee left to make a report.

April 28, Judge Littlejohn in the Circuit Court made an order directing the purchase of Green's Practice for the use of the Clerk and Court, and closing the order as follows: "The Board of Supervisors will audit and allow its cost."

May 6.—L. D. Grove delivers a temperance lecture in Pentwater and reports 120 members of the Temperance Association.

May 30.—Improved mail service now enjoyed by the people; mail arrives semi-weekly. Meeting of the citizens of Pentwater to see about improving the harbor. E. B. Burrington starts a brick yard. A meeting of all the Masons in Oceana County is called at C. W. Deane's office July 3rd, to make arrangements for organizing a lodge.

July 20.—ANDREW RECTOR SHOT.—Orson A. Fuller, of Hart, committed an indecent assault upon a young girl 12 years of age, which so excited the populace that a crowd gathered and went to Fuller's house with the avowed intention of tarring and feathering him. Fuller received the crowd with a loaded gun that he fired in their midst, killing Andrew Rector. Fuller the next day gave himself up to Justice Andrus (not Dexter) and upon examination he was discharged, he claiming that he fired the weapon in self-defense. Immediately upon being discharged he was arrested for committing an indecent assault upon the girl above mentioned. He plead guilty to the charge, and was fined five dollars and thirty days imprisonment in the county jail.

September.—A camp meeting is held at Roseville (Whisky Creek), which is largely attended by old settlers and Indians.

H. C. Flagg, Manager for C. Mears, issues the first due bill, and the paper in referring to the event heads its item "An Omen of Relief."

November.—Rev. Ahaz A. Darling makes appointments for holding services in Oceana County.

1863.—January 9th a singing school is started at Pentwater by Prof. Nicholas.

Alonzo Hyde claims to have a full-blood Ayereshire bull and a full-blood Suffolk pig.

Farmers complain of high prices and take steps to organize a union store. This is the first attempt at organization of farmers for a common purpose.

In June of this year E. B. Clark opens a daguerrian and ambrotype Gallery.

July.—PATRIOTISM AMONG THE INDIANS.—The patriotism of the settlers had sent to the front a larger proportion of the able-bodied men of the the county than many of the older counties. The call for volunteers each time was promptly answered. On the

4th day of July this year a great celebration was held at the Indian Reservation. Lieut. E. V. Andress, 1st Mich. Sharpshooters, was present and delivered the oration to the aborigines, after whom Chief Pay-baw-me (whose portrait appears elsewhere) speaks. Louis Genereau acted as interpreter on this occasion. The speeches were made to encourage the young braves to enlist, and so effectual were they that twenty-five responded by enlisting. These, led by Louis Genereau, Jr., stepped forward and were sworn into the service of the U. S. Government. On the Sunday following Lieut. Andress marched them to Pentwater, accompanied by nearly all the Indians on the Reservation. The scene at the departure of the steamer was very interesting and affecting. Many of the squaws had come to see them off, and there could be seen the old grey-headed squaw taking leave of her son. A mother with a pappoose on her back bidding her husband good bye after the Indian manner. In another quarter a younger squaw casting shy glances at her departing brave. As the boat left the dock three hearty cheers were given to them and responded to by them. This company did good service and several times reports of the gallant conduct of its members came back. Some of them never returned, but gave their lives to perpetuate the white man's government.

October 13.—REMOVAL OF COUNTY SEAT.—The following resolution was offered before the Board of Supervisors, viz.:

"*Resolved*, That the county seat be removed either on the north one-half of Sec. No. 17 Town 15 North of Range 17 West, or on the south half of Sec. 8 of said town. And further *Resolved*, that the Board of Supervisors be a committee of the whole to locate the site on one of the descriptions above mentioned in this resolution; and further unless the said L. B. Corbin does give sufficient bonds to the said county for one thousand dollars, if the county seat is located on the northeast quarter of section seventeen in said town, said resolution is null and void, and the said committee meet at L. B. Corbin's grist mill on the last Thursday in October, at 10 o'clock A. M. to locate said site."

On the adoption of said resolution the following is the vote:

YEAS.	NAYS.
H. C. Flagg,	O. K. White,
Robert F. Andrus,	Benjamin Hill,
Andrew J. Benson,	Charles Camp.
Henry Hoffman,	
Wm. H. Leach,	
Wm. Weston.	

The Board met again June 6, 1864, and not deeming the county seat legally removed by the above resolution, the following was introduced, viz.:

"*Resolved*, That the county seat of Oceana County be and the same is hereby removed so far as a vote of the Supervisors can remove it, from its present location, and that it be located on a lot known and described as a lot containing two acres in a square form, 31 rods south of the north line of section 17, Town 15 North of Range 17 West, and bounded on the east by the now laid out township road."

The vote on this resolution stood as follows:

YEAS.	NAYS.
Henry C. Flagg,	Wm. Weston,
Wm. H. Leach,	Charles Camp,
Andrew J. Benson,	Benjamin Hill.
Oliver K. White,	
Robt. Andrus,	
Henry Hoffman.	

At the same session it was moved and carried to submit the removal of the county seat as above resolved to a vote of the people. The vote of the people decided its removal in accordance with the resolution of the Board.

From the breaking out of the rebellion until the surrender of Lee and the final triumph of the Union forces were assured, there was no wavering or faltering in patriotic spirit among the settlers. The first call for volunteers was answered with alacrity and more than the county's quota on each subsequent demand was sent to the front. No murmur escaped the people although more than Oceana's share was called for. But when in November of this year it became known that a draft for Oceana county would take place at the Provost's office in Grand Rapids, the disgrace was all the more keenly felt because of the injustice of the draft. Clubs were formed of patriotic volunteers who went to Grand Rapids to take the place of those drafted whose families would suffer by the draft. The following is the result of the draft:

Claybanks—Monroe Brown, Joseph Baker, E. W. Ferrill.

Greenwood—M. A. Frink, Alex. McLaren, Theodore Taylor, Benjamin F. Moe, James Ferguson, Edward Lore.

Leroy—Jeremiah Sullivan, Wm. J. Haughey, Martin Froderson.

Otto—Theodore Reed, Wm. B. Law, Amos W. Putney.

Pentwater—Chas. Gehrey, Wm. Ulrich, James Corlett, John Bamford, Edward B. Flagg, Wm. Lamplan, Peter Dolan, James Piper.

Hart—Milon N. Collins, Henry McQueen (deceased several months before the draft took place), D. C. Prosser, Wm. F. Lake.

Weare—Benjamin H. Cole, Henry Gay.

The Board of Supervisors met on the seventh day of December following, and mildly but patriotically offered to the State the following protest:

WHEREAS, Since the present rebellion broke out it appears that there is enlisted in the service of the U. S. ninety-four white men who were citizens of the county of Oceana, in the State of Michigan, and thirty-four Indians whom we regard as citizens of said county and State, for which the said county has never received any credit,

Wherefore, *Resolved*, That the Board of Supervisors in session assembled, appoint a committee of three to make a statement of the above facts to the Governor of this State, and request him to use his efforts in procuring for said county the proper credit, which in justice we are entitled to receive for such enlistments."

To show the spirit which actuated the people at this time we copy a resolution adopted by the Board of Supervisors at this session:

"WHEREAS, Our country is struggling to put down the most gigantic rebellion ever recorded in history, and therefore it becomes necessary to make an increase in our armies to effect the above object and to demonstrate to the world that a republican form of government can be sustained by that intelligence and patriotism which are ever the concomitants of freedom, therefore

Resolved, That in order to effect the above objects, that there be raised in the county of Oceana the sum of three thousand two hundred dollars, to be paid to men who may enlist into the service of the United States in bonds of seventy-five dollars each to the amount of one hundred and fifty dollars for each man who shall thus enlist, when he is duly mustered into the service. Said bonds shall be signed by the Clerk and Treasurer of said county, made to bear seven per cent. interest, one-half of the aggregate amount to be paid on the first day of February, A. D. 1868, and the residue on the first day of February, A. D. 1869, the interest on the whole to be paid annually, and the amount to be incorporated in the general tax."

CATHOLICISM IN CLAYBANKS.—We find record of the labors of Rev. Father Schriner, of Muskegon, in behalf of the Catholic Church in Oceana County this year, which is the first record noticed of a public nature concerning the religious work of this church in the county. At our earnest request Mr. J. G. Farrell, a gentleman of education, and the son of Owen Farrell, at whose house the first Catholic services were held in the county, has written the following church history, which adds much to our information concerning it:

"The first Catholic services among the whites in the township of Claybanks, were held in the house of Owen Farrell in the year 1857, the Rev. Father Stannus, of Muskegon, officiating. The Catholics of Claybanks then consisted of the families of Owen Farrell, John Miller, Adam Schiller, Henry Teichthesen, and Mrs. Wm. Leak. In the spring of 1868 the same reverend gentleman paid Claybanks his second and last visit, coming on foot, through what was then a trackless wilderness, from Muskegon, with an Indian for his guide, to minister to this meager flock which had not been augmented during his absence, services being held at the same house as before.

The next Catholic priest to visit Claybanks was the Rev. M. M. Marioq, of Muskegon, in June, 1862, services being held in the same place as before. During the years 1863, 1864 and 1865, Rev. Father Schriner, of Muskegon, attended the mission of Claybanks, holding services at the house of Thomas Kelley.

During the years 1866 and 1867, Claybanks was attended by Rev. Henry Reeves, of Muskegon. 1868, 1869 and 1870 by Rev. Wm. Tahken, services being held at private houses. About the close of 1870 a small school house on the farm of A. S. Anderson was purchased by the Catholics, and was found more convenient and commodious than private houses, although it but poorly answered the purposes for which it was bought.

Father Herbstrit, of Big Rapids, held services in this building, which was now (although not entirely free from irony, the writer thinks) called the 'church,' three or four times yearly, and was followed by Rev. M. J. P. Dempsey, then of Ludington, and now the efficient and talented Secretary of Bishop Foley, of Detroit.

In the spring of 1882 Montague, Muskegon Co., was given a resident priest and Rev. Louis Baroux installed as its first pastor. Father Baroux attended Claybanks mission once a month until June, 1884, when he was succeeded by Rev. Edward LeFevre. Father LeFevre, recognizing the inadequacy of the building used for church purposes to accommodate the growing congregation and its inconvenient and undesirable location, it is due chiefly to his perseverance and tireless energy that the Catholics of Claybanks now own and occupy the fine frame church built during the summer of 1885 on the farm of John Miller.

Father Lefevre was succeeded in 1886 by Rev. J. G. Wyss, and he in 1887 by Rev. Father Willigan, the present pastor of Montague, who holds services at Claybanks monthly.

The value of Church property is about $1500.00.
Catholic population, 80.   J. G. FARRELL."

1863—SUNDRY NOTES.—Anson Freeman, said to be the first white settler of Colfax appears. Hart builds a new school house.

Elbridge G. Farmer, after whom the township of Elbridge was named, while working in Tabor's saw mill was struck by a piece of grindstone, which burst, and for a time was supposed to be fatally injured. He finally recovered and is, we believe, alive and residing in the city of Grand Rapids at the present time.

Otto reports this year the organization of a Congregational church with a membership of four persons.

COURT HOUSE IN THE VILLAGE OF HART.

The above is a fine representation of the "new Court House," so-called, erected on Court House Square. This building was built by David Benham on a contract for $6,030.80, under the supervision of a committee appointed by the Board of Supervisors, consisting of David Johnson, Geo. W. Woodward, N. C. Smith, and J. A. Chellis. It was completed and accepted by the Board in 1874. Since, the building has been lengthened and otherwise improved, making at the present time a large, well arranged and finely furnished Court House, and is worth at least $10,000. There is a furnace in the basement. The first floor is arranged in commodious offices for Register of Deeds, Judge of Probate, County Treasurer, Sheriff, County Clerk, Prosecuting Attorney, and vault. The upper floor contains Court Room, Judge's Room and Jury Room.

It is situated in a beautiful park in the center of the village, containing also a jail and residence for the Sheriff, band stand, and U. S. signal service pole. Many young ornamental trees are growing on the grounds. The water works mains have been extended to the center of the grounds and two hydrants placed there. The park is fast becoming a lovely and attractive place for amusement and recreation in the summer season.

CHAPTER VII.

—x—

RECORD OF EVENTS—1864 to 1868.

The Oceana Times was loyal to the Union. Every article referring to the war that appeared in it bristled with patriotism, and from the commencement of hostilities until the close the Union flag adorned the head of its editorial column. Soldiers who enlisted received flattering notices of their conduct in battle. Touching obituaries appeared for the brave men who died in hospital or were killed in battle, and the names of those who answered the calls for volunteers were here entered, a record that will endure beyond the lifetime of the most sturdy volunteer. We find at the beginning of the year 1864 the following, enlisted by C. A. Rosevelt from this county and mustered into service at Grand Rapids, viz.:

John Herrington,   Pentwater.
Wm. Robar,   "
Henry Beebe,   "
David Beebe,   "
G. W. Faulkner,   "
Chester L. Carpenter, "
Chas. Brookfield, "
Stephen Hartwell, "
Henry M. Cook,   Weare.
Charles Davis,   Claybanks.
Anton Sever,   "
Wm. Olinder,   "
Theodore F. Reed, Otto.
Wiliam Gillan,   "
Henry Dodge,   "
Louis A. Randall, Benona.
Samuel Wing,   Hart.
Levi Power,   "

The following are the names of those enlisted by Lieut. A. Bemis:
Francis Dagle,   Pentwater.
Charles Fletcher, Hart.
Aaron S. Mooney,   "
Jesse Mills,   "
Charles Scharriett, Weare.
Nelson Glover,   Greenwood.

This filled the quota for Oceana County and saved it from draft.

Following close upon the above reports came "News from Battle," which we copy in full:

"CLAYBANKS, July 25, 1864.

F. W. RATZEL, ESQ.,

DEAR SIR:—Will you please insert the following notices:

Killed at the battle of the Wilderness, before Richmond, May 11th, 1864, private Peter S. Chichester, of Co. B, 1st Regiment Michigan Sharpshooters, aged 18 years and 7 months.

Died in Armory Square Hospital, Washington, D. C., of wounds in the head received at the battle of the Wilderness, May 10th, 1864, private Oliver E. Perry, of Co. B, 1st Regiment Michigan S. S., aged 18 years.

Killed, at the battle before Petersburg, Va., June 27th, 1864, private Francis Marion Perry (brother of the above), of Co. B, 1st Regiment Michigan S. S., aged 20 years.

Killed, near Petersburg, Va., July 6th, 1864, Sergeant John Huston, of Co. B, 1st Regiment S. S., aged 22 years.

Thus have fallen, in early life, four young men of much promise. All residents of Claybanks, they were intimate associates before they left their homes for scenes of conflict in defense of our country. Alike fired with holy patriotism, they could not be restrained; but answering the 'bugle call' and shouting the 'Battle Cry of Freedom' they went hand in hand and side by side to meet the foe. How nobly they have accomplished their task, the glorious record of the gallant 1st Sharpshooters will attest.

But they have fallen, nobly fallen, facing the foe, but not to those alone who return victors from the field of strife, shall be awarded the meed of honor.

None shine brighter on the scroll of the Nation's glory than the names of the noble Ellsworth and the gallant Lyon. Deeply enshrined in the hearts of their countrymen is the memory of those who have nobly fallen sacrifices on the Nation's altar.

Two of them were in regular standing in the M. E. Church, a relation which had not been dishonored, while reports from their officers give intelligence that the others found peace with God not long before their death. The hearts of the stricken parents are comforted with the thought that, 'though fallen, they have passed from scenes of strife below to victory above.' IRA R. A. WIGHTMAN."

Then came another call for 500,000 troops, and the apportionment for the county was as follows: Greenwood, 5; Otto, 5; Leroy, 5; Claybanks, 6; Pentwater, 12 (with a credit of 4); Elbridge, 0; Weare, 4; Hart, 9; Benona, 3. Hart was the first town to respond with her full quota, and Weare next.

In August of this year Wesley White died of wounds received in the battle of the Wilderness.

THE MUD HEN.—Charles Mears, under the impression that the north and south branches of Pentwater River were navigable if the right kind of a craft was employed for the purpose, set his inventive genius at work, which resulted in the building of the famous *Mud Hen*. This boat was scow bottom, twenty-two by fifty-two feet, with a large open space in the center. Before the machinery was placed it resembled a large catamaran, except that it was solid at both ends. In the center open place was a large paddle-wheel, a secondhand engine purchased from a Chicago junk shop and a mill boiler constituted the machinery. The cost when complete "did not exceed five hundred dollars," says Mr. H. C. Flagg, under whose directions the boat was constructed.

It was expected that this novel craft would by reason of its light draft and large paddle-wheel, easily crawl over shallow places and thus render practicable the navigation of the South Branch, at least as far as Hart. The craft was duly launched in the presence of many skeptical spectators, but she floated and was pronounced by all to be 'safe.' Her peculiar build and antics in the water caused her to be dubbed the "Mud Hen," by which name all the old settlers knew her.

It was not a success in river navigation. It did, however, possess great propelling power and for several years was used in towing logs and vessels about Pentwater Lake. In fact, it was the first tug owned and used on this lake.

The subsequent history of the Mud Hen is not without interest. It was taken by Mr. Mears to Chicago, fitted up as a pleasure craft and often chartered to sportsmen going north on a hunting trip. Finally some one offered Mr. Mears ten acres of land near Washington Heights in exchange for the boat, which he accepted. Investigation showed the title to his land to be badly mixed and consequently he abandoned all interest in it, not even paying the taxes upon it. A number of years later Chicago's rapid growth caused this land to increase in value, and some gentlemen having purchased all the other titles, finally paid Mr. Mears $12,000 in cash for his title. Thus it will be seen that Mr. Mears realized handsomely upon his Mud Hen.

MYSTERIOUS DISAPPEARANCE.—In the latter part of July this year (1864) an old gentleman from the southern part of Michigan came to this county "looking land." He was supposed to have considerable money on his person from the fact that he talked about purchasing if he found just what suited him. It was about the first day of August that he came to the house of H. S. Sayles in Elbridge and made inquiry concerning lands in that vicinity. Mr. Sayles not being at home he started out to find him, following up an Indian trail running east, and this was the last that was seen or heard from him. He was a Scotchman and was supposed to have come from Washtenaw County.

AN ADVENTURE.—The 14th day of October this year Mrs. W. H. Cheney left Pentwater, mounted upon a trusty horse, for her home near Hart. As she was about a mile from the village a man suddenly sprang from behind some bushes into the road and tried to stop her horse by grasping the bridle. He missed his hold, however, and caught the martingale instead. Mrs. Cheney noticing this gave her horse a cut with the whip and started at a gallop, dragging the man some two or three rods. He grabbed hold of her dress in the hope of pulling her from the horse, but striking her horse again he was obliged to relinquish his hold and fell by the road. She reached home all safe and sound, but minus a portion of her dress left in the ruffian's clutch.

COUNTY SEAT.—The vote on the removal of the county seat to Hart, in accordance with the resolution of the Board of Supervisors, resulted as follows:

	For Removal.	Against.
Claybanks	6	53
Weare	39	4
Greenwood	0	29
Pentwater	68	0
Otto	2	45
Leroy	3	51
Elbridge	15	33
Hart	73	6
Benona	23	2
	229	223

Thus it will be seen that through the kindly work of Pentwater Hart obtained the county seat.

HART, 1864.—The building on page 31 was first occupied this year as a county building. There were only two other buildings in the village at this time, one Corbin's boarding house and the other a house standing on the lot now occupied by C. E. Croff's residence.

The first Postmaster of Hart, Wm. H. Leach, received his commission this year.

Small pox appeared in Pentwater this year.

A school house was erected this year, on the southwest corner of section 10, Shelby, being the second in the township. This building had a board floor and bark roof. The first school house was built in 1862 on Sec. 18, with logs, elm bark floor and bark roof.

The first birth in the town of Weare, that of DeWitt C. Gay, occurs in August of this year.

School District No. 1, town of Golden, was organized this year.

In the town of Otto, this year, at a barn raising for C. Newman, a young man by the name of Edwin Barber, was struck by a falling plate and killed. He was the first to be interred in the town cemetery. Diphtheria appeared in this town, causing several deaths in the Evans family.

OYSTERS HIGH.—The members of the County Board of Supervisors while in session boarded at McNabb's store. It seems that McNabb had received some oysters but hadn't dished any up to the Board as yet. Some of the members had a failing for oysters, and one evening as the members were discussing the various problems of State in the room that was used for general lounging purposes, they were startled by the sudden appearance of the landlord looking wild and excited. Something serious must have happened—a secret plot— a crime committed—some one killed—a robbery; finally he recovered, shouting, "Say, you fellers! where's them oysters?" Blank expressions of wonder appeared upon the countenances of some, but three of the members were noticed to chuckle slightly. Pointing his finger at the three he said "there you are," and retreated. When the Board assembled the next morning the following bill was among the accounts:

Oceana County to Landlord, Dr.

To Keg of Oysters stolen by B., F. and M $5 00
There being but nine oysters in the keg, I deduct 50

Leaving Balance $4 50

As the members did not wish the matter to go upon the records they compromised with him.

1865.—All the machinery of government is in good working order. Settlers are constantly arriving and centers of population begin to appear in various parts of the county. The first store is built in Hart village this year, the first shingle mill in Pentwater. The war is closed and the soldiers who escaped its ravages return home again. The events of the year are without special interest. The liquor selling continues, and Mr. Hyde's temperance efforts redoubled. An excitement over the reported discovery of oil near Pentwater is occasioned, but soon subsides to break out again at intervals for several years following. The pigeons appear and make business brisk during their stay. John Bean, Jr., in June of this year ships the first sawed shingles from Pentwater. The Board of Supervisors purchase the Orange Ward farm of 160 acres, now owned by A. D. VanWickle, for $4,800, and engage Mr. and Mrs. Ward as overseers of the farm at $50 per month. Goodsell Bros. start a hardware store in Pentwater, and a call was made in September for a meeting of all the Masons in Oceana County at C. W. Deane's office for the purpose of organizing a lodge of that fraternity.

Peaches and plums fill the markets. At a meeting of the Board of Supervisors in December of this year an attempt was made to remove the county seat to Middlesex which was defeated by one vote. The first barber shop is opened in Pentwater by Geo. Elms. General prosperity is enjoyed at the close of the year.

1866.—Oil excitement breaks out early this year at both Hart and Pentwater. A feeling of rivalry between the two places begins to manifest itself. There are now 87 scholars enrolled at Pentwater public schools. Another attempt was made this year to organize an Agricultural Society. On settlement with the County Treasurer Oliver Swain, a deficiency in his accounts of $854.58 is found, and by resolution the Prosecuting Attorney is instructed to collect the same of Mr. Swain by April following, or prosecute him. A gambling den is discovered in Pentwater and broken up. Rev. Amos Dresser now takes part in the temperance work. He reports 336 names to the Washingtonian pledge. Aug. 14 of this year occurs the first meeting of Masons in Pentwater. Aug. 26. the M. E. Church (since destroyed by fire) was dedicated. The county sells its Poor Farm to A. D. VanWickle for $3,500. The village of Pentwater becomes greatly excited over the selling of diseased meat by its butcher. Oct. 12 Wm. Tuttle commits suicide. In November Goodsell Bros. establish a foundry in Pentwater. The year closes with numerous whisky prosecutions started.

ANECDOTE.—During the month of November, 1866, the Hon. A. B. Turner, of Grand Rapids, then as now editor and proprietor of the Grand Rapids Eagle, having a curiosity to learn something concerning the new territory north, made a trip through Oceana county in the U. S. mail stage. Being a gentleman of intelligent appearance, well dressed, and accompanying the mail, making frequent inquiries of the settlers, he was taken to be a government officer and as such looked upon as an important personage. Afterwards writing of this trip, he says:

"We draw up at a Postoffice. Here we are glad to get off and warm while the mail is changing. The contents of a large bag are emptied on the floor, and the Postmaster and his wife are down in the necessary posture, assorting the packages. We are in Oceana county from which we have not heard the result of the election, and we open a conversation thus:

'Are you the Postmaster here?'

Receiving an affirmative reply, we ask:

'How are political matters with you?'

Evidently understanding the question as referring only to himself and family, he promptly answers:

'We are republicans, sir.'

'Don't you support President Johnson?'

'No, sir' (very curtly).

Assuming an air of as much solemnity as possible, we remark that the President has a right to the support of the office-holders of the country, and that support is expected.

The P. M. here raises himself to an erect position, full six feet high, and giving us a withering look, square in the face, emphatically says:

'Sir, we don't keep principles for sale here; but you can have the office if you like.'

The wife keeps her recumbency, but pauses in her work long enough to give us a searching look over her spectacles and ejaculates:

'Guess you'll have hard work to find a Johnson man on *this* road to make a Postmaster of.'

Our solemnity here gives out, but before an explanation can be made, to satisfy our friends that we are not an agent of the President on a 'bread and butter' mission we resume our seat in the stage and proceed northward."

1867—February.—Contract for building a new jail was let to H. C. Flagg on behalf of Charles Mears for $3,500. At the December term of the Board of Supervisors the committee reported the jail completed. In accepting it the Board unanimously expressed its appreciation of the manner in which the job was completed.

VILLAGE OF PENTWATER.—By special Act of the Legislature, approved March 16, 1867, the village of Pentwater became incorporated, and on the 8th day of April following held its first election. There were two tickets in the field, viz.: a union ticket, and working men's ticket. C. W. Deane for President and Oliver P. Cook for Assessor were upon both tickets. The number of votes polled was 181, and resulted as follows:

President,	C. W. Deane	176
	Scattering	5
Recorder,	H. Douville, W. M.	122
	E. B. Flagg, U	59

Treasurer,	John Highland, W. M.			109
	Bennett J. Goodsell, U.			71
Assessor,	Oliver P. Cook			181
Trustees,	D. C. Pelton,	2 years,	W. M	110
	I. N. Lewis,	"	"	118
	Wm. H. Merritt	"	"	89
	Jas. J. Kittridge, 1 year		"	121
	A. Bryant,	"	"	107
	J. M. Lacy,	"	"	73
	H. C. Flagg,	2 years,	U.	81
	A. B. Judd,	"	"	68
	A. J. Underhill,	"	"	66
	G. W. Maxwell, 1 year,		"	61
	John Bean, Jr.,	"	"	83
	James G. Gray,	"	"	60
	Scattering			17

This made the first Board, Deane, Pelton, Lewis, Kittridge, Bryant, Bean and Merritt. Politically Bean and Merritt were democrats and the others republican. The result was hailed by the workingmen as a great victory, and in the evening, jubilant over their success they turned out *en masse*, formed a procession and headed by a martial band marched through the streets cheering and firing guns. The procession halted in front of different residences of their elected candidates, gave three cheers and marched on. This was kept up until about eleven o'clock when the crowd dispersed. Thus ended the first election of the village of Pentwater, the first village of the county.

May 17.—Edwin R. Cobb visits Pentwater and threatens the people, residing in the village who trace their titles to Charles A. Rosevelt, assignee of Cobb & Rector, with suits. He had previously brought suits claiming that he had been defrauded of his rights and property by Rosevelt, but had been defeated. At this time he threatened to commence again on another basis. As the matter was afterwards adjudicated in both county and U. S. Courts, we will give the history of this celebrated legal contest over Pentwater titles under a separate head.

June 18.—DeHaven's Imperial Circus visits Pentwater and as it is the first "show" that has ever visited the county, it draws the people from all sections. The paper in speaking of the event estimates that over one-half of the county's population was in Pentwater on that occasion. The red men with squaws and pappooses were all out in force.

July 4.—Hart village has its first celebration. It consists of dinner in the woods, speaking, music, etc.

July 5.—For the first time a daily mail is now enjoyed at Pentwater. This improvement in mail service is hailed as an omen of future prosperity, and real estate suddenly takes an upward boom.

BASE BALL.—With the progress of events we here notice the organization of a Base Ball Club at Hart, which being the first regularly organized club in the county we herewith give the list of officers, viz.: President, Wm. Wigton; Vice President, L. G. Rutherford; Secretary, W. H. Leach; Treasurer, T. J. Main; Directors, Edward Stone, M. A. Luther, John Dagle, John F. Cloud. This club was appropriately named the "Pioneer Base Ball Club."

CIVILIZING THE INDIANS.

Through statistics furnished by David K. Foster, himself a half-breed and a teacher of the Government school at Crystal, we are enabled to ascertain the success of the Government in its efforts to civilize the Indians in this section.

The following account of how the Indians came to this county is found in Page's History, viz.:

"The Indians assembled at Grand Haven early in the fall of 1857 and were transported to the number of perhaps 700 or 800 with their goods to Pentwater by the side-wheel steamer Ottawa, owned in Grand Haven. When they landed, as many of them came from inland towns, they were much struck by the great sand hills, and camped for a time around Pentwater Lake before going up to their reservation. It was a remarkable sight to see how they would disport in the sand hills—to see two nearly nude figures lock arms and roll over and over from the top until they would land in the water. They found at that early day around Pentwater plenty of hunting and fishing.

In the summer of 1858 the propeller C. Mears, owned by Charles Mears, brought the balance of the Indian bands from Grand Haven to Pentwater—about 500 or 600, making in all about 1,300. The men rode their ponies along the beach. The principal chiefs were Peshosiky, whose other name was Henry Clay, or the great orator; Cob-moo-sa, *i. e.*, Great Walker; Shaw-be-co-ung, or 'wings,' meaning that he could soar as an orator; Pay-baw-me, who was a Catholic and a lay reader; Cob-moo-sa being a pagan to the day of his death, which happened when he was over 100 years old. Shaw-be-co-ung was an Episcopalian, and was a good talker. Louis Genereau was an interpreter and was half French. He was a Methodist Episcopalian, but changed in his old age to Catholic, and married Pay-baw-me's widow. Joseph Elliott, who with Genereau lived in Elbridge, was a full-blooded Indian and an interpreter. He was a Methodist, and it is said that he preached with considerable fluency. He gave the first sermon ever preached in Pentwater in C. Mears' boarding-house, the 'boys' to the number of 100 being present, and paying in pork and potatoes as their tithe."

The Government caused Indian school houses to be built, one on the northwest corner of Sec. 11, township of Elbridge, called the Pay-baw-me school house, one on the northwest corner of Sec. 17, called the Genereau, one on the northeast corner of Sec. 27 of the same township called the "Cob-moo-sa," and one in Crystal. S. Fletcher had the contract for building these school houses and Josiah Russell and son George worked with him in constructing them.

THE PAY-BAW-ME SCHOOL HOUSE.

This was located near H. S. Sayles' place, which has always been a favorite place of rendezvous for the red man. The Government teachers were James Haley, an Irishman and a strict Catholic who came from Detroit. Mrs. H. S. Sayles, of Elbridge, and Eliza Foote, an estimable lady who now resides in the city of Lansing.

The Cob-moo-sa school was taught first by the Rev. D. R. Latham; then by John Bean, Jr., who was followed by Mrs. Arial Crosby.

The Genereau school was taught by W. H. Leach, D. W. Crosby and John Smith, the latter being an Indian.

The Crystal school was taught by D. K. Foster, a half-breed, and Charles Selkirk.

Mr. D. K. Foster gathered statistics showing the enterprise of the Indians of Mason and Oceana counties in adopting civilized methods, from the first day of July, 1866, to the first day of July, 1867, and filed the same with the Government. From his report we take the following:

Bushels of	Wheat	raised		825
"	Buckwheat	"		150
"	Corn	"		7,738
"	Potatoes	"		11,931
"	Turnips	"		87
"	Oats	"		1,482
No. of Ponies				131
"	Cattle			54
"	Swine			160
"	lbs. Maple Sugar made			26,000
"	Log Houses built			126
"	Frame Houses			2
"	Bark Wigwams			10
"	Deaths			15
Value Lands Sold				$3,220

1867—FRUIT.—For several years fruit of a very superior quality had been supplying the local markets and exciting the admiration of all. It even caused many to predict at this time Oceana's great future as a fruit producing section, still very few made any attempt even to cultivate fruit on a scale commensurate with the advantages of the county, already apparent. The men who supplied the markets with fruit at this time are with one or two exceptions, the men who are recognized as the leading horticulturists of today.

In September of this year wagon loads of peaches, plums and pears were brought to Pentwater and sold to hookers, merchants and people of the village. Myrtle B. High at this time was raising plums on section eight in Weare. He had also been very successful in raising peaches on this place. E. B. Burrington, who also lived in Weare, had an orchard that produced very fine peaches, and the River House farm then was regarded as the model fruit farm. The trees were literally breaking down with peaches, and they seemed to bear every year. The choicest varieties came from this farm where to-day not a half dozen peach trees can be found, and where fruit men of to-day regard as the most unfavorable locality to be found in the county for fruit raising. Mr. Mears shipped from this farm to Chicago in 1867 over 500 bushels of peaches.

W. P. Harding, of Weare, also raised a large quantity of fruit this year, his pears exciting universal admiration. The River House peach orchard above referred to had been set out just five years, and this year the average yield was one bushel per tree.

CONGREGATIONAL CHURCH.—In November of this year the first church bell of the county arrives by vessel and is placed upon the dock. Every man, woman and child of the village visits the dock during the day and inspects this new evidence of civilization. Each visitor tested it by striking it with a hammer or some other hard substance, and a continual ding dong was heard all day and late in the evening. On the 30th day of Jan., 1868, the new church edifice which this bell was to adorn, was dedicated with appropriate services, the sermon being delivered by the Rev. H. A. Reed, of Marshall, assisted by several other ministers. Mr. E. D. Richmond presented it with a new organ, and the Rev. Amos Dresser was installed as the first minister of this church.

BENONA—The township of Leroy is changed to Benona. This township is getting to be an important commercial town. A bridge pier was built which increased the trade largely, and was said to be one of the best on the lake shore at the time. Robert Rogers was the builder of this pier, which cost $12,000. When completed there was fifteen feet of water at the end of it. Four steam vessels stopped at the pier daily. There was a good wagon road from this point to Shelby, Otto, Greenwood, and other points of the county interior. Building progresses finely, and village lots are selling rapidly.

SUNDRY NOTES.—In July H. H. Woods puts in the first soda fountain at Pentwater. In November the schooner Kate Doak is wrecked and two lives lost.

CHAPTER VIII.

—x—

RECORD OF EVENTS—1868 to 1873.

TEACHERS' INSTITUTE.—The first organized session of the teachers of the county as a County Teacher's Institute was held at Pentwater, the session concluding on the second day of January, 1868. It was largely attended, excited great interest, and gave a new impetus to educational matters all over the county.

There is little of special importance that occurs this year, and we condense briefly the minor events as they occur, viz.: In December a winter stage line is established between Pentwater and Whitehall by Roddy & Collins.—A. M. U. express office is opened in Pentwater with E. D. Richmond as agent.—The Chapter R. A. M. organized at Pentwater.—A sash and blind factory running, Nickerson & Lewis props.—We hear of the firm of Maxwell, Sands & Co. quite often in connection with the manufacture of shingle.—A Lodge of Good Templars is organized and officers installed at Hart.—The coldest day of the winter of 1867-8 the thermometer showed $2\frac{1}{2}°$ below zero.—Agricultural and Mechanical Association organized at Hart.—Pentwater is designated a Port of Entry, and L. D. Grove appointed U. S. Deputy Collector of Customs.—The Oceana Times enlarged to a seven column folio.—E. Rice starts a newspaper in Pentwater named the Democrat.—The schooner Travis, of Pentwater, wrecked Sept. 2, off Grand Haven, and two lives lost.—Goodsell Bros.' foundry burned Oct. 31.—T. R. Evans organizes a brass band in Pentwater.—In December Goodsell Bros. commenced rebuilding the foundry.—Dec. 26 John Rowe was drowned in Pentwater Lake.—The salary of the Circuit Judge being only $500, the Board of Supervisors votes $100 to the Hon. Moses B. Hopkins.

1869—HART.—This village has increased in population and business since our last mention of it.—Messrs. Culver & Slater have a hardware store here with a large trade.—M. R. Chadwick has built a building for a drug store.—Moore's Hotel is running with B. Moore as landlord.—White & Knox are engaged in a general merchandise business.—J. K. Flood & Co. are running a drug store.—B. F. Huff is engaged in general merchandise trade.—Also W. H. Cheney, M. L. & W. Leach, and Stover and Britton have a boot and shoe shop.—The county business in all its departments has increased, which makes business at the county seat lively during sessions of the Circuit Court or Board of Supervisors.—April 30 of this year the Oceana County Journal appears with Judson L. Palmiter as editor and proprietor.

JUDSON L. PALMITER.

Mr. Palmiter had been many years an editor at Kendallville, Indiana, and having purchased the material of the Ionia Democrat, brought it to Hart and started the publication of the Oceana County Journal, a seven column folio, and republican in politics. This paper had what was then styled "patent insides," and was thus the first county paper to make use of ready print sheets. Mr. Palmiter, who thus appears before Oceana County people for the first time, was destined to become a prominent factor in its development. A sketch of his life appears under another head.

RAILROAD TALK.—The people became excited over projected railroads having Oceana county as an objective point. The Lansing, Ionia & Pentwater Railroad began early in the season to coquette with the people for right of way, bonus, etc. Later the Grand Rapids & Northern road sent its agents out among the people, and then the L. S. R. R. presented its advantages and claims. Each line had its friends. Meetings were called and committees appointed who held conferences with the railroad officials for the different lines reported, but nothing was done beyond making surveys and a great amount of speculation. The year dies and with it all hope of securing a railroad.

JUDGE HOPKINS.—In September of this year Judge Moses B. Hopkins was taken ill and the next regular term of Court was not held. On the 31st day of October he died. His death was due to a cold caught by exposure to inclement weather in making his appointments. A sketch of his life appears in the chapter entitled "Bench and Bar." His death left the office of Circuit Judge vacant.

Augustine H. Giddings was appointed Circuit Judge to fill the vacancy occasioned by the death of Judge Hopkins. Mr. Giddings was a gentleman of commanding appearance, courteous in his bearing, firm in his convictions of duty, dignified upon the bench, impartial and just in his decisions. He was a graduate of Yale College, and was at the time of his appointment regarded as one of the brightest and most promising lawyers of the State. His appointment was a happy one for this county, as it at once elevated the standard of legal ethics and secured for the Courts of law the proper respect of litigants and attorneys.

AUGUSTINE H. GIDDINGS.

THE NEWSPAPERS.—From the time the Oceana County Journal was first issued at Hart, a bitter rivalry began to be manifested between that paper and the Oceana Times. This rivalry manifested itself in scathing editorials by the respective editors, bristling with strong personal allusions. This was kept up until Nov. 1st of this year, when Judson Palmiter, of the Journal purchased the Times and forming a copartnership with Amos Dresser, Jr., on the 12th day of November the Times appeared with Palmiter & Dresser as proprietors, and Amos Dresser, Jr., as editor. The personal sketches of these persons appear elsewhere under head of "The Press." The Democrat, which was started the year before, did not survive the year out, and 1870 dawns with the two papers, Times and Journal, under practically the same management.

MIKE HAYES. Many of the old settlers will remember this character. He was a powerfully built man, quiet and harmless when sober, and a good hand in the lumber woods, but a perfect terror to the community when intoxicated. He used to visit Pentwater periodically, fill up with liquor and then set about destroying property, fighting and otherwise terrorizing the people. His total disregard of the consequences of his acts made him an individual to be feared, and officers were loth to make complaint or attempt to arrest him. Finally, however, about the latter part of July in this year, a warrant was issued for "big Mike" as he was called, and placed in the hands of James Roddy, Constable, himself a powerful man and without fear. A tragedy was expected when Roddy started to make the arrest, but for some reason Mike quietly surrendered without a struggle. Roddy took possession of a large club which Mike had and started with him for the Justice's office. On the way Mike slyly drew a large knife and was slyly watching a favorable opportunity of plunging it into the officer's breast, when some one warned Roddy of his peril. He quickly turned about and brought the club he had taken from Mike upon his head with terrific force, felling him to the ground like an ox, making an ugly scalp wound and rendering him unconscious. He was finally taken to the Doctor's, his wounds dressed, then to the Justice's office, where he plead guilty and was fined. This event seemed to break his spirit, and although afterwards he was several times arrested for disorderly conduct, his power as a terrorizor had passed. Liquor made a total wreck of him in a few years, and he finally dropped out of the community. Several years later report came that he was dead but this was denied by some who were well acquainted with him.

1870—THE RAILROAD.—The Michigan Central through James F. Joy, took hold of the railroad project and made the citizens a proposition, which at a public meeting called for the purpose, was fully endorsed and all other projects at once disappeared. The name of the railroad was Grand Rapids & Lake Shore. This Company was organized in February, 1869, made survey of route from Grand Rapids to Whitehall. The Company proposed if $30,000 stock should be pledged, to organize in February, 1870, a road through to Pentwater. In January of this year the following stock was reported pledged:

Name.	Address.	Shares.	Amt.
Outside the County		163	$16,300
A. A. Darling	Hart	2	200
L. G. Rutherford	"	2	200
Barnard Putney	"	1	100
John Grosse	"	1	100
W. J. Britton	"	1	100
W. D. Markham	"	1	100
James K. Cooper	"	1	100
Richard Chadwick	"	1	100
E. L. Craw	"	2	200
C. P. Miller	"	1	100
Frank Markham	"	1	100
J. W. Hiles	"	2	200
B. J. Beers	"	2	200
David Benham	"	2	200
Carried Forward		183	18,300

Name.	Address.	Shares.	Amt.
Brought Forward		183	$18,300
E. B. Clark	Pentwater	3	300
A. Dresser, Jr.	"	3	300
A. J. Griffin	"	2	200
L. W. Steffy	"	2	200
G. W. Imus	"	2	200
E. L. Craw	"	18	1,800
J. Bean, Jr.	"	7	700
E. N. Dundass	"	2	200
A. Turner	"	5	500
L. E. Payne	"	1	100
B. J. Goodsell	"	3	300
Charles Flood	"	2	200
Samuel A. Browne	"	18	1,800
James G. Gray	"	2	200
A. J. Underhill	"	3	300
Geo. Goodsell	"	3	300
H. C. Flagg	"	3	300
E. Nickerson	"	2	200
R. C. Kellogg	"	2	200
E. L. Craw	"	11	1,100
R. F. Dundass	"	1	100
James Ellsworth	"	1	100
S. W. Pomeroy	"	1	100
J. Reid	"	5	500
L. D. Grove	"	2	200
E. L. Craw	"	5	500
A. Bryant	"	3	300
E. L. Craw	"	5	500
Total		300	$30,000

A subscription is also in circulation, pledging additional aid to the road, provided it shall be completed to Pentwater on or before the 1st day of June, 1871.

At the meeting in Pentwater where the above Pentwater stock was taken, John Bean, Jr., A. J. Underhill were appointed delegates to attend the annual meeting at Grand Rapids on Feb. 3rd, and James G. Gray and H. C. Flagg a committee to draft letter of instructions and credentials. The delegates attended and returning, made the following report, viz.:

PENTWATER, Feb. 5, 1870.

MR. EDITOR:—Having been chosen a delegate to attend a meeting of Stockholders and Directors of the Grand Rapids & Lake Shore Railroad Company, convened at the city of Grand Rapids the 3rd inst., I ask permission to communicate, through your paper, to the people of Pentwater, an account of the proceedings of that meeting and also what appears to me to be the prospect of our getting a railroad into Pentwater.

After making inquiries as to the propositions and purposes of the Michigan Southern Railroad Company, I came to the conclusion that it would not pay to seek after new projects, but ascertain if the Grand Rapids & Lake Shore Railroad Company had the men and means to carry out their project of building their road. I have become well satisfied that the Company is composed of good substantial men; that the Michigan Central Railroad Company is in earnest about the building of this road; and that it rests with the people of Oceana County to say whether it will be built or not. We are asked to raise by municipal donation, ten per cent. upon our assessed valuation of the towns along the line, to aid in preparing the road bed between this place and Whitehall; and after having shown a disposition to do what we are able, I have no fear but that the balance of the funds necessary to complete the grading of the road, will be supplied on very short notice. I am assured from sources that we can rely upon, that the balance will be subscribed in forty-eight hours, after it is found to be necessary in order to make up a deficiency of seventy-five or one hundred thousand dollars to complete the road from here to Whitehall.

The meeting at Grand Rapids was well attended; All appeared to be in earnest, and their looks and actions meant business. The meeting was called to order by Hon. Lowell Hall, President. Directors present, W. F. Wood, H. J. Hollister, Thos. Iiffon, Geo. Sinclair, and represented by proxy S. R. Sanford, Chauncy Davis, and several others. There was in attendance—several stockholders, a good delegation from Hart, and Mr. Bean and myself from Pentwater. The delegations from Pentwater and Hart were invited to state their views in regard to the extension of this road, and as to the probable amount of aid that would be given: which was responded to by Bean and myself, and Mr. Russell and Rutherford from Hart, stating that aid by the way of stock subscription and municipal donation, could be relied upon to the amount of eighty thousand dollars in Oceana County. Several gentlemen stated that the proposition of Oceana County was liberal, and if that amount could be relied upon, no difficulty would be found in obtaining subscribers for the balance of funds necessary to complete the grading and laying of ties. The charter was then amended so as to read as follows:—

'The said railroad is to commence at such point in the city of Grand Rapids, as the President and Board of Directors shall determine; running thence to the village of Lamont. thence to the village of Nunica, thence to Fruitport, thence to Muskegon, thence to the village of Whitehall, thence to the village of Pentwater, by the way of section seventeen in township of Hart, Oceana County.'

A committee of three was appointed to draft by-laws and present same at the next meeting of stockholders. L. Patterson, H. J. Hollister, and Mr. Nelson were named as such committee.

The President and Mr. W. F. Wood were appointed as committee to employ Mr. Brewster, to commence the survey immediately, between Whitehall and Pentwater.

The Secretary was directed to notify all the stockholders not present, of the meeting to be held on the 9th inst.

One Director was appointed for Hart, and one for Pentwater, which will be chosen at the next meeting. It now remains for us of Oceana County to do what we are able to do in this matter, and we need have no fear as to the result, knowing as we do, that we have the Michigan Central Railroad Company to back us up, and that it is their object and purpose to reach Pentwater harbor.

    Respectfully Yours,   A. J. UNDERHILL."

On the 17th of February Ransom Gardner, in the interest of the Lake Shore R. R., visited Pentwater. A mass meeting was called and he stated the advantages to the county of his line. He was accompanied and assisted by Senator Williams, of Allegan, E. P. Ferry, of Grand Haven, and L. G. Mason, of Muskegon. The citizens desired Mr. Gardner to make his proposition in writing, which he did as follows, viz.:

"COSMOPOLITAN HOTEL, WHITEHALL, MICH., Feb. 17, 1870.
To the Citizens of Pentwater—Gentlemen:

Providing your people decide to give your aid and undivided support in favor of Our Road, upon receiving official notice of such decision, and the aid being secured to the legal amount allowed to be voted by the respective towns through which we pass, and such reasonable amount of stock subscriptions as you may be able to take, we *shall at once commence the construction of Our Road* north from Muskegon, and we are able to pledge you its completion to your place upon the same liberal terms for traffic and travel, as we have already secured, and at as early a date as the time already named, viz.: Oct. 1, 1871, and earlier if possib'e.

It now rests with you when we shall commence.

    Respectfully Yours, &c.,   R. GARDNER,
              Pres't M. L. S. R. R. Co."

Having obtained this letter, correspondence was had with Mr. Joy, and as a result the Grand Rapids and Lake Shore R. R. pledged the completion of the road through to Pentwater by July 1, 1871, and at a meeting held in Hart, March 21, at which Josiah

Russell was Chairman, the G. R. & L. S. R. R. was decided upon as the one the people would support. But it seems that the people were still divided in their preferences, and another meeting was called at Pentwater early in April, at which it was practically decided to vote the aid for the G. R. & L. S. R. R. The result of the vote at the polls was largely in favor of aid to the railroad, and this settled all further controversy. The contracts were let for grading, and active work all along the proposed route commenced.

Shortly after the election voting bonds to the railroad, the Supreme Court decided the law permitting such action unconstitutional, which had a tendency to discourage further efforts in building.

Private subscriptions were at once solicited and the work progressed.

During the season an agreement was entered into between the three companies on the shore of Lake Michigan between Manistee and New Buffalo, to consolidate under one management. The road between New Buffalo and Pentwater to be completed Jan. 1, 1871, and the link between Pentwater and Manistee to be completed afterwards. The new organization to be known as the Chicago & Michigan Lake Shore Railroad Co.

The amount of aid voted at the spring election and affected by the Supreme Court decision was $16,300. The Company agreed to accept $10,000 in stock and donation outside of the amounts given by S. A. Browne, Charles Mears and Maxwell & Caswell and to complete it by June 1, 1871. Great rivalry existed between Pentwater and Hart, and through the influence of some of the leading Pentwater citizens the line of the proposed road did not touch Hart village and reached Pentwater on the south side of Pentwater Lake. The road was graded and trains run to Pentwater during the early part of 1872. In 1881, the name of the road was changed to the Chicago & West Michigan Railway Company. Later, Hart's enterprising citizens, by subscribing $12,000 and securing right of way and depot grounds, induced the Company to build a spur from Mears to Hart four miles long.

The Chicago & West Michigan Railway Co. is one of the most powerful railroad corporations in the State.

HESPERIA VILLAGE, 1870.—Two years prior to this date a single log cabin on the river bank marked the site of the village of Hesperia. 1870 finds it with about fifty buildings and two hundred inhabitants. There are three dry goods stores, owned by Weaver & Co., D. J. Foster, and A. P. Bigelow; a grocery and provision store, owned by L. P. Whitney & Co.; a shoe shop, a blacksmith shop and a saw mill; a three-story hotel with J. W. Bowen, proprietor. The village is located upon the line between Oceana and Newaygo counties, Main street running with the line. It is putting forth every energy to secure a railroad.

ORDERS AT A PREMIUM.—Pentwater, in common with most lumbering towns at this time, when navigation was closed had little money in circulation. "Orders" for goods drawn by one firm upon another, and "due bills" formed a large part of the circulating medium. A merchant from another village visited Pentwater, and in conversation with a resident noticed one of these "orders" in his hand.

"What's that?" he inquired.

"That is Pentwater currency," was the reply.

"We don't have any such our way," remarked the merchant, ready for a bargain. "What'll you take for it?"

"Four dollars," was the reply.

The merchant noticing that it was drawn for eight dollars, and having heard of great discounts offered for cash, concluded to invest and counted out the money, without thinking to glance at the back where appeared an indorsement of four dollars and ten cents. He did not discover the joke until he presented his order in payment for eight dollars' worth of trade and had to come down with four dollars and ten cents in addition to his order.

POLITICS AND THE TIMES.—The Oceana Times at this period appeared with Palmiter & Dresser as proprietors, and Mr. Dresser editor and manager. Both were republican. The regular republican convention to nominate county officers was held and considerable strife was manifest and bitterness engendered by the respective candidates. There were forty-three votes cast and the following ticket was nominated, viz.: Sheriff, Wm. Webb; Clerk and Register, Daniel W. Crosby; Treasurer, John R. Butler; Prosecuting Attorney, J. M. Rice; Circuit Court Commissioner, F. W. Ratzel; Surveyor, Nelson Green; Coroners, Joseph Walker and Louis Genereau.

At this time Mr. Dresser accepted and published articles written by F. W. Ratzel in answer to articles appearing in the Oceana Co. Journal, published by Mr. Palmiter, and as the above ticket did not give general satisfaction, a bolt was organized in which Mr. Dresser took part, and which resulted in nominating another ticket, styled the independent ticket, as follows: Sheriff, Hervey S. Sayles; Clerk and Register, Amos Dresser, Jr.; Treasurer, P. R. Cady, and the rest of the republican ticket was renominated. Messrs. Sayles, Crosby and Butler were elected. Immediately after the independent convention, war broke out between Messrs. Palmiter & Dresser, which culminated later in the year by Mr. Palmiter obtaining an injunction prohibiting Mr. Dresser from publishing the Times. Mr. Dresser obtained a like injunction against Mr. Palmiter, and for some sixty days no paper was published in Pentwater. Jan. 20, 1871, however, Mr. Dresser having obtained through the efforts of friends sufficient funds had purchased new material, retaining the old subscription list, issued the first copy of the East Shore News, an eight column folio, and sent it to old subscribers. The bitterness engendered between the two partners continued for several years, and the matter was brought before the Courts several times, but never disposed of. A compromise was effected which settled all the legal questions involved. The Times material which came to Mr. Palmiter's possession, was in 1872 used in starting the Times again at Pentwater, with Wm. Warner as editor. In the spring of 1873 Mr. Palmiter sold the plant to W. S. Platt and W. Sutherland. Mr. Sutherland sold to G. E. Mathews, and the Times continued to be published by this firm, until in the spring of 1874, when it was removed to Fremont Center and used in publishing the Fremont Times.

Mr. Dresser continued the publication of the NEWS until May 12, 1871, when he associated with himself J. E. Rastall, who, however, only remained until December of the same year. Jan., 1872, Clark Taylor, of Ionia, became half owner with Mr. Dresser. The name of the paper was in May, 1872, changed to Pentwater News. In Jan., 1873, Mr. Taylor was succeeded by A. T. Lyon, of Penn Yan, N. Y. Jan., 1874, the form of the paper was changed to a six column quarto. In Dec., 1874, Lyon retired, and in Nov., 1875, W. R. Porter appeared as proprietor with Mr. Dresser. He sold his interest to W. J. Canfield, in Feb., 1876, who in Oct., 1879, purchased Mr. Dresser's interest and conducted the publication until March, 1880, when he sold to L. M. Hartwick, the present editor and proprietor. Jan. 1, 1888, S. Andrus purchased a half interest in the plant, but sold out to his partner, Mr. Hartwick, in September of the same year.

Chief Joseph Pay-baw-me died on the 4th day of May, 1870. A portrait and sketch of his life will appear elsewhere.

1870—The Board of Supervisors meet this year with sixteen towns represented. The committee on the matter of Mr. Swain, a former Treasurer reported $600 paid and $399.53 still due.

1871.—After the completion of the jail building in 1868, the upper story was made use of, by the county for holding terms of Circuit Court, meetings of Board of Supervisors and other public bodies. This year the Board of Supervisors ordered the building of an addition to the jail building. In June of this year the county purchased of Jacob Schrumpf 120 acres of land, including certain chattels upon it for the sum of $5,200, to be used for County Poor Farm.

ACCIDENTS AND INCIDENTS.—Jan. 20th Wm. Maynard, of Claybanks, was helping Charles Passenger, of Shelby, dig a well. They had got down about seventy-one feet when Mr. Passenger concluded not to go any deeper, and they commenced taking up the curbing. Mr. Maynard was in the bucket at work taking out the curbing from the bottom and had got up to within thirty-five feet of the top, when the sand commenced caving in from behind the curbing. This let the curbing where Mr. Maynard was working loose, and before assistance could be rendered the well filled up, burying him. His lifeless body was not reached until the evening of the 23rd of January. He was found standing in the bucket as though in the act of taking up curbing.

On the 24th day of April, the same year, H. H. Cole, of Crystal, went down into his well thirty-two feet deep, to recover a bucket which had been accidentally dropped. He stepped on one of the bottom stones and it gave way and the whole well caved in upon him, settling down six feet from the top, thus making a depth of twenty-six feet of earth and stones above him. D. R. Walters, a scientific well digger came and cautiously removed the stones and earth above him and in twelve and one-half hours reached him. When found a stone weighing 25 lbs. was resting directly on his head, and stones and earth were pressing him on all sides as close as could be, from his feet to his shoulders. Strange to say he had his senses during the whole of the time that elapsed before his relief, and for four hours before he was reached he could be heard praying, and by conversing with him his exact situation learned. When released from his perilous position he was found to be bruised but not seriously injured, and is today alive and a resident of Crystal township. He attributes his deliverance "directly to the help of God."

On the night of March the ninth, fire broke out in Bacon & Jensen's store, Pentwater, and speedily spread, destroying th buildings on the south of it until all the buildings on the west side of Hancock street, from Fifth street to the Postoffice were destroyed, being five buildings. Three buildings on the same ground were burned in 1874, and the entire block was destroyed by fire in September, 1880.

SMALL POX.—On the 11th day of November, a stranger made application for a room at the Northwestern Hotel, Pentwater, (the building which has been remodeled and is now the bank building) kept by W. S. Dumont. His appearance indicated that he was very poor and sick. Mr. Dumont, after seeing him comfortably provided for, secured the services of Dr. Bills, who treated him for an affection of the throat with which he appeared to be suffering. Later in the day he grew worse and during the night died. Upon examination of his effects, a coarse bag containing seventeen twenty dollar gold pieces was found, and a pocket book containing $8.50 in currency. A pocket memorandum book was found upon which was the name of John Thuln, and another memorandum indicating that he had traveled in California, Louisiana, and elsewhere. He was buried Sunday following, many citizens accompanying his remains to the grave. Afterwards the photographer, Mr. Justus Koon, who took a photograph of the dead stranger, was taken with small pox and died. Mr. Walradth and wife of the hotel were also taken with it and died. The undertaker and many others who visited the place, as well as all the inmates of the hotel, were taken with it, but after a time recovered. There were fifty-one cases, all told, in Pentwater. There were also cases in Golden, Crystal and Ferry. Bills known as the small pox bills were presented to the Board of Supervisors for allowance as follows: Pentwater, $2,930.98, and other towns bringing the total to $3,666.01, which after much diplomacy and many investigations was allowed.

On the 30th day of December, this year, the telegraph line having been completed through to Manistee, the first message was transmitted from Pentwater and the first message received at Pentwater. A Miss Casto was the first operator. She was succeeded by M. A. Rice, the present operator, in May, 1872.

1872.—THE ELDRED SHINGLE MILL.—The largest shingle mill in the State, and reputed as being the largest in the U. S. in the spring of 1872, was known as the Eldred mill of Pentwater. It contained nine shingle machines and its daily capacity was 270,000. The mill buildings consisted of two parts, one 50x80 feet, and the other 30x100 feet. It was located near the place now occupied by the Chicago & West Michigan Railway Co.'s water tank. In connection with the mill was a large boarding house and several dwelling houses for the employes. Eighty men and twenty girls were employed in the mill. On the night of May 6th this large mill took fire and was entirely consumed. It was not rebuilt and its loss was a severe blow to Pentwater. Pentwater had recently purchased the steam fire engine Oceana, and this was the first fire occurring after its purchase. It was powerless to save the mill, but it did save the other buildings near it.

BANK.—The first bank in the county was started by J. G. Gray and Rice & Ambler, under the name of Gray Bros. & Co., in the fall of 1870 and was kept in the rear end of Gray's drug store, now the

P. O. building. Afterwards I. J. Gray purchased J. G. Gray's interest and moved the bank into the little building now occupied by M. A. Rice as a jewelry store. In the spring of 1872 Samuel A. Browne & Co. became interested in this institution. It was then organized as the Oceana County Bank, S. A. Browne elected President, W. E. Ambler Vice President, and I. J. Gray Cashier. In 1875 S. A. Browne and W. E. Ambler retired. In 1877 Messrs. F. Nielsen and W. E. Ambler became the sole proprietors of this bank with all its franchise, having purchased the interest of I. J. Gray. The name was changed to that of Nielsen & Co. Mr. Nielsen acted as cashier and general manager. Being a gentleman of well defined business habits, strictly honest, accurate, and having the confidence of the community, the business under his management has increased until the firm of Nielsen & Co. ranks as one of the first houses in the county as regards its financial standing. This firm was the first to build a fire and burglar proof vault, and to adopt the now popular time lock.

THE WRECK OF THE SCHOONER SOUVENIR.—On the night of Nov. 26, 1872, the weather being mild and pleasant, the schooners Souvenir and Minnie Corlett, owned in Pentwater and manned from this port, left harbor loaded, bound for Chicago. The former was ladened with 800,000 shingles, and the latter with lumber in the hold and square timbers on deck. At about 11 o'clock p. m. the wind veered suddenly to the northwest and soon increased to a terrific gale, accompanied with blinding snow and the mercury dropped to zero. The next morning the Souvenir was discovered near the Claybanks south of Ludington, going on the outer bar with one man on deck at the wheel, but no one else in sight. There was no life crew to help, and the sea would not permit the venture to reach the vessel. Those on shore signalled the man on deck to tie a line about his body and let the other end float ashore. He signalled back "No," either being unable to make the effort or thinking it useless. About noon Wm. Girard, the lighthouse keeper at Ludington, succeeded in reaching the vessel in a small boat, going alone, no one having the courage to accompany him. He found the man yet alive but unconscious, and he breathed but a few moments afterwards. He was the last of the crew, the rest were all gone. The rigging and deck load were gone and the spars had fallen aft and still remained on deck. It was Frank Whitcomb who stood at the wheel and perished in sight of land and help. The crew was as follows: Chas. Craine, Captain; Frank Whitcomb, Mate; John Perry, Steward; Charles Dagle, Peter Hallene, Richard Moore and Thomas Thayer, seamen.

The Minnie Corlett being scow built, washed high and dry upon the shore and all escaped with their lives, but some with badly frozen feet and hands. Peter Drevis, now a resident of Pentwater was on board the Corlett and had his limbs and ears badly frozen.

The event was described in verse by Prof A. J. Woods, of the Pentwater Union Schools, as follows:

THE LOSS OF THE SOUVENIR.

Gone was summer with its sunshine, with its mild and favoring gales,
  And the chilling blast of autumn with its snow and sleet prevails;
Fierce and still more fierce the west wind beat against our wave-washed shore;
  And the lake gave fearful warning none must tempt its dangers more.

But the gallant hardy seamen, used to toil, to dangers bred,
  Laughing at the winds and billows, viewing storms with naught of dread,—
Heeded not the warning given, manned their gallant craft once more,
  Bade adieu to friends and kindred, and prepared to quit the shore.

While, as if to lure them onward, milder blew the winds that day,
  And the raging, restless billows sunk again to sportive play;
And to those who watched and waited for their loved ones came no fear,
  When by brave men manned and guided, sailed the gallant Souvenir.

But no man can read the secrets Nature chooses to withhold;
  Winds and waters scorn man's prowess and refuse to be controlled;
And before the night was ended, ere they reached their destined port,
  Winds and waves in all their fury made the fated bark their sport.

What those brave boys met and suffered through that long and fearful night,
  When the mad sea came upon them in its wild, resistless might,
How they toiled, till chilled and helpless, powerless to combat the waves,
  They were swept from off their vessel, and consigned to watery graves.

Whether all went down together, or were swept off one by one;
  Whether in the night they perished, or held out till rise of sun;—
God in mercy only knoweth, it is not for us to know,
  Best it is we may not fathom every fearful sight of woe.

All we know is, that ere midday, torn, dismantled, tempest-tossed,
  At the sport of winds and billows, there was thrown upon our coast,—
All that evermore might greet us, of that vessel staunch and true,
  Which but yesternight departed, with the Souvenir from view.

Of the *seven* brave men who manned her, only *one* now trod the deck,
  When upon the shore she drifted, an unsightly, shapeless wreck;
And he, too, when home seemed nearer, when the help of man seemed nigh,
  Bruised and crippled, chilled and helpless, he could only gasp and die.

Mourn we for the loved departed, taken in their pride away;
  Mourn we with the stricken kindred who are with us here to-day.
May we be by grace enabled, as our hearts with anguish swell,
  To take home the warning given, knowing "God doth all things well."

1873—HEMLOCK BARK EXTRACT.—Messrs. Johnson & Goodell visited the central and northern portion of Michigan with a patent process for extracting the liquid from Hemlock bark, which extract it was said was all that was necessary to be used in tanning hides, etc. They proposed to start factories, put in local managers, etc. It promised big money and quite a number from Pentwater invested in the Hemlock Bark Extract business. After about sixty days, however, the bottom dropped out of the enterprise and those who invested began to investigate, and although the patentees made good promises, the enthusiasm died out and in a year's time the enterprise dropped and the patentees failed. The product wouldn't sell.

M. E. CHURCH DEDICATED AT HART.—The M. E. Church Trustees at Hart had erected a new church. On the eighth day of February there was an indebtedness of $800, and it was estimated that it would require $300 to finish the tower. Doctor Perrine, of Albion College, came and on Sunday, the ninth day of February preached a sermon, after which eight hundred dollars was collected or pledged, and in the evening another sermon by the Doctor and more subscriptions taken, and the church was then dedicated according to the ritual formula, and the Rev. C. H. Howe installed as pastor.

On the evening of May 12th the Congregational Society of Shelby adopted articles of association and elected the following persons as officers, viz: Alexander Pittenger, Parley R. Cady, Rhodes Willetts, E. J. Shirts and E. B. Gaylord, Trustees; Jarvis Fleming, Clerk; Geo. W. Piper, Treasurer.

JUDGE GIDDINGS.—This year an attempt was made to impeach Judge Giddings for neglecting his official duties. The Board of Supervisors of Oceana County at once passed a resolution approving of the manner in which he had discharged the duties of his office in this county, and affirming that his removal would be a public calamity. The Bar of Oceana County took similar action, and further progress in the impeachment movement came to a halt.

At the December session of the Board of Supervisors an attempt was made by Messrs. Charles Mears and S. Odell to secure the removal of the county seat to Mears. This was followed by an effort to remove it to Shelby. On the motion to remove to Shelby the vote stood eight yea and eight nay. Failing to carry, it was then decided to erect county buildings at Hart, provided the people of Hart would give $2,500.

CHAPTER IX.

—x—

PIGEONS—WOMEN'S CRUSADE—DEFALCATION—PENTWATER'S TITLE CASES—SUNDRY MATTERS FROM 1873 to 1875.

PROVIDENTIAL VISITATION.—Pentwater, with its fine harbor, inland lake and tributary streams, the north and south branches of Pentwater River, penetrating the lumber regions interior, early became a principal settlement, and as regards its commercial transactions and its manufacturing interests, it still leads all the other settlements of the county. By reason of its location it becomes the natural business center for those occupying the fine farming lands of South Mason County, Crystal, Weare and Golden townships of Oceana County, although separated from these sections by from two to four miles of land of a lighter character. Its recognized advantages were its harbor and its interior connections by river, thus enabling lumbermen to conduct their operations at this point with the greatest advantage. Hart possessed an excellent natural water power. In early times a water power was regarded as the one thing necessary and essential to the starting of a village in a new territory. If it had nothing else, a water power assured success. It was undoubtedly this fact that led to the selection of the present site of Hart village. It fact, it was this power that was utilized for the first grist mill of the county. A fine territory covered with an excellent body of hardwood timber surrounded it. Hardwood lumbering at this time was not thought of, and its timber was regarded as an incumbrance rather than as a source of wealth, and millions of feet of logs fed the flames in great heaps to make room for raising crops. The water power and the county seat made Hart the thriving village we find it in 1874.

Shelby had no lake harbor, or pine forests tributary to start it. It had no water power or county seat. In fact it had nothing but a hilly territory of excellent farming land, but not highly regarded. For years it had been the half-way stopping place for travelers from Whitehall to Pentwater, and some of its pioneers regarded that fact of itself as of sufficient importance to induce them to start a village here. Cotemporaneous with the building of the railroad the village of Barnett was platted. The advantages of railroad communication with the outside world and the novelty of it, stirred up the enthusiasm of its citizens and the embryo village made rapid progress. But the effect soon died away and a period of decline was becoming painfully manifest, when the most singular event in the history of the county occurred. Just as the little village was sinking into the slough of despond, came a visitation that appeared providential in its coming and was wonderful in its results. It was in the spring of 1874 that the first great flight of wild pigeons to this section occurred. They selected a locality within a few miles of the village for their nesting place. The news went abroad and nearly every train from the south brought sportsmen by the score, and with them came plenty of currency. Everyone became a pigeon hunter or dealer. They were caught and shipped by the barrel, in coops, and thousands were fed for a later market. It is estimated that this business realized to the people of Shelby over $50,000 in one season. The express company gave its agent, Mr. A. Z. Moore, ten per cent. of charges for handling pigeons, and his fees for the season were $630.29, and many were shipped by freight, or carried to other points for shipment. The effect of this season's work was that of an elixir. It put new life into all the enterprises that had been started. In 1876 the pigeons came again in greatly increased numbers. The fame given to this little inland village as the locality of the greatest pigeon roost in the U. S. gave it for a time a national notoriety. This year there were shipped 1,781 barrels and 1,982 coops of pigeons, and 2,000 dozens were retained and fed. The agent's percentage this season amounted to $1,553.30. It is estimated that there were over 700,000 birds shipped, and that over five hundred strangers found shelter in Shelby and vicinity during the stay of the pigeons. The golden shower thus poured upon the village was expended in local improvements, and farms were rapidly cleared up, the population increased, and the village became the equal of its rivals in importance and business. Having placed the village squarely upon its feet, the pigeons sought new quarters and never returned again in numbers. Later another period of depression seemed settling upon the place, when the wonderful adaptability of its soil for potato culture was discovered and farmers commenced the cultivation of this tuber in great quantities. This brought buyers from distant places, as the potatoes here marketed were of a superior size and quality, and were grown in great quantities. For several years it was noted as the greatest potato market in Northern Michigan. Still later its hills, which in early times were regarded with disfavor by the settlers, were found to be the ideal fruit sections, and at the present the peach and plum orchards of Shelby and vicinity have extended the fame of this burg to many States. The stories told of Oceana County's fruit productions are familiar, and find a full verification in the yearly productions of the orchards surrounding the village of Shelby.

The above is an etching from a photograph of a limb broken from a plum tree in Mr. E. J. Shirts' orchard at Shelby. It is not an exaggeration of the appearance of plum trees ladened with fruit, but on the contrary exhibits the average. Thousands of plum trees in the orchards of Oceana County would never sustain the fruit that yearly appears upon them unless supported by many props.

WOMEN'S TEMPERANCE CRUSADE.—On the evening of Dec. 22, 1873, Dio Lewis, a Boston physician and lyceum lecturer, delivered in Music Hall, Boston, a lecture on "Our Girls." The following night he delivered a lecture at the same place on "Temperance." He told how in a New England manufacturing village a band of women had driven from their midst the rum traffic by a crusade of prayer and song. Following this lecture a number of ladies signed the following compact:

"We, the ladies whose names are hereto appended, agree and resolve, that with God's help, we will stand by each other in this work, and persevere therein until it is accomplished, and see to it, as far as our influence goes, that the traffic shall never be revived."

Then they started out and visiting drug stores and saloons prayed, sang, and entreated until one by one the dealers gave in and signed the pledge already prepared. The spirit of the movement was caught up by other sections and in a few weeks it had spread over a great portion of the Northern States. In the spring of 1874 it reached Oceana County, and in the latter part of March an organization was perfected at Pentwater, with the following officers: President, Mrs. G. D. Lee; Vice Presidents, Mrs. J. G. Gray, Mrs. G. W. Fisher, Mrs. A. Dresser, Jr.; Secretary, Mrs. G. W. Maxwell; Treasurer, Mrs. Chas. Lamont; Executive Committee, Mrs. L. F. Waldo, Mrs. Sewall Moulton, Mrs. A. E. Andrus, Mrs. Geo. Goodsell, and the officers of the Society *ex officio*. It started out with a membership of nearly one hundred. On Sundays appropriate sermons were preached, referring especially to the movement. At the regular prayer meetings the prayers were in behalf of it, and the work commenced. Saloons were visited, and the proprietors entreated to abandon the traffic. Prayers and song took place. In some instances they were refused entrance to the saloons and they took up their position on the sidewalk in front.

At a mass meeting called at Gardner's Hall for the purpose, just prior to the township election, the following ticket was nominated: Supervisor, Edwin Nickerson; Clerk, John H. Bouton; Treasurer, Mark A. Rice; Justice, Charles R. Whittington; Commissioner of Highways, Wm. B. O. Sands; School Inspector, John Ripley; Drain Commissioner, L. M. Thorp; Constables, M. S. Perkins, F. O. Gardner, Wm. H. Bailey, Geo. B. Elms.

At the republican caucus on Wednesday night following, the entire ticket was endorsed. A citizens' caucus was called and nominated the following ticket: Supervisor, H. C. Flagg; Clerk, John S. Reynolds; Treasurer, F. Nielsen; Justice, J. Fegan; School Inspector, L. D. Grove, full term; E. A. Wright, to fill vacancy; Drain Commissioner, E. Irons; Constables, W. A. Rounds, G. F. Piper, E. Moody, A. H. Palmer.

C. R. Whittington declined to run and G. W. Grant was placed on the ticket in his stead. The election resulted in the success of the women's ticket, with the exception of Town Clerk. R. M. Montgomery (since Judge of Kent County) was Prosecuting Attorney. The old prohibitory law was on the statute books, and Mr. Montgomery informed the ladies that if complaints were made and evidence furnished him, he would prosecute. Complaints were made before Justice Hartwick and the cases were prosecuted with vigor and defended with equal vigor, the eloquent R. A. Montgomery, now of Lansing, Mich., being the attorney employed for that purpose. No ordinary room would hold the crowds that assembled to see the trials, and the Opera Hall was utilized for a Court room. Many convictions resulted and the saloon business became so unprofitable that many devices were resorted to to evade prosecution. Some of the saloons advertised buttermilk for sale and the proprietors insisted that no intoxicating liquors were sold by them. Still, people would buy buttermilk and get intoxicated, and one prosecution was had where the evidence disclosed that buttermilk alone was purchased, but a prominent physician upon cross-examination stated that the buttermilk contained intoxicating qualities, and a conviction resulted.

About this time the basement of the building now occupied by P. Dreves, was fitted up with a device to evade the law. Entering an open door the visitor found himself in a small room in one corner of which was placed a rudely constructed wheel, only one-half of which appeared in sight, with the following placard directly above:

> PUT YOUR MONEY IN THE WHEEL
> AND
> CALL FOR WHAT YOU WANT.

A little to one side was a smaller card, containing this additional direction:

> PUT THE GLASSES IN THE WHEEL.

On the walls on either side were several cards containing the information that "All drinks must be paid for on delivery." "Positively no credit given to any," etc.

This makeshift called forth the following poetic effusion from the Grand Rapids Times:

> Shoost put your money on der vheel, for vhat you vants den call,
> It works shust like der fishing reel, but bobs rount in der vall,
> Und prings you prandy, rye, or ghin, cigars, lager peer, or vine—
> For glittering haunts of vice und sin in Pentvater you can't find.
>
> Der bartenter his name vas Chase, but who revolves der vheel
> In our model town no von can blace; consequently anypodies vill not squeal.
> In der leedle nook you blace a dime, (der liddle vheel goes round,)
> Call vhisky—presto glass on time.—Pentvater ish der model town.

The prosecutions were so effectual that on the 19th day of June the last saloon closed its doors and the man with the wheel departed for Wisconsin. Then the women added another stanza to the above poetry, which read as follows:

> Der vimmins dey got after Chase, mit his revolving vheel,
> And make it hot for him in dis blace, if anypodies vouldn't squeal.
> So he shumped up trough de dirty floor out of his hole in der vall,
> Und made for Visconsin shore, petticoats, vheel und all.

The effects of the crusade were apparent for years, although the saloons gradually crept into existence again as active crusade work ceased.

The crusade reached Hart April 4th, and a course similar to that in Pentwater was pursued. One VanKuren was keeping a saloon and after being visited by the ladies he promised to quit if they would pay him $25. Some of the men backing the ladies told them to accept his proposition, and the ladies supposing that the men suggesting the idea would furnish the money, made the promise. VanKuren shut up for a while, but not getting his money, opened again, but was finally induced to quit the business.

OCEANA COUNTY AGRICULTURAL SOCIETY.—On several occasions attempts had been made to organize a County Fair Association. For one reason or another all had failed until in February, 1870, a meeting was called at L. G. Rutherford's office in Hart, which was attended by several business men of Hart and a number of farmers. The meeting was called to order and Hazen Leavitt, of Leavitt, made Chairman, and J. Palmiter, Secretary. A permanent organization was decided upon, and the following officers were elected: President, James E. Reed; Vice President, Alexander Pittenger; Secretary, J. Palmiter; Directors, Hazen Leavitt, A. R. Wheeler, O. K. White, Caleb Davis, Jr., W. J. Tennant, Theodore Taylor, Wm. J. Sprigg, J. J. Kittridge and S. A. Browne. It was decided to issue 500 shares of capital stock at $10 a share.

The first fair was held in Hart, Sept. 24 & 25, 1872, and was a success in every particular. In 1873 a three days' Fair was held, which was also a success. The Board of Supervisors voted $205 and a tax of one-tenth of a mill on the dollar was allowed. In 1874 the Association purchased of Wigton & Bosworth on contract, the ground since used by it for holding Fairs. It has held Fairs on these grounds every year since purchasing, with more or less success, as the weather was favorable or unfavorable. Its last meeting, held in 1889, was very successful, and the organization may now be recognized as one of the permanent institutions of the county.

THE PEACH DEFALCATION.—In April, 1873, Josephus S. Peach, a farmer residing in Hart township, possessing the confidence of the people, having to all appearance lived the life of an honest, upright citizen, was nominated and elected Township Treasurer. At the close of this term when he settled with the Township Board, a balance of $1,252.02 was found due from him to the township, but it was supposed that he had the funds in his possession and the matter was not inquired into. He was renominated in 1874 and re-elected. Did the business without exciting any suspicion of irregularity. In September, just before leaving home temporarily, he made arrangements with Mr. A. S. White to pay what orders should be presented to him, and Mr. White continued to do so until about

$400 had accumulated. After the last roll was placed in his hands he refused to accept orders in payment of taxes unless the holders would allow him four per cent. for collection, and by this means he collected a larger proportion of the taxes in money than ever had been done before. Just before Christmas he settled with several gentlemen to whom he was indebted, and on Christmas day closed his account with Mr. White for the orders he had paid, and deposited a small amount.

Christmas day being the last day he was expected to be in his office to receive taxes, nothing was thought of his leaving immediately thereafter to make,—as he said,—a short visit to friends in the southern part of the State. His wife desired to accompany him, but he made plausible excuses for not acceding to her request, and left her with the understanding that he would return in a few days and that shortly after she should take a trip outside.

He left about $100 with his wife to pay any orders that might be presented in his absence, and told her she had better not receive any money in payment of taxes until he should return. She accordingly refused, but finally relented and took in and deposited in the bank about $400 before the final development took place.

His bondsmen to the county were Otis W. Knox and Rollin R. Wheeler, and to the township Jesse B. Garwood and Wm. J. Sprigg.

About the first of January, 1875, Mr. Garwood received the following letter:

"Dec. 31, 1874.

Mr. J. B. Garwood:—As you know, the whirl-a-gig of time often brings about changes, of which mortals never dream. Jesse, as you have been in our family longer and know more of our family affairs than any other man, I make free to tell you more. First, I shall never come back to Michigan for some reasons best known to Mollie (his wife) and myself. I want you to dispose of my property, both real and personal, to the best advantage. Jesse, I don't want any one, neither the township of Hart, to lose one dollar on my account. I had of necessity to take some money that did not belong to me. I think there is enough property there to make all right. God bless you all.

The train that carries this letter, also takes me out of the State of Ohio.

This from your erring Friend,   J. S. Peach."

The receipt of this letter created the greatest excitement that had ever been known in Hart, and appeared like a thunder-bolt from the clear sky to his bondsmen. An investigation followed and it was found that he was a defaulter to the amount of $2,275.51 of the township funds, and $1,350.00 of the county funds. It also appeared that in a number of instances he had received money and given receipts for taxes without making any record of the transaction.

Shortly after the above denouement one of his bondsmen received a letter from a Mr. Baldwin, of Bellefontaine, Ohio, stating that Peach was in that place. Acting upon this information steps were at once taken to secure Peach's arrest. It then became known that Peach's past record was of an unsavory character. It seems that he had at one time resided in Ohio, near neighbor to this Mr. Baldwin. Each had a wife of his own, but Peach becoming enamored with the wife of his neighbor, Baldwin, finally left the country with her and came to Michigan. This was the last that was seen of him in Ohio until after his defalcation in Hart. It also appears that he made arrangements to live again with the wife he had so basely deserted, but was prevented from carrying his plans into execution by the sudden appearance of officers and bondsmen from Hart, and he made haste to depart.

He was followed by a detective through Tennessee, Alabama and Georgia, and finally back to Tennessee, where he was arrested at Sparta, and a telegram sent to his bondsmen, who started at once for him, followed the next day by O. K. White, Sheriff. The detective after arresting Peach lodged him in the jail of Sparta, and walked to Tullahoma (over 50 miles) to send the telegram. He returned on foot and upon his arrival was met by a bitter complaint concerning the unsuitable condition of the jail, and finally consented to remove him to a hotel where the jailer agreed to assist in guarding him. After removing him to the hotel the detective was drugged and Peach escaped into the mountains. Messrs. Sprigg and Knox at this time were within twenty-two miles of Sparta and Sheriff White about thirty miles behind following them. After a couple of days fruitless search Sheriff White returned home. During the summer following the Sheriff received two or three communications inquiring how much would be paid for Peach, but beyond this nothing has ever been heard from him since his escape.

The Board of Supervisors offered a reward of $300 for Peach's arrest. It also authorized the commencement of a suit against the township of Hart to recover the moneys belonging to the county, embezzled by Peach. Judge Brown rendered judgment in favor of the county and against the township for $1,800. This case was removed to the Supreme Court by L. G. Rutherford, attorney for the township. The Supreme Court reversed the judgment because the action had been improperly brought, but in the same decision intimated that the township was liable to the county and should spread the amount on its next tax roll. That the proper remedy to compel this action was by *mandamus*. This remedy was resorted to by the county and the amount of $1,330 with about $400 costs and expense, was subsequently levied and collected.

PENTWATER TITLES SETTLED.—Elsewhere appears the record of the burning Eldred's mill and its serious influence upon the growth of Pentwater. This was followed by another event that in its disastrous effects was still more calamitous.

In 1849 Andrew Rector and Edwin R. Cobb purchased from the U. S. Government certain lands in the township of Pentwater, including that now occupied by the village. Afterwards, on the 9th day of April, 1859, having become involved, they made a deed of assignment to Charles A. Rosevelt, by which deed they purported to convey all their property, real and personal, to said Charles A. Rosevelt, as appears by the following clause in said deed, viz.: * * "Witnesseth, that the said parties of the first part, in consideration of the premises, and the sum of one dollar to them in hand paid by the said party of the second part, the receipt whereof is hereby acknowledged, have granted, bargained, covenanted, released, assigned, transferred and set over by these presents, do grant, bargain, sell, covenant, release, assign, transfer and set over unto the said Charles A. Rosevelt, of the second part, and to his heirs and assigns forever, *all and singular*, the lands, tenements, hereditaments and appurtenances *situated, lying and being in the State of Michigan*, and more particularly described in a schedule hereto attached and marked 'A,' "—. This deed appears to have been executed on the same day and presented to Alexander S. Anderson, Register of Deeds, for record. On pages 374, 375 and 376 of Liber 'A' of Deeds, the deed is recorded at length and on page 429, following a statement by the Register that the following are schedules 'A,' 'B,' and 'C,' referred to in the deed recorded on pages 374, 375 and 376, appears the record of these schedules, the date of record being Sep. 29, 1859.

By examination of schedule 'A,' referred to in deed, for a more specific description of the lands assigned, it appears that forty acres, including that on which the principal portion of the vil-

ALEXANDER S. ANDERSON.

lage of Pentwater was located, was not included. As nearly all the people owning lots in this territory traced their titles through Charles A. Rosevelt as Cobb & Rector's assignee, the validity of the assignment deed was essential to the protection of their titles.

Sometime subsequent to the making the deed of assignment, but prior to this period (1873), Edwin R. Cobb, claiming that Rosevelt had abused his trust and defrauded Cobb & Rector, in order to secure what he considered his rights, brought suit in the Circuit Court and attacked the validity of the assignment deed, but we cannot find that he denied the execution. He failed to establish his claim, and many of the people whose titles came through Rosevelt, learning of the result supposed that settled the matter and established their titles beyond question.

In 1873 Daniel E. Corbett, Isaac E. Messmore, Eugene Vaughn, Benjamin Luce and Seth Holcomb, all residents of Grand Rapids, having learned of the omission appearing in the schedule 'A,' of the description of forty acres, quietly went to work and purchased of Cobb & Rector's heirs, quit claims. Rumors of the combination of these Grand Rapids speculators and its purchases being whispered about caused some uneasiness, but it was said, "that's the same old matter of Cobb's, and has been settled once. It can amount to nothing." Still the uncertainty caused outsiders to hesitate before investing in Pentwater real estate, and following upon the heels of the burning of Eldred's mill, caused the general depression to be more severely felt. To add to this feeling of depression and intensify matters, early in 1874 Mr. D. E. Corbett appeared in Pentwater, and on behalf of the Grand Rapids syndicate above referred to, asserted full ownership over the property within this territory, estimating its value at several hundred thousand dollars. He offered to deed to residents who desired it for what he stated was a reasonable price, but which was regarded as nearly the full value of the property. He claimed that inasmuch as the forty acres was not inserted in the schedule 'A,' that Cobb & Rector retained title to this, and as he and those he represented had purchased the Cobb & Rector title, they were absolute owners. On the other hand, having through attorneys looked up the matter, the citizens claimed that the general words of assignment in the deed, viz: "All and singular the lands, tenements, hereditaments and appurtenances situated, lying and being in the State of Michigan," conveyed *all* the land that Cobb & Rector owned in Michigan, without reference to the schedule.

Mr. Corbett admitted that the clause would have been sufficient had it not been for the fact that the general words of assignment were immediately followed by a reference to schedule 'A' for a more particular description. This he claimed deprived the general clause of the effect claimed for it by the citizens. The decisions of the Courts being in support of this theory, it did look as though Mr. Corbett was master of the situation, and a few compromised with him by buying quit claims, but the great majority refused to deal with him.

A suit in ejectment was commenced by James S. Post against Emanuel Rich, and Mr. Post having a similar title to the Grand Rapids parties, and backed by them the case was pushed to an early decision, in order to frighten the people into acceding to their demands. Before trial had been reached in the Rich case, to accelerate matters three more ejectment cases were brought against James G. B. Atwood, A. Brillhart, John Atwood and Louis M. Hartwick. Through the same influence the Grand Rapids dailies published long articles purporting to describe the situation, and which did have the effect of making Pentwater's titles notorious. Improvements stopped, business lagged, people lost interest in the place, and it soon became apparent that the titles must be settled at once or the village was doomed. About this time, L. M. Hartwick, a co-defendant in one of the ejectment suits above noticed, and with his partner, Mr. L. D. Grove, an attorney for the defendants in the other cases, began a careful investigation of the records, spending several days in the Register's office for that purpose, and when he returned he announced to his partner, Mr. Grove, his belief that if the original deed could be found the missing description would appear in it, as he claimed to have found other errors in Mr. Anderson's work that warranted the suspicion that Mr. Anderson had failed to record all the deed contained. Mr. Grove adopted the idea at once and set about trying to find the deed. Being a pioneer attorney of the county he was acquainted with all the persons who had anything to do with Cobb & Rector's matters, and in the course of a few weeks he succeeded in getting a letter from Wm. Parks, of Grand Haven, who stated that for one hundred dollars he would undertake to find the deed. Of course it was not known whether the deed would possess any value to the defendants or not, and finally he informed Mr. Parks that if he would allow him to look at the deed, if it contained what he wanted and expected Grove & Hartwick would pay the hundred dollars. He replied that the deed could not be inspected until paid for. After some consultation it was decided to purchase it, and it was sent by Mr. Parks to his son Albert, who at that time was Station Agent at Pentwater, and to whom the money was paid, and from whom the package containing deed, schedules, etc., was received.

It was a moment of great expectation when the package was opened in the office of Grove & Hartwick. To prevent the possibility of intrusion the doors were locked. Grove opened the package, took out the schedule, and after inspecting it a moment commenced to dance a hornpipe. "What is it, Grove?" inquired Hartwick. "Our fortune is made," he replied. "It's all right, the description is here. 'Twas Anderson's blunder that caused its omission on the Record. Why, see here, he just skipped one line and that line describes the land." True enough, such appeared to be the fact. Now it seemed to be an easy matter to clear Pentwater's titles. With "occupancy and the deed" the Record was not feared. But now came the question of how to make "the fortune" Grove had prophesied. Finally it was decided to say nothing about the deed, but offer to clear the titles for the village in the disputed territory for $1,000. The offer was made, but the people in mass meeting, while satisfied with the price, wanted assurance that it could be accomplished. This assurance could not be given without disclosing the deed, consequently no arrangement was made and Rice, Ambler & Montgomery were employed to defend the people's titles on behalf of the village. Mr. Grove, provoked at what he styled the foolishness of the people, went to Grand Rapids, and after a consultation with Mr. Corbett returned to Pentwater with a proposition from him to retain Grove & Hartwick, paying a large retainer and requiring no work, but simply to keep the deed out of sight. Grove & Hartwick's clients were to be protected by quit claims from Corbett et al. Mr. Hartwick refused to accept the retainer, and shortly thereafter the firm of Grove & Hartwick dissolved. Mr. Hartwick retained possession of the deed and appeared in the cases of Hartwick, Atwood and Brillhart, and Grove acted thereafter with the Grand Rapids parties. In the meantime the Rich case had been tried and decided in favor of plaintiff, the deed not having been introduced in evidence. A new trial under the statute was granted, and in the course of time the other cases of Atwood, Brillhart and Hartwick took the same course, the only fight being upon the question of improvements, and after obtaining the construction of the Court of the statute governing improvements and judgment rendered for plaintiffs, new trials were allowed, and the cases stood as before.

The Rich case was pressed for trial by Mr. Corbett, who now showed his full hand by appearing as attorney and conducting the trial. The trial was finally entered upon and R. M. Montgomery, of the firm of Rice, Ambler & Montgomery, assisted by C. I. Walker, of Detroit, defended it. The plaintiffs through Mr. Grove had become informed of the possession by defendants of the deed and what it it contained, and had already formulated a theory to defeat its effect, viz.: That the schedule which contained the description of land omitted in the Records, not having been actually attached to the deed and delivered with it, was not entitled to be admitted in evidence as proof of conveyance, and the fact that the deed and schedules were on separate papers and recorded in different places in the Record, was relied upon in support of this theory. On the trial of this case the defendants' attorneys sought to introduce the Records in order to show notice, but were refused by the Court. They were afterwards permitted to introduce them as secondary evidence. The plaintiff, thinking that the Court in admitting the Record erred, made but little opposition to the further progress of the case, and judgment was rendered for defendant. Plaintiff immediately removed the case to the Supreme Court, which sustained the judgment of the Court below, but as the only question raised before the Supreme Court was upon the admissibility of the Records, the validity of the assignment deed was not passed upon, and it did not settle the question of title.

During the trial of this case in the Circuit Court an incident occurred that was of sufficient moment to require notice in this connection. The original deed of assignment was introduced in evidence and passed up to Judge Giddings, and lay upon his desk as the Court adjourned for dinner. When the Court convened after dinner the deed could not be found and there was considerable commotion caused, as the result of the suit depended upon it. The members of the Bar looked at each other, and finally glanced at L. D. Grove, whom, by reason of his interest in the case and statements before made claiming proprietorship in the deed, the members suspected of having taken it. Grove's face remained "childlike and bland" under the searching scrutiny of a dozen pairs of eyes. Finally the stillness of death seemed to pervade the Court room. Judge Giddings arose and with a dignified bearing no other man could assume, raised his hand and bringing it down upon the desk with force, said: "I find as a matter of fact that the deed was placed there (indicating the desk) by the hand of the Court, and that it was removed from there by the hand of Lyman D. Grove. I find as a conclusion of law that the hand of Lyman D. Grove must put it back there forthwith." It is needless to say the deed was returned.

This incident reaching the ears of some Pentwater people, and realizing the slender thread upon which their titles depended, a meeting was called, and a delegation headed by Stillman Parker was sent to Hart with instructions to importune the Court to take and keep the custody of the important deed. The delegation appeared in Court, other business was suspended temporarily and the request was made of the Court by Mr. Parker. The Judge having ascertained that the Grove & Hartwick interest in the deed had been purchased, at their request made an order, first that the deed be re-recorded, and that the Register take custody of it and allow no person to have it except upon the written order of the Court, and it is supposed to be in the custody of the Register at this time. In the trial of the Rich case the Records were excluded and defendants defended relying solely upon the deed and the occupancy of the premises. The plaintiffs would not accept the result as conclusive and commenced an action against School Dist. No. 1 in the U. S. Courts. This case was defended by Rice, Ambler & Montgomery and C. I. Walker. On the trial J. H. Standish testified that he drew up the deed and attached the schedule to the deed before it was executed and delivered, he borrowing a pin from a female present for the purpose of attaching the papers. The papers had pin-holes in them indicating that they had been attached as testified. Alexander S. Anderson, the Register, also testified that when the deed was left with him for record he was under the impression that the papers were attached. That the reason he did not record the schedule with the deed was because he thought it unnecessary, but afterwards changing his mind recorded it as appears on the records. The following is the decision as rendered by Judge Withey:

The Court, having examined the special finding of the jury in the above-entitled case, and having considered the matter therein submitted for its judgment and opinion, renders the following judgment therein—that is to say:

First—That Charles A. Rosevelt acquired the title in fee, by the deed of assignment from Rector and Cobb, of and to the premises in question, and the defendant acquired from Rosevelt the title which he received from Rector and Cobb.

Second—That as defendant was in possession, under a claim of title, from 1850 up to and including the time of purchase by plaintiff and commencement of suit, plaintiff purchased with notice of defendant's claim and title, and it does not matter whether the record title was in defendant or not, so long as the conveyance from Rector and Cobb to Rosevelt and the conveyance from Rosevelt to defendant were operative as deeds of conveyance of the premises. Defendant's possession, under claim of title, is notice to every one, and as effectual for defendant's protection as record notice.

Third—As to the schedule of property, the jury having found that there was such a schedule, and annexed to and delivered with the deed, the Court sees no occasion to discuss the question of schedule in any of its relations to the case. If there was a schedule and it contained a description of the premises in question (and it did under the testimony and finding of the jury), then by the act of execution and delivery of those papers title passed to the assignee. Title once shown to have passed could not get back to Rector and Cobb without conveyance. The fact that the schedule was by the Register of Deeds, or some one, detached from the deed, or that it was not recorded with the deed as it should have been, or the fact that the schedule was altered by additions to or subtractions from it, after both deed and schedule had been delivered into the Register's office, cannot affect the question whether title passed to Rosevelt by delivery of deed and schedule in the first instance duly and properly executed by Rector and Cobb.

Finally, the Court is of the opinion that upon the whole case as found by the jury, the defendant is not guilty, etc. Let judgment be entered in form accordingly, with costs, against the plaintiff, and in favor of defendant.   S. L. WITHEY,
District Judge.

This settled all the titles of the occupied lands in Pentwater but did not settle that of the vacant lots. W. E. Ambler was employed by the township to perfect the titles for the unoccupied lands, and he at once filed a number of bills in Chancery to quiet title of occupied premises, knowing that under the decisions already rendered he had clear cases. These suits were accumulating costs to the Grand Rapids people very rapidly, and Mr. Corbett, after fighting the costs awhile, called for terms of capitulation. Terms made by Mr. Ambler were by quit-claims for all vacant lots in Pentwater on which they claimed title, and then he would receipt for costs. This was carried out and Pentwater's titles became perfected and forever settled.

We find this year (1875) the firm of Sands & Maxwell, which has heretofore received brief notice, occupying the above building and doing a business that gives promise of the great institution it afterwards became. The House was established in 1862 under the name of Hart & Maxwell, and Geo. W. Maxwell was foreman. In 1866 the firm dissolved and George continued the mercantile business. In April, W. B. O. Sands became his partner. In 1871 N. F. Harris became a partner, and in 1872 he retired. In 1875 Geo. W. Maxwell died and E. G. Maxwell became a partner. The merchandise sales of this House in 1875 were $128,653.73; its lumbering business $144,782.25. The further history of this House will appear under the history of the Pentwater Bedstead Factory.

CHAPTER X.

—x—

Citizens' Exchange Bank—Fruit Organizations—Death of L. D. Eaton—Trotting Stock—Death of Judge Giddings—Jennie Mills' Disappearance—Death of Judge Littlejohn—Suicide of I. H. Cogswell—Wreck of the Lamont—Alonzo Irons Mystery, Etc.

CITIZENS' EXCHANGE BANK.—The growing demand for a banking house at the county seat, was in the year 1874 duly considered by A. S. White, J. K. Flood and F. J. Russell, gentlemen each of whom possessed abundant means and an honorable standing with the people. A bank organized with this combination would make a strong and safe institution. The only question to be considered was "would it pay?" It was finally decided, however, to risk it, and on the 30th day of November, 1874, the Citizens' Exchange Bank was organized with the above named persons equal partners, and A. S. White manager. The house was a success from the start and the business went far beyond the expectations of its owners. The deposits have reached a figure upwards of $50,000. Being a private banking house, the individuals are liable to the extent of their individual property, and as each member of the firm is possessed of considerable means, its reliability is unquestioned. Its correspondents are The Chemical National Bank of New York, one of the wealthiest banks in the U. S.; The Third National Bank of Detroit, and The Fourth National Bank of Grand Rapids. George Alverson, an affable and courteous gentleman, has been assistant cashier in this house for eight years.

FRUIT ASSOCIATIONS.—We have noticed the growing importance of the fruit item of Oceana's productions. Knowledge of its culture for profit, however, was vague. The reputation of this section as especially adapted to its culture was confined to the county. For the double purpose of acquiring information in regard to fruit culture and extending the reputation of the locality by making proper fruit exhibits, a Pomological Society was organized with the following named persons actively identified with it, viz.: D. L. Garver, C. A. Sessions, A. H. Judd, Wm. Swingle, E. J. Shirts, F. J. Russell, L. Chubb, T. Taylor and J. M. Teeple. Profitable meetings were held during this season, then the interest waned and the Society ceased to exist. March 2, 1878, another organization was perfected at

Pentwater, called the West Michigan Horticultural Society, with many of those in the other Society and several new members. This continued to grow and meetings were held at Pentwater, Hart and Shelby that were largely attended. Interest increased, exhibits were made under its auspices at the State and other Fairs, and the reputation of the county for its adaptability for fruit culture attracted general attention. The State Horticultural Society held its spring meeting the following year at Pentwater, which was very successful, and new life was instilled into the rank and file of horticulturists throughout the county. This organization after accomplishing much, like its predecessor finally ceased to exist. The fruit interest continued to grow and extend, and the necessity of an organization was apparent. Some of the old members, assisted by younger material, put their shoulders to the work again and revived the old Horticultural Society and placed it upon a good substantial basis. Through its influence statistics have been secured, exhibits made at Detroit, Lansing and other places, and the reputation of the locality spread abroad until the attention of people in many States has been attracted toward Oceana County. It is still in existence and preparing for great work the coming season.

DEATH OF LORENZO D. EATON.—On page 27 we refer to Lorenzo D. Eaton as one of the first settlers of this county. He was born in New York State, March, 1827, where he passed his early days and arrived at man's estate. Nov. 24, 1842, he was married in New York State to Rebecca Bragg. He removed to Wisconsin and was living at Waukesha when a man by the name of Kelly, of Milwaukee, who claimed to have land in Oceana County, Michigan, engaged Mr. Eaton as foreman to take a gang of men and go upon it and get out shingle bolts for him. Kelly promised to provide for his family during his absence. Under this arrangement, in 1849 Mr. Eaton appeared in what was then the almost unbroken wilderness of Oceana. He had been here at work about three or four

LORENZO D. EATON.

months when an Indian brought a message to him from a friend living at White River, informing him that the land he was at work on did not belong to Kelly, and that the U. S. Marshal was after him. He immediately started on foot back to his home in Wisconsin, where after a journey of three hundred miles, enduring great hardships, he arrived only to find that Kelly had wholly neglected his family, and that they were in a condition of destitution and suffering, and had it not been for his timely return would have starved.

In 1850 he was again engaged by Kimball and Burchard to come to Oceana County and superintend their work in getting out shingle bolts. This time he brought his family with him. They came on a vessel and anchored at night off Stony Creek. He left the vessel and went ashore to get a scow to take off his family and supplies, but he had scarcely reached shore when a storm arose, and it becoming apparent that the vessel could not maintain her moorings, Mrs. Eaton and family and a very few provisions were placed in a small boat and sent ashore. This was on the 3rd day of November, 1850. The storm continued in great fury for three days and nights; rain and snow falling upon these pioneers who were without shelter except that which was rudely constructed at the time. He remained a resident of the county during his life. He, in after years, became a land locater and as such engaged his services to different persons. In the spring of 1876 he formed a copartnership with a young man by the name of Sammons, (son of J. H. Sammons,) who was locating lands in the Upper Peninsula. In July of this year they had made a trip to the forests and returned to Ontonagon, where Mr. Eaton secured passage on the ill-fated steamer St. Clair. The vessel took fire and burned to the water's edge. Mr. Eaton, with others, in attempting to make shore was drowned, and his body never recovered. He left his wife and seven children to mourn his loss. He was devoted to his family, a good father, kind husband and member of the M. E. Church. He was a member of the Odd Fellows' organization, and politically a democrat.

OCEANA'S TROTTING STOCK.—In every locality, cotemporaneous with its growth comes the horseman. The horse is man's best friend in improving a new section, and in contributing to his pleasure and convenience afterwards. Oceana county early developed a class of horsemen who did all in their power to increase the speed qualities of their animals. There were S. A. Browne, Wm. Webb, Jas. Malcom, Ed. Worden, and others, each of whom owned horses said to be *fast*, and many a race was trotted upon the ice to test the speed of contestants for favor.

In the winter of 1871 and 1872, Doctor D. G. Weare, a druggist of Pentwater and the person in whose honor a township was named, brought in a three-year-old chestnut colt, which he asserted was a direct descendant from Sherman Morgan, and which he named Oceana Chief. He used to appear upon the streets driving this colt every day. The awkward, shambling gait of the animal only served to excite the ridicule of local sportsmen, and the Doctor and his horse were made the butt of many a jest. He finally hired one Wm. Snyder to train it, paying Snyder sixty dollars per month. This also caused many unfavorable remarks, as the payment of $60 per month to care for a horse was considered simply ridiculous. The Doctor's efforts, however, to bring this animal into prominence as a trotter were unsuccessful, and he finally sold it to Chas. Nichols, a lumberman, for $700, receiving a part of the consideration and the balance to be paid when the pedigree was furnished. He furnished a part of the horse's pedigree, but as it had some bad omissions Mr. Nichols refused to pay the balance. A suit resulted which was before the Courts for several terms and finally decided against him. Nichols placed the horse in the hands of John Boga, his son-in-law, to train and drive.

In 1875 S. A. Browne brought to his Pentwater stables a beautiful black mare named Lady Turpin, which at the Rochester, N. Y., races this year had won first money, making a record of 2:23. The bringing of this horse to Pentwater stimulated the interest before manifested to fever heat, and The Driving Park Association prepared its grounds for great races, to follow. The course had been opened the year previous and inaugurated by the celebrated Small Hopes and other horses making a track record of 3:08. Under Boga's management the "Chief" began to develop wonderfully and in 1875 had won a race in three straight heats over the best local horses, and already sportsmen were beginning to look upon him as the coming horse.

Aug. 15, 1876, a race upon the Driving Park Association's grounds, Pentwater, for a purse of $250, with $125 as first premium, was advertised, free for all. The following is the description of the race:

"For this race seven horses were started:

1st, r g Red Oak.	2nd, c s Oceana Chief.
3rd, b'y s W Morrell.	4th, b'y g Gen. McArthur.
5th, b m Flossy.	6th, bl'k g John Barney.
7th, b'y g Roadmaster.	

There was considerable difficulty in getting a fair start, each driver seeming determined if possible, to have the advantage if he could get it. After scoring several times, they were given the word 'go,' and it was known that the *fastest horse* would win this race, if jockying *had* shown itself in some of the others and great interest was manifested; every stump and mound convenient was used by the spectators in order to get a better view. The remark was repeatedly made that 'the Chief was a bad breaker,' and 'if he would only keep his feet,' showed the interest taken in the result—and when they had reached the quarter post and the Chief *did* break, a look of dismay among his friends was visible; but he soon 'got down to business,' and came in the winner of the heat in 2:40, amid loud huzzas.

The call was made for the second heat, and after a half dozen futile attempts the horses were finally sent off in fine style. Oceana Chief soon went to the front, and maintained his position without a skip, notwithstanding the daring attempt of Barney to throw him off his feet. The Chief came in the winner of this, the second heat, in 2:37½, the fastest time thus far made.

The Chief had now won two of the three heats, and won them by fair and honest work, and his many friends were anxious lest the drivers of the other horses in the race should so manipulate affairs that he would be taken at a disadvantage. He had already taken two heats, 'would he take the third and end the race?' The horses were called and as in both the other heats, considerable time was spent in scoring, and when the word 'go' was given, they went off in fine style, and as the Chief again got the lead and opened quite a gap, the excitement was intense. The efforts of the police to 'keep quiet,' and preserve order was respected to a certain extent—but when the Chief came down the home-stretch and under the string leading the whole posse by a full length, there went up such a shout from the crowd, as only those can give who have restrained their feelings from a sense of duty, and all were jubilant over the result.
Time—2:40—2:37½—2:42."

From this time on Oceana Chief grew in favor. He was alternately placed in races and kept in the stud. On the Saginaw track he made a record of 2:23, equalling Lady Turpin's Rochester record, and which at the time was one of the best records made by a horse in his class.

Some of Mr. Browne's friends becoming jealous of the growing favor of Oceana Chief, made arrangements for big races on Pentwater Driving Park grounds in June, 1878, at which time noted horses from outside were induced to come and enter the free for all, and combine to defeat the Chief. The race came off, and the following were the entries:

1 Little Dan, s g—F. D. Clark.................................Grand Rapids.
2 Lady Jolly,—M. A. Jones......................................Caro.
3 Russ Ellis, b g—George G. Robins........................Grand Rapids.
4 Oceana Chief, c s—John Boga..............................Pentwater.
5 Scrabler, c g—M. A. Jones..................................Caro.
6 Jessie, c m—Bates & Harper...............................Spring Lake.
7 Lady Truesdell, b m—Thos. Merrill......................Muskegon.
8 Frank, bay g—John Connelly...............................Ludington.

The first heat the Chief won fairly. The next heat the combination forced the Chief back and permitted Russ Ellis to take it. The excitement now became great as the undisguised acts of the jocky to beat the Chief became manifest. The Chief's position was the outside. He started at a gait that was soon crowding the pole horses, and as he worked for the pole the jockeys played in front of him. Boga then turned out, taking the outside, trotted without a break right round the field and came under the wire a good winner, and acknowledged by the shouts of the spectators. The other heat was easily won by him, and Oceana's superiority as a trotter was established and never afterwards questioned by local sportsmen.

Nichols became involved and the ownership of the horse changed several times from one member of his family to another, and was also heavily mortgaged. In 1880, about sixteen miles from Grand Rapids, he was taken sick and died. It was thought by many that he did not die but was spirited away to get rid of the incumbrances upon him. It is certain, however he never appeared again in this section. He left a numerous progeny, some of which likewise became quite noted. Maggie Knox, owned by O. W. Knox, of Hart, was sired by the Chief, and made a record of 2:24¼. As there are many horses in this vicinity that trace their record through the Chief, we herewith give his pedigree so far as known:

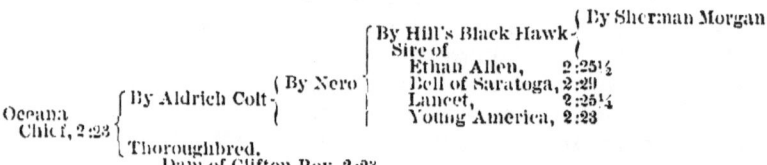

To S. A. Browne, however, is due great credit for giving to this locality an enviable reputation for its trotting stock. He became proprietor of a fine farm in Golden, which he named the Golden Stock Farm, and here brought and kept many horses of a fine strain of blood and wide reputation. Here also he bred many fine animals that have since become distinguished. Among those bro't here by Mr. Browne, was Indicator, 2:23½; Gold Dust, 2:29; Grand Hambletonian (stallion), 2:28½; Spinella, 2:30; Shadow, 2:27; Abdallah Belle; Richmond Belle; Peru Belle, 2:27; Lady Humphrey, 2:34; Scotia, 2:30; Amethyst; Sea Bird; Lady Arnold; Susie Wilkes; Soprano; Spiletta; Indiana, 2:39, and the young stallion Grand Sentinel, which was one of the finest horses ever brought to Michigan, and afterwards acquired almost national reputation. He has one son, Grand Sentinel, Jr., owned by Asa M. Pringle, of Golden, which has a numerous progeny, for the benefit of which we herewith give the following history:

"Grand Sentinel, 2:27½, son of Sentinel, 2:29¾, brother to Volunteer, was bred by John R. Richardson, Lexington, Ky.; got by Sentinel, out of Maid of Lexington, by Mambrino Pilot, 2:34¾, son of Mambrino Chief. Grand Sentinel, was, without being a very handsome horse, one of good parts, and very speedy and resolute. But, like his sire, he died just at the outset of a successful stud career. On the 8th of January, 1887, while playing in his paddock, he slipped on an icy spot and falling sustained injuries to his kidneys which led to acute inflammation and culminated in his death. His sire, Sentinel, died at the early age of ten years, and Grand Sentinel at thirteen years. But their line is achieving greatness, and promises to live on radiantly."

JUDGE GIDDINGS DIES.—Augustine H. Giddings, whose portrait appears on page 67, closed his earthly career in the saddest possible manner in a Philadelphia hospital, in the latter part of the year 1876. He ascended the bench of the Judicial Circuit to which Oceana County was part, in 1869, upon the death of Judge Hopkins. By his urbane manners, dignified bearing and courteous ways he secured the respect and esteem of all with whom he came in contact. He was, however, addicted to the use of intoxicating drinks, and to this terrible habit that held him in its vicelike chains and from which he made many a heroic struggle to free himself, was due his failure to obtain the highest reward to the ambitious disciple of the law, namely, a position on the Supreme Bench, and his death among strangers while yet in the prime of life. His appetite seemed to take possession of him at long intervals, between which he never tasted liquor, but when the desire came upon him nothing could prevent his gratifying it. He realized the disgrace which his course brought upon him, and several times during a half lucid interval, attempted suicide. Notwithstanding the fact that Court business was seriously interfered with by his acts, wherever he appeared he was accorded unusual marks of esteem by attorneys and litigants. He died without having been married, but many people sincerely mourned his departure.

COUNTY TREASURER DIES.—Aug. 23, 1877, Henry G. Hoffman, one of the pioneer settlers and County Treasurer, died, and the office was thereby made vacant. Mr. Hoffman's son and Deputy at once took charge of the office and was performing the duties satisfactorily when he too, was taken ill and died. The Board of Supervisors at its session in October elected John R. Butler, who served the balance of Mr. Hoffman's term.

JENNIE MILLS' DISAPPEARANCE.—Jennie Mills, of Pentwater, was a young lady of attractive personal appearance, and had many friends among the young people. She was employed as help in the family of J. G. Gray at the time of which we write, *i. e.*, Christmas, 1877. Many preparations for Christmas festivities had been made among which was a social party which she expected to attend. Always of a sunny disposition, it was remembered that on Christmas eve. she appeared even more gay than usual as she exhibited to friends the gifts she had received. She received a visit from a gentleman friend in the evening and parted with him about nine o'clock, nothing having occurred to give any clue to her subsequent disappearance. The next morning her clothes and jewelry were found on her stand, and the following note, but she had disappeared:

"Pentwater, Mich.

Dear Charley

You may think I am A foolish girl to think of you as I do but I will not try to explain matters here or any place else But Remember the past and don't forget Jen unless you find one who is a Better Friend to you than she was for Jen has loved you Beyond Reason But she will soon be at Rest and you can take a Boat Ride over her to morrow with Pleasure I suppose But when you come to morrow night Jen will not open the door for you and Charley is the only one who knows the Reason I will bid you a long farewell. Wishing you comfort and Happiness for ever

Your true friend,

JENNIE MILLS."

It was supposed she had thrown herself into the lake, but no trace of her ever came to the surface. Then it was thought she had wandered away in a fit of temporary insanity, and searching parties scoured the country in vain. Rumors of her having been seen in Canada and elsewhere were heard again and again. Many believed that she was still alive. The evidence of her drowning was very slight and few believed that she died in that manner. Sept. 5, 1885, a man by the name of Niel St. Clair, of Howard City, while cutting hoop poles near Wood Lake, found the skeleton of what appeared to be a young woman. The left side of the skull had been crushed in, indicating a violent death. The skeleton had evidently lain there several years. There had been no disappearances in the vicinity to account for its presence. There was nothing found with it to mark its identity. There were many Pentwater people who thought the letter published above was merely a blind and that she did not commit suicide as indicated, but was taken away and disposed of in some manner, but no evidence to prove the suspicion ever came to light, unless there was a connection between the finding of the skeleton and Miss Mills' disappearance. Near thirteen years have passed and the mystery of her death is as great as it was the next week after her disappearance.

HART ARGUS.—November 8, 1887, L. A. McIntyre, a doctor at Hesperia, and a Mr. Frink, a resident of the same place, started the Argus at that place, Dr. McIntyre conducting it. At this time there seemed to be an opening for another paper at Hart owing to dissatisfaction expressed at the course of the Journal, and in April, 1878, the office was removed to Hart, Mr. Frink retiring, and the paper became the *Hart Argus*. It received a fair patronage and continued as a republican paper under Mr. McIntyre's management until Sept., 1884, when it was purchased by Mr. E. S. Palmiter, its present owner and proprietor. It immediately, under his management, became the organ of the prohibition party and has advocated the principles of that party to the present time.

DOG TAX.—The Legislature had passed an Act requiring the assessment of a dog tax and providing for its collection. The Supervisors of the different towns were met by a perfect howl of indignation by dog owners, who declared they would not submit to it, etc. When the Board convened in October each Supervisor had the same experience to relate, and as a result the following remarkable resolution was adopted by a vote of nine to seven:

"WHEREAS, The present law authorizing a tax on dogs is believed to be unconstitutional by all—and,

WHEREAS, The said tax is oppressive and burdensome on that class of our people least able to bear the same—and,

WHEREAS, There are but very few sheep in the county to be worried or killed by dogs, and,

WHEREAS, The protection of sheep seems to be the prime object of said law, now, therefore, be it

Resolved, By the Board of Supervisors of the County of Oceana that the Supervisors of the several townships of this county be instructed not to assess the *Dogs* in their several townships."

HAWLEY'S MILL EXPLODES.—April 16, 1879, without previous warning the boilers in Hawley's sawmill, Shelby, burst into hundreds of pieces, portions of the same being hurled over forty rods distant. The dome and two large pieces of the boiler weighing about a ton each, were thrown high in the air and dropped about two hundred feet away. The engine bed dug out, turned over and thrown half around. Many timbers were shivered to pieces. Nearly all the machinery below was destroyed and a perfect wreck made. James Curtis Rider, the engineer, was instantly killed. E. C. Hurd, head-sawyer, while filing a saw, and E. F. Cook were badly cut in the head. George Getty, H. Benedict, Sylvester Elliott and John Vradenburg each had narrow escapes. Low water is supposed to have been the cause. The damage was about $6,000.

DEATH OF I. H. COGSWELL.—The subject of this sketch was born in Auburn, N. Y., in the year 1813, coming from there to Marshall in 1851, where he remained one year. Leaving that place he moved into Eaton County, where after two year's residence he came to Newaygo County, near the line. This was in 1856. In the spring of 1859 he emigrated to Kansas, and after a four years' stay returned to this point again, and after about one year moved across the line into Greenwood, Oceana County, where he lived until the tragic event which is hereafter described occurred. He was a man of commanding appearance, highly sensitive on questions of honor, and was respected and loved by all who knew him. He had been Judge of Probate for Newaygo County one term, and after coming to Greenwood was made Supervisor of that township, which position he held for five consecutive terms, and had just entered upon the sixth.

The home he lived in was a log structure with a board lean-to, or shanty, situated on section one of Greenwood township. On the death of J. D. Stebbins, a lumberman in that vicinity, he was appointed administrator of the estate. He had been notified by Judge of Probate F. J. Russell, to appear before the Probate Court on Monday, the 30th day of June, 1879, and render his account as administrator. The amount of estate to be accounted for was about $2,000. It was not thought that there was any shortage when matters were figured out. Neil McCallum, his son-in-law, and Lachlan McCallum were his bondsmen. In April he had made a proposal to Judge Russell to settle, which was refused, and on the 26th day of June he went to Lachlan McCallum in hopes of getting the matter straightened out, but he was not at home. He came home under the impression that his administration was suspected and would be attacked, and the next day he spent in figuring. The 28th he also remained at home and did nothing but look over the figures and help his wife about the house. The next day was Sunday. He had spoken for a horse to go to Hart Monday for a settlement. He claimed he had everything but some money due from Lachlan McCallum, and that appeared to worry him. On Sunday morning, the 29th, about sunrise he made a fire in the stove and then asked his wife to go with him into the room, and when he got there he took four packages of money and a book and put them in the stove and burned them, in spite of his wife's entreaties not to do so. He said, "I'll show them a trick the devil never did." After he had burned the money he took a paper and going to the closet lighted the clothing. Mrs. Cogswell tried to throw a dress out of doors but he prevented her. He said he was tired of life and wanted her to go with him. She inquired, "How will we go?" "I will have to kill you first," he said. He had a razor in his hand. She refused, and he followed her out of doors and said "The money is gone and we must go." He implored her to come with him. He said he was going to his grave. He then went into the house again and returning came out with a pocketbook in his hands and throwing it at his wife, said, "That is your wheat money." He then went in and that was the last ever seen of Isaac H. Cogswell. The house was burned to the ground. The coroners' verdict was "Death by deliberately walking into his burning house." The community was divided in opinion as to his being dead, many claiming the fire was only a blind, and that he had left the country. This opinion lost its force as year after year rolled by and nothing was ever heard of him. He was sixty-six years of age when his tragic death occurred.

BULL OF THE WOODS.—John S. Hyde, a machinist, musician and genius, imbued with the same idea that actuated Charles Mears in 1864, namely, that the navigation of the South Branch of Pentwater River was practicable, set about the construction of a scow-bottom boat, to be propelled by steam. The boat was constructed with especial reference to the accommodation of passengers and the carrying of freight between the two villages, Hart and Pentwater. Mr. Hyde completed his boat and in addition to making several pleasure excursions from Pentwater, he actually did make several trips, but as the Wigton grist mill when requiring the water, left the stream so shallow that the boat was obliged to lay for hours at a time waiting for water, this made it too expensive, and Mr. Hyde after trying ineffectually to secure the natural water of the stream at stated periods, abandoned his enterprise. He still asserts that with the natural flow of water he would have made the navigation of the river practical and profitable to both places. His boat was "dubbed" the "Bull of the woods." Unlike the Mud Hen, described on page 53, it did not prove a profitable investment.

MRS. GAINER CAPTURES A HORSE-THIEF.—Gilbert Brayton stole a span of horses and set of double harness from Messrs. Sweet & Taylor's mill in Ludington, on Saturday night, Sept. 27, 1879, about 10 o'clock, and going across to the village, took a double wagon and hitching his team to it, drove off. As near as can be ascertained, he traveled until about 2 o'clock Sunday afternoon without stopping, and it is very doubtful if any one knows just what roads he took up to this time in his efforts to baffle his pursuers and elude pursuit. But the pangs of hunger now compelled him to stop at "Mother Gainer's" for dinner, and this finished, he again set forth, going to Crystal Valley, Hart, Smith's Corners, Pentwater, and then east and north, until at 2 o'clock Monday morning, he was back at the very place where he took dinner the day before.

He had evidently been bewildered, and had in the 12 hours made a complete circle.

Just after he had been to dinner at Mother Gainer's on Sunday, Sheriff Moulton came hurriedly along, and telling the tale of the theft and offering $25 for the thief, he greatly excited the old lady, who had unconsciously given shelter to the scoundrel, and now was not slow in giving all the information possible which might lead to his capture. "Drive, Sheriff, drive like h—l," she concluded, "and you'll catch him."

On Brayton's return he seemed in haste to depart, but Mother Gainer called him to one side and told him she was a fortune teller, that she knew everything that he had done from the day he was ten years old, and everything he would do up to the end of his mortal career, and that she would prove it by telling him a fact known only to themselves, and then looking him full in the face she said:

"You stole those horses."

Brayton did not attempt to deny it, and she then told him she would buy the team of him, but he would have to go with her to Pentwater after the money. He seemed loth to consent, but finally did so. On the way he got ready to jump from the wagon several times, but Mother Gainer was too wide awake to permit anything of the kind and safely brought him to the village, where Constable Roddy stood ready to escort him to jail, having been warned by Sheriff Moulton who had followed Brayton in all his wanderings as far as Smith's Corners, where he lost the trail.

Mother Gainer said she expected Brayton would attempt to escape before he was brought to Pentwater.

"But," said she, "I made up my mind if he jumped from the wagon I would fall on top of him, and holler like the devil."

Sheriff Moulton had his prisoner safely in his own custody before noon, and took him to Ludington where he had his examination and was bound over for trial.

WRECK OF THE MERCURY.—Nov. 20, 1879, the citizens of Pentwater were startled by the information that the schooner Mercury, ladened with 250,000 feet of lumber, cleared from Ludington to Chicago, was going to pieces in the heavy sea south of Pentwater, and that the crew were in imminent peril of their lives. The beach was soon lined with people anxious to assist the crew ashore. The sea that was running was so heavy that not a boat could be found that would ride the breakers a minute. The telegraph wire between Pentwater and Ludington was down and help from there could not be secured. The line was repaired finally and a message sent, and about twelve o'clock that night Capt. H. B. Smith, with the little steamer Magnet, brought a volunteer life crew from Ludington with the life boat in tow, and all the men were rescued. In the afternoon, prior to the arrival of the Magnet, the crew on the ill-fated bark tried in vain to float a line ashore, and a skiff was manned by three brave men, Henry Hawkins, Frederick Sorenson and father, and an attempt was made to reach the end of the line. They got near enough for Hawkins to grasp the end of the line when the skiff capsized and all three were thrown into the water. The two Sorensens reached the shore in an exhausted condition, while poor Hawkins became entangled in the line and sank to rise no more. The sailors drew the body near the Mercury, but the line breaking the body was lost, and was never recovered.

Capt. H. B. Smith, for his gallant conduct that night in braving the terrible sea that rolled with his little steamer, was afterwards rewarded by a medal for gallantry, by Act of Congress.

THE WRECK OF THE LAMONT. One of the most terrible lake catastrophes that ever occurred near Pentwater was the wreck of the tug Geo. Lamont and the loss of all on board, March 14, 1880. Some time previous C. R. Whittington and P. H. Adams purchased and brought to Pentwater the tug Gem, repaired and fitted it up for general tugging business upon the lake. From the time the Gem arrived a rivalry sprang up between the owners of the tugs Messenger and Lamont and the Gem. The spirit of rivalry was maintained and strengthened by bantering, hectoring remarks by each and the circulation of false stories concerning the seaworthiness of the respective crafts. At last it culminated in an agreement for a race to take place next day. The Lamont was a small tug of less than five tons burthen, while the Gem was about ten tons. Statements of all kinds were circulated and side bets made, and the captains were each wrought up to such a pitch of excitement that nothing short of a catastrophe to start with would have stopped them.

The fatal Sunday dawned with a heavy sea rolling in, and everything being in readiness they started upon the race. The persons on board the Gem were Captain P. H. Adams, John Millidge and Moore Hardway, and on board the Lamont were Captain Charles Lamont, his son Georgie, a lad of about twelve years, and Palmer Hill. It was evident from the start that the Lamont was no match for the Gem in such a sea, yet she ploughed along through the breakers in a vain endeavor to keep up. Many people watched them until they were a couple of miles out, and not being able to see them longer on account of the falling snow, returned to their firesides. About the middle of the afternoon the Gem came back, having made the trip and returned. Upon inquiry as to the Lamont, Adams stated that when about four miles out she turned about, and as he supposed, returned to Pentwater, as the snow enveloped her so he could not see her any great distance, and he had not seen her since. The people of Pentwater immediately scoured the beach and about three miles north the Lamont was discovered wrecked, with no sign of any one on board. The bodies afterwards came ashore and were interred in the village cemetery. Mr. Lamont was one of the best engineers in the place, a good mechanic and a daring sailor. Many a time has he breasted the rolling waves with a tug to relieve some vessel in distress, or aid them in making port. He seemed to be absolutely without fear.

DEATH OF JUDGE LITTLEJOHN.—Ex-Judge Flavius J. Littlejohn, whose portrait appears on page 36, and who was the first Judge occupying the bench in Oceana County, died at his residence in Allegan, Michigan, in May, 1880, of senile disease of the bladder. For many years the Judge presided over a circuit extending from Allegan along the lake shore north to the straits, and rode the circuit with lawyers who attended the Court in its journeyings. Many hardships and privations were encountered and endured in the early times. County seats were not even "flag stations," but the approaches to the local seats of justice were through paths where no vehicle could be drawn and travel was on horseback or afoot, and it was a lucky trip that was without meeting with mishaps in the shape of swollen rivers, bridgeless, forest fires, or blockades of fallen trees. As settlers came in the judicial circuit was divided and sub-divided until at present there are several formed out of the original territory traversed by the late Judge. His reputation was unblemished and his decisive manners coupled with good, practical judgment and legal attainments created a strong personal friendship and great respect for his decisions, approximating to almost infallibility. We recollect a time when if a question was to be placed at rest all that was necessary was to quote the venerable Judge's opinion—that settled it beyond cavil. For many years he had been in feeble health yet had continued to practice law after his retirement from the bench, as his condition would permit—died in the harness. The last visit to our county that we are aware of was in 1875, when he assisted in the trial of the case of Post vs. Rich, which involved the title to quite a portion of the village of Pentwater. He was bright and lively as of yore, but said work tired him; still he was happy to meet old time friends once more and spent the most of the night in talking of the old times and acquaintance, and laughed as heartily as any one at the recalling of jokes and ludicrous scenes, and recounted many that came to his mind. Indeed, this was one of his favorite pastimes. He is the author of "Legends of Michigan and the Old Northwest," which abounds with anecdotes of the old pioneer life of our State and which has met with favor all over our country as a narrative of border experiences. He was a man of decided political opinions, yet although an ardent democrat he could recognize the right of others differing with him, and grant to them the same privileges that he claimed for himself. Truthfully may we say he was a pure and upright Judge and a genial gentleman.

SHELBY INDEPENDENT.—Judson Palmiter, founder of the Oceana Co. Journal, and at one time one of the proprietors of the Oceana Times, having removed the material of the old Times office to Shelby, started the first paper in that village, which appeared on the 10th day of April, 1880. The name of the paper was the Shelby Independent. February 9th, 1884, Frank W. Newman purchased the plant and has since conducted the paper. Under Mr. Palmiter's management it professed to be independent in politics, but Mr. Newman made it an out-and-out republican paper, and has continued it as such.

THE ALONZO IRONS DISAPPEARANCE.—On Friday, June 3, 1881, one of the most mysterious cases of disappearance that ever occurred in the county, took place. Alonzo Irons, a young man whose home was in Pentwater, and who was highly regarded by all who knew him, having been employed by Nickerson & Collister to act as manager and store-keeper for them at Crystal, disappeared very mysteriously on the above date, and although people from all sections turned out in numbers and scoured the country, and notwithstanding the fact that large rewards were offered and a Pinkerton detective employed for some time, a solution of the mystery has never been reached.

In brief, the facts are as follows: On the day mentioned, after having eaten his dinner, he, in company with a young man by the name of Fisher, started from the mill with the intention of going to the house of a Mr. Chase to pay for some hay that had been purchased of him for Nickerson & Collister. The young man who accompanied him was going part of the way to deliver some axes to the Johnson brothers, who were making bolts in the woods. While they were walking along the string holding the axes broke and they fell, one of them cutting Fisher's heel. They stopped and bound up the wound, and Mr. Fisher came back. Irons taking the axes went on alone. He delivered the axes at the shanty and then proceeded towards Chase's. He never reached Chase's house, and has never been seen by his friends since leaving the Johnsons.

We herewith publish the detective's report of his investigations, as it has been seen by but few persons, and will give additional information concerning the efforts made to find Irons:

PINKERTON'S NATIONAL DETECTIVE AGENCY.

L. G. RUTHERFORD, Attorney at Law, Hart.

DEAR SIR:—According to your request an operative was detailed to proceed to Hart, Mich., to see you and make investigations in relation to the disappearance of a young man by the name of Alonzo Irons on June 3rd. Irons being the foreman for Nickerson & Collister, proprietors of a saw mill in the woods 13 miles from Hart.

Wednesday, June 15th, 1881.

At 9 a. m. Operative C. left Chicago for Hart, where he arrived about 10 p. m. of the same day. He immediately called upon you and received a statement of the case as far as then known.

Thursday, June 16th, 1881.

C. left Hart this morning, having received a letter of introduction from you to a Mr. Taylor in the vicinity of the saw mill where Irons worked. Arriving at the saw mill, C. saw the new foreman, Glover, who said that he knew Irons well; that he left the mill Friday, June 3rd, directly after dinner, without his coat, to go and see a man named Chase about some hay, and was seen three or four miles up the road by some bolt cutters, since which time he had not been seen. His accounts were all right and there was money due him by the firm. If nothing had happened to him he should have returned the same afternoon at 6 p. m. to take the men's time. There was a dance that evening at an Indian's named Coxsheegan, and Irons was heard to say that he was going to attend it. After gathering a good deal of information of this sort, C. went to see King's wife. * * C. found her after a good deal of hunting among the Indians, at the house of a man named Cotton, and asked her to account for her time during the day on which Irons disappeared. She said she and her husband were at home all day with his little boy. In the afternoon Nelse Olcutt came and staid to supper, and went away about nine in the evening. She could not account for the blood which was found on the floor, but for the bullet hole through the window, she said that her husband locked her out one night and she broke the window with a stick trying to get in.

Friday, June 17th, 1881.

C. left Hart again this morning and went up to see King. He found him at his house with his little boy. King was sick, but got up and seemed very willing to answer C.'s questions. His statement was to the effect that himself, his wife, the little boy, and a fellow named Olcutt were at home all of Friday afternoon and evening. His wife was making a dress, and none of them were away from the house only up to the cross-roads where the boys had a bonfire in the evening. A man named Vaughn who lives with his family a few rods further down, on the opposite side of the road, testified to the same thing. King showed C. what had been said to be a bullet hole in the window, and he at once saw that it was not made by a bullet, but by a stick close to the bottom of the pane. As to the spots of blood on the floor, King said that he remembered having opened a blister on his foot and a few drops of blood fell on the floor and chair. He showed C. the place on his foot where a large burn had recently healed. On making inquiry of Taylor, where King worked, C. learned that he had burned his foot on a stump which was yet on fire. C. asked King a good many questions about his wife, and he said he had done the best he could for her, but that she had brought him into disgrace, and he could not take her back. He came away from Ada on her account. He did not know that Irons had been intimate with his wife, and he would not be able to recognize him if he passed him on the road. He felt sure that C—— was intimate with his wife, and if he caught C—— or any one else fooling around his house at night, he said he would shoot them, and he believed the law would sustain him. He told C. that he did keep his wife out one night when she came back with another man who hung about the gate. This was the night she broke the window trying to get it. D. feels sure had there been any disturbance at King's that Vaughn's, who live a few rods away, would have heard in. C. then went to the mill where Irons was foreman, and saw Crowfoot, with whom Irons was quite intimate. Crowfoot was willing to tell all he knew, and talked quite freely of the affair, but he did not think that Irons ever had anything to do with King's wife, * * * C. managed by a great deal of questioning to draw out the fact that two Indians, at least, had threatened Irons' life, one by the name of Lew Dominick. Crowfoot had heard that Irons was in the store alone with this "4th of July" about a month ago, when Louie Baptiste, an Indian and 4th of July's brother-in-law, came in and ordered her out and drove her into the rain, and then turning to Irons threatened to kill him. Jennie was with Irons in the store all the morning of June 3rd, the day he disappeared. She had been working for Mrs. Kellogg, the wife of the boarding boss, who turned her away immediately after. Jennie left the camp about an hour before Irons, but went in a different direction. Louie Baptiste has two brothers, Joe and Mitchel, and as they were working in the mill C. went in and took a look at them. He pretended not to notice them, but they appeared very uneasy and did not take their eyes off from him while he was there. The other Indians working there did not seem in the least suspicious. Louie and Joe were both at work the day Irons left, but Mitchel left that noon and was pretty drunk. Irons did not show up at the dance at Coxshegawn's. After supper at Taylor's, C. drove over to see Peter Starr, but gained no additional information.

Saturday, June 18th, 1881.

C. went up to the mill this morning and almost the first man he saw was Crowfoot, who told him that Johnny Gesucks, an Indian, asked him quietly what C. would give to know who killed Irons. C. had anticipated this question and had posted Crowfoot what to say. Crowfoot told Gesucks that he thought C. would give $600 or $1,000. From this and other incidents suspicion points strongly to the Indians. C. then drove to Crystal, and saw Jennie Hinman, the squaw who is married to an Indian named Sabbee or Shawbee, who works in the Crystal saw mill. He did not question her or let her know who he was, as he merely wished to locate her. He next drove across the country to see Hank Kidder. Kidder with one of the Baptiste Indians, found a place back of King's house and down in a swampy place which they claimed was the scene of a struggle, and Kidder's little boy and Joe Baptiste each found a silver half dime and a nickel; also what they claimed to be mustache hairs that were scratched off by the body being dragged under the fence. The hair Kidder had (he only had one,) was black and long, whereas Irons' mustache was only perceptible and about a cream color. Kidder impressed the operative as a blow-hard, and he is inclined to think that he either "planted" these coins for the purpose of creating a talk, or that they were dropped by the searchers, as they were found about a week after Irons disappeared. Today, on his return to Hart, C. saw Mr. John Bean, the County Surveyor and an old settler, who is thoroughly conversant with the woods.

 Yours truly,   ALLEN PINKERTON.

L. G. RUTHERFORD, Esq., Attorney at Law, Hart, Mich.

 DEAR SIR:—The following is the continuation of your report:

Sunday, June 17th, 1881.

C. went to King's place this morning and had a talk with him; C. also examined the spot back of his place where the money is said to have been found. The ground was torn up and the grass considerably scratched, but this, of course, was done by the searchers, as there are several reliable men who made an earlier search and they assured C. that there was no sign of any struggle. C. has examined King thoroughly and separately from his wife, and is convinced that he had nothing to do with the murder and that he knows nothing of it. C. thinks that jealous Indians did the work. C. saw the Vaughn family who live across the street from the Kings. The families are very intimate and the Vaughns are reliable. They say King and his wife and little boy were about home all of the day that Irons disappeared and they corroborate King's story in various ways. C. went again to see if he could discover any smell in the woods where young Sayles claimed to have smelled something, but C. was unable to find anything. C. went over to Bean's mill and saw Ira Fritz and Bleek Crowfoot and others. C. ran a rumor down about the Sweeney's, who keep a store and sell whisky at the mill on the sly, but it amounted to nothing. A good many say that these Indians have not grit enough to commit murder, but C. has found several men who have been nearly killed, when taken unawares, for some little offense, and Van Brocklin, foreman of the shingle mill and a reliable man, said that the Indians are just like wolves, cowardly and treacherous. Now and then a decent one is found. C. returned to Sayles' and staid all night.

Wednesday, June 20th, 1881.

C. went to Bean's mill early this morning and VanBrocklin told him that Austahasong, an old Indian and a reliable one, had found a trail near Paybama Lake that he wished C. to look at. Van Brocklin is an old trailer and he said that the Indian's word is reliable, and C. asked him if he would go and show him (C.) the trail. He said he would. During the talk the villainous faces of Joe and Louis Baptiste were watching C., but he paid no attention to them. VanBrocklin borrowed Shonageesick's river boots for C. and they started on what proved to be a sixteen mile tramp. VanBrocklin and C. with Austahasong and his son and two other Indians left camp and after walking about seven miles came to the marsh near Paybama Lake. It is a wild, desolate place and they saw several bear tracks. After they waded through the swamp a long distance they came to the trail. Austah gave a grunt and pointed to it. They then went to the place in the woods where it starts and followed it down to the creek where it crossed, and then through the swamp grass to within three or four rods of Paybama Lake, where it could not be seen on account of the nature of the ground. C. saw that a soft, heavy body had been dragged over it towards the lake. It looked as if a bag of wheat or oats had been dragged over the place. It certainly was no canoe. C. suggested a bear or deer, but could see at once that if it were either hair would have been left on the trail. Austah said "If bear or deer trail go from lake." One of the Indians suggested that a bundle of light wood for burning in a jack-light was dragged there, and Austah laughed at dragging light wood a long way through water when there was plenty of it on the banks of the lake; besides where the trail started there was no light wood. The trail led to within a few rods of a canoe that Austah made over a year ago, and it has been on the lake ever since. C. got into the canoe and paddled around the lake, which is small but deep and shut in by thick woods all around; he could see the bottom in some places covered with moss and weeds, but that was only on the edge. After making the circuit of the lake C. directed the party to go back and see if they could find anything in the shape of a trail leading from the place where the body was dragged. There were three little smokes or small fires where the trail began, and after searching about for some time Austah and VanBrocklin found the tracks of persons leading away from the trail and also the same tracks deeply indented pointing towards the trail. C. was a little skeptical about the identity of these tracks, but he could see that they were old and deep, as if a heavy body had been carried. After about two hours' work the Indians followed the track to the old wagon road cut down to the swamp from the main road and about half a mile from where Irons was last seen. There was just one faint wagon track on this road, and all said that the road had not been used for months. It certainly looks as if a body had been carried in a wagon as far as the road goes and then slung from a pole or carried on a litter to a lonely place near the swamp and then dragged to the lake, taken in the canoe and thrown into the water. C. did not rely on his own opinion entirely, but on that of experienced woodsmen like Austah, VanBrocklin and others, all of whom said that nothing could be dragged by a hunting and fishing party that would make a similar trail. One Indian, Bailey, differed, but he is a Catholic and Austah is a Methodist. The other is a Pagan and agreed with Austah.

Tuesday, June 21st, 1881.

This morning C. saw John Bean and he was going up to see Lon Yates where Mrs. King was stopping. C. decided to go with him. On the way up with Bean, C. decided to drag the lake Thursday, going to Pentwater to-morrow after the tools. When they arrived at Yates' C. found that Mrs. King had gone with Yates' peddler and did not know where. On his return C. stopped at Monroe Wicks', where Oleutt works, but he was not there. C. had a talk with Mr. Holt, a neighbor just across the road, who had heard Oleutt's story, and believed it. Further down the road C. met Mr. Wicks and he said Oleutt was strictly truthful and he believed him. Oleutt was at King's from two in the afternoon until nine in the evening with King, his wife, and Willie, King's son. C. drove on and met one of the Supervisors. On driving by Cotton's near Bean town, C. saw Mrs. King. They had a talk and she said she would like to go to Hart, and C. invited her to ride down with him as that would give him an opportunity to talk with her. She said she would go, and after C. drove over to the mill, on the way back he picked her up. She told C. a good deal of her past life, how she was arrested when 13 years old for being a prostitute. She said she would never go back to King, but was going to Grand Rapids or Ada, her former home. She told C. she was going to get some of King's notes into her hands and sell some of his horses if she could, and invited C. to come and see her at Grand Rapids. On arriving at Hart C. got supper for her and got her a room, and bought her a comb, button-hook and several little trifles.

Wednesday, June 22nd, 1881.

C. heard today that Louie Baptiste beat his wife some time ago for having $2.00 which she could not account for and he swore that Irons was at the bottom of it. This came through Billy General, an Indian. C. spread the report that he was to drive to Paybama Lake and drag it on Thursday, and then asked Austah to watch and see if any one came there before then. C. then drove to Pentwater with Ed. Irons and met Mr. Nickerson, one of the proprietors of the mill, who promised to do everything he could to aid in the matter. Returning to Bean-town C. took supper at Capt. Irons. C. saw Lou's boots and learned that Ed. wore them while searching. This accounts for the tracks on King's oat field.

Thursday, June 23rd, 1881.

This morning after making a very efficient drag, C. assisted by his party commenced to drag the Paybama Lake. They worked hard all day, but did not find anything to reward their efforts.

Friday, June 24th, 1881.

They resumed dragging this morning and continued till 3 p. m. with no success. VanBrocklin, who is an old sailor and fisherman, was the best man C. could have had. They found another little lake close by and decided to drag it when they got a better rig.   Yours Truly,   ALLEN PINKERTON.

CHICAGO, July 6th, 1881.

L. G. RUTHERFORD, ESQ., Attorney at Law, Hart, Mich.

DEAR SIR:—The following is a continuation of Mr. Coe's report:

Saturday, June 25th, 1881.

This morning C. went over into Mason county to see Joe Adams, a man who took a prominent part in the search for Irons, and who proposed to lynch King. C. met him near his house and had a long talk with him, and there seemed to be still better cause for suspicion against the Baptiste boys. Billy General, an intelligent Indian who lives near him, thinks that Louie Baptiste, if not guilty, at least knows something about the disappearance of Irons. Johnny Pete, a son of old Pete Puckanobanaw, took his father and mother over to the town of Elbridge, either the day before or on the morning of the disappearance of Irons. Johnny Pete was said to have been with the Baptiste boys late in the night in which Irons disappeared. After they had come back, a few days after the disappearance, from searching for Irons, Joe Adams asked Louis Baptiste why he did not assist in the search, and Baptiste said: "What for you ask me? I no killum Irons." C. then drove back to camp where Johnson and several Swedes who had lately arrived, were stopping. These were the men who last saw Irons, a short distance beyond Bean's camp. Johnson was willing to tell all he knew. He said that Irons was walking along the road a little after 4 o'clock in the afternoon. He walked slowly as if thinking of something, with his head down and one hand behind his back. These men were sitting on a log smoking and did not speak to Irons nor did he notice them. C. then returned to Bean-town.

Sunday, June 26th.

Today C. went down to Hart to write up his reports, which he is unable to do in the woods.

Monday, June 27th.

C. left Hart early this morning and went to the mill and took a walk over into Mason county to see Adams. He was not at home, but C. found him in the woods talking to Billy General and several other Indians. C. and Adams walked back to the house and in a short time were joined by Billy General. Billy said in substance the same as Adams told C. on Saturday. He said that the Indians would not kill a man for money, but they would do so for revenge. He seemed to think that Louis Baptiste acted strangely when talking to Adams. He promised to try and find out where Johnny Puckanobanaw went with his team on the night before Irons disappeared. He thought he couldn't do much because the Indians seemed to be suspicious of him. General agreed to come to Hart Wednesday or Thursday. On his way back C. stopped at Crystal and saw Ira Ford, a Constable of that place. C. asked him if he knew anybody who could be trusted to rope in with Jennie Sawbee. Mr. Ford suggested a French Indian named Louis Tremblee, and said he would do all he could to assist C.

Tuesday, June 28th, 1881.

C. came to the conclusion that it would be impossible to rope in with the Indians on account of their imperfect knowledge of English and the fact that they will not talk about each other. He decided that the only way to do was to arrest the whole party, and then either trust to their giving each other away or imprison them together and have a hole cut in the ceiling of their cell and have Niley Sayles, who speaks the Indian language, and Billy General concealed in the room above to listen to their talk. C. went to Hart today for the purpose of submitting this plan to the authorities there. They approved of it, but it was finally decided that C. should question the parties who are suspected as soon as he could get Sayles to act as an interpreter. He is away, but will be back in a short time and C. will then see what can be done with the Baptiste boys and Jennie. C. then went back to Bean-town and spent the day in getting all the information he could about the suspected parties. He learned that Louis Baptiste had nearly killed a white man named Betsy in Pentwater two years ago, which shows that he is of a bad disposition.

Wednesday, June 29th, 1881.

Today C. went over to Crystal to see if Ford had learned anything about the matter from Jennie. He said that Tremblee had had her out the night before but could get nothing out of her in regard to the matter. C. then returned to Bean-town. He is trying to find out how Austabasong found the trail by Paybama Lake in such a desolate place. C. learned that an old squaw, the grandmother of the Baptistes, dreamed that she saw two men carrying a body through the swamp and just as they were about to sink it in Paybama Lake she woke up. C. will try to find out whether the old lady dreamed this, or really knows anything about it. He will also try to find out who started the story that Louis Baptiste gave his wife a whipping on finding out that she had $2.00. C. also got a letter from Mrs. King asking him to come and see her in Grand Rapids. C. learned that she had said before leaving that C. was pretty cute but she had not told him *everything* she knew.

Thursday, June 30th, 1881.

C. went to Hart today and waited for Billy General, but he did not come. About noon Adams came and said General had refused to come, saying that he could not afford to pay the expense. Adams offered to pay his expenses, but he would not come, as he seems to be afraid to tell what he knows.

Friday, July 1st, 1881.

C. started this morning, taking Sayles with him, to see Jennie. He found her in bed. She refused to talk until C. threatened to arrest her when she became more tractable. C. asked her when she last saw Irons. She said the day he left she was in the store with him. She said that she knew that he was going away in the afternoon. C. said, "Well, what time was it you met him in the woods." She said she did not meet him; she left Bean-town after he went. She went to John Cotton's near by, and after staying a little while went over to Shagonabee's house. This is true. C. asked her how long she staid at Shagonabee's. She said two weeks. This was a lie as she was arrested three days after at Crystal. She said she knew nothing about Irons. They then went over to Crossman's mills where old man Bailey lived. Bailey is the Indian who was with C. on the trail at Paybama Lake. He says he is certain that the body was dragged there. He thought that Johnny Coby, an Indian now at White River, started the story about Louis Baptiste finding his wife with two dollars. C. then went over to Bean-town. He had a talk with Louis Baptiste who acted very strangely and contradicted himself several times. C. asked him if he had ever had any trouble with Irons.

He said that the Indians all loved Irons as he was so good to them. C. asked him where he went last Tuesday. He said he went to see Charlie General, who was a notorious drunkard and supposed to be a brother of Billy General. He said he told Ira Fritz that he went to Mason County, as he wanted him to think his horse was a good one, as he wanted to buy it of him Ira had said that Louis had followed them when they went to Mason County. Louis said that on the night Irons disappeared he went home and went to bed; he didn't go to the dance at Coxsegan's because he was tired. It is the first time he missed a dance anywhere. He said he didn't know anything about his wife getting $2.00 from Irons. He said his brother Mitchell was at the mill that afternoon. VanBrocklin, foreman in the mill, says that Mitchell left the mill at noon with Charley Pete. C. then saw Charlie Pete who seemed very nervous while C. was talking to him. He denied having been away from the mill on Friday, June 3rd, and stuck to it. Mr. Spicer, who lives near by, says that he was in the store the day before Irons disappeared, and Louis Baptiste was there also and was talking in an angry manner to him. * * Irons came from behind the counter in a threatening manner and said; "What's that you say?" Louis said that he might be mistaken. They spoke a few words in the Indian tongue and then Louis went away, but they were both angry. C. then went to see Louis' wife. Fourth of July was there also. Mrs. Baptiste was very anxious to know who told C. that Irons had given her two dollars, and seemed very indignant at it. * * C. asked Louis' wife what time Louis came home and where he went after supper on the night of Irons' disappearance. She said he went to bed after supper as he was tired. Ira Fritz will swear that he saw Louis go towards home at supper time and then come back. He hung around until dusk and then left. C. then went to see Mitchell Baptiste. He was not at home. His wife said that Mitchell went to bed on the night of the disappearance right after supper. Louis Shagoubee's wife was there and C. asked how long Jennie staid at her house after Irons disappeared. She said two nights. This is true. C. waited some time for Mitchell, but he did not come and C. went back to Sayles'.

C. thinks that the result of his inquiries among the Indians shows that they must know something about the matter or they would not lie so about it. Sayles, who at first did not believe that the Indians knew anything about it is now inclined to think that they know more about it than they will tell.

    Yours Respectfully,   ALLEN PINKERTON.

A SAD ACCIDENT AT CRYSTAL.—A very sad accident occurred at Crystal Valley on the evening of July 31, 1879. Two boys, the sons of Mr. and Mrs. Wm. McClure, were both drowned in the mill pond, a small body of water covering about two acres. Geo. P. Quinn, son of Mrs. McClure by a former husband, a lad of about fourteen years of age, and Warren McClure, son of Mr. McClure by a former wife, nine years of age, were the victims. They were both bright lads having many friends who predicted for them a bright future. The circumstances of the affair were briefly these: On the evening named the boys came from school and requested of their father, who was sick in bed, permission to go in swimming. He consenting, they repaired to the mill pond and were seen at about six o'clock playing in the shallow water. This was the last seen of them in life. The fact that they did not come to supper was commented upon, but the parents concluded they had gone after the cows and so the matter rested until dusk, when a search was instituted which resulted in the finding of both bodies in the pond. Warren was lying upon his back in about eight feet of water, while George was clinging to him face down. The supposition was that Warren had gone beyond his depth and George in attempting to assist him also perished. The affair cast a gloom over the community for many days.

THE SCANDINAVIAN, EVANGELICAL, LUTHERAN CHURCH OF OCEANA COUNTY.—Among the pioneers of Oceana County there were a few Scandinavians who settled in what are now Benona and Claybanks townships. Coming from countries having a State Church, and where the principles of Christianity are early and firmly inculcated into the mind, it is but natural that early in their pioneer life they should yearn to establish among themselves the church of their fathers. In the summer of 1862, urged by their inherent desire, they sent an invitation to Rev. Hatlestad, of the Augustana Synod, to visit them. He came, and on the 10th of August, 1862, they met for the first time in these almost unbroken wilds for worship. Accustomed as they had been in the Old World to regularly attend services, how must it not have thrilled them as again they bowed in prayer, and, with the moaning of the Great Lake wafted calmly through the solitudes of the primeval wilderness surrounding them on every side, as accompaniment, they again sang the psalms they had sung in youthful days.

In the afternoon of the same day, they held a meeting to organize a Church, at which the following persons united and formed the Church whose name appears at the head of this sketch:

Anders H. Brady and wife Ingeborg.
John Munson and wife Fredericka.
Andrew H. Brady and wife Julia.
Henry Hendrickson and wife Martha.
Tollef Hendrickson and wife Nicoline.
Tollef Brady and wife Gurine.
Halvor H. Brady and wife Nicoline.
Nils Haroldson and wife Maren.
Christopher Knudson and wife Isabella.
Ole Fergesen and wife Oline.
Halvor H. Brady.
Annetta Brady.
Christopher Omholdt.

A constitution was adopted in part, and Henry Henrickson, Anders H. Brady and John Munson were elected deacons.

In 1865, thirteen members were added, and in 1866 the balance of the constitution was adopted, the organization completed and eleven persons admitted to membership.

The following is a list of those who have served the Church as pastors:

Rev. J. Nesseth from the organization until 1868.
Rev. J. C. Jacobsen from 1868 until 1870.
Rev. T. H. Wald from 1870 until 1878.
Rev. O. Amble from 1878 to 1884.
Rev. H. Z. Hvid from 1884 until 1885.
Rev. S. Olsen from 1885 until 1886.
Rev. J. Sæther from 1886 until 1887.
Rev. O. C. Baker from 1887 and continuing.

In 1869, Tollef Brady sold the Church three acres of land and gave it two acres. The same year one acre of this was dedicated to a grave yard. Already, fine monuments mark the resting places of many who have been closely connected with the interests of the Church. Foremost among these may be mentioned Anders H. Brady and John Munson, two of the first deacons.

In 1884, a neat little church was built, in Claybanks. It is 50 feet long, 32 feet wide and 18 feet high, with the addition of a vestry in the rear. The steeple, of ancient architectural design, is 12 feet square and 64 feet high. The cost of the edifice and its furnishings was about $2,000.

At present the membership exceeds two hundred, and the Church is in a healthy and prosperous condition.

THE MAKIN MURDER.—On the 11th day of October, 1884, Jas. A. Barker, or Al. Barker, as he was known, shot and killed his brother-in-law, Willie Makin, in the presence of his wife, Makin's sister, and Jesse Howe and son. The shooting took place from Barker's barn, whither Makin and his sister had gone to get a grist which Barker had ground at Pentwater the day before for Makin. Barker stood in the open door with a stick in his hand, and as Makin stepped upon the bridge he struck him over the head with the stick breaking it. Makin then stepped one side as if to pick up a stone and started up the bridge again, when Barker commenced firing upon him, one of which shots took effect, hitting Makin in the breast, causing almost instant death. Jesse Howe, who witnessed the tragedy, brought the news to Hart and officers immediately started after and arrested Barker at a neighbor's house near by. He was under the influence of liquor and had a revolver on his person fully loaded. The trial took place in the February term of Court following, and being the first murder trial in the county, excited considerable attention. The Prosecuting Attorney, C. B. Stevens, and the Hon. F. W. Cook, of Muskegon, conducted the prosecution; L. G. Rutherford and Hon. W. E. Ambler the defense, Judge Ramsdell presiding. He was found guilty of manslaughter and sentenced to ten years in Jackson State's prison.

Several efforts were made to secure his pardon, but were unavailing. The murder was cold-blooded and heartless, but there were many extenuating circumstances brought to light. Had he not been under the influence of liquor, however, the murder would never have occurred.

On the 31st day of January, 1888, Barker died in State's prison, of typhoid fever.

PENTWATER FURNITURE FACTORY.—We remember when we first came to Northern Michigan hearing the oft-repeated expression: "Yes, its a lively town now and will be for a few years, but what will be done when all the pine is gone?"

While Oceana County has never been much of a pine timber point as compared with her neighbors on the north and south, still her first manufactures were of the saw mill species, and while in the main, the development of agriculture has gradually followed the lumber period, still the question of maintaining and increasing village growth must be by furnishing labor for men, and if steady thrift is secured some new manufactures must succeed the lumber mills. Pentwater took its first step in attempting to solve this problem in the spring of 1882, when a few of her enterprising citizens reached the determination to give over their efforts to induce foreign capital to come to their assistance, and resolved that they would make the venture unaided. It was arranged between Sands & Maxwell, Nickerson & Collister, and Nielsen & Co., three of the principal firms, that they would contribute twelve thousand dollars of the amount necessary to start a furniture factory, and with this as a "leader" Messrs. Fred Nielsen, W. E. Ambler and E. Nickerson undertook to raise the necessary funds by a general subscription to capital of a joint stock company.

It was a great undertaking when we consider the small number and ability of the citizens to invest in the enterprise. After some hard and persistent work, about $32,000 was subscribed and the company incorporated. On the 25th day of May, 1882, the stockholders met at the office of W. E. Ambler and organized by electing Edwin Nickerson, William B. O. Sands, Edgar G. Maxwell, Thomas Collister, Fred Nielsen, Jacob Fisher, John Jeffries, Directors. William E. Ambler was elected, but declined to serve and was excused. The Board of Directors organized by electing W. B. O. Sands, President; E. Nickerson, Vice President; J. Jeffries, Sec'y; Fred Nielsen, Treasurer.

Director Nickerson offered the following resolution:

"That W. E. Ambler is hereby appointed as the agent of the company to purchase of Hon. Charles Mears certain ground for the use of the company, as he shall deem advisable and for the best in-

GAZETTEER OF THE VILLAGE OF PENTWATER.

—x—

Churches.—Congregational. M. E. Church. Rev. A. L. Coors, Pastor. Baptist. Rev. M. L. Marvin, Pastor. St. James Mission, Lay Reader, G. H. Cleveland, M. D., Catholic Church, no Resident Priest.

Schools.—Union. Prof. F. O. Wickham, Principal. Assistant, Miss McBurney. Grammar, Jennie Bouton. Intermediate, Jessie Eaton. 2nd Intermediate, Etta Burr. Primary, Mrs. Mary Herrington.

Secret Societies.—See Page 164 and following.

Attorney's.—Wm. E. Ambler, L. M. Hartwick, W. H. Tuller, Charles R. Johnson, H. W. Harpster.

Physicians.—G. O. Switzer, M. D., Eclectic. G. H. Cleveland, M. D., Regular. C. W. Cramer, M. D., Homeopathic.

Bankers.—Nielsen & Co.

Merchandise General.—Sands & Maxwell Lumber Co., C. Mears. A. J. Underhill. F. O. Gardner.

Hardware.—C. F. Lewis & Co.

Druggists.—E. A. Wright, F. W. Fincher.

Furniture.—C. R. Whittington.

Books and Stationary.—C. C. Ambler.

Jeweler.—M. A. Rice.

Photographer.—O. W. Stone.

Millinery and Dress Making.—Mrs. C. D. Pool, Miss. M. Nash. Mrs. C. H. Smith. Dressmaking, Mrs. L. Bane. Miss Glover. Ida Walradth.

Restaurant and Boarding.—Mrs. G. Wm. Grant, R. Golden.

Pentwater News.—L. M. Hartwick, Prop.

Bakery—C. N. Wise.

Hotels.—Imus House, E. W. Elliott, Prop. Forest House, W. S. Dumont, Prop. Lake View House, W. C. Adkins, Prop.

Weaver.—Mrs. E. Long.

Billiards.—P. Dreves.

P. O.—H. H. Bunyea, P. M.

Saloons.—A. Fisher. T. Weidensee.

Barbers.—C. Meaux, B. A. Smith. J. Cahill.

Clothing.—Wm. Klingbeil.

Livery.—Wm. A. Rounds.

Painters.—J. Jeffery. L. O. Vincent. G. W. Davis.

Manufactories.—Pentwater Bedstead Co., Sands & Maxwell, Props. Middlesex Brick & Tile Co., Foundry and Water Works, E. J. Birkett, Prop. Tables, Wagons and Agricultural Implements, J. Halstead. Table Slides, J. S. Bird. Flouring Mill, Nickerson & Collister. Planning and Carpenter, Labonta & Mero. Saw Mills, Sands & Maxwell Lumber Co., F. O. Gardner, A. J. Underhill. Shingle, C. H. Chapman. Oceana County Canning and Evaporating Co.

Blacksmithing.—Wm. Ticknor, J. Halstead.

Fishermen.—A. Warner, A. Cutler, J. Cutler, M. D. Pool, Robt. Venn, M. H. Putnam.

Boat Line.—Pentwater and Ludington, twice each day. Steamer Geo. W. Sanford Jr.

Railway.—C. & W. M. Two passenger trains daily.

Fire Department.—Geo. Flood Chief.

Atlethtic Club.—Niel VanAllsburg, President.

News Agency.—Wm. M. Hartwick.

terests of the company, paying therefor such sum as he may think proper," &c.

Mr. Ambler visited Chicago and purchased for the company the present site, paying therefor $2,000 in stock and $300 cash. The company commenced building without delay. A fine factory 50x-100 feet, four stories high, with brick boiler and engine room was erected and the very best of new machinery put in. The first bill of furniture as disclosed by sale book was on April 12, 1883, "8 Beds, $21.00."

Furniture was shipped all over the U. S. and a large trade worked up. Only one *fault* was found, and that was, the goods were too well made for such cheap furniture. The company employed from 50 to 100 men.

The grave mistake made was the investment of too much capital stock in the factory and leaving the company practically without any working capital. The annual statement of 1884 shows of the capital stock of $32,750, the amount then invested in buildings, real estate and machinery to be $28,325.94, leaving the company to borrow all necessary funds for operating. This, together with *experience purchasing* at last created a debt beyond the ability of the company to meet, and on Nov. 11, 1886, the factory was sold to the Sands & Maxwell Lumber company, and the mortgage debt thus extinguished and the stock of Sands & Maxwell cancelled. This left the Pentwater Furniture Company with the stock on hand and bills receivable to meet current debts and balance to divide among stockholders. The Sands & Maxwell Lumber Company commenced operations Jan. 1, 1887, under the name of The Pentwater Bedstead Company.

Since this company has taken possession of the factory it has pushed the business in its usual way, which is to crowd to the fullest capacity and increase facilities as fast as business will warrant: During the winter of 1887-8 it built a two-story brick addition, 48x164 feet, to the works, which is connected with the main building by a tramway from the second stories. As we have stated, the first order was received April 12, 1883, and was for 8 beds, $21.00. Now the company furnishes work for one hundred hands, runs full time and is receiving orders as fast as they can be filled. In 1889 the company used in this establishment two million feet of lumber and expects to use three millions this year. Its sales in 1889 amounted to $84,833.78, and the furniture was shipped to all parts of the country, a quantity going to California. The present shipments are about $10,000 per month. It has an order from Denver, Col., at this writing, for a ten car lot. Mr. Sands personally superintends the factory, while Mr. J. H. Bouton acts as shipping clerk.

OCEANA COUNTY SAVINGS BANK.

July 2, 1885, the Oceana County Loan and Security Company was organized at Hart, Mich., and the following Directors elected:

L. McGraft, L. N. Keating, C. T. Hills, of Muskegon; Charles E. Lawrence, of Hillsdale; W. B. O. Sands and W. E. Ambler, of Pentwater; E. D. Richmond, of Hart. The authorized capital was $100,000. The Board of Directors organized by selecting the following officers: President, W. E. Ambler; Vice President, C. T. Hills; Secretary, E. D. Richmond. The purpose of the organization was to invest its capital in first mortgages and other securities on long time and hold these papers for sale to any person wishing to make investments. The cut on previous page shows the home office as first established. It is fire-proof and detached, built of brick and stone, with iron roof, cornice and shutters, 30x40 feet, with French plate glass front. It is highly and elegantly finished inside with native woods, has a vault 10x10 feet, with Hall & Co.'s fire proof doors, time lock, &c. Oct. 31, 1887, some of the stockholders sold to the present owners, and it was reorganized under the State banking law as the Oceana County Savings Bank. It now has $70,000 capital paid in; surplus, $4,644.76; undivided profits, $6,409.31. The Board of Directors for 1890 are C. T. Hills, A. L. Carr, E. D. Richmond, C. H. Hackley, L. N. Keating, A. A. Dunton, D. J. Mathews: President, C. T. Hills; Vice President, A. L. Carr; Cashier, E. D. Richmond; Assistant Cashier, W. N. Sayles.

THE BANKING HOUSE OF CHURCHILL, OAKES & CO., at Shelby, was organized July 1st, 1883, with a paid up capital of $10,000, which has since been increased each year. The business has proved a very satisfactory one to those engaging in it and has paid a fair dividend. At the organization Walter H. Churchill was elected President; Samuel W. Webber, Vice President, and Dustin C. Oakes, Cashier, and these gentlemen have continued to discharge the duties of the respective offices since. The firm have a large fire-proof vault containing a large burglar and fire-proof safe, with time locks. The office is in the new Opera Block and is furnished with all modern improvements for safety and convenience. The gentlemen composing the firm are all well known, and being possessed of a large amount of real and other property in this and other counties in the State, as well as good names for business integrity and honesty no person need have any fear of disaster in doing business with Churchill, Oakes & Co.

OCEANA CO. TRIBUNE.—Some members of the greenback party realizing the advantages of a party organ to represent their views during the progress of a campaign, in Sept., 1886, organized a joint stock company composed of leading greenbackers, and installing F. Towns, a young man of editorial experience, as editor, commenced the publication at Hart, of the Oceana County Tribune, a seven column folio. While Mr. Towns was editor, W. Wigton, I. D. Reed and James Brassington were the real managers. Afterwards Mr. Towns retired and I. D. Reed became editor, which position he held until 1889, when he also retired and James Brassington became editor and manager, with Frank VanValkenburg, an experienced printer, as chief assistant. The paper is now recognized as an organ of the democratic as well as greenback party. It is well edited and presents a fine appearance. Mr. Brassington is a practicing attorney and devotes only a portion of his time to the management of the paper.

SHELBY HERALD.—Harry M. Royal, a young man reared in the village of Shelby, who served his early apprenticeship in the Independent office of that place, afterwards occupying an important position in the office of the Tradesman, at Grand Rapids, established and in the month of May, 1888, issued the first number of the Shelby Herald. It is a six column folio, well edited, clean in appearance and bristling with locals each week. It is independent politically and receives a good patronage. The editor is a young man of promise and thoroughly alive to the interests of his village.

CHAPTER XI.

MUNICIPALITIES.

PENTWATER.

The township of Pentwater is the extreme northwestern town in the county and is designated as Town 16 North, Range 18 West. It comprises only fifteen sections of land. It is divided into two parts by the channel and little lake. The village is located on the north, east and west sides of the lake. The principal improvements and property value are located on the east and north side. The place was first settled by Edwin R. Cobb and Andrew Rector, as appears elsewhere. The name is undoubtedly a corruption of the words *penned water*, indicating the little lake upon the banks of which the settlement was made. The following is a list of the Supervisors, Clerks and Treasurers of the township to 1890:

SUPERVISORS.—E. R. Cobb, 1856-7; D. G. Weare, 1858; Henry C. Flagg, 1859-'61-2-3-4-5-6; A. J. Underhill, 1860-'73; Edgar D. Richmond, 1867-8; Sewall Moulton, 1869; F. W. Ratzel, 1870; Stillman Parker, 1871; G. W. Imus, 1872-5-6-'89; E. Nickerson, 1874; John Fegan, 1877-8; A. Brillhart, 1879; S. W. Bunyea, 1880-1-2; E. A. Wright, 1883; H. H. Bunyea, 1884-6-8; W. L. Tilden, 1885; Henry Hurley, 1887.

CLERKS.—James Dexter, 1856-7; E. R. Cobb, 1858; E. D. Richmond, 1859-'60-'75-6; Charles W. Deane, 1861; Andrew M. Dahl, 1862; F. W. Ratzel, 1863-5-6; E. C. Hildreth, 1864; Henry H. Woods, 1867; E. E. Edwards, 1868-9-'70; R. L. Rice, 1871-2; Henry F. King, 1873; John S. Reynolds, 1874; A. J. Underhill, 1877; E. B. Clark, 1878-'80-9; W. P. Lee, 1879; W. H. Tuller, 1881-5-6-7-8; H. A. Gross, 1882-3-4.

TREASURERS.—Norman Rogers, 1856-7; W. P. Harding, 1858; J. G. Blowers, 1859; Wm. Webb, 1860-1-2; W. H. Merritt, 1863; B. R. Hall, 1864; Thomas Craine, 1865-6; W. B. O. Sands, 1867-8; E. W. Bovee, 1869-'70; W. A. Rounds, 1871-2-3; Mark A. Rice, 1874-5-6; H. H. Bunyea, 1877-8-'80; A. Sorensen, 1879; A. W. Newark,

1881; J. H. Bouton, 1882-3-6; C. R. Whittington, 1884-5; F. Smith, 1887-9; Otto Grant, 1888.

VILLAGE OF PENTWATER.—Since the platting of Pentwater village its history may properly be divided into three periods, which the words *inflation, depression,* and *healthy growth* aptly designate. The first was the lumber period, the two branches of Pentwater River reaching many miles into the famous pine lands north and south, the fine harbor shielded from the heavy lake winds made it a desirable point to manufacture lumber and it grew rapidly, too rapidly in fact, for the pine becoming exhausted its mills thinned out and lumbermen sought other fields. About this time a syndicate of speculators at Grand Rapids discovering that there was a flaw in Pentwater's recorded titles bought up quit claims from the heirs of the original owners and commenced a number of ejectment suits against those in possession. This caused the period of depression and Pentwater acquired the name of being a dead town. But the cloud upon the titles was removed by the Courts. It was soon discovered that it was almost entirely exempt from malarial influences and that serious illness was uncommon. Then a bed of very fine clay for brick or tile was discovered extending three-fourths of a mile along the banks of the little lake. The attention of the lumberman being diverted from pine it was noted that the beech, maple, cherry, ash, basswood and elm timber near Pentwater was of a very superior grade for the manufacture of furniture, wagons, etc., and we begin to enter again upon the third period of healthy growth. A Chicago capitalist, Mr. Charles Mears, organized the Middlesex Brick & Tile Co., which having laid out some seventy-five thousand dollars in making ready to develop the clay plant, is now manufacturing and sending to Chicago on its own scows and barges the finest common brick made, and employs some 80 hands. The Pentwater Furniture Co., and the Pentwater Bedstead Co., employing as many more, sprang into existence, followed by the Halstead Wagon Works, the Pentwater Novelty and Iron Works, and the Oceana Co. Canning & Evaporating Co. During this time improvements of all kinds have been taking place in every part of the village. New and fine residences erected, small manufacturing or trading enterprises developed into large prosperous institutions, and on the main street large brick blocks, and at the present time indications for a remarkable growth are good. The village has a steam fire engine and a good system of water works, a paid fire department, maintains a night watch, has one of the best union schools in the North, and the following church organizations: Methodist, Congregational, Baptist, Episcopal and Catholic, all of which worship in edifices of their own. The village is beautifully located upon and half surrounded by Pentwater Lake, and within eighty rods of Lake Michigan, but separated from it by high hills covered with evergreens the year 'round, making it one of the most romantic and picturesque villages on the shore. It, aside from being a popular resort in summer for tourists, invalids and sportsmen, is the natural shipping outlet for the county, and through it a large proportion of the county's wonderful fruit products have to pass to reach the outside world.

It is the health of the place, however, that makes it especially desirable as a place of residence. During the prevalence of diphtheria, scarlet fever, typhoid fever and kindred diseases that have been so fatal in other portions of the State, Pentwater has been almost entirely exempt. There have been developed but two cases of typhoid fever here in several years, and in each instance the disease was contracted elsewhere and the patient brought here and cured.

In the winter season fishing upon the ice is a favorite pastime, and in the summer cisco, herring, perch, bass and pickerel are caught by the basketful.

THE PENTWATER NEWS.—On page 40 appears an account of the establishment of the first newspaper of the county, the Oceana Times. It was published at Middlesex, now a part of Pentwater. The founder was Mr. F. W. Ratzel, whose portrait, through the courtesy of his brother-in-law, Mr. E. B. Flagg, we are enabled to present to our readers. On page 73 appears additional history of the paper and the sale by Mr. Ratzel. Mr. Ratzel, after disposing of his interest in the paper, engaged in mercantile pursuits, and in '79 removed to Manistee, where in the latter part of January, 1885, he died.

Mr. Hartwick, the present proprietor, in 1885 purchased the brick block which is herewith represented, and moved the plant into it.

F. W. RATZEL.

PENTWATER NEWS BLOCK.

It occupies the whole of the first floor and basement. In June, 1887, there was put in an Olds gasoline steam engine, and the job press was run by steam. In January, 1888, a Prouty power press was added and at the present time the paper has a circulation of 1200, a good advertising and job patronage.

WATER WORKS.—In May, 1888, the following named persons constituted the Common Council of the village of Pentwater, viz.: President, L. M. Hartwick; Recorder, Chas. M. Underhill; Treasurer, Chas. R. Whittington; Trustees, D. C. Wickham, Wm. Kuhn, Thos. Collister, Mark A. Rice, Alvin Warner and James E. Grover. At the second meeting of the new Council the President recommended taking steps looking towards the putting in a system of water works. A committee was appointed, consisting of the President, D. C. Wickham and T. Collister, who after making inquiries and formulating a system, made a report which with some variations was afterwards adopted. The question upon a proposition to bond the village was submitted to a vote of the people and carried, only fourteen votes appearing against it. The contract was let to M. Walker, of Fenton, for putting in pumps, capacity 1,500,000 gallons, and about two miles of cast-iron mains, as follows: From pump house to Hancock street, eight inch main: from Third to Seventh on Hancock, six inch main; from Seventh to Ninth on Hancock, and from Third to Second, four inch; from Hancock to Rush on Seventh, from Second to Eighth on Wythe, from Hancock to Rutledge on Third, from Fifth to First on Rutledge, and from pump house to Bedstead Co.'s works, four inch. Crosses were put in at every street crossing and gates at intervals along the line of mains, 16 Ludlow hydrants were placed. A contract was made with E. J. Birkett, proprietor of the foundry, to furnish the power and run same for five years. The system was completed and the test made Jan. 11, 1888. Prior to the completion of the contract a vacancy was created on the Council by the removal of Wm. Kuhn, and at a special election Geo. W. Imus was elected to fill the vacancy. Messrs. Rice and Birkett perfected and put in an electrical fire alarm, and by the time election occurred again the system, barring some minor details, was completed. The cost for mains, crosses, gates, hydrants, etc., was $7,843.76. The total cost about ten thousand dollars.

RESIDENCE OF W. E. AMBLER, PENTWATER.

MIDDLESEX BRICK & TILE CO.—For many years the Hon. Chas. Mears advocated the advantages and feasibility of manufacturing clay products at Pentwater, insisting that the clay banks on the north shore of Pentwater Lake, at the east limit of the village, was unrivalled in its quality and location for easy shipment, and at last he succeeded in interesting gentlemen from Chicago sufficiently to make a tour of inspection, which has resulted in confirming all that Mr. Mears has ever claimed, and in fact, exceeding his expectations, and to his persistent energy and abiding faith in the scheme is due the fact that in July, 1883, the Middlesex Brick & Tile Company was incorporated, with a capital of sixty thousand dollars. Charles Mears, Harvey Cockell, of Chicago; W. E. Ambler, Fred Nielsen and F. O. Gardner, of Pentwater, Directors. Under Mr. Cockell's supervision docks were built, buildings erected, machinery purchased and put in, a tug built, and the same year some brick were manufactured. It was the plan of Mr. Cockell to dry the brick under cover by artificial heat, so that the clay could be kept moving from the time it left the banks until it reached the last kiln where the brick were burned. There were some defects in the system of curing and the product was not of as good quality as expected but as the institution was passing through its experimental stage the courage of the investors did not fail them, but greater and more extensive preparations than ever were made for work the next season. April 9, 1884, however, the works took fire and all the buildings and some of the machinery were destroyed. This was an unfortunate blow and resulted afterwards in Mr. Cockell selling his stock and retiring from the management. The Board was reorganized with Mr. Mears in control. Henry Hurley was made manager and the works again started

M. D. GIRARD, RECORDER, '89.

E. B. CLARK, ASSESSOR, '89.

up. The brick were cured by the weather under cover and then transferred to the kilns and burned. The product now was a very fine quality of common brick that found ready sale. The Company employed from eighty to one hundred hands during the summer season. In 1889 Mr. Hurley died and his successor has not yet been selected.

RESIDENCE OF W. B. O. SANDS, PENTWATER.

PARKS.—Several times in years past knots of our citizens have casually discussed the project of making some improvements at Bass Lake, agreeing that with a small outlay a pleasant drive of about three and a half miles from the village could be had, nice picnic grounds in the shady woods, and boating, bathing and fishing in the lake, yet some way nothing had been done for want of a "starter." In July, 1886, three of our villagers talked the matter over, and it resulted in procuring a team, and Mr. Perkins, Dr. Cleveland and Mr. Ambler paid a visit to the lake and after looking over the ground decided to test the feeling of the good folks and see what could be accomplished. The land wanted belonged to Hon. Chas. Mears, of Chicago. Mr. Mears favored the project and made the generous proposition to convey the land to the Company for the nominal sum of seventy-five dollars and take that amount of stock in the Company. Whereupon articles of incorporation were prepared and in less than a week from the time of the first talk and without any fuss or furor, the Company was organized, and six hundred dollars of the one thousand stock taken, outside of Mr. Mears' subscription of three shares. The following named gentlemen signed the articles of incorporation, viz.: Sands & Maxwell Lumber Co., W. E. Ambler, E. A. Wright, Fred Nielsen, Jacob Fisher, A. J. Underhill, H. H. Bunyea, W. L. Tilden, Geo. W. Imus, F. O. Gardner, Labonta & Mero, L. M. Hartwick, E. Nickerson, Thos. Collister, M. S. Perkins, M. A. Rice, G. H. Cleveland, Wm. Moody, Smith Brothers, J. W. Loomis, C. W. Cramer, C. R. Whittington, F. W. Fincher, W. A. Rounds.

G. O. SWITZER, HEALTH OFFICER '89.

Monday evening following a meeting of stockholders was held at the Pentwater NEWS office and the election of Directors resulted as follows: W. E. Ambler, Fred Nielsen, J. Fisher, H. H. Bunyea, G. W. Imus, M. S. Perkins and L. M. Hartwick.

The next day the Directors organized by electing, President, W. E. Ambler; Secretary, L. M. Hartwick; Treasurer, Fred Nielsen.

The report of the Board of Directors at the annual meeting in 1887 showed $800 received from sale of shares, all of which was expended on the grounds; roads leading from Pentwater to the grounds were repaired and put in fair condition; the grounds cleaned of rubbish and underbrushed; a large Greek cross shaped pavilion finished inside and out has been erected, also kitchen and and store room; a

M. A. RICE, TRUSTEE.

boat house and docks for landing; two bath houses; two croquet grounds made; swings and rustic benches placed in portions of the grounds; a well with pump; ten fine row boats placed in the boat house; an ice house, etc. Afterwards Messrs. Fred Nielsen and W. E. Ambler built fine cottages on the grounds. The park is a very popular place for pic-nic gatherings.

During the summer of 1888 a project for organizing an Odd Fellows' Park Association was started in this place. Its purpose was to purchase and fit up grounds where members of the order with families and friends could go and enjoy themselves in rest and recreation, and where Lodges could picnic and summer reunions take place. The grounds selected were twenty-three acres on the east side of what is known as the Big Bayou of Pentwater Lake, extending south and taking in the point. Nature has been very lavish in preparing these grounds for park purposes. The natural lay of the land is picturesque, and from its greatest elevation a view of the village, Lake Michigan, the little lake and many miles of fine landscape is obtained. It is covered with shrubbery of oak, pine, ground hemlock, and nearer the water, cedar. Several lovely grottos are located on the grounds in which are springs of ice-cool, crystal water, pure and tasteless. Its nearness to Lake Michigan exempts it from the mosquito pest during warm weather, while it is far enough removed to be protected from severe lake winds by intervening hills. It is within a mile and a half of the depot, and a mile of the village. The Big Bayou furnishes the best of fishing waters and the only

G. W. IMUS, TRUSTEE.

J. M. CAHILL, TRUSTEE.

good trolling grounds in the lake. Pentwater Lake, as is well known, is remarkable for its high banks and deep water, which furnishes the secret of the total exemption from malaria. By its peculiar shape it furnishes the finest body of water on the shore for yachting, rowing and other aquatic sports, and being connected by a short channel with Lake Michigan gives the opportunity of enjoying excursions right from the grounds into this beautiful body of water. Many yachts, row boats and steam craft are owned at Pentwater which can be secured for use by the Association until it gets craft of its own. It was intended to secure at least one hundred members with one share each.

May 10, 1889, the Park Association was organized by the election of the following Board of Directors: E. T. Mugford, I. C. Ford, Wm. Cooper, T. H. Baker, Wm. G. Fisher, L. M. Hartwick, W. H. Tuller, Wm. Hudson, C. M. Underhill, G. O. Switzer, C. W. Cramer. Some seventy shares were pledged. During the year 1889 a large pavilion was erected, several acres of ground cleared, several fine springs developed, walks built, a dock built, grottos made accessible by walks, etc., and a start made, which, if continued, will make it a very fine park.

PENTWATER HEALTH RECORD.—The death rate among adults throughout the civilized world averages about 14 per thousand of population. In the State of Michigan it is about 8. In the county of Oceana, 6. In the village of Pentwater during the year 1889 there were nine deaths among adults, or an average of about five per thousand of population.

The following is a table of deaths from all causes from one year old and upwards, occurring in Pentwater since Jan. 1, 1882, to Jan. 1, 1890:

	'82	'83	'84	'85	'86	'87	'88	'89
Consumption	2	4	7	2	2	2	3	2
Old Age	1	3	2	1	0	5	2	3
Heart	1	2	0	1	0	0	1	1
Dropsy	1	0	0	0	1	1	1	1
Fever	1	0	0	0	1	0	0	1
Accidents	2	0	1	1	0	1	0	0
Kidney Trouble	1	0	0	0	0	0	0	0
Scarlet Fever	0	1	0	0	0	0	0	2
Childbirth	1	0	0	0	0	0	0	0
Paralysis	0	0	0	0	1	0	0	0
Cancer	0	1	0	0	0	0	0	3
Neglect	0	0	1	0	0	0	0	0
Cholera Morbus	0	0	1	0	0	0	0	0
Softening of Brain	0	0	0	0	0	1	0	0
Diphtheria	0	0	0	0	0	0	0	0
Inflammation of Bowels	0	0	0	0	1	0	2	0
Rupture of Blood Vessel	0	0	0	0	0	1	0	0
Consumption of Blood	0	0	0	0	0	0	2	0
General Debility	0	0	0	0	0	0	1	0
	10	11	12	5	6	11	12	11

PENTWATER.—RESIDENCE OF E. G. MAXWELL.

PAY-BAW-ME.

Pay-baw-me, the noted chief, is described as a man of medium height, keen of eye, spare and dark. When young he was one of the wildest of his tribe, but when about middle age he was converted to Christianity. He is said to have been a man of ability, and could preach a telling sermon. He was for years Town Treasurer of Elbridge and kept everything straight, but in a peculiar Indian fashion by hieroglyphics and in the Indian tongue. He was the head of the Catholic bands and read on Sundays. He was a monogamist and had no issue. His widow married Louis Genereau. He died in 1870, a man of about sixty years of age.

The following table shows the mortality by months, covering the same period:

	'82.	'83.	'84.	'85.	'86.	'87.	'88.	'89.
January	1	2	1	0	0	2	2	2
February	2	1	2	2	0	1	0	0
March	0	1	2	0	2	0	1	0
April	2	0	1	0	0	2	3	3
May	1	1	2	1	0	0	1	0
June	0	1	1	1	0	0	1	1
July	2	1	0	0	0	2	1	2
August	0	2	0	0	1	0	1	0
September	0	0	3	0	1	1	2	0
October	2	0	0	0	2	2	0	0
November	0	1	0	0	0	0	0	3
December	0	1	0	1	0	1	0	0
	10	11	12	5	6	11	12	11

From May 17, 1888, to Jan. 1, 1890, a period of twenty months, there was just one death between the ages of one and twelve years.

TOWNSHIP AND VILLAGE OF SHELBY.

The first meeting of the town, which was at first, Stony Creek, was at Wheeler's Mills, on the first Monday in April, 1855; Harvey Tower, Chairman. This being the first election of the township, the electors went into caucus, and proceeded to nominate officers, after which they adjourned one hour. They then proceeded to poll the votes, polls closing at "half-past 3 o'clock." $75 was voted to defray town expenses. There were sixteen votes cast, in all, and the elections were practically unanimous.

In 1862 the town of Shelby (called then Benona), was set off by itself, and there were but eight voters, and all voted for Bird Norton as Supervisor. 1863 and 1864 seem to have been years of confusion, as the officers were always resigning. In the latter year there were eleven voters. In April, 1870, a vote was taken to give aid, to the amount of $7,195.20, to the G. R. & L. S. R. R., which was carried, but owing to some legal flaw never paid. The people of Shelby built the depot, at a cost of $1,200.—Page's History of Oceana County.

The following is the list of Supervisors, Clerks and Treasurers, to the present time:

SUPERVISORS—Warren Wilder, '55; Wm. Gardner, '56; L. D. Eaton, '57-8; S. E. Knowles, '59; H. Hoffman, '60-'61; Bird Norton, '62; Wm. Weston, '63; Silas C. Powers, '64; Warren Vradenburg, '65; Walter H. Churchill, '66-'85; Parley R. Cady, '67-8-9; Andrew Maples, '70-1-2; George W. Woodward, '73-4-5-6-7-9-'80-2-4; A. H. Bearss, '78; W. H. Barry, '81-3; Jesse Bearss, '87-8-9.

CLERKS.—Malcolm Campbell, '55-6; Henry Hoffman, '57; D. M. Merrifield, '58; George Semback, '59; Wm. Weston, '60-1-2; E. W.

Elliott, '63; A. C. Randall, '64; Orrin Deming, '65-6-7-8; W. H. Churchill, '69-'70-1-2-3-4-7-'81; H. O. Bickford, '75-6; Alpheus Neff, '78-79-80; Manly C. White, '82; F. A. Pitts, '83; W. E. Osmun, '84; F. W. Newman, '85-6-7; F. M. Myers, '88; T. T. Usborne, '89.

TREASURERS.—James McNutt, '55-6-'60-1-2; John Stearns, '57; L. M. Curtis, '58. Wm. Gardner, '59; James A. Hall '63; Alva Babcock, '64; R. Vradenburg, '65; Calvin S. Reed, '66; O. G. Marvin, '67; James S. Runner, '68; A. H. Bearss, '69-'72; David Stringham, '70-1; Alex Pittenger, '73-4-5-6-7-8; Parley R. Cady '79-'80; A. Z. Moore, '81-2; Rufus W. Wheeler, '83; D. H. Rankin, '84; George Dewey, '85-6; C. J. Fleming, '87-8-9.

VILLAGE OF SHELBY.—We have headed this article Village of Shelby because that is the name under which was incorporated in 1882 a thriving village on the C. & W. M. R. R., on Sec. 17 of the township of Shelby. There are two village plats, one of which was made in 1871 and named Barnett, and another south of this platted in 1873 by Martin L. Sweet and Andreas Bevier, and named Shelby. The business part of the village and the more populous residence part is upon the plat or village of Barnett. If a man were to purchase a lot in this plat, not knowing the name, he would be surprised upon examining his deed to find he had been deeded a lot in the village of Barnett. There was something of a joke perpetrated when this name was given to the village of Barnett. At the time it was platted there was a brakeman by the name of Barnett on the railroad who proposed to pay the expenses of platting if the proprietors would name it after him. His proposition was accepted, but when he was called upon for the fees he asked if it had been recorded, and being answered in the affirmative laughed and declared he was merely joking, but was much obliged for the honor conferred upon him. Thus the village became Barnett, while the postoffice and railway station were named Shelby, and as the latter name is the one generally used in referring to the village and the one under which it was incorporated, many being ignorant of the fact that any other name exists, we have used it at the head of this brief sketch.

The first settlement that had any appearance of developing into a village was made at what is known as "Churchill's Corners." Here Mr. W. H. Churchill built a house during the summer of 1864 on the northwest corner of section sixteen. This was followed by a blacksmith shop built by Alpheus Neff in 1868; a general merchandise store built by Jas. Williams in 1869, and a drug store built by a Mr. Adams in the spring of 1870. All of these buildings were on section sixteen, except the latter, which was across the road on section nine. It might be well to mention in passing that when Mr. Churchill settled here in Feb., 1864, there were but eleven voters in the township. This little village did considerable business. Here the postoffice of Shelby was first located with Mr. Churchill as Postmaster, commencing Dec. 15, 1866, who continued to hold the position for nineteen years and nine months. Here travelers were entertained by Mr. Churchill, who may be named as the first hotel keeper of Shelby. The State road built in 1865-6 ran past this little cluster of buildings, and a great many passengers were carried over it from Whitehall to Hart by that veteran stage driver, James Roddy. Horses were changed at this place and taking all things into consideration, it was far from a dead town.

W. H. SHIRTS, TRUSTEE.

In the fall of 1871 the railroad was surveyed and grading begun, and the spot selected for a depot being some distance from the little settlement, it left a space between sufficiently large with land upon the other side of the road bed to plat a village, and Samuel A. Browne, A. Pittenger, Jas. G. Gray and O. Deming decided to take advantage of the opportunity and platted and recorded the village of Barnett. That building might be compelled to commence near the railroad depot and not merely continue in that direction from the Churchill settlement they left the land adjoining the settlement in blocks, refusing to sell single lots. The scheme was successful and building began near the depot. The first store building on the plat

J. WRIGHT, TRUSTEE.

was built by Mr. E. J. Shirts in the winter of 1871-2, on lot 1 of block 18. In the spring of 1872 Messrs. Churchill & Neff built a hardware store on lot 20, block 14. Since then building has gone steadily forward and today we find a flourishing village filled with fine edifices and progressive business men. The following from a copy of the Pentwater NEWS published in 1873, shows the condition of Shelby at that time:

"The village of Barnett in Shelby township, started last year, seems to be building, just now, quite rapidly. W. H. Churchill, the Postmaster of Shelby has removed the office to Barnett station—where it presents a very neat and imposing appearance—and, in company with Mr. Neff, Mr. Churchill is keeping a hardware and variety store. Mr. E. J. Shirts, lately of Lansing, is keeping a small dry goods store, and is now arranging to build quite a capacious one. Mr. William Branch, in company with another gentleman, has just opened a boot and shoe store, and all seem to be in prospect of doing a good business. Dr. C. F. Sweet is building a new drug store, and G. W. Woodward, Esq., the newly elected Supervisor, is about erecting a grain warehouse for the purpose of buying and storing farmers' produce. This will be quite an important feature of the town, as the opening of a cash market for produce is a very great help to any village. Messrs. Malcolm & Williams have a very fine mill in operation here, and thousands of dollars have been paid by different parties for logs, this winter, to be sawed up into lumber by this mill. Messrs. Williams & Son are about putting up a new store, and will, as soon as it is finished, remove their stock of goods into it from their present location at Shelby Corners. Stumps are very thick in the village of Barnett, but time and labor will soon efface them, and Barnett may ere long be a very pleasant village."

E. H. CUTLER, TRUSTEE.

From this time the village continued to grow. We have shown on pages 80 and 81 of this book how the pigeons came at an opportune moment to help out their dull times, and today Shelby is one of the most thriving villages in the county. Hart owes much of its importance to the county seat; Pentwater to its lake outlet, but Shelby owes all to the energy and public spirit of her business men. Today we find within her limits two beautiful places of worship, Methodist and Congregational, and one of the finest school edifices in the county. There are well established Lodges of Masons and Odd Fellows; a Rebekah Lodge; G. A. R. Post; Camp of Sons of Veterans; Woman's Relief Corps, and Salvation Army. For fire protection it has a well organized fire department, a Button steam fire engine made at Waterford, N. Y., with good engine house, one thousand feet of hose with one cart and other necessary appurtenances. The water in steamer is kept warm from the furnace in the Opera House block. The water supply consists of nine large reservoirs and numerous small ones located in different parts of the village. The village is in a healthy locality where the best of water is obtained, is pleasantly situated and a desirable place for a home; and as a business point is surrounded with a beautiful farming country fast developing, which must continue to improve the village as the surroundings improve. Among the many fine buildings now in the village may be mentioned the new Opera House block, the Churchill block, and the residences of W. H. Churchill, D. C. Oakes, D. H. Rankin, R. H. Wheeler, Geo. E. Dewey, and many others.

G. W. WOODWARD, ASSESSOR, '89.

T. H. BAKER, CLERK, '89.

The village of Shelby was incorporated in 1885 and the first election held May 4th. The Board of Inspectors was composed of G. W. Woodward, W. H. Churchill, A. E. Souter and Alex. Paton. The first President elected was Geo. B. Getty, who served one year. F. W. VanWickle was the next, serving from 1886 to 1887. Geo. B. Getty again from 1887 to 1889, and Geo. E. Dewey from 1889 to the present time. The present Council is composed as follows: President, Geo. E. Dewey; Trustees, E. H. Cutler, Wm. Butler, Jeptha Wright, A. Z. Moore, W. H. Shirts and H. L. Andrus; Clerk, Thos. H. Baker. Their election occurs on the second Monday of March.

The following is a list of business firms represented in the village:

A. G. Avery, General Store.
D. Bejeon, Harness, &c.
Mrs. H. O. Bickford, Millinery.
H. Brotherton, Wagons and Sleighs.
E. N. Brown, Blacksmith.
Will. Butler, Stave Manufacturer.
R. G. Cavanagh, Physician.
Churchill, Oakes & Co., Bank.
W. H. Churchill, Justice, &c.
H. C. Crossman, Lumber and Saw Mill.
M. L. Ferris, General Store.
C. W. Fisher, Groceries, &c.
Jas. Forbes, Drayman.
R. G. Forbes, Livery.
E. B. Gaylord, Hardware.
"   "   Fruit Evaporator.
G. B. Getty, Lumber Dealer.
W. L. Griffin, Lumber Dealer.
Hanover & Co., Merchant Tailors.
J. A. Harrison, Blacksmith.
"   "   Wagons and Sleighs.
J. H. Hetley, Prin. School.
Mrs. F. O. Howe, Millinery, &c.
H. Johnston, Boots and Shoes.
A. R. McKinnon, Hardware, &c.
Ben. J. Moore, Boots and Shoes.
C. C. Moore, Jewelry, &c.
J. H. Moore, Lumber Dealer.
J. B. Moore, Boots and Shoes.
Moore's Hotel, Moore Bros.
Martha Neff, Dressmaking.
Mrs. F. W. Newman, Independent
E. H. Norton, Meats.
W. L. Paige, Restaurant.

Paton & Andrus, Saw Mill.
F. H. Payne, Groceries.
Peck & Cutler, Handles.
F. A. Pitts, Groceries and Meats.
Pitts & Wood, Photos.
Rankin House, Fred Sandbery, Prop.
D. H. Rankin, Charcoal.
D. Rankin & Co., Drugs.
Rankin & Dewey, Gen'l Store.
L. Rathbone, Barber and Cigars.
D. A. Reed, Blacksmith.
H. W. Reid, Auctioneer.
C. H. Rose, Cigars, &c.
H. M. Royal, Herald.
J. W. Runner, Drugs and Books.
R. Sabin, Physician.
D. G. Scroggs, Attorney.
Shelby Furt. Co., F. A. Scott, Mgr.
Shelby Roller Mills Co., Flour, &c.
Shirts Bros., Groceries.
Smith & Crossman, Millinery.
A. E. Souter, Justice and Ins. Agt.
S. Spellman, Blacksmith.
W. S. Stringham, Drugs, &c.
C. F. Sweet, Physician.
J. A. Tillotson, Barber.
C. H. Tullar, Furt. and Jewelry.
T. T. Usborne, Harness.
D. Vanwort, Drayman.
F. W. VanWickle, Drugs & Groceries.
R. Walton, Blacksmith.
Wheeler Bros., Gen'l Store.
F. W. Wilson, Physician.
G. W. Woodward, Justice.

SHELBY.—OPERA BUILDING. OPERA HALL IN SECOND STORY. CHURCHILL, OAKES & CO., BANK; D. H. RANKIN & CO., STORE; W. H. CHURCHILL, JUSTICE OFFICE; D. E. McCLURE, SCHOOL EXAMINER, FIRST STORY. BUILDING IS HEATED BY STEAM.

SHELBY.—RESIDENCE OF W. H. CHURCHILL.

DAVID RICHARDS.

The above is the picture of a peculiar character who lives in Shelby. His name is David Richards, and for many years he has been laboring under the delusion that he is the President of the C. & W. M. R'y Co. He has been humored in his delusion by citizens and railroad employes. He is on hand when trains arrive, gives orders, hires and discharges men as though he was an actual official. The medals upon his coat and vest have been presented to him by R. R. employes and he wears them with pride. He claims the bank and moneyed men about town are holding back $1,000,000 of salary accumulated in his 15 years' as railroad president. He also tells how long it took him to build the Niagara bridge, and that he built it as high as the river was wide, and then pushed it down, the opposite end landing on the pier exactly as he had planned. He decorates himself with all imaginable badges and insignia of office, and usually walks through the train at Shelby, asking for suggestions from the passengers how to improve his road. Everybody who travels on this line knows "Davey."

HART TOWNSHIP AND VILLAGE.

In the spring of 1856 Nelson Glover settled on the farm on which he still resides, and the same spring there also settled a man with his family just across the river from him, named William Dunham, and east of Glover on the same side of the river, was Jacob Schrumpf, another Scotchman named McAllister, and also Joseph Booth, and a Mr. Green. In the same spring Dr. Ira Jenks came from Kent, in company with two other men, wending his way via Croton, on the Muskegon, across the Marengo Plains, through the wilderness, with a pocket compass, to the lake shore below Pentwater, and two sawmills and a boarding-house, with one partly built, was all there was then of Pentwater. Dr. Jenks came up the woods, and called on Mr. Glover. In June he came again, and chopped on his place, having had to cut a road four miles into his place. His bark shanty had no floor, no door, no windows, and the bark had curled so that one could put one's head out of the cracks, if one wished. In about three weeks, Geo. W. Light and Edward Davis, with their families, settled on what is now VanWickle's place. Judge Russell, with his two sons, Hiram and George, came in for a few weeks, and did some chopping on their place this season, but the Judge and his family did not move in until 1859. In the spring of 1857 there were ten families,—N. Glover, W. Dunham, J. Schrumpf, J. McAllister, S. Rollins, James Brooker, Ira Jenks, V. Satterlee, G. W. Light, E. Davis, H. H. Fuller.

W. H. Leach put up the first frame dwelling in the village, and was the first postmaster, succeeded by the present Circuit Judge Russell. Robert McAllister was the first stage, as he carried the mail on his back from Pentwater to White River. If he had passengers, it is not known how he carried them, as even "the boot" of the stage was full. After this, the mail was carried by one man and three horses. The man rode one horse and the two remaining horses brought up the rear. Until 1876 the people of Hart got their mail at Pentwater. In 1869 Collins & Roddy carried the mail. The Methodist Episcopal Elder A. A. Darling was the first preacher. In 1869 Elders Crane and Pratt preached in Huff's Hall and a church was commenced that year. H. Brooks and Miss Ettie VanWickle were the first teachers in the new union school. B. Moore erected and kept the first hotel. Nelson Green was the first Judge of Probate, followed by Josiah Russell, Charles Camp, and Amos Crosby, etc. Nelson Green was the first County Surveyor, succeeded by Josiah Russell, and then H. C. Hawley. Tyler Garmer was the first jailer, succeeded by O. P. Fortner. J. Palmiter published the first newspaper. In 1869, 36,036 pounds of maple sugar were made in this town. The first Episcopal service in Hart was in 1869, by the Rev. Dr. Pitkin.

G. Rollins, Daniel Wentworth and Mr. Spoor, who were among the earliest settlers of Hart, were three ship carpenters, who came to build a vessel for C. Mears, at Pentwater, and Rollins came in first and picked out land for himself and the others. It was his house that the first town meeting of Elbridge was held in, that town then including four towns. Rollins and Spoor are dead, and Mr. Wentworth is in Maine, visiting the scenes of his boyhood.— Page's History of Oceana County.

SUPERVISORS.—Josiah Russell, '61-2; Robert F. Andrews, '63-5; David L. Garver, '64; Abijah W. Peck, '66; Theron S. Gurney, '67; Ahaz A. Darling, '68-9-'70; William J. Sprigg, '71-2; David Johnson, '73-4; Enoch T. Mugford, '75-6-7-8-9-'80-1-2-3-4-5-6-7-8-9.

CLERKS.—Abijah W. Peck, '61-2; Leonard E. Clark, '63; Peleg A. Hubbard, '64; William H. Cheney, '65; William H. Leach, '66; William A. Peck, '67; John M. Rice, '68; Theron S. Gurney, '69-'70-1; Charles W. Slayton, '72; Marcus H. Brooks, '73-4-5-6-7-8; James H. Slater, '79-'80-2-3-4; C. A. Gurney, '81; W. P. Sackrider, '85-6; F. H. Edwards, '87-8-9.

TREASURERS.—Charles W. Wilson, '61; Daniel M. Wentworth, '62-4-5; Nehimiah Miller, '63; George B. Rollins, '66-'82; David Benham, '67; Frederick G. Reading, '68-9; John Westbrook, '70-1-2-5; Josephus S. Peach, '73-4; Peleg A. Hubbard, '76; Mills H. Bosworth, '77-8; William D. Markham, '79; Isaac D. Reed, '80; G. L. Crumb, '83-4; W. Stitt, '85-8-9; J. A. Collier, '86-7.

VILLAGE OF HART.—The village of Hart is located in the midst of the finest farming lands of the county. It is the product and active evidence of the development of Oceana's farming and fruit interests. Cotemporaneous with the clearing up of farming lands, the raising of wheat, potatoes and fruit for which the county is noted, came into existence and grew the pleasant and attractive village of Hart. The village is situated on high ground sufficiently undulating to give it a pleasing appearance. The South Branch of Pentwater River runs thro' it on the north, while east and west several small brooks of clear, crystal water, which have their origin in springs, run thro' the village and empty into the river. These streams abound with speckled trout, salmon and grayling, and during trout season the villagers enjoy the rare sport of trout catching without the usual discomforts attending such sport. It has also become noted throughout the State, and sportsmen come every season, filling the hotels while the season lasts. Although a large commodious hotel is here, they are frequently compelled to lodge regular guests in private families to accommodate visiting sportsmen.

H. J. CHADWICK, PRESIDENT, 1889.

It is the county seat, the location of the county fair, has the largest flouring mill in the county, one which cost some $60,000 to build, two banks, three newspapers, one fruit evaporator, and a number of business houses, all of which apparently are doing a good business. It has a village government, having been incorporated under the laws of the State in 1885, and enjoys the advantages of a fine system of water works. Its main street has been graded and paved.

W. E. THORP, TRUSTEE.

BOARD OF SUPERVISORS,—1889.

HART.—RESIDENCE OF JAS. K. FLOOD.

Its business buildings have mostly been built or rebuilt within a period of twelve years, and are neat in appearance.

Many fine residences have been built here in the past twelve years that are models of architectural beauty. Few places present the home feature as well as Hart. The majority of its business men have grown with the county, and made their accumulations here. The spirit of enterprise is apparent in all its public improvements. Its people are generous, courteous, hospitable and intelligent. For several years it has successfully maintained a literary society and Chatauqua reading circle. The farms surrounding the village are well improved and are classed among the best in the county. The village is in the center of Oceana's best fruit lands, and also near her celebrated trout streams that attract outside sportsmen. It has the finest hotel in the county, a large brick block finely finished and elegantly furnished, under the management of a popular and genial landlord. Its principal points of vantage are its water power, its fruit lands and its trout streams. Its pure water and healthy climate make it a desirable place of residence.

J. A. COLLIER, MARSHAL, '89.

E. T. MUGFORD, Assessor, '89.

FIRE DEPARTMENT—The Hart Fire Department is in a prosperous condition. It was first organized as a Hook and Ladder Company, and afterwards as a regular Fire Department. The organization was perfected Aug. 4, 1886, with John F. Widoe as Chief. The Department consists of 20 members, besides the Chief. Wm. N. Sayles is the present Chief. The Chief is appointed by the Council.

WATER WORKS.—Hart has the Walker system of water works, put in at a cost of $4,500. The main is about one-third of a mile in length, with seven hydrants. Can throw four streams eighty feet high at one time. Accepted by the Council Oct. 18, 1886.

HART IMPROVEMENT COMPANY (Wigton House Block).—The original stockholders were:

Warren M. Wigton,	J. K. Flood,	F. J. Russell,
Geo. Rhodes,	E. B. Gaylord,	D. J. Mathews,
M. A. Luther,	Wm. J. Sprigg,	A. R. Chappell,
David Johnson,	L. P. Hyde,	H. P. Parsons,
A. S. White, Trustee;	E. P. Wigton,	T. S. Gurney,
Isaac Ford,	J. F. Widoe,	Helen A. Gurney,
Orson Kelley,	C. W. Slayton,	E. S. Houghtaling,
Lydia L. Richmond,	J. D. S. Hanson,	E. D. Richmond.
	A. S. White.	

The capital stock was $10,000. There were nine Directors, the first Board consisting of the following named gentlemen:

T. S. Gurney,	Warren M. Wigton,	E. B. Gaylord,
F. J. Russell,	David Johnson,	D. J. Mathews,
A. S. White,	J. F. Widoe,	J. K. Flood.

Wm. H. Bailey leased the hotel for five years.

ATTICONIAN SOCIETY. The Atticonian Literary and Debating Society was organized in May, 1881, with the following officers:

President, George Alverson. Secretary, H. J. Chadwick.
Vice President, Chas. A. Gurney. Treasurer, Chas. R. Johnson.
Prophet, Geo. A. McIntyre.

Reorganized Sept. 27, 1888, with the following officers:

President, John O. Richmond. Secretary, Robert R. Gale.
Vice President, J. D. S. Hanson. Treasurer, J. F. VanValkenburg.

Present officers:
President, George Alverson. Secretary, Harry Thorpe.
Vice President, C. W. Slayton. Treasurer, J. D. S. Hanson.

Present membership, 20. This Society is in a flourishing condition and has had considerable influence in its way since its organization. Has secured many excellent lecturers here.

HART UNION SCHOOL.—The following are the names of teachers and number of pupils in each department of the Hart Union School:

Principal, F. E. Young; Assistant, Miss LaVange Brooks; No. pupils, 84.
Intermediate, Miss Emma McRae; Assistant, Miss Docia Griswold; No. pupils, 81.
Primary, Miss Maggie Palmiter; No. pupils, 64.
Total enrolled, 229.

HART.—RESIDENCE OF HON. T. S. GURNEY.

HART.—WIDOE BASE BALL CLUB.

CHATAUQUA CIRCLE. Hart has a Chatauqua Circle, which was organized in October, 1885, with a membership of seven, and the following officers:

President, Mrs. A. A. Dunton. Secretary, Miss Carrie Wigton.
Treasurer, Miss Laura Butler.

At present there are nine members, with the following officers:

President, Mrs. J. V. Cahill. Secretary, Mrs. J. K. Flood.
Critic, Mrs. Nell Russell. Treasurer, Mrs. H. J. Holmes.

List of graduates:

Mrs. A. A. Dunton, Mrs. C. E. Croff, Mrs. Nell Russell,
Mrs. J. K. Flood, Mrs. J. V. Cahill, George Alverson,
Mrs. Chas. A. Gurney, Miss Emma R. Thorp, Mrs. H. J. Holmes.

BUSINESS HOUSES.—The following is a list of the business houses of Hart:

Wm. D. Ackerson, Photographer.
Am. Express Co., T. J. Main, Agt.
Argus, E. S. Palmiter, Prop.
Lemuel Atwood, Physician.
Geo. R. Bates, Hardware.
Charles Bergman, Painter and Paper Hanger.
John A. Billings, Meat Market.
W. W. Bosworth, Saw & Shingle Mill.
James Brassington, Attorney.
M. H. Brooks, Attorney, C. C. Com'r.
F. Bunnell, Agt. C. & W. M. R. R.
J. R. Butler, Dep. Reg. Deeds and Abstract Office.
Cady & Gurney, Druggists.
H. J. Chadwick, Physician, Drugs.
Marvin Chandler, Drayman.
Citizens' Exchange Bank.
James A. Collier, Postmaster.
Mrs. M. N. Collins, Dressmaker.
Geo. Cooper, Car. & Wagon Builder.
Wm. Cooper, Carpenter, Sheriff.
F. L. Corbin, Livery.
Harry Cornell, Dentist.
Mrs. W. T. Covell, Millinery.
Robert Currie, Carpenter and Ship Timber Jobber.
A. A. Dunton, Jr., Physician.
Frank H. Edwards, Painter.
Daniel Field, Blacksmith.
James K. Flood, Lumber.
Griswold & Cahill, Hardware.
Theron S. Gurney, Attorney.
J. D. S. Hanson, Pros. Attorney.
Hart Journal, S. Edson Prop.
Hart Leather Leg. Co., E. D. Richmond Manager.
Hart Mufg. Co., Lumber.
Henry H. Hatch, Physician.
Nelson Henion, Painter.
Henry J. Holmes, Carpenter.
E. S. Houghtailing, Grocer.
John Knickerbocker, Drayman.
Mrs. O. W. Knox, Music Teacher.
Otis W. Knox, Dry Goods.
A. Larnard, Blacksmith.
H. Marshall, Restaurant and Bakery.
Mathews & Chappell, Lumber Dealers.
Charles Meaux, Barber.
C. C. Messenger, Drug Store.
Frank A. Merton, Fruit Evaporator.
A. E. Molley, General Store.
Mugford & Servis, Pump M'f'g'rs.
Oceana Co. Tribune, J. Brassington Manager.
Mrs. H. P. Parsons, Dressmaker.
H. P. Parsons, Jeweler.
Mrs E. P. Pearl, Dressmaker.
Mrs. Nellie Pepple, Restaurant.
Mrs. J. O. Richmond, Dressmaker.
J. O. Richmond, Jeweler.
Ridell & Collins, Carpenters.
Rhodes & Leonard, General Store. (P. of I. Store.)
F. J. Russell, Attorney.
Ryerson & Dempsy, Meat Market.
Mrs. Nina Sackrider, Millinery.
W. P. Sackrider, Attorney, Co. Clerk.
S. A. Shufelt, Saloon.
Cyrenus Slaght, Gen'l Merchandise.
Jas. D. Slater, Harnessmaker.
Jas. H. Slater, Shoemaker.
A. Smith, Saloon.
Mrs. C. B. Stevens, Dressmaker.
C. B. Stevens, Attorney.
Stitt & Sanford, Grocers.
Wm. E. Thorp, General Store.
Miss Anna Waller, Dressmaker.
Waller & Son, Blacksmiths.
D. C. Wickham, Register of Deeds.
Wm., Wideman, Shoemaker.
John F. Widoe, Clothing.
Wigton House, W. H. Bailey, Prop.
Wigton & Bosworth, Flour Mills.
Williams Bros., Barbers.
George Wyckoff, Co. Treasurer.

The following named gentlemen have been President of Hart village: W. M. Wigton, '85; Theron S. Gurney, '86; Daniel Landon, '87; John F. Widoe, '88; H. J. Chadwick, '89. The present Council is composed as follows: President, John F. Widoe; Trustees, Wm. E. Thorp, H. H. Gilliland, Chas. E. Leonard, Jas. H. Slater, John Westbrook, Geo. Dennison; Clerk, F. H. Edwards.

TOWNSHIP OF CLAYBANKS.

Claybanks was the first township in the county to be settled and the history of the county for many years is the history of the township. When the county was organized it was one of the three big townships, and included the territory of Claybanks, Grant, Otto and Greenwood. The territory included within its present limits embraces some of the oldest and best farms in the county. In its early history the prospects were good for a large and prosperous village being located within its limits, but events so shaped themselves as to cause the villages of the county to be located elsewhere. It has four school buildings and two fine church edifices. The Roman Catholic and Scandinavian churches are described at length on pages 48 and 116. The first Postoffice in the township was located at Whisky Creek and called Claybanks. Flower Creek Postoffice is also kept on Sec. 27.

The following is the list of Supervisors, Clerks and Treasurers:

GEO. C. MYERS, SUPERVISOR, '89.

Supervisors:—A. S. Anderson, '55-6-7-8-'64-5-6-7-8-9'70-1-5; Nelson Green, '59-'60; Jason Carpenter, '61-2; O. K. White, '63; Harvey Tower, '72-3; M. Baker, '74-6-7-8-9-'80; Joel D. Linsday, '81-2-4-5; Geo. C. Myers, '83-6-7-8-9.

Clerks.—Timothy Brigham, '55-6; James Cody, '57; Jeremiah Collins, '58-'61; Jason Carpenter, '59-'64-5; A. A. Lillie, '60-6; Malcolm Campbell, '63; S. G. Huston, '67-8-9-'70-4; Martin Baker, '71-2; Horace H. Keyes, '73; Hugo Deyman, '75-6-7-8-9-'80-4-5-6-7-8-9; O. E. Huston, '81-2-3.

Treasurers.—Thomas Phillips, '55; C. A. Rosevelt, '56; Owen Farrell, '57; Barton Haggerty, '58-9; E. B. Burrington, '60; O. C. Perry, '61-2-3-4-5-6; M. B. Lillie, '67-

8-9-'70-1; O. E. Huston, '72; A. S. Anderson, '73-4-6; Andrew Brady, '75-7-8; Joel D. Linsday, '79-'80; Seneca Fuller, '81-2-5-6; J. G. Farrell, '83-84; I. Haggerty, '87-8-9.

TOWNSHIP OF WEARE.

April 2, 1860, the township of Weare was organized. The act of organization took place at the house of Charles Mears on what is known as the River House farm. The township is composed of 36 full sections of land which in an early day was considered principally valuable for its timber. It has all the varieties of soil mentioned in Chapter I, and more recent improvements have demonstrated the fact that its soil is adapted to the successful raising of all farm products grown in Michigan. Fruit can be raised successfully on fully one-third of the lands of the township. At the present time the cultivation of fruit is occupying the attention of many, although heretofore it has not engaged the attention of the farmers as generally as in the townships of Shelby and Hart. Some of the finest farms and most successful farmers of the county are in this township. We herewith present our readers with a view of a representative farm in South Weare:

Residence of Joseph Schaner, Sec. 29.

The township was named after Dr. Daniel G. Weare, who settled on Sec. 27 in 1855. There are no villages in the township but there are five fine school buildings, two of which are built of brick and well furnished with modern school furniture. There are three fine church buildings, M. E , Baptist, and Catholic.

The following is the list of Supervisors, Clerks and Treasurers:

Supervisors.—Myrtle B. High, '60-2-'70; Norman C. Smith, '61-5-6-7-8-'73-4-5-6-7-8-9-'80-1-2; A. J. Benson, '63; A. J. Smith, '64; E. P. Gregory, '69; George Tiffany, '71; Samuel Graham, '72; P. Cramer, '83; R. C. Roberts, '84; E. M. Roberts, '85; A. L. Carr, '86-7-8-9.

Clerks.—A. D. Boomer, '60; F. VonHolmrich, '61; Jas. Dexter, '62; James R. Mooney, '63-4; D. R. Gifford, '65-6-7; John Glading, '68; D. Fulton, '69-'70-1-2-4-5-6; James Walker, '73; R. C. Roberts, '77; E. M. Roberts, '78-9-'80-1; S. Andrus, '82-3-4; P. Rasmusson, '85-6-7-8-9.

A. L. CARR, SUPERVISOR, '89.

Treasurers.—F. J. Hartman, '61; Hiram Blowers, '60-3; W. Jennings, '64-8-'70-1-2-3-4-5-6-7; E. B. Burrington, '65; Jas. Walker, '66; N. Snyder, '67; S. R. Wilson, '69; Jos. Schauer, '78-9; H. Lefevre, '80-1-3-4-7-8; C. M. Jensen, '82; G. B. Dikeman, '85-6-9.

TOWNSHIP OF BENONA.

Intimately associated with the history of this township is the honored name of Ferry. The first saw mill erected in the county was built in the year 1849 by the Rev. Wm. M. Ferry and his son the Hon. T. W. Ferry. It was built at the mouth of Stony Creek and was run by water power. Benona village was here started but aside from a Postoffice, a store, and a few other buildings, there is no indication of a village. It is a very picturesque and healthy locality, and the lake and streams entering it furnish excellent fishing. It is a popular locality with visiting sportsmen.

The name Benona was selected and given to the Stony Creek Postoffice by A. R. Wheeler. It is a very pretty name and was probably the name of some locality of another State familiar to Mr. Wheeler. If it is a corruption of the word "Benoni," signifying "child of grief," it is hardly appropriate for the territory it marks. Although the township was originally Stony Creek and embraced

Shelby, Newfield and Benona of today, and although it has been used to make three other towns, and also suffered the loss of its name, Shelby having for a time been called Benona, still as regards its beautiful farms, intelligent citizens and great fruit interests, its schools and churches, it is to be congratulated and ought not to have its name interpreted to signify grief. This township, like Claybanks, is the home of many of the earliest pioneers of the county and was the scene of their earliest labors. Some have passed away but many still remain in the enjoyment of the beautiful country their labors have developed.

The following is the list of Supervisors, Clerks and Treasurers:

Supervisors.—H. Hoffman, '62-3-7-'70-1-2-3-4-5-6; A. R. Wheeler, '64-5-6-8-9; Jos. H. Sammons, '77-8-9; Chas. A. Sessions, '80-1-2-3-4-5; W. H. Fleming, '86-7-8-9.

Clerks.—Wm. F. R. Smith, '62-3-4; Alonzo Hyde, '65-6; G. Powers, '67-8; George E. Conklin, '69; Edwin G. Everdeen '70-1-2-3-'80-1-2-8-9; Jacob Snell, '74-5-6; G. Thiele, '77; J. B. Applegate, '78-9; B. Thiele, '83-4; C. A. Williams, '85; W. H. Anderson, '86; F. Myers, '87.

Treasurers.—H. Hendrickson, '72-3-4-5 6-7-'75-7-8; H. Hoffman, '68-9; A. R. Wheeler, '70-1-2-3-4-6; David Graham, '79; James Gibbs, '80-8-9; William Olinder, '81-2-6-7; J. B. Thompson, '83-4; W. H. Fleming, '85.

W. H. FLEMING, SUPERVISOR, '89.

TOWNSHIP OF GOLDEN.

We have before described the organization of this town, but the history of the manner in which it came to be organized and named has never been correctly given. One of the earliest settlers of this township was William J. Haughey, who thus describes the settlement and organization of the town:

"Well, as pine gave out, some of the settlers moved north to Elbridge, now Golden. At that time Mr. Henry Hartman and myself wanted more pine land, and it so happened we both got the same man to help us look it up, Tom Bearss, now living in Barry County. Well, by some means Henry got the idea that I was after his land, then you should see fun, Hartman following me. Finally we compared notes and found we were after different descriptions; we then shook hands, took our lager and were sworn friends. We two were now going into a new township to open it up to settlement. Mr. J. Barnhart moved to Round Lake, Mr. Asa Pringle, William Pringle and A. F. Bemis settled near by. Our first election was held in a log school house southeast of Hart, going by compass. I finally blazed a trail through the woods.

Well, we wanted to have a town of our own, so friend Barnhart and others got up a petition to the honorable Board of Supervisors to set us off from Elbridge and call the new town—well, the Supervisors could not read the name; our friend, the County Clerk, Mr. E. D. Richmond, could not make it out, and as Mr. J. Barnhart wrote it, it was referred to him, but the writing had got cold and he could not tell what it was. I happened to come in about this time, when it was proposed to call it the township of Haughey, as I was supposed to be the oldest inhabitant. By my request it was to be named Golding."

The name Golding was the maiden name of Mr. Haughey's mother. By some error the name upon the records appears Golden instead of Golding, and as such it is known to this day.

There are portions of the township in which the soil is light and sandy, but there are other portions where it is good for general farming purposes, and fruit raising. Some of the most successful fruit orchards of the county are located in this township. The celebrated Stanhope orchard is located on section 2, the Golden Stock farm on section 12, the Branch's orchards are on section 21, A. M. Pringle's and B. C. Knapp's on section 24, and Caleb Davis' on section 22. There are many other farms equally as good, but these through the public reports have become specially noted. The village of Mears is also located in this town upon the C. & W. M. R'y and is one of the most extensive shipping points for fruit in the county. There have been several saw mills in the township, but with its fine timber all but one have disappeared and farming and fruit raising constitute the chief employment of the people. Charcoal making has been a great industry at a point about one-half mile north of the village, the kilns being a part of the Rankin system. These kilns have enabled farmers and fruit raisers to clear their lands without expense, and have furnished the locality with currency that has materially lessened the burdens of those engaged in improving lands.

List of Supervisors, Clerks and Treasurers:

Supervisors.—J. Barnhart, '65-6; E. J. Sparks, '67; W. M. Pringle, '68; C. Davis, '69-'70-1-2; J. K. Howe, '73-4; Geo. Wyckoff, '75-6-7-8; Clark B. Genung, '79-'87-8; George A. Wagar, '80-1-2; E. E. Allen, '83-4; R. T. Morris, '85-6; J. F. Cumming, '89.

Clerks.—Alfred C. Wilson, '65; Hiram J. Wilson, '66; H. S. Bronson, '67; E. Goodman, '68; G. C. Hannum, '69-'70-1; Wm. Hiles, '72-3-4-5-6-7; Samuel J. Sparks, '78 (resigned in October); E. H. Hotchkiss, from October, '78-9-'80-1-2-5-8; W. F. Downing '83-4; A. Tennant, '86-7; C. A. Campbell, '89.

J. F. CUMMING, SUPERVISOR, '89.

Treasurers.—W. J. Haughey, '65; Asa M. Pringle, '66-8; Wm. Hiles, '69; H. Howorth, '70-1-2-3-4-5-6; R. T. Morris, '77-8-9-'83-4; A. M. Pringle, '80-1; C. B. Genung, '82; Geo. Wyckoff, '85; E. Stanhope, '86-7; E. E. Allen '88; H. M. Branch, '89.

TOWNSHIP OF ELBRIDGE.

The Christian name of one of Oceana's pioneer settlers was selected as the name for this township. Elbridge R. Farmer, now an old man residing in Grand Rapids, is the person who was thus honored. The territory included within the limits of the township is noted as the last camping ground of the red man in this vicinity. The township ranks sixth in the value of its assessable property. Its soil is heavy and in agricultural pursuits it is making rapid strides to the front. Hervey S. Sayles and the Hon. D. W. Crosby, are among the first white settlers.

"The first Sunday school in Elbridge was commenced in 1870, in the cedar school house, by the American Sunday-School Union. W. J. Tennant was the first Superintendent, and has continued in office until the present, with the exception of two years, when V. E. Kerr held the position. The children were nearly all Indians, there being four white families at that time in the town—Sayles, Crosby,

Cochran and Tennant. Among the pleasant reminiscences of the organization, might be mentioned the one of the Indians attending the school. Indian children, having heard that there was going to be a Sabbath school, came from all parts of the town to see what kind of an institution it was. They came marching into the school house, with their bows and arrows, and accompanied by their dogs. They were instructed as well as could be done, to leave their bows and arrows at home, so the next time they came with nothing but their dogs. During the exercises, one of the dogs looked in at the door and growled, which caused nearly all in the house to laugh. One of the Indian boys did not like such actions, and as soon as he got out of doors he gave the dog a kick, but no sooner had he done that, than the owner of the dog fell to kicking him, and by the time the Superintendent got out of doors to stop it, they were having a regular knock-down fight."—Page's History of Oceana County.

List of Supervisors, Clerks and Treasurers:

Supervisors.—S. G. Rollins, '58; Seth T. Robinson, '59: Josiah Russell, '59-'60-1; J. Bean, '62; W. H. Leach, '63; H. S. Sayles, '64 5 6 7 8 '85; D. W. Crosby, '69-'70-'81-2 3 4-6-7 8; W. J. Tennant, '71-2-3; T. G. Houk, '74-5-6-7-8-9-'80; D. J. Hill, '89.

Clerks.—H. H. Fuller, '58; Thos. W. Farrell, '59; Henry B. Burrill, '60; A. W. Peck, '61; W. H. Leach, '62; Ariel Crosby, '63; Hazen Leavitt, '64; D. W. Crosby, '65-6-'74-5-6-7-8-9; Olney Bishop, '67; C. C. Cochran, '68 9; W. J. Tennant, '70; Jas. N. McCreary, '81; J. R. Thompson, '72-3; Jas. H. Wyman, '80; Jesse Weirich, '82-3; G. May, '84; J. Tennant, '85 6-7-8 9.

Treasurers.—Ira Jenks,'58; James R. Mooney, '59; Charles B. Wilson, '60 1; Joseph Babahmuseh, '62; H. S. Sayles, '63-'76-7-9-'80; Seth T. Robinson, '64-5 6; Joseph Pay-ba-ma, '67 8 9-'70; Charles E. Hickey, '71 2-3; Louis Genereau, '74-5; James H. Wyman, '78; William N. Sayles, '81; A. C. Shepherdson, '82; C. Leak, '83-4-9; G. May, '85 6; D. J. Hill, '87 8.

D. J. HILL, SUPERVISOR '89.

TOWNSHIP OF LEAVITT.

The township of Leavitt derived its name from its first white settler, Hazen Leavitt, hale and hearty, although in his eighty-fifth year.

For many years this has been considered a back town of the

county, but the building of the Butters & Peters railroad to Stetson from Ludington, caused the village of Walkerville to be platted, the growth of which has been the most remarkable of any in the county.

There are many fine farms in this township, of which the L. L. Taylor and C. W. Leavitt are the most noted.

Residence of L. L. Taylor, Leavitt.

WALKERVILLE.

Much has been said and much written regarding the wonderful growth of cities and towns in the West, but probably as remarkable a growth as many of those may be found in our own county. Walkerville is a village of today and the prospects are that the sudden growth of the town is also a permanent growth. In 1883 Fayette Walker, who owned a mill at this point, platted a village and named it Walkerville. It is located upon parts of sections three and ten, of Leavitt township, the section line road between these sections being the main street of the village. When first platted the growth was slow, it being only within the past three years and since the arrival of the Butters & Peters railroad that the town has boomed. It is located near a bad swamp which will not conduce to the good health of its inhabitants, but the village itself is situated upon high ground, with a broad main street bordered by walks upon either side. The town has a very decidedly new aspect, some of the later buildings being as yet without paint, and others showing the recent application of the brush. As usual in new towns many of the store buildings have residence rooms above. By means of the railroad mentioned the citizens have daily direct communication with Ludington, and much trade goes that way. The name of the Post office is Stetson, and Mr. J. E. Doty is the genial Postmaster. Of business places, there are now two meat markets, two hotels, two general merchandise establishments, two drug stores, a saw and feed mill, two blacksmith shops, a hardware store, a barber shop, a shoe shop, a livery barn and a saloon. The M. E. society have commenced the erection of a church edifice. They have a good school, and taking it all in all, Walkerville is a thriving town which, if its last year's growth is equaled each year hereafter, will soon rival the other villages of the county. It is surrounded by a splendid farming country which will undoubtedly give permanancy to the growth of the village.

List of Supervisors, Clerks and Treasurers of Leavitt:

Supervisors.—

V. E. Clark, '65 7, H. Goodrich, '68 9, A. C. Gowdy, 70-1-2 3, David Scott, '74 5-6-7 8, W. F. Palmiter, '79-'80, J. Bogue, '81-2 3-4-5-6-7, A. B. Holt, '88, Wm. Hilyard, '89.

Clerks.—

G. G. Scott, '82, G. H. Merrifield, '83-4-5-6-7 9, John Robinson, '88.

Treasurers.—

William Vaughn, '82, William Hilyard, '83-4 8, B. Craker, '85, C. Andreas, '86 7, J. Giddings, '89.

WM. HILYARD, SUPERVISOR, '89.

TOWNSHIP OF NEWFIELD.

This township was organized as an independent township under its present name in 1866. The origin of the name is thus explained in Page's History of Oceana County, by Joseph W. Sweet, an early settler of the place:

"A number of the settlers chanced to be in his house, and a proper name for the shortly to be organized town was discussed. Elbridge Green wished it to be called Greenfield; Alex. McLaren proposed Sweet-town, which was modestly declined, on the part of Mr. Sweet, who, in turn, suggested Perrytown, in honor of old Booth

Perry, the first settler in the town, but at last the name of 'Newfield' prevailed, and was inserted in the petition."

List of Supervisors, Clerks and Treasurers:

Supervisors.—Henry C. Hawley, "'66-7-8 9 '75-6-7-8 9 '81-2, J. W. Dunning, '70-1 2, J. N. Chellis, '73-4, J. E. Philo, '88-4-5-6-7-8-9.

Clerks.—Charles H. Potter, '66-7 9-'72, Charles Strobridge, '68-H. C. Hawley, '70, H. K. Bush, '71, J. W. Dunning, '73-4-5 6-7, O. A. Rowland, '78-'84, I. H. Barlow, '80, Charles Perkins, '81, W. Fleming, '82 3, J. F. Bush, '85, A. T. Rowland, '86, A. A. Matherson, '87, A. C. Eldridge, '84 9.

Treasurers.—Joseph W. Sweet '66-7-8, M. A. Frink, '69, B. F. Marquick, '70-1-2 3, S. Atherton, '74-5, J. McGill, Jr., '76-7, G. D. Webster, '78 9-'80, P. Monroe. '81-2, John McCowen, '83, Chas. E. Strobridge, '84-5, O. A. Rowland, '86-7, M. Resseguie, '88-9.

J. E. PHILO, SUPERVISOR, '89.

VILLAGE OF HESPERIA.

The village of Hesperia is located on the south side of White River, partly in Oceana and partly in Newaygo counties. That portion located in Oceana county is in the township of Newfield. The main street of the village is the county line, this dividing not only the business but the residence portion nearly in the center. Being in the center of a rich farming country with no other villages very near, there is but one reason why it has not grown much faster than it has, and that reason is its lack of railroad communication with the outside world. Efforts have been made at various times to secure a road, but thus far they have been unsuccessful. In spite of this drawback Hesperia has become a thriving village and includes among its business men many energetic and enterprising citizens. The village was platted and recorded in 1866, T. L. Waters being the Surveyor. The land was owned by John P. Cook and Daniel Weaver. An addition has since been added upon the south by O. A. Rowland. The first log house was built in 1857 and the first frame house in 1866. The first settler on the Oceana side was J. W. Sweet. A saw mill was erected in 1866, a flouring mill in 1871, and another in 1882. The village was incorporated in 1883, and the following named gentlemen have had the office of President: Daniel Weaver two years, H. C. Hawley two years, H. K. Bush two years, and the present incumbent is Dr. L. E. Norton. The village at present contains two grist mills, one saw mill, a stave mill, a grist mill which also does planing and general work, a bee hive factory, six combined dry goods and grocery stores, two hardwares, two drug stores, two meat markets, one milliner, four blacksmith shops, two liveries, three hotels, one newspaper the Hesperia "News", a barber shop, a gent's furnishing establishment, a furniture store, two jewelers, and a shoe shop. There are four practicing physicians and one lawyer located here. There are three church edifices, Presbyterian, Baptist and Methodist Episcopal, and four religious organizations. About 1885 the village made a contract with W. J. Tennant to put in waterworks for fire purposes, and it now has a good system. There are five hydrants. The power is furnished by Webster's saw mill and direct pressure is used. The pumps are rotary. There is a well regulated fire department of which Mr. L. S. Weaver is Chief. The department is composed of two hose companies of thirteen men each, and is equipped with two carts and other necessary appliances. The one thing that the people pride themselves upon more than any other is their graded school. They have a fine school building and a good corps of teachers composed of Mr. Will S. Millard as principal, and three assistants. The Postoffice at present is located on the Newaygo side with Mr. W. C. Simmons as Postmaster. Hesperia is quite a town for secret and other societies, there being at present in operation and in flourishing condition a Masonic Lodge with a branch of the order of the Eastern Star, an Odd Fellows' Lodge, a Post of the Grand Army of the Republic with a Woman's Relief Corps in connection, and a Camp of the Sons of Veterans. They also have a Lodge of the Ancient Order of United Workmen with a membership of twenty.

TOWNSHIP OF FERRY.

The township of Reed was organized pursuant to a resolution of the Board of Supervisors in April, 1869. The Reeds, Elnathan J. and Theodore F., were prominent in securing the organization of the town and the name of Reed was given to it. Afterwards, by Act of the Legislature the name was changed from Reed to Ferry in honor of the Hon. T. W. Ferry, U. S. Senator. A Postoffice was established on the northeast quarter of section twenty-eight, named Reed, a school house built, a saw mill, grist mill, store and church added, and quite a thriving village is now located here, the center of a fine tract of farming lands.

The soil of the township varies from light to heavy, and its timber is excellent. The township has passed its lumber period and is now entering upon a more successful and permanent development. The following is the Gazetteer of the village:

B. F. Archer, Hardware.
Charles B. Archer, Tinshop.
Frank Carpenter, Wagonmaker.
O. L. Cederquist, Shoemaker.
Fox Bros., Livery, and stage to Shelby.
Wm. E. Gunn, Blacksmith.
John M. Heim, Eagle Hotel and Heim's Hall.
Orion Hightower, Groceries.
Dr. L. Irish & Co., Drugs.
Nathan Irish, Ferry House and Meat Markets.
Mrs. P. A. Jackson, Barber.
W. R. Mathews, Real Estate and Loan.
Mrs. Manderville & Co., Millinery.
Powers Bros., Grist and Saw Mill.
I. M. Young & Co., Groceries and Dry Goods.

List of Supervisors, Clerks and Treasurers:

Supervisors.—B. F. Reed, '69-'70-1; T. F. Reed, '72-3; R. P. Ferris, '74-5; D. Landon, '76-7-8-9-'80-1-2-3-4; B. F. Archer, '85; G. M. Smith, '86; E. L. Benton, '87-8-9.

Clerks.—T. Smith, '69-'70; Chas. Gaylord, '72; T. P. Landon, '73-'87-8; E. L. Benton, '74-6-7-8-9-'80; Gus. M. Smith, '75-'82-3-4; Chas. W. Powers, '81-6-9; W. E. Gunn, '85.

Treasurers.—J. F. Evans, '69; Levi Powers, '72; Daniel Landon, '73-4-5; G. M. Smith, '76-7-8-'80-1; T. H. Pittenger, '79; E. L. Benton, '82-4; J. A. Chellis, '83; W. E. Hightower, '85-6; W. W. Powers, '87; J. H. Critchett, '88-9.

E. L. BENTON, SUPERVISOR, '89.

TOWNSHIP OF CRYSTAL.

In the winter of 1865, Jared H. Gay, who had been a settler since July, 1861, made an effort to have the town set off from Weare. There not being enough legal voters, he contracted to deed lands on section 16, to George Lammon, Charles Willet and Albert O. Aldrich. A remonstrance against separation was got up by parties in Elbridge and Weare, but Mr. Gay employed Chas. W. Deane, a lawyer of Pentwater, to advocate his cause, and was successful.—Page's History of Oceana County.

Jared H. Gay is probably the first permanent white settler of this town. He has been prominent in the offices of the town ever since and is still a resident of it. The beautiful and appropriate name of Crystal was selected by his wife. The beautiful crystal streams of water for which it is noted suggested the name to Mrs. Gay.

In its early history Crystal was the lumberman's pride, and soon became ravaged by the voracious mills. Lately it is developing as an agricultural town. Its brooks of clear, cold water fed by springs abound with trout. The Butters & Peters R. R., as it is known, runs from Ludington thro' this township to Stetson, in the town of Leavitt. Crystal Valley is the name of its village which has a population of about 200. Mail by stage tri-weekly. It has an M. E. Church building, Odd Fellows' Hall, general store, saw mill, hotel, wagon shop, harness shop, shoe shop, etc.

List of Supervisors, Clerks and Treasurers.

T. T. JONES, SUPERVISOR, '89.

Supervisors.—Dr. Jas. J. Kittridge, '66-8-9; William Murch, '67; Geo. C. Crouch, '70; Jas. Corsaut, '71; Charles Willet, '72-3-'83; Henry Cogill, '74-5-6 7-9-'80-1-2-4-8; T. T. Jones, '78-'85-6-7-9.

Clerks.—D. K. Foster, '66-7; William Murch, '68-9; Moses F. Stone, '70; Geo. Lammon, '71; Henry Cogill, '72-3; F. B. Kittridge, '74; Joseph Cogill, '75; J. Webster, '76-7; C. A. Noble, '78-9-'80-8; E. F. Avery, '81-2-'84; I. C. Harwood, '83-5; B. F. Stone, '86; J. H. Chadwick, '87; P. B. Harwood, '89.

Treasurers.—Jared H. Gay, '66-7-8; Henry Cole, '69; Paul Bushaw, '70; J. J. Kittridge, '71-2-3-4-5-6-7-8-'81-4; F. B. Kittridge,

'79-80; D. P. Kelly, '82-3-5-6; A. O. Aldrich, '87-8; Charles Comstock, '89.

TOWNSHIP OF GREENWOOD.

H. D. Clark was the first settler, and located in the extreme southeast corner, closely followed by L. and A. McCallum, Amos Wright, L. T. Brown, B. Ish, and others. Oliver Swain and Judge Camp followed soon after, settling in the extreme northeastern part, and B. F. Moe located midway between the two settlements.

The town was slowly settled, as it was a dense lumbering region, and only as the lower portions of the country, bordering on White River, began to be exhausted of their timber, did Greenwood begin to be sought out by the early lumbermen. Situated on the south branch of the White River, it was possible by means of pole boats, to transport the settlers and their effects to the Rapids, and to team thence to their future homes by means of oxen, or oftener, by the forest trails, on the backs of the settlers and their obliging neighbors. Goods were often thus brought up from the mouth of White River, where there was early a settlement, with the usual accompaniment of a sawmill, store, and the inevitable saloon or two. Sometimes, a settler and his family with their household effects, were dumped down on the north side of Muskegon Lake, to make their way the best they could, by foot, to White River Postoffice, and thence by pole boats up the White River, or by ox team, and often in fording the streams they stood in imminent danger of drowning.

Another mode of entering the country was by the way of Newaygo.

The first settler was Henry D. Clark. He is still hale and hearty, and enjoying the fruits of his labors on a beautiful farm in the extreme southeastern corner of the county, on section 36. He made his way into his present lot in September, 1855, and built a rude shanty of score blocks and bark, and commenced to make a clearing. After about five weeks of lonely blessedness, he heard, one evening, the welcome sound of a human voice—that of Amos Wright, who asked if he wanted company. One may be sure that never was Robinson Crusoe so delighted at finding Friday, as Clark was to hear the cheery sound of a human voice, and to grasp the hand of Wright and that of the sturdy, honest Scotchman who accompanied him, Mr. Lachlan McCallum, now one of the best farmers in the county. Messrs. Wright & McCallum came in October, 1855. They had met by accident, in John Ball's office, in Grand Rapids, and found land in Greenwood. Lyman J. Browne came in about the same time. When H. D. Clark raised his log house, he had to scour the country for nine miles around to get men enough to assist in the raising. Archibald McCallum, who was afterwards a martyr in the war, came about the same time as Lachlan, his brother, and the two worked in the lumber woods."—Page's History of Oceana County.

On page 103 appears the account of the Cogswell tragedy, which convulsed the citizens of Greenwood with horror.

The township was organized in April, 1858, and the name Greenwood selected as being expressive of the appearance of her forests. An attempt was made to name the town Oliver in honor of an old settler, Oliver Swain, but failed.

List of Supervisors, Clerks and Treasurers:

C. SERFLING, SUPERVISOR, '89.

Supervisors.—O. Swain,'58-9-'60-1-2; Chas. Camp, '63-4-5-6-7-part of '79-'86; Henry F. Cushman,'68-9-'70-1-3; Joseph Stevens, '72-'80; I. H. Cogswell, '74-5-6-7-8-9; Benjamin F. Hermance, '81-2; A. M. Phelps, '83-4-5; Chas. Serfling, '87-8-9.

Clerks.—Cyrus W. Bullen, '58-9; Lachlan McCallum, '60-1-'75-6-7-8; J. M. Swain, '62-3; Chas. E. Sischo, '64; R. F. Wells, 65-6-7-8-9-'70-1; O. F. Williams, '72; A. M. Phelps '73-4-'87-8; C. Serfling, '79-'80-1-2-3-4-5-6; B. F. Hermance, '89.

Treasurers.—Craig B. Moe, '58; Benjamin Ish, '59-'60-1-2; Ezra I. Rugg, '63; Henry C. Hawley, '64-5; Joseph Stevens, '66-7-8-9-'70-1-5-6-7-8-9; H. F. Cushman, '72; Enos Scott, '73-4; Rudolph Bell, '80-1; A. M. Phelps, '82-9; B. F. Hermance, '83-4; H. D. Clark, '85-6; R. Ayers, '87-8.

TOWNSHIP OF OTTO.

This township comprised its present territory and that of Ferry. It was organized and held its first election in 1860. In 1868 the township of Reed (now Ferry) was organized, taking the north half of Otto. This left Otto very weak as its land was principally valuable for its timber, and a large portion of it was owned by non-residents. Although with the growth of the county it has gradually improved, its progress has been slow. Its vote is only about 26, and its assessed valuation is $51,000, the lowest of any town in the county. It derived its name, Otto, from the German "Otho."

List of Supervisors, Clerks and Treasurers:

Supervisors.—E. J. Reed, '60-1; B. Hill, '62-3-4; B. F. Reed, '65; J. F. Evans, '66-7-8; S. B. Potter, '69; Jacob Williamson, '70-4-5-6-'81-2-3-4-6-7-8-9; Robert Pointer, '71-2; L. H. Shaw, '73; O. E. Fogg, '77-8-9-'80-5.

Clerks.—Timothy Smith, '64-5-7; Daniel Williams, '66; Charles Rathbun, '68; E. O. Peck, '69; L. B. Shaw, '69-70-1; J. Williamson, from July, '72; S. B. Potter, '73-4-5-6-7-8-9-'80-1-2-3-4-5-7-8-9; E. E. Ellis, '86.

Treasurers.—J. F. Evans, '63-4; J. M. Haines, '65; J. Hinds, '66-7; G. R. Quick, '68; J. Gowell, '69; J. Williamson, from Nov., '69, to March, '70'-85; E. H. Ellis, '70; W. Duke, part of '71; D. Adams, '71-2-3-4-5-6-'86-7; O. E. Fogg, '76-7-'84-8; S. B. Stephenson, '78; F. Newman, '79-'80-2-3; C. Newman, '81.

TOWNSHIP OF GRANT.

The township of Grant is located in the south tier of towns of Oceana County, Mich., and is the legal subdivision known as Township No. 13 north, of Range No. 17 west, and was subject to entry at the United States Land Office at Ionia, Mich.

The township was organized Dec. 31, 1866. The first township meeting was held on the first day of April, 1867, at the house of Jason Carpenter, at which meeting O. K. White was elected Supervisor, Jason Carpenter, Clerk, and Henry W. Turk, Treasurer, each receiving twenty-seven votes—all that were polled. The first settlement was made by Fernando Seaver, in the then township of Claybanks, Ottawa County, on section 31, in 1851, followed by William Winderknecht and John Brocker, soon after. Alfred Pope also settled on the same section, on the farm now owned and occupied by Harvey Tower, in 1856. The same year Alonzo Green made a settlement on section 30. In May, 1857, O. K. White settled on section 7, after opening nearly six miles of road. In the fall of 1857, the first election was held for the election of county officers for Oceana County. Jason Carpenter made a settlement on section 5, in 1859, and Dexter M. Wheeler settled on section 4, in 1860; John Smith on same section, in 1861. Milo H. Sweet made a settlement on section 6, Henry W. Turk on section 9, Alonzo Smith and James Baker on section 10, the same year. At this time wolves were thick and quite familiar, so much so that John Brocker tells us that when he had got his shanty so far completed as to move into it, with a blanket for a door, one of the fellows pushed his head through the door and took a survey of the interior of the shanty. It was evidently satisfactory to him, for he trotted away with the utmost indifference when the family entered a protest against his company.

O. K. White says: "In November, 1861, four of the fraternity paid us a visit. They were heard near the house in the afternoon, so near, indeed, that the children took to the house for fear of them. About 8 o'clock in the evening the ball was opened in good earnest, and they kept up their howling the entire night, approaching the house and then retreating. The music was fearful, and effectually prevented sleep in that house. An infant, scarcely four months old, exhibited signs of fear, although held in her mother's arms. I was unable to scare them away, with any means at hand, although I tried repeatedly. I imagined there might be at least a dozen, but tracks in the light snow revealed the fact that there were only four."—Page's History of Oceana County.

This township was named after the the great Union General by the organizers, who were admirers of him long before the people of the country at large had begun to fully appreciate his services.

List of Supervisors, Clerks and Treasurers:

E. S. RANDALL, SUPERVISOR, '89.

Supervisors.—O. K. White, '67-8-9-'70-1-4; N. Green, '72; H. W. Turk, '73; H. H. Hand, '75-6; Harvey Tower, '77; M. H. Sweet, '78-9-'80-1-2-3-4-5-6-7-8; E. S. Randall, '89.

Clerks.—J. Carpenter, '67; L. W. Bennett, '68; D. Hecor, '69; H. S. Marble, '70; J. S. Osborn, '71; A. Sainsbury, '72-3-4-5-6-8-9-'80-1-2-3-4-5-6-7-8-9; A. White, '77.

Treasurers.—Hy. W. Turk, '67-8-9-'75; L. B. Godfrey, '70-1; B. F. West, '72-3; N. Green, '74; J. M. Keyes, '76; M. H. Sweet, '77; O. K. White, '78; F. Seaver, '79-'80; F. A. Foster, '81-2-7; J. G. Johnson, '83-4; F. A. Robbins, '85; E. D. White, '86; J. B. Conger, '88-9.

TOWNSHIP OF COLFAX.

This is another patriotic town, named in honor of an illustrious Vice President. The township is a close competitor with Otto for the smallest number of inhabitants of any town in the county. It is, however, still possessed of valuable pine lands, and some good for farming purposes. Its assessed valuation in 1889 was $154,-000. Calvin Woodworth, a patriarch in appearance, is the oldest living resident of the town. He located there in 1864, and has been an active factor in all its public interests ever since. His son is the present Supervisor.

List of Supervisors, Clerks and Treasurers:

Supervisors.—G. C. Benton, '69-'70; C. Woodworth, '71-2-3-'82; Fayette Walker, '74-5-6-7-8-9-'80-1; J. M. Baldwin, 3-4-5-6-7-8; C. A. Woodworth, '89.

Clerks.—A. S. Perring, '69; J. B. Winans, '70-5; S. A. Blanchard, '71-6-'82; Alfonso C. Gowell, '72-3-4; Andrew J. Cole, '77-8-9-'80-1; T. W. Draggoo, '83-4-5-6-7-8-9.

Treasurers.—A. Freeman, '69-'77-8-9-'80; F. Walker, '70-1-2-3-4; A. Draggoo, '75-6-'81-2; Calvin Woodworth, '83; Rufus Jewell, '84; C. A. Woodworth, '85-6; Fred. E. Woodworth, '87-8-9;

C. A. WOODWORTH, SUPERVISOR, '89.

CHAPTER XII.

––x––

SECRET AND SOCIAL ORGANIZATIONS.

––x––

MASONIC.

Freemasonry, from the time of the organization of the first Lodge in 1866, has maintained a steady, healthy growth, there now being four flourishing lodges of Free and Accepted Masons, besides a Chapter of Royal Arch Masons and a Council of Royal and Select Masters. There are also in the county two Chapters of the Order of the Eastern Star, one at Hesperia, Eureka Chapter No. 188, and one at Hart, Hart Chapter No. 60, with 66 members. The four lodges have an aggregate membership of 274, among them being some of the leading men of the county.' They all have good lodge rooms, the one at Pentwater, owned by the order, being especially commodious, well furnished, and conveniently arranged.

OCEANA LODGE NO. 200, F. & A. M.

Was organized at Pentwater in 1866. The preliminary meeting was held at Middlesex Hall on June 12, 1866. The next meeting was a called communication at same place on Aug. 14, 1866, and the first regular communication was held on Aug. 21, 1866. The following were the charter members of the lodge, and it may be observed that the only one of them now living at Pentwater is Ebenezer B. Clark:

J. Boynton,   W. H. Sibley,
Rev. G. D. Lee,   E. B. Clark,
D. C. Pelton,   M. Gloyd.

The first officers were:
J. Boynton, W. M.
A. B. Judd, Sec.   G. Goodsell, Treas.

G. W. IMUS, 7th P. M.
W. H. Sibley, S. W.   S. W. Pomeroy, J. D.

The following are Past Masters, in the order named: J. Boynton, E. E. Edwards, R. L. Hardy, L. D. Grove, J. M. Rice, W. E. Dockry, G. W. Imus, O. H. Dean, Stuart Mackibbin.

The present officers are:
E. B. Flagg, W. M.
H. A. Grant, S. W.
J. Halstead, J. W.
F. Nielsen, Treas.
E. B. Clark, Sec'y.
M. V. Badgley, S. D.
O. H. Tayer, J. D.
Anthon Jensen, Tyler.
Geo. H. Cleveland, Chap.
C. M. Underhill, A. H. Palmer, Stewards.

The stated communications are held on the Tuesday on before full of moon, at Masonic Hall.

The present members are as follows:

O. H. DEAN, 8th P. M.

W. E. Ambler	M. S. Ainslie	W. V. Badgley.	Hobart Brink
John Bloore	C. W. Brown	W. H. Browne	A. Bahr
M. Bundy	C. H. Chapman	O. H. Dean	M. Ewald
		J. Fegan	John Fisher
		H. M. Gibson	J. Grover
		J. Halstead,	J. Hagestrom
		C. W. Hills	Carl Hanson
		Anthon Jensen	Peter Jensen
		J. J. Kittridge	Fred Kuhn
		Wr. Klngbeil	A. O. Aldrich
		Wm. Age	W. H. Bailey
		C. M. Baker	H. H. Bunyea
		J. H. Bonton	F. Binnie
		Hiram Brink	E. B. Clark
		G. H. Cleveland	Julius Demers
		E. B. Flagg	Jacob Fisher
		H. A. Grant	F. Goodsell
		Otto Grant	M. Hardway
		Wm. Hudson	G. W. Imus
		L. M. Hartwick	C. R. Johnson
		J. C. Jensen	W. A. Kuhn
		Wm. Kuhn	A. Lafremer
		I. N. Lewis	C. L. Moody
		F. E. Moody	E. Nickerson
		S. Mackibbin	O. D. Richards
		C. Pool	G. G. Senback
		Peter Richter	A. Sorensen
		C. Seversen	A. J. Underhill
		Wm. Webb	C. Zibball

E. B. FLAGG, W. M.

N. Liljenberg	J. R. McClure	T. Mero	F. Nielsen
A. H. Palmer	W. A. Rounds	J. M. Rice	W. B. O. Sands
	O. H. Tayer	C. M. Underhill	Geo. Warner

WIGTON LODGE NO. 251, F. & A. M.

Was organized at Hart on the 7th day of May, 1868. The charter members were as follows:

J. M. Rice
John Elliott
A. E. Palmiter
W. H. Walker
D. Benham
L. G. Rutherford
W. Coolidge
H. C. Mason
Byron S. Pratt
M. R. Chadwick
Jas E. Williams
Wm. Wigton
Wm. H. Leach
K. R. Collins
A. Mason

The following have since died: A. E. Palmiter, Jas. E. Williams, Wm. Wigton and K. R. Collins.

The first officers were:
J. M. Rice, W. M.
Byron S. Pratt, S. W.
M. R. Chadwick, Sec'y.

W. E. THORP, 8th P. M.

John Elliott, J. W.

The following have been Worshipful Masters during the years as named:

J. M. Rice, '68; W. S. Pratt, '69; W. H. Walker, '70; L. G. Rutherford, '71-2; David Johnson, '73-4-8-9-'80-1-2; W. Coolidge, '75-6; Wm. J. Britton, '77; W. E. Thorp, '83; E. D. Richmond, '84; E. T. Mugford, '85-6-7; A. L. Carr, '88-9.

The present officers are:
A. L. Carr, W. M.
T. J. Collins, S. W.
L. P. Hyde, J. W.
T. J. Main, Treas.
W. N. Sayles, Sec'y.
A. J. Felter, S. D.
John Cary, J. D.
F. H. Edwards, Tyler.
W. Coolidge, Chap.
J. S. Hyde, Organist.

E. D. RICHMOND, 9th P. M.

The stated communications of this lodge are on the Wednesdays on or before the full of moon. The lodge hall is located in the Wigton block and is nicely furnished throughout; and the financial standing is good. The members Jan. 1, 1890, were as follows:

C. M. Avery	M. H. Brooks
G. C. Bradley	W. Coolidge
A. L. Carr	J. G. Cary
M. N. Collins	J. V. Cahill
Wm. J. Cole	H. J. Chadwick
H. L. Devine	F. H. Edwards
J. K. Flood	D. Denham
W. H. Bailey	M. R. Chadwick
Tyler Carmer	A. R. Chappell
W. R. Collier	G. L. Cumb
John Cargill	C. Comstock
T. J. Collins	A. A. Dunton
D. G. Ervin	A. J. Felter
G. A. Frambes	J. A. Frambes
D. B. Hutchins	H. J. Holmes
T. G. Houk	L. P. Hyde
David Johnson	O. W. Knox
G. L. Lacey	N. Miller
J. McFayden	L. A. McIntyre
Wm. J. McRae	J. C. Pierce

E. T. MUGFORD, 16th P. M.

S. Plass	L. G. Rutherford
H. E. Russell	M. M. Ramsey
R. W. Riddell	J. W. Riddell
Wm. Shafer	W. Stitt
W. N. Sayles	Wm. Snyder
Wm. Thorp	W. E. Thorp
T. A. Tice	Geo. Tate
W. M. Wigton	W. H Waters
Elmer Wyckoff	C. A. Gurney
H. B. Hatch	F. W. Hubbard
A. G. Hyatt	J. S. Hyde
L. E. Johnson	A. Mason
E. T. Mugford	S. McEwen
T. J. Main	Will McRae
A. W. Peck	H. Palmer
F. J. Russell	F. D. Richmond
E. N. Roberts	H. S. Sayles
Levi Stuck	C. W. Slayton
Chas. Sackrider	J. E. Smith
W. H. H. Turner	Joseph Tyler
T. C. Turner	W. L. Tilden
Geo Wyckoff	A. S. White
W. H. Wigton	

A. L. CARR, W. M.

BENONA LODGE NO. 289, F. & A. M.

This lodge was organized under dispensation from the Grand Master, Oct. 7, 1870, at Benona, and a charter was issued by the Grand Lodge, January 12, 1871. The following were charter members:

RICHARD E. CATER, 3rd P. M.

Chas. H. Howe   Wm. Olinder
H. Hoffman   Wm. Anderson
R. Sabin   A. R. Wheeler
G. Conklin   T. Barber

The first officers of the Lodge were:

Chas. H. Howe, W. M.
Ransom Sabin, S. W.
Wm. Olinder, J. W.
A. R. Wheeler, Treas.
Henry Hoffman, Sec'y
Geo. Conklin, S. D.
Wm. Anderson, J. D.
Thos. Barber, Tyler

L. H. Moore, Dep. Grand Master, on June 9, 1871, instituted and dedicated the lodge, and the first work under the charter was the conferring the third degree upon Richard E. Cater.

The following brothers have held the position of Worshipful Master: Chas. H. Howe, Henry Hoffman, Richard E. Cater, John Thompson, A. Z. Moore and Wm. H. Barry.

The present officers are:

A. Z. Moore, W. M.
W. M. Gardiner, S. W.
A. R. McKinnon, J. W.
Hugh Johnston, Treas.
D. E. McClure, Sec'y
L. D. Hull, S. D.
E. D. Chittenden, J. D.
H. W. Hutchinson, Tyler
H. W. Reid, H. C. Griffin, Stewards.

The lodge was moved from Benona to Shelby village on Feb. 3, 1877, and now meets in its comfortable hall, situated in the upper story of the Churchill & Phelps brick block.

WM. H. BARRY, 6th P. M.

The nights of meeting are the Tues-

A. R. McKINNON, J. W.

days on or before full of moon. The lodge is in a flourishing condition, and numbers among its members some of the best men in the county. Arrangements have been made to place the portraits of deceased members upon the walls of the lodge room and among others will be that of Hon. A. R. Wheeler looking down upon the workings of the lodge he helped so much to organize.

The following is a list of the present members:

Harry L. Andrus
Wm. H. Anderson
Alanson Beckwith
Newton L. Bird

W. M. GARDINER, S. W.

Edward F. Coon	Albert G. Avery	J. B. Applegate	Wm. H. Barry
S. A. Butts	W. H. Churchill	Wm. Compton	Elbert Chittenden
Johathan Critchett	Geo Everdeen	W. Myron Gardiner	Ira F. Gifford
Ira D. Hull	G. B. Hitchcock	Israel Hull	Hugh Johnston
Joseph Lyttle	Irvin W. Loomis	A. R. McKinnon	Wm. Olinder
Thos. Pittenger	Dan'l H. Rankin	Henry W. Reid	Ransom Sabin
E. J. Shirts	I. L. Staples	F. A. Scott	John Thompson
Wm. A. Tyler	F. W. Wilson	J. W. Warner	Egbert Chittenden
John F. Cumming	Geo. E. Dewey	Martin Foster	H. C. Griffin
Geo. B. Getty	E. W. Hutchinson	Elmer Hightower	Stephen Inman
Angus Kennedy	W. Larrabee	A. Z. Moore	Dan'l E. McClure
Andrew Oleson	David C. Russell	Angus D. Rankin	Alfred E. Souter
Chas. A. Sessions	J. D. M. Shirts	A. Sigourney	A. J. Stewart
	Chas. H. Tullar	Charles Watson	Elias Wightman

HESPERIA LODGE NO. 346, F. & A. M.

The dispensation for the institution of the lodge at Hesperia was granted on Oct. 27, 1874, and the charter was granted Jan. 24, 1875. The following were the charter members:

Philip H. Weaver   Lealand G. Weaver   Sylvanus Atherton   Jacob Carlisle
    Joseph W. Sweet   J. W. Dunning   Nathan Heath
            Alvin Decker   Shepard Tibbitts

The following became the first officers of the lodge:
Philip H. Weaver, W. M.   J. W. Dunning, S. W.   Lealand G. Weaver, J. W.
    Philetus Munroe, Treas.   J. F. Howard, Sec'y

The Worshipful Masters in the order in which they served were as follows: P. H. Weaver, J. W. Dunning, Chas. Stark, John Smith and Orvil E. Morton.

The present officers are:

J. W. Dunning, W. M.   Chas. Stark, S. W.   A. L. Scott, J. W.
Ephraim Utley, Treas.   E. R. Haight, Sec'y   P. H. Weaver, S. D.
Phineus Brown, J. D.   R. S. Burt, Tyler   Chas. Wilcox, W. C. Mull, Stewards.

The stated communications of this lodge are on Friday of each month on or before full of moon, in Masonic Hall, in J. W. Dunning's store building on the Oceana Co. side of Main Street. They have a very nice hall, pleasantly located and neatly furnished. They have buried two members since Jan. 1, Philetus Munroe and Horace Carbine. The members Jan. 1, 1890, were as follows:

Phineas Brown	Geo. R. Boyer	Wm. Brown	Burr Bettis
Jas. Colwell	Benj. Candee	Paul Dodge	A. W. Dowdell
Geo. W. Fergnson	Wm. Gregson	H. C. Hawley	Nathan Heath
O. Z. Hawley	M. M. Mansfield	P. Munroe	Benj. F. Moe
E. S. North	Fred Newman	B. Patterson	Chas. Stark
John Smith	E. B. Slocum	Geo. S. Seymour	S. B. Stevenson
Ephraim Utley	Chas. Wilcox	L. S. Weaver	R. S. Burt
W. I. Bulson	E. R. Bulson	John D. Croy	Horace Carbine
J. W. Dunning	Alvin Decker	Nebraska Dodge	Wm. Fleming
E. R. Haight	O. D. Hawley	J. P. Harley	Wm. C. Mull
O. E. Morton	J. McCosh	Niel McCallum	Chas. Newman
Jos. O'Hara	O. A. Rowland	A. L. Scott	Myron Stark
J. W. Sweet	F. B. Seymour	Chas. E. Strobridge	Ezra Spaulding
	P. H. Weaver	S. V. Walker	

OCEANA CHAPTER NO. 56, R. A. M.

Located at Pentwater, was instituted on Feb. 11, 1868, with the following charter members:

FRED NIELSEN, P. H. P.

Rev. B. F. Doughty   C. W. Deane   L. D. Grove   N. C. Mason   A. Mason
J. Boynton   L. E. Payne   C. A. Noble   E. W. Worden

Since the organization of the Chapter there have been 130 members. B. F. Doughty was the first High Priest and the following in order named have held that position: J. M. Rice, W. E. Dockry, L. G. Rutherford, and Fred Nielsen.

The present officers are:
D. C. Wickham, H. P.
Fred Nielsen, King
Jas Grover, Scribe
E. Nickerson, Treas.
J. H. Bouton, Recorder
G. W. Imus, C. of H.
E. B. Flagg, P. S.

The stated convocations of the Chapter are the third Monday of each month, at Masonic Hall, Pentwater.

D. C. WICKHAM, H. P.

The list of present members is as follows:

W. E. Ambler	Wm. H. Barry	Hobert Brink	Wm. H. Browne
C. H. Chapman	Watson Carroll	E. F. Coon	O. H. Dean
M. Ewald	Jacob Fisher	G. A. Frambes	Jas. Grover
John Hagestrom	G. W. Imus	Anthon Jensen	Wm. Kuhn
A. R. McKinnon	C. L. Moody	Jas. McClure	Fred Nielsen
C. A. Noble	Alva Palmer	W. A. Rounds	W. B. O. Sands
John Thompson	F. W. Wilson	Geo. Warner	J. H. Bouton
Chas. W. Brown	John Bloore	Frank Binnie	E. D. Chittenden
Wm. H. Cheney	Chas. Comstock	Geo. Donaldson	E. B. Flagg
John Fisher	R. Flanders		W. Myron Gardiner
Wm. Hudson	Peter Jensen	W. A. Kuhn	Nels Liljenberg
F. E. Moody	A. Z. Moore	D. E. McClure	E. Nickerson
A. Olesen	J. W. Pollok	F. J. Russell	A. Sorensen
	O. H. Tayer	D. C. Wickham	Wm. Webb

OCEANA COUNCIL NO. 27, R. & S. M.

Was instituted at Pentwater Feb. 3, 1869, and to the present time there have been 71 members. The Past T. I. M's are J. Boynton, J. M. Rice, Fred Nielsen, W. E. Dockry and D. C. Wickham.

The present officers are:

G. W. Imus, T. I. M.   O. H. Dean, D. M.   E. B. Flagg, P. C. W.
Fred Nielsen, Treas.   J. H. Bouton, Recorder   W. E. Ambler, Capt. G.
F. E. Moody, Con. of C.   Jas. Grover, Steward   I. N. Lewis, Sentinel

The stated Assemblies are the second Monday of each month, in Masonic Hall, Pentwater.

The present membership is thirty-seven.

ODDFELLOWSHIP.

The fraternity of Odd Fellows at this time is very strong in Oceana County, yet it is but a few years since the organization of the first lodge at Hart in 1879. At that time it was with much difficulty that the Grand Master could be prevailed upon to issue a dispensation for the institution of that lodge, he being fearful that it could not live. Bro. H. J. Holmes, of Hart, has a letter from him in regard to the matter, in which he so expresses himself, giving as a reason for such fear that the county was too new to support a lodge. But the growth of Oddfellowship has been on a par with the growth of the county generally, and that is simply phenomenal. From the small beginning made at that time, a lodge of seventeen members, has grown the present strength of the order in the county, which is represented by six lodges in good working condition with an aggregate membership of 342, and owning property to the amount of thousands of dollars; besides two Encampments and four lodges of the Degree of Rebekah.

OCEANA LODGE NO. 327.

The first lodge in the county was organized at Hart, June 10, 1879, with five charter members as follows:

H. J. Holmes
A. Hoisington
Thomas Hull
J. A. Collier
Lorenzo Brooks

After admitting a number of Ancient Odd Fellows and intiating others, the following became the first officers of the lodge:

H. J. Holmes, N. G.
J. A. Collier, V. G.
T. S. Gurney, Sec.
A. Hoisington, Treas.
Thomas Hull, W.
Lorenzo Brooks, C.

H. J. HOLMES, 1st P. G.

The Noble Grands in succession to the present time have been as follows:

H. J. Holmes, J. A. Collier, Andrew Hoisington, Lorenzo Brooks, T. S. Gurney, James McVean, C. A. Gurney, E. P. Wigton, R. W. Henderson, C. A. Campbell, A. Corliss, E. H. Hotchkiss, Robert Currie, L. C. Parnin, H. J. Servis, I. C. Ford, G. E. Mathews, C. B. Stevens, W. P. Sackrider, J. Olin, Alex. Wright, William Cooper, C. E. Croff, and E. T. Mugford.

The present officers are:

Robert Currie, N. G.
Benj. Martin, V. G.
W. P. Sackrider, Sec.
H. J. Servis, P. Sec.
J. A. Collier, Treas.
John Olin, W.
Wm. Cooper, C.
E. T. Mugford, P. G.

J. A. COLLIER, 2nd P. G.

The Lodge meets on Saturday evenings in their new hall, recently purchased, in the Chadwick and Dennison block. The lodge is well supplied with necessary regalia and other appurtenances, and has money in the treasury. The following is a list of members:

E. E. Allen
C. A. Adams
F. Besensen
E. L. Brooks
Lorenzo Brooks
S. A. Butts
J. A. Collier
C. A. Campbell
J. A. Cole
Wm. Cooper
R. L. Crosby
Edson Collins
R. A. Chapin

THERON S. GURNEY, 5th P. G.

Robert Currie
C. E. Croff
Geo. Cooper
Judson Collins
Geo. Dennison
T. Downing
E. Dyer
Jos. Evans
Ed. Ervin
W. T. Evans
L. C. Ford
A. W. French
G. E. Frambes
James Franklin
R. Franklin
E. A. Fuller
C. A. Gurney
T. S. Gurney
E. S. Houghtaling
M. Huftile

C. A. GURNEY, 7th P. G.

J. D. S. Hanson
R. W. Henderson
Milton Hiles
Frank Hitchcock
A. Hoisington
E. H. Hotchkiss
H. S. Kinney
John Knickerbocker
Benjamin Martin
James McVean
L. D. Miller
H. Miller
Jesse Mills
Charles Morgan
E. T. Mugford
John Mugford
John Olin
Peter Nelson
James Peckham
A. M. Pringle

H. J. SERVIS, 15th P. G.

L. C. Parnin
J. A. Phillippo
Ira Richmond
C. B. Reamer
J. W. Robinson
A. Skillen
H. J. Servis
W. P. Sackrider
Ed. Stansberg
C. N. Sowers
M. W. Satterlee
W. A. Sanford
C. B. Stevens
W. N. Sayles
N. G. Sayles
Carl Schrumpf
W. J. Servis
A. W. Shufelt
P. Thomas
Jesse Tennant
W. J. Towning
A. J. Wright
E. P. Wigton

C. B. STEVENS, 18th P. G.

Wm. Wear
C. K. Williams
Alex. Wright

W. P. SACKRIDER, 19th P. G.

WM. COOPER, 22nd P. G.

E. T. MUGFORD, 24th P. G.

HESPERIA LODGE NO. 334.

Was organized at Hesperia, Nov. 26, 1879, with the following as charter members and first officers:

W. S. Stevens, N. G. W. S. Millard, V. G.
G. R. Boyer, Sec. Israel Clark, I. G.
        P. Munroe, Treas.

The Noble Grands to the present time have been as follows: W. S. Stevens, W. S. Millard, John Smith, Israel Clark, H. C. Hawley, G. R. Boyer, W. B. Chandler, L. E. Norton, J. B. Smith, J. Jackson, W. C. Mull, John Ash, E. R. Haight, W. Balcom, E. J. Bennett, James Gordon, Galen Northrup.

The present officers are:

W. H. Turner, N. G. E. J. Philo, V. G.
A. C. Eltridge, Sec. W. C. Mull, Treas.
Israel Clark, P. Sec. G. Northrup, P. G.

The lodge meets on Saturday evening in Odd Fellows' Hall, on the west side of Main Street. They own a lot which cost $1,500 and report $400 in funds. The number of members in good standing on Jan. first was sixty-seven; the names we have not been able to secure.

SHELBY LODGE, NO. 344.

During the summer of '80 the few Odd Fellows residing at Shelby, notably Geo. B. Getty and Otis A. Elliott, agitated the question of establishing a lodge there. After talking the matter over and seeing the different members of the order, a meeting was finally called at the Elliott House and steps were taken to organize. As a result a lodge was instituted under dispensation on Aug. 30, 1880, and a charter received Feb. 18, 1881. The following became charter members:

O. K. White
W. H. Dunn
W. F. Lewis
I. B. Bowerman
I. Winterstien

W. H. DUNN, 1st P. G.

Geo. B. Getty
Moses W. Burk
D. W. Dodd
Otis A. Elliott

The first officers of the lodge were:

W. H. Dunn, N. G.
O. K. White, V. G.
O. A. Elliott, Sec.
Geo. B. Getty, P. Sec.
Wm. F. Lewis, Treas.
O. F. Hill, W.
Moses Burk, C.
Beer Pittenger, Chap.

The following have held the office of Noble Grand in the order named: W. H. Dunn, O. K. White, W. F. Lewis, O. F. Hill, C. P. Rathbone, Geo. B. Getty, Wm. Woodland, Chas. Babcock, Moses Burk, Milo H. Sweet, E. H. Cutler, A. E.

W. F. LEWIS, 3rd P. G.

Souter, F. E. Reamer, H. B. Hobby, A. D. Rankin, T. H. Baker, F. W. Newman, D. Flynn and J. A. Harrison. The present officers are:

C. E. Abraham, N. G.
F. M. Meyers, V. G.
Elmer Tyler, Sec.
M. Sargent, P. Sec.
A. C. Kocher, Treas.
H. B. Hobby, W.
F. E. Reamer, C.
J. A. Harrison, P. G.

The lodge meets on Saturday evenings, in the Churchill and Phelps block, on Main street. The financial condition is good, having $500 invested in supplies, and a surplus of $600. The membership Jan. 1, 1890, was as follows:

C. E. Abraham
J. E. Baker
J. Beam
T. H. Baker
Fred Baker
Eli Beam
Warren Beam

O. K. WHITE, 2nd P. G.

Wallace Babcock
F. J. Chalker
W. L. Culver
John Cramer
Orrin Crowfoot
W. H. Dunn
Frank Deming
J. D. Evans
Daniel Flynn
R. G. Forbes
E. B. Gaylord
Chas. Getty
Geo. B. Getty
H. J. Goodenrath
M. A. Gilbert
H. Hendrickson
Dennis Hinchen
H. B. Hobby
H. W. Harpster

C. P. RATHBONE, 5th P. G.

J. A. Harrison
H. Johnston
A. C. Kocher
E. Lambert
A. A. Lewis
W. F. Lewis
Albert Lintz
Albert Long
W. F. Mitchell
F. M. Meyers
Marshall Meyers
S. Matney
F. W. Newman
Jerry Pigeon
A. M. Prosser
Delos Prosser
A. D. Rankin
Chas. P. Rathbone
Frank Roberts
Peter Rankin
F. E. Reamer.
Robert Rowley

GEO. B. GETTY, 6th P. G.

D. A. Reed
M. H. Sweet
A. E. Souter
L. A. Shirts
M. Sargent
Bert Thiele
Elmer Tyler
Chas. VanWickle
Wm. Woodland
Chas. Wilson.

WM. WOODLAND, 7th P. G.

E. H. CUTLER, 11th P. G.

A. E. SOUTER, 12th P. G.

F. E. REAMER, 13th P. G.

T. H. BAKER, 16th P. G.

J. A. HARRISON, 19th P. G.

C. E. ABRAHAM, N. G.

184 OCEANA COUNTY PIONEERS

F. M. MEYERS, V. G.

PENTWATER LODGE NO. 378.

Pentwater Lodge was organized April 27, 1883, with the follow-

A. E. BURGESS, 2nd P. G.

ing charter members: Daniel Calkins, A. E. Burgess, Otto Grant, C. J. Heath and W. S. Reed.

The first officers were:
D. Calkins, N. G.
A. E. Burgess, V. G.
L. M. Hartwick, Sec.
Otto Grant, P. Sec.
W. S. Reed, Treas.
Alvin Warner, W.
Robert Venn, C.

The following have held the office of Noble Grand following D. Calkins, who served until Dec. 31, 1883: A. E. Burgess, L. M. Hartwick, C. W. Cramer, G. O. Switzer, Otto Grant, Robert Venn, A. Warner, M. F. Hyde, J. B. Steele, Thos. Morin, A. Jacobs and W. H. Tuller.

L. M. HARTWICK, 3rd P. G.

C. W. CRAMER, 4th P. G.

The present officers are:
C. M. Underhill, N. G.
W. E. Hodges, V. G.
C. P. Barnard, Sec.
M. F. Hyde, P. Sec.
T. Morin, Treas.
J. H. Bouton, W.
Peter Jensen, C.
W. H. Tuller, P. G.

The lodge meets on Saturday evenings in their own hall which is in the upper story of the Pentwater NEWS block. The lodge owns the upper part of the block and also the lot in the rear. It has besides this property about $500 in ready money. Probably no lodge in the county is better situated than this lodge.

The following were members Jan. 1, 1890:

G. O. SWITZER, 5th P. G.

C. W. Cramer
E. B. Comstock
O. F. Compton
H. Cutler
W. S. Dumont
E. A. Daggett
Peter Dreves
G. V. Dunn
T. Erickson
Frank Girard
D. B. Gardner
M. H. Gannon
M. D. Girard
Otto Grant
Wm. Hudson
J. W. Hurley
T. J. Haughey
Jens Hanson
Chas. Hitchcock
L. M. Hartwick
H. D. Hartwick
E. W. Hodges
Erie Huftile
Gustav Hanson
M. F. Hyde

Chas. Anderson
Sam'l Andrus
J. Brookshes
C. P. Benedict
E. N. Briggs
J. H. Bouton
Niel Browne
C. P. Barnard
Aleck Browne
Fred Brown
J. H. Brill
A. E. Burgess
Peter Browne
Clare Cross
Jeff Cutler
George Cook
Thomas Carney
A. Cutler

OTTO GRANT, 6th P. G.

W. E. Hodges
Fred Hanson

Eddy O. Irons
M. L. Johnson
Peter Jensen
A. Johnson
A. Jacobs
Wm. Klingbeil
Harry Lodge
David Mills
W. R. Maxfield
Ira Munson
O. W. Marsh
Charles Maynard
Charles Martins
Thos. Morin
Theodore Mero
Thomas Merriam
A. L. Nichols
Fred Nygaard
A. M. Perkins
Charles Palmer

M. F. HYDE, 9th P. G.

THOMAS MORIN, 11th P. G.

Alvin Warner
James Warrington

Hans C. Peterson
Cedric B. Randall
S. E. Russell
M. Routly
W. A. Rounds
John Reid
W. L. Stoddard
W. J. Sloan
M. A. Sloan
Fred Sorensen
G. O. Switzer
N. C. Smith
James B. Steele
Frelan Smith
William H. Tuller
Andrew P. Tuttle
L. O. Tupper
Chas. M. Underhill
Robert Venn
James Wright
George Wright
George Warrington
John J. Wakefield

CHARLES M. UNDERHILL, N. G.

CRYSTAL VALLEY LODGE NO. 386.

Organized at Crystal Valley, April 29, 1887, started out with the following as charter members:

<table>
<tr><td>Charles Comstock</td><td>George Vine</td></tr>
<tr><td>J. H. Beckwith</td><td>F. A. Bristol</td></tr>
<tr><td colspan="2" align="center">Albert Kenyon</td></tr>
</table>

The first officers were:

<table>
<tr><td>J. H. Beckwith, N. G.</td><td>Charles Comstock, V. G.</td></tr>
<tr><td>A. Kenyon, Sec.</td><td>F. A. Bristol, P. Sec.</td></tr>
<tr><td colspan="2" align="center">George Vine, Treas.</td></tr>
</table>

J. H. Beckwith held the office of Noble Grand until Dec. 31, 1887, and the office has been filled as follows for term ending as follows: Chas. Comstock, June 30, 1888; F. A. Bristol, Dec. 31, 1888; J. H. Beach, June 30, 1889, and M. O. Fisher, Dec. 31, 1889.

The present officers are as follows:

<table>
<tr><td>Charles A. Lammon, N. G.</td><td>W. G. Fisher, O. G.</td></tr>
<tr><td>F. B. Kittridge, Sec.</td><td>L. C. Brewster, P. Sec.</td></tr>
<tr><td colspan="2" align="center">Charles Comstock, Treas.</td></tr>
</table>

The lodge meets on Saturday evenings at their hall in Crystal

Valley, which is owned by the lodge. Probably no lodge in the county can show a better record than this. Starting with but five charter members, in less than three years it has grown into a substantial, flourishing lodge, with a membership of 35, and this, too, in a very small town.

The names of the present members are as follows:

A. O. Aldrich
Alex Amily
F. A. Bristol
J. Beckwith
Oliver Barney, Jr.
L. C. Brewster
Charles Ballard
H. M. Beadle
J. H. Beach
C. W. Brown
J. Cleveland
E. J. Cleveland
Charles Comstock
F. B. Comstock
G. H. Darling
Wm. Darling
J. Demerest
David Dunn
Eugene Davis
M. O. Fisher
Wm. G. Fisher

Earl Fisher	Reno Fisher	Elmer Gafford
A. G. Hyatt	Albert Jones	F. B. Kittridge
C. A. Lammon	W. A. Mason	Martin Nielsen
E. S. Rogers	Silas Steadman	George Vine
	Charles Willet	Warren Willet

M. O. FISHER, 5th P. G.

STETSON LODGE, NO. 390.

Was organized Sept. 5, 1889, at Walkerville, with the following charter members: T. J. Sherlock, Edwin Stansberry, B. F. Stone, J. M. Tennant and Elisha North.

The following were the first officers:

B. F. Stone, N. G.   T. J. Sherlock, V. G.
J. M. Tennant, Sec.   E. S. North, Treas.

The present officers are:

T. J. Sherlock, N. G.   E. Stansberry, V. G.
Raymond Ross, Sec.   George North, Treas.

The meetings are held on Thursdays at Sherlock's Hall. The prospects for this lodge are good, and there is no reason why, located as it is, it should not increase and multiply. The membership is as follows:

Robert Bunting	Mr. Mosher	George North
E. S. North	Mr. Perry	Raymond Ross
T. J. Sherlock	Edwin Stansberry	B. F. Stone
Mr. Tuttle	J. M. Tennant	Hiram Webb	Wm. Webb

HART ENCAMPMENT, NO. 12

Located at Hart, was organized on Jan. 31, 1881, by Grand Representative Norman Bailey, with the following charter members:

| J. A. Collier | C. A. Gurney | T. S. Gurney | A. Hoisington |
| Jas. McVean | E. P. Wigton | Daniel Calkins |

The first officers installed were:

| J. A. Collier, C. P. | A. Hoisington, S. W. | H. J. Holmes, J. P. |
| T. S. Gurney, S. | C. A. Gurney, Treas. | Daniel Calkins, J. W. |

The following have served as Chief Patriarchs in the order named: J. A. Collier, H. J. Holmes, T. S. Gurney, James McVean, J. A. Collier, C. A. Campbell, Alex. Wright, C. A. Gurney, A. Hoisington, Ira C. Ford, L. M. Hartwick, H. J. Servis, Robert Currie, John Olin, E. S. Houghtaling, W. P. Sackrider, Geo. Dennison, F. A. Scott and C. E. Croff.

The present officers are:

Robert Currie, C. P.	E. S. Houghtaling, S. W.	C. K. Williams, J. P.
W. P. Sackrider, S.	H. J. Servis, F. S.	J. A. Collins, Treas.
John Olin, J. W.		W. J. Servis, I. S.

The meeting nights are the first and third Thursdays of each month, in Odd Fellows' Hall. The encampment is well equipped, is clear of debt and has money in the treasury. The present members are as follows:

S. A. Butts	L. Brooks	T. H. Baker	J. A. Collier
Robert Currie	A. Comstock	Wm. Cooper	Chas. Comstock
C. E. Croff	Geo. Dennison	Ira C. Ford	C. A. Gurney
T. S. Gurney	M. H. Gannon	E. B. Gaylord	H. J. Goodenrath
A. Hoisington	R. W. Henderson	E. S. Houghtaling	M. L. Johnson
Chas. Morgan	John Olin	E. S. Rogers	N. C. Smith
H. J. Servis	F. A. Scott	C. B. Stevens	W. L. Stoddard
M. H. Sweet	W. P. Sackri'er	W. N. Sayles	W. J. Servis
	E. C. Whiting	C. K. Williams	

LAKESIDE ENCAMPMENT, NO 109

Was organized at Pentwater, February 7th, 1887. A number of Pentwater brothers belonging to the Hart Encampment and finding it inconvenient to attend the meetings, hence decided to form an encampment at home. The encampment started with the following charter members:

L. M. Hartwick	W. H. Tuller	C. W. Cramer	Thomas Morin
M. F. Hyde	J. H. Beckwith	Wm. Klingbeil	G. O. Switzer

The following were installed as the first officers:

L. M. Hartwick, C. P.	W. H. Tuller, S. W.	C. W. Cramer, H. P.
G. O. Switzer, S.	M. F. Hyde, F. S.	Thos. Morin, Treas.
	J. H. Beckwith, J. W.	J. B. Steele, G.

The Chief Patriarchs have been as follows, for terms expiring on date named: L. M. Hartwick, June 30, '87; W. H. Tuller, Dec. 31, 87; C. W. Cramer, June 30, '88; G. O. Switzer, Dec. 31, '88; T. Morin, June 30, '89; M. F. Hyde, Dec. 31, '89.

The following are the present officers:

W. E. Hodges, C. P.	Otto Grant, S. W.	E. N. Briggs, H. P
M. F. Hyde, S.	Chas. Anderson, F. S.	Wm. Klingbeil, Treas.
	J. B. Steele, J. W.	L. O. Tupper, G.

The encampment meets each alternate Tuesday evening in Odd Fellows Hall. It is well situated financially and otherwise, having all necessary working material and fine regalia. The present members are:

Chas. Anderson	J. Brookshes	Niel Browne	E. N. Briggs
J. H. Beckwith	C. W. Cramer	Peter Dreves	Otto Grant
D. B. Gardner	F. Girard	M. D. Girard	W. E. Hodges
L. M. Hartwick	M. F. Hyde	Eddy O. Irons	A. Jacobs
Wm. Klingbeil	T. Mero	T. Morin	A. M. Perkins
H. C. Petersen	S. E. Russell	F. Smith	J. B. Steele
G. O. Switzer	W. H. Tuller	L. O. Tupper	Geo. Warrington

DEGREE OF REBEKAH.

Integrity Lodge No. 58, D. of R. The first lodge organized in the county, was organized at Shelby on Oct. 14, 1882. The Noble Grands in succession have been, Wm. F. Lewis, Maria J. Gilbert, Geo. B. Getty, Jane E. Sweet, M. H. Sweet, A. Hoisington and Ida L. Reamer. The present Noble Grand is Mrs. C. E. Wilson. The Lodge meets on the first and third Wednesday evenings of each month in Odd Fellows Hall. The present membership is twenty-five.

Deborah Lodge No. 93, D. of R. Was instituted at Pentwater, May 5, 1886, by P. G. M. Harrison Soule. The following persons have been Noble Grands: L. M. Hartwick, Mrs. Jennie Smith, Mrs. Mary I. Hyde, Mrs. Emma Briggs, Mrs. Mary E. Grant, and Miss Esther Browne (now Mrs. Knapp). Present Noble Grand Mrs. Sarah Tuttle. Meetings are held on alternate Tuesday evenings at Odd Fellows Hall. Present membership sixty-two.

Ruby Lodge No. 109, D. of R. Organized March 26, 1888, at Crystal Valley. Past Grands are J. H. Beckwith, Mrs. C. A. Beckwith, Mrs. L. C. Brewster, and Mrs. Aggie Barney. Present Noble Grand Libbie Cole. The meetings are held on alternate Tuesday evenings, at Odd Fellows Hall. Present membership forty.

White River Valley Lodge No. 86, D. of R. Is located at Hesperia. The present Noble Grand is Clara Mull. Membership sixty.

GRAND ARMY POSTS.

COMMANDER DEPARTMENT OF MICHIGAN, 1887.

The old soldiers living in Oceana County, following the example of others have banded themselves together for mutual benefit and assistance in case of need; and we find six well organized and flourishing Posts within its limits. There are also several ladies' Relief Corps and several Camps of Sons of Veterans. Following we give the leading points of interest in regard to these organizations, with a list of the members of the Posts and Camps, in the order of their organization.

JOE HOOKER POST NO. 26

Is located at Hart, and was organized August 16, 1881, with the following charter members:

I. D. Reed
J. H. Slater
L. G. Rutherford
W. R. Collier
W. E. Thorp
G. L. Crumb
J. V. Cahill
C. W. Slayton
C. E. Croff
F. H. Edwards
J. A. Collier
Wm. J. McRae
Daniel Calkins
Myron Hammond
Chauncey Griswold
L. C. Parnin
W. H. Waters.

W. E. THORP, 1st P. COM.

J. V. CAHILL, 2nd P. COM'D'R.

The first officers of the Post were:
W. E. Thorp, Com'd'r
C. W. Slayton, S. V. Com.
I. D. Reed, J. V. Com.
J. H. Slater, Adjt.
J. V. Cahill, Q. M.
W. R. Collier, Sur.
G. L. Crumb, Chap.
L. G. Rutherford, O. D.
W. J. McRae, O. G.
C. E. Croff, S. M.
F. H. Edwards, Q. M. S.

Mr. W. E. Thorp held the office of Commander during the balance of the year '81, and also during '82-3 and 4. J. V. Cahill was Commander in '85; J. A. Collier, '86; J. H. Slater, '87; H. J. Holmes, '88, and D. C.

Wickham, '89. The present officers, mustered at first meeting in January, 1890, are:

J. A. COLLIER, 3rd P. COM'D'R.

Geo. B. Dikeman, Com.
F. H. Edwards, S. V. Com.
W. A. Bill'ngs, J. V. Com.
J. H. Slater, Adjt.
H. J. Holmes, Q. M.
P. H. Chappell, Sur.
Geo. B. Rollins, Chap.
J. B. Winans, O. D.
Geo. Wells, O. G.
J. A. Collier, S. M.
M. A. Luther, Q. M. S.

The Post meets at Odd Fellows Hall in the village of Hart, on the second and fourth Mondays of each month. The financial condition of the Post is good, and it stands as one of the most substantial and solid Posts of the county.

J. H. SLATER, 4th P. COM'D'R.

H. J. HOLMES, 5th P. COM'D'R.

D. C. WICKHAM, 6th P. COM'D'R.

The following were members, Jan. 1, '90:

	Co.	Regt.	State.	Branch.
E. E. Allen	H	2	Ohio	C.
J. W. Althouse	A	3	Mich.	I.
F. Besenson	I	59	Ills.	I.
C. F. Ballou	K	92	N. Y.	I.
S. S. Branch	K	8	Ohio	I.
J. C. Beddinger	I	12	Mich.	I.

	Co.	Regt.	State.	Branch.
W. A. Billings	M	21	Pa.	C.
C. O. Bishop	F	39	Wis.	I.
N. Benedict	F	18	Mich.	I.
W. R. Collier	H	8	Mich.	I.
J. V. Cahill	G	10	Wis.	I.
C. E. Croff	C	17	Ills.	C.
J. A. Collier	B	115	N. Y.	I.
J. G. Cary	Ind. Bat.		Ohio	L. A.
B. F. Campbell	C	18	Mich.	I.
P. H. Chappell	H	29	Mich.	I.
C. A. Campbell	K	2	Conn.	H. A.
Pat Corcoran	H	2	N. Y.	C.
P. Carter	I	7	Mich.	I.
G. B. Dikeman	A	151	N. Y.	I.
G. F. Dennison	L	E. & M. Corps.		
F. H. Edwards	I	7	U. S.	I.
A. Evans	C	3	Mich.	L. A.
A. Fletcher	A	26	Mich.	I.
H. H. Feight	E	138	Pa.	I.
W. H. Flory	I	3	Mich.	C.
" "	K	8	Mich.	C.
A. Farmer	K	13	Mich.	I.
C. Fletcher	A	26	Mich.	I.
W. H. Fuller	D	30	Mich.	I.
G. A. Frambes	B	59	Ohio	I.
C. Griswold	F	2	Ohio	H. A.
S. M. Gilbert	D	83	Pa.	I.
Nelson Glover	A	26	Mich.	I.
S. W. Gilbert	B	83	Pa.	I.
L. L. Gardner	K	2	U. S.	C.
H. J. Holmes	G	10	Wis.	I.
B. Holscher	G	100	N. Y.	I.
D. B. Hutchins	D	111	N. Y.	I.
Wm. Hobbs	B	8	Wis.	I.
George Hill	L	5	N. Y.	C.
L. A. Hammun	A	28	Wis.	I.
J. Knickerbocker	D	9	Mich.	I.
M. A. Luther	C	76	N. Y.	I.
T. M. Lauder	Bat K	2	Ohio	A.
A. H. Lacnard	A	6	Ohio	I.
" "	H	23	Ohio	I.
W. J. McRae	Bat. M	2	Ills.	A.
Gus May	G	49	N. Y.	I.
G. L. McCarty	K	20	Wis.	I.

	Co.	Regt.	State.	Branch.
F. A. Morton	—	9	Ind.	I.
L. C. Parnin	I	59	Ind.	I.
J. D. Painter	I	12	Mich.	I.
A. Petrie	H	21	N.Y.	I.
T. Pinder	A	8	Ills.	C.
H. P. Parsons	C	49	Mass.	I.
L. G. Rutherford	H	189	N.Y.	I.
C. Richter	D	8	Mich.	I.
G. R. Rollins	B	100	Ind.	I.
R. W. Riddell	F	120	N.Y.	I.
L. Renninger	H	37	Ohio	I.
W. A. Rounds	C	16	U. S.	C.
J. H. Slater	K	83	Ills.	I.
R. L. Shaw	I	1	Mich.	C.
Henry Sample	I	28	Mich.	I.
Henry Sage	A	107	Pa.	I.
R. R. Sanford	G	1	Mich.	S. S.
O. W. Stever	G	30	Wis.	I.
O. Stebbins	D	98	N.Y.	I.
W. E. Thorp	D	21	N.Y.	I.
George Tate	A	7	Mich.	I.
C. W. Taylor	F	14	Ills.	I.
T. C. Turner	A		Ohio	H. A.
W. H. H. Turner	C	153	Ind.	I.
H. D. Tucker	E	7	Wis.	A.
S. Thorp	F	118	Ind.	I.
J. R. Thompson	F	4	Mich.	C.
J. B. Winans	H	20	Ohio	I.
C. W. Weeks	C	83	Pa.	I.
D. C. Wickham	H	129	N.Y.	I.
" "	—	8	N.Y.	A.
George Wells	D	60	N.Y.	I.
John Westbrook	A	104	N.Y.	I.
A. Wasson	K	84	Ind.	I.
J. A. Weyant	K	19	N.Y.	I.

SHIELDS POST, NO. 68

Was organized at Shelby, June 27, 1882, with the following charter members:

G. W. Woodward   W. H. Dunn   Nathan Adams
W. H. Churchill   Manly C. White   Wm. H. Barry
Hiram C. Morris   E. F. Coon   Geo. B. Getty
Wm. M. Payne   A. Fleming   Sam'l Wright
        Peter Pasinger   R. F. Ames

G. W. WOODWARD, 1st P. C.

The first officers of the Post were:
G. W. Woodward, Com.
W. H. Dunn, S. V. Com.
Nathan Adams, J. V. Com.
W. H. Churchill, Adjt.
Manly C. White, Q. M.
W. H. Barry, Sur.
Hiram C. Morris, Chap.
E. F. Coon, O. D.
G. B. Getty, O. G.
Jas. McKay, S. M.
W. M. Payne, Q. M. S.

The Commanders have been as follows during the years named: G. W. Woodward, 1882; W. H. Dunn, 1883; W. H. Barry, 1884-5; Nathan Adams, 1886; D. O. Vaughn, 1887; W. H. Dunn, 1888; G. H. Eddy, 1889.

The present officers are:
L. D. Wildey, Com.
Hiram C. Morris, S. V. Com.
Dennis Hinchen, J. V. Com.
J. D. Randall, Adjt.
W. H. Barry, Q. M.
N. B. Farnsworth, Sur.
Sam'l Wright, Chap.
Philo Penfield, O. D.
A. Fleming, O. G.
Nathan Adams, S. M.
Thos. Twining, Q. M. S.

The Post meets on the first and third Mondays of each month, at Hedges' Hall, on Main street, Shelby. The standing of the Post is good, finances are in good shape and the interest of the members in its meetings is made apparent by the attendance.

W. H. DUNN, 2nd P. C.

W. H. BARRY, 3rd P. C.

GEO. H. EDDY, 6th P. C.

The following comprises the membership, Jan. 1, 1890:

Name	Co.	Regt.	State.	Branch.
Nathan Adams	H	11	Mich.	I.
Ralph F. Ames	F	151	Pa.	I.
W. H. Barry	A	1	Mich.	L. A.
O. A. Brown	I	20	Mich.	I.
Frederick Butzer	F	24	N.Y.	C.
Alonzo Beckwith	I	39	Wis.	I.
W. H. Churchill	G	15	Mich.	I.
E. F. Coon	I	99	N.Y.	I.
Wm. Compton	E	6	Mich.	C.
John Curren	H	21	Mich.	I.
Francis Conroy	C	12	Mich.	I.
A. L. Cobb	B	1	Mich.	E. & M.
Jas. B. Dorrance	C	11	Mich.	C.
David Dill	F	5	Mich.	C.
G. H. Eddy	D	33	N.Y.	I.
John Eaton	A	21	Ohio	I.
Ezra Elliott	B	8	Ills.	C.
A. Fleming	H	11	Mich.	C.
W. H. Fleming	K	1	Mich.	I.
" "	H	11	Mich.	C.
C. W. Fisher	C	3	Pa.	C.
N. B. Farnsworth	B	9	Mich.	I.
" "	A	19	Mich.	I.
George B. Getty	D	45	Pa.	I.
Leander Godfrey	C	111	Pa.	I.
Dennis Hinchen	B	97	N.Y.	I.
John W. Inman	H	2	Ohio	C.
Orlow Inman	C	176	Ohio	I.
Thomas Kelly	I	8	N.Y.	C.
Edward Kinney	E	1	Mich.	E & M.
James S. Knowlton	B	1	Mich.	L. A.
Sam'l S. Lewis	I	112	N.Y.	I.
John Little	A	1	Col.	C.
Hiram C. Morris	H	107	N.Y.	I.
J. N. Marvin	C	17	Ind.	I.
Edward M. Moody	A	110	N.Y.	I.
Joel W. Morse	F	142	Ind.	I.
Geo. W. Morehouse	E	101	N.Y.	I.
Wm. M. Payne	D	5	Mich.	C.
Peter Pasinger	L	4	Mich.	C.
Alex. Pittinger	K	8	Ohio	I.
Philo Penfield	B	1	Ohio	L. A.
Francis A. Pitts	M	10	Mich.	C.

	Co.	Regt.	State.	Branch.
B. G. Perrin	G	100	Pa.	I.
J. D. Randall	A	13	Mich.	I.
LeGrand Rathbone	D	11	Mich.	C.
Edwin S. Randall	C	13	Mich.	I.
Wm. H. Reamer	G	24	N. Y.	I.
Wm. P. Shafer	A	26	Mich.	I.
Ransom Sabin	H	2	Mo.	C.
Stephen Stonehouse	H	27	Mich.	I.
J. P. Smith	G	2	Mich.	C.
" "	A	10	Mich.	C.
Thos. Twining	F	57	Ohio	I.
Ross Vradenburg	F	15	Mich.	I.
G. W. Woodward	D	1	Mich.	E. & M.
" "	G	21	Mich.	I.
Samuel Wright	F	44	Ind.	I.
Jeptha Wright	B	12	Ind.	C.
B. S. Wade	F	13	Mich.	I.
L. D. Wildey	C	18	Mich.	I.
Simeon R. Wright	G	17	Mich.	I.

R. M. JOHNSON POST, NO. 138

Located at Ferry, was organized in May, 1883, with the following named persons as charter members:

John Archer
Daniel Landon
Alvin B. Decker
Benjamin F. Archer.
John M. Heim
Simeon R. Wright
Theodore P. Landon
Henry Dodge
A. W. Sparks
J. M. Keeney
A. Eitnicar

The Post was mustered by W. E. Thorp, of Hart, and the following were elected as the first officers:

John Archer, Com.
T. P. Landon, S. V. Com.
Henry Dodge, J. V. Com.

BENJ. F. ARCHER, 1st P. C.

E. O. PECK, 3rd P. C.

J. M. Heim, J. V. Com.
W. R. Matthews, Adjt.
Henry Dodge, Q. M.
Frank Dunn, Chap.
B. F. Archer, O. D.
A. B. Decker, O. G.

The Post meets on the first and third Saturdays of each month in Heim's Hall. The members take a lively interest in the affairs of the Post, the meetings are well attended and the general condition of the Post, financial and otherwise, is good.

The following were members Jan. 1, 1890:

J. M. Keeney, Adjt.
Dan'l Landon, Q. M.
A. W. Sparks, Chap.
John M. Heim, S. M.
Jos. Mallison, Q. M. S.

These officers held their offices during 1883-4. Benjamin F. Archer was Commander in '85; Theodore P. Landon in '86; E. O. Peck in '87; B. F. Archer again in '88, and Geo. W. Newton was elected for '89 but held only a short time when he resigned, and Orrin Weiswell was elected and served the balance of the term. The following took their offices in Jan., '90:

Paul Dodge, Com.
T. P. Landon, S. V. Com.

ORRIN WEISWELL, 4th P. C.

	Co.	Regt.	State.	Branch.
John Archer	G	1	Mich.	I.
Benj. F. Archer	G	4	Mich.	C.
Samuel Apple	L	99	Ohio	I.

	Co.	Regt.	State.	Branch.
J. H. Critchett	A	100	Ind.	I.
Alvin Decker	M	9	Mo.	C.
Henry Dodge	G	1	Mich.	A.
Paul Dodge	H	99	Ind.	I.
Frank Dunn	N	2	N. Y.	B.
A. H. Dickerson	E	7	Mich.	I.
A. Eitmear	K	169	Ohio	I.
H. Frees	A	100	Ind.	I.
Samuel Frees	A	100	Ind.	I.
E. M. Fessenden	I	105	Pa.	I.
J. M. Heim	G	38	Ohio	I.
D. S. Hindes	F	5	Mich.	C.
Levi Joslin	K	2	Ohio	B.
Hiram Keech	F	14	N. Y.	I.
T. P. Landon	I	2	Pa.	I.
Joseph Loomis	F	4	Ohio	I.
James Mendham	E	7	Mich.	C.
W. R. Matthews	C	11	Mich.	I.
Joseph Mallison	H	11	Mich.	I.
George W. Newton	I	20	N. Y.	C.
James Osborne	M	2	Mich.	C.
P. W. Parish	F	5	Mich.	C.
Chas. Royle	H	9	Wis.	I.
A. W. Sparks	I	3	Mich.	I.
S. B. Stephenson	E	19	Mich.	I.
Orrin Weiswell	D	4	Mich.	C.
Jacob Williamson	I	94	N. Y.	I.
Jesse Walker	H	21	Ohio	I.

GEN'L SILL POST, NO. 299

Located at Crystal Valley, was organized March 7, 1885, with the following charter members:

T. T. Jones   Alva Darling   Wilson Cole
A. O. Aldrich   M. Huff   E. W. Chadwick
J. H. Beach   E. F. Avery   Wm. H. Poe
S. W. Steadman   D. F. Cummins   Alex Amily
                   Ira Puffer.

The first officers of the Post were:
  T. T. Jones, Commander.   Alva Darling, S. V. Com.
  Wilson Cole, J. V. Com.   E. F. Avery, Adjt.
  A. O. Aldrich, Q. M.   W. H. Poe, Sur.
  J. H. Beach, Chap.   E. W. Chadwick, O. D.
M. Huff, O. G.   S. W. Steadman, S. M.   D. F. Cummins, Q. M. S.

T. T. Jones held the office of Commander for three years, and J. H. Beach for two years. The present officers are:

T. T. JONES, 1st P. C.

Ira Puffer, Commander.
Jay Whittaker, S. V. Com.
Stephen Manly, J. V. Com.
S. W. Steadman, Adjt.
J. H. Beach, Q. M.
Wm. H. Poe, Sur.
E. F. Avery, Chap.
T. T. Jones, O. D.
D. F. Cummins, O. G.
D. P. Kelly, S. M.
A. O. Aldrich, Q. M. S.

The Post meets on the second and fourth Thursdays of each month at Crystal Valley. The finances are in good shape and the Post is generally prosperous.

The following is a list of the present membership:

	Co.	Regt.	State.	Branch.
A. O. Aldrich	K	182	Ohio	I.
E. F. Avery	G	70	Ills.	I.
Alex. Amily	A	26	Mich.	I.
J. H. Beach	I	1	Mich.	L. A.
David Beadle	F	1	Mich.	L. A.
Wilson Cole	F	11	Pa.	C.
E. W. Chadwick	E	1	Ind.	H. A.
D. F. Cummins	C	11	Mich.	C.
" "	E	11	Mich.	I.
Alva Darling	G	20	Mich.	I.
David Demerest	J	1	Mich.	L. A.
M. Huff	C	13	Mich.	I.
T. T. Jones	B	4	Mich.	I.
D. P. Kelly	E	1	Mo.	Eng.
Stephen Manly	F	13	Mich.	I.
W. H. Poe	F	1	Mich.	L. A.
Ira Puffer	K	19	Mich.	I.
Richard Roberts	G	3	N. Y.	C.
S. W. Steadman	C	21	Mich.	I.
Jay Whittaker	H	15	Mich.	I.
Smith Welch	H	50	N. Y.	Eng.

JOHN F. REYNOLDS POST, NO. 52

Was organized at Pentwater, Oct. 22, 1887, with sixteen charter members, as follows:

C. O'Brien
E. Nickerson
George Warrington
H. C. Hart
Edward Brooker
E. D. Mathews
D. Swarthout
J. E. Hall
A. Jacobs
C. B. Randall
O. H. Dean
Philo Barnard
Wm. Buchanan
A. J. Underhill
H. H. Bunyea
D. B. Gardner

E. NICKERSON, 1st P. C.

The first officers were as follows:

E. Nickerson, Com'd'r.
A. J. Underhill, S. V. Com.
O. H. Dean, J. V. Com.
H. H. Bunyea, Adjt.
D. B. Gardner, Q. M.
Geo. Warrington, Sur.
J. E. Hall, Chap.
A. Jacobs, O. D.
C. O'Brien, O. G.
C. B. Randall, S. M.
Philo Barnard, Q. M. S.

E. Nickerson filled the office of Commander in 1887-8, and A. J. Underhill in 1889. The officers mustered in 1890 were as follows:

H. H. Bunyea, Com'd'r.
A. D. Maxfield, S. V. Com.
William E. Gill, Adjt.
H. C. Hart, Sur.

A. J. UNDERHILL, 2nd P. C.

G. V. Dunn, J. V. Com.
W. S. Dumont, Q. M.

M. L. Marvin, Chap.
Wm. Kahler, O. G.
E. N. Briggs, O. D.
O. H. Dean, Q. M. S.

On Jan. 24, 1890, this Post was called to mourn the loss of its Adjutant, Wm. E. Gill, who was summoned to answer to the last roll call in that commonwealth where battlefields are forgotten and peace reigns forever.

This Post meets on the second and fourth Wednesdays of each month in G. A. R. Hall in the Mears block. The general condition the Post is good.

The following were members Jan. 1, 1890:

	Co.	Regt.	State.	Branch.
H. H. Bunyea	B	10	Mich.	C.
E. N. Briggs	A	9	Mich.	C.
B. F. Browning	C	122	Ohio	I.
Wm. Buchanan	I	42	Mo.	I.
Edward Brooker	60	Ball. Vet. R. Corps.		
Philo Barnard	D	105	Ohio	I.
Wm. Coppell	—	3	U. S.	I.
O. H. Dean	A	21	Mich.	I.
W. S. Dumont	C	2	Vet. R. Corps.	
G. V. Dunn	K	81	Ind.	I.
D. B. Gardner	D	166	Ohio	I.
F. O. Gardner	E	10	Ohio	C.
E. S. Griswold	C	3	Mich.	I.
W. E. Gill	K	4	Mich.	I.
James Greer	C	97	Ohio	I.
H. C. Hart	I	14	Ohio	I.
J. E. Hall	K	22	Vt.	R. C.
J. W. Hurley	K	3	N. Y.	C.
M. Huftile	F	100	Ohio	I.
J. C. Harrison	C	122	Ohio	I.
George Holton	—	16	Mich.	I.
A. Jacobs	E	151	N. Y.	I.
J. C. Jacob	K	35	Pa.	I.
W. F. Kahler	C	97	Ohio	I.
Peter Labonta	C	14	Mich.	I.
Edward Mathews	K	35	Wis.	I.
A. Mathews	C	1	Wis.	H. A.
A. D. Maxfield	F	14	Mich.	I.
M. L. Marvin	F	13	Mich.	I.
E. Nickerson	E	3	Mich.	I.
C. O'Brien	H	1	Pa.	H, A.
M. S. Perkins	M	11	Mich.	C.
A. H. Palmer	C	48	Ind.	I.
C. B. Randall	K	8	Wis.	I.

	Co.	Regt.	State.	Branch.
D. C. Reed	H	8	Mich.	Bat.
James Roddy	A	26	Mich.	I.
W. B. O. Sands	I	37	Ills.	I.
D. Swarthout	F	8	N. Y.	C.
A. Savige	G	14	Ohio	I.
T. Terwilliger	E	4	Mich.	I.
A. J. Underhill	A	26	Mich.	I.
Geo. Warrington	Mar.	—	—	—
N. B. Wilson	L	1	Ohio	H. A.
E. A. Wright	G	18	Mich.	I.

DAN. LANDON POST, NO. 397

Was organized at Walkerville, Dec. 20, 1888. The Post meets on the second and fourth Saturdays of each month. G. W. North was the first Post Commander and has held the position to the present time. The present officers are:

G. W. North, Commander.   Samuel Bowles, S. V. Comdr.
V. Carpenter, J. V. Comdr.   Jas. Carter, Q. M.
W. B. DeLong, Chap.   W. M. Wicks, O. D.
David Carter, O. G.   Ezra Woodward, S. M.
A. J. Painter, Q. M. S.

The following is a list of the members, Jan. 1, 1890:

	Co.	Regt.	State.	Branch.
Geo. Anson	H	13	Mich.	I.
Samuel Bowles	D	86	N. Y.	I.
Stephen Beebe	H	4	Pa.	I.
David Carter	D	7	Mich.	I.
J. E. Carter	F	1	Mich.	Eng.
V. E. Clark	D	9	N. Y.	I.
V. Carpenter	G	126	Ohio	I.
W. DeLong	I	12	Mich.	I.
Geo. Inman	K	40	Iowa	I.
T. J. Knowles	I	1	U. S. Vet.	Eng.
Lucius M. Keyes	E	4	Mich.	C.
A. O. Lowe	H	75	Pa.	I.
M. V. Leach	C	1	N. Y.	L. A.
B. F. McMahon	F	30	Ind.	I.
Wm. McDonalls	F	88	Ind.	I.
Hiram Mack	F	140	N. Y.	I.
Geo. W. North	I	177	Ohio	I.
A. J. Painter	F	25	Mich.	I.
Wm. Rumsey	H	13	Mich.	I.
David Stafford	D	83	Pa.	I.

	Co.	Regt.	State.	Barnch.
Wm. Spoon	B	10	Mich.	C.
Levi Vaughn	C	35	N. Y.	I.
" "	H	39	N. Y.	I.
W. M. Wicks	U. S. S. Iosco.			
Ezra Woodward	D	68	N. Y.	I.

MARK SATTERLEE CAMP, NO. 28—S. O. V.

Of Hart, was organized Jan. 8, 1886, with the following charter members: C. A. Gurney, J. W. Landon, W. R. McRae, Chas. Williams, Wm. Griswold, W. H. Chappell, M. W. Satterlee, Frederick Fowler, Chas E. Summers and Albert Akin.

The first officers were: C. A. Gurney, Capt.; Chas. Williams, 1st Lieut.; M. W. Satterlee, 2nd Lieut.; J. W. Landon, 1st Sergt.; W. R. McRae, Q. M. Sergt.; Wm. Griswold, Chap.; W. H. Chappell, Sergt. of G.; Frederick Fowler, Color Sergt.; C. E. Summers, Camp G.; Albert Akin, Picket G.

M. W. Satterlee was Captain in 1887; John W. Landon in 1888, and W. H. Chappell in 1889.

The present officers are: A. H. Landon, Capt.; Calvin Hobbs, 1st Lieut.; J. W. Landon, 2nd Lieut.; W. F. Dennison, 1st Sergt.; F. M. Sage, Q. M. Sergt.; W. H. Chappell, Chap.; F. J. Hutchins, Sergt. of G.; J. M. Landon, Color Sergt.; Chas. Hobbs, Camp G.; Wm. Mills, Picket G.

The members Jan. 1, 1890, are as follows: C. A. Gurney, J. W. Landon, Wm. R. McRae, Wm. Griswold, W. H. Chappell, C. E. Summers, J. M. Landon, E. L. Luther, Calvin Hobbs, A. H. Landon, F. J. Hutchins, W. W. Huftile, Fred Taylor, Henry Huftile, Edmund Hart, Geo. Wolf, J. H. Creviston, Alfred Tate, G. A. Tate, Wm. J. Mills, F. M. Sage, W. F. Dennison, Alvah Beach, Elmer Beach, O. W. Wolf, F. W. Edwards, H. A. Hutchins, Geo. W. Kelly, Ira C. Carter, W. G. Hardy, C. H. Hobbs, E. A. Mack, W. H. Mack, S. S. Hersey and Jas. E. Carter.

The Camp meets on the second and fourth Fridays of each month in Odd Fellows' Hall. The financial condition of the Camp is good, Its members take an interest in the meetings, and altogether it is a flourishing organization.

MARVIN GILSON CAMP NO 60—S. O. V.

Located at Shelby, was organized on the 30th day of Aug., 1886, with the following charter members:

F. H. Randall, Arthur Adams, Chas. E. Getty, Geo. W. Rogers, Edward Fleming, Frazier Bulkley, C. C. Fisher, Carlos Eddy, G. H.

Woodward, Wm. Ames, W. F. Gillett, H. J. Goodenrath, DeEstian Compton, Guy Vaughn.

The first officers were: H. J. Goodenrath, Capt.; C. E. Getty, 1st Lieut.; Wm. Ames, 2nd Lieut.; F. H. Randall, 1st Sergt.; G. H. Woodward, Q. M. Sergt.; Frazier Bulkley, Chap.; Guy Vaughn, Sergt. of G.; Geo. W. Rogers, Color Sergt.; W. F. Gilbert, Camp G.; DeEstian Compton, Picket G.

H. J. Goodenrath was Captain in 1887; Chas. E. Getty in 1888; Arthur Adams in 1889, and the present officers are: D. C. Oakes, Capt.; Peter Eddy, 1st Lieut.; Frazier Bulkley, 2nd Lieut.; Fred Smith, 1st Sergt.; Ed. Morris, Q. M. Sergt.; Geo. Rogers, Chap.; A. Adams, Sergt. of G.; F. H. Randall, Color G.; Fred Sabin, Picket G.; Wilber Adams, Cor. G.

The following was the membership on Jan. 1, 1890: Arthur Adams, Wilber Adams, Frazier Bulkley, Vene Barber, H. Compton, Chas. Churchill, Peter Eddy, C. C. Fisher, Edward Fleming, Chas. E. Getty, D. C. Oakes, DeForest Payne, Frank H. Randall, Chester Robbins, Geo. Rogers, Frank Scoville, Fred Sabin, Fred Smith, C. C. Twining, Chas. Vradenburg, J. C. Wade, H. J. Goodenrath, Ed. Morris.

The Camp meets on the first and third Wednesdays of each month at Hedges' Hall. It is in good financial condition and prospering.

We append the following as many of the members reside in this county:

JOHN A. DIX POST, NO. 9

Located at Hesperia, was organized and mustered Oct. 11, 1879, with the following charter members:

W. C. Simmons,   Robt. Binns,   A. H. Deits,
N. D. Holt,   F. R. McKeen.

Mr. W. C. Simmons was the first Commander, holding the office until 1886, when H. E. Waterman held for one year, and W. C. Simmons again until Jan. 1, 1890. The present officers are:

A. M. Phelps, Comdr.   Amasa Deits, S. V. Com.
W. H. Potter, J. V. Com.   H. E. Waterman, Adjt.
G. S. Carlisle, Q. M.   Chas. Hess, Surg.
J. J. Howell, Chap.   C. R. Reynolds, O. D.
J. R. Wyman, O. G.   Geo. Robbins, S. M.
Wm. Gilbert, Q. M. S.

The Post meets every alternate Saturday evening at G. A. R. Hall, over L. E. Norton's drug store on the Newaygo side of Main street, at 7:30 o'clock. The Post is in good condition. The following were members Jan. 1, 1890:

	Co.	Regt.	State.	Branch.
W. I. Bullson	G	2	Mich.	C.
Geo. R. Boyer	B	1	Mich.	E. & M.
G. S. Carlisle	E	9	Mich.	C.
A. H. Deits	G	8	Mich.	I.
W. Davis	D	16	Wis.	I.
Jas. Frink	K	12	Vt.	I.
E. M. Fessenden	I	105	Pa.	I.
Wm. Gilbert	I	7	Mo.	C.
N. D. Holt	K	133	N. Y.	I.
E. R. Haight	B	3	Mich.	I.
J. J. Howell	I	10	Mich.	C.
M. W. Holmes	G	27	Mich.	I.
T. C. Haynor	B	12	Ills.	I.
Chas. Hess	F	35	N. Y.	I.
H. C. Jenny	D	4	Mich.	C.
L. P. Jacquay	D	129	Pa.	I.
S. Kempfield	I	11	Mich.	I.
A. Knowles	B	105	Ohio	I.
G. W. Kenyon	B	4	Mich.	I.
Thos. Lockard	D	44	Ills.	I.
I. A. Labert		2	Wis.	A.
F. R. McKeen	C	2	Me.	I.
A. C. Martin	F	4	Iowa	I.
M. M. Mansfield	B	8	Mich.	I.
A. M. Phelps	K	4	Mich.	C.
W. H. Potter	E	3	Mich.	C.
Geo. Robbins	D	186	N. Y.	I.
W. C. Simmons	B	5	Iowa	C.
E. Spaulding	H	6	Mich.	C.
G. Townsend	A	6	Mich.	C.
J. R. Wyman	C	2	Mich.	C.
H. E. Waterman	I	186	N. Y.	I.

WILL B. CHANDLER CAMP, NO. 114

Located at Hesperia, was organized Nov. 4, 1887, with the following as charter members: R. E. Bennett, J. B. Robbins, G. L. Barnhart, J. L. Gilbert, W. E. Wyman, E. L. Haynor, J. H. Dailey, W. W. Robbins, A. E. Howell, Oglive Morton, J. F. Kempfield, Ralph Carlisle, C. B. Mansfield, H. J. Phelps, H. E. Phelps, Elmer Carlisle, Wm. Webster, G. Kempfield, F. W. Tillotson and B. W. Robbins.

The first officers were: R. E. Bennett, Capt.; J. B. Robbins, 1st

Lieut.; G. L. Barnhart, 2nd Lieut.; J. Gilbert, 1st Sergt.; R. Carlisle, Chap.; J. H. Dailey, Sergt. of G.; J. Kempfield, Color Sergt.; W. E. Wyman, Camp G.; H. E. Phelps, Picket G.

R. E. Bennett held the office of Captain until the present year. The present officers are: G. L. Barnhart, Capt.; A. E. Howell, 1st Lieut.; Elmer Carlisle, 2nd Lieut.; B. W. Robbins, 1st Sergt.; E. R. Parkton, Q. M. Sergt.; L. Gilbert, Chap.; R. Carlisle, Sergt. of G.; J. Kempfield, Color Sergt.; W. Wyman, Camp G.; H. E. Phelps, Picket G.

The following is a list of members Jan. 1, 1890, viz.: R. E. Bennett, G. L. Barnhart, J. L. Gilbert, L. T. Gilbert, W. E. Wyman, E. L. Haynor, J. H. Dailey, W. W. Robbins, B. W. Robbins, C. C. Mansfield, A. E. Howell, J. H. Kempfield, Elmer Carlisle, Ralph Carlisle, H. J. Phelps, H. E. Phelps, E. R. Parkton, Ezra Spaulding, Warren Spaulding, Sherman Davis, John Dunn, John Whitehead, Geo. McGahn, Hollis Hopkins, Fred Darlington, Geo. Kosier, Rodolph Kinney, S. S. Radley and Lyman Spaulding.

The Camp meets each alternate Saturday evening, at seven o'clock, in Grange Hall, over drug store of L. E. Norton. The Camp is in a flourishing condition and as an auxiliary to the Post is doing its part in relieving the distress of veterans and their families.

OCEANA COUNTY VETERAN ASSOCIATION.

There had been in existence for a number of years an organization known as the "Oceana County Soldiers' and Sailors' Union." On March 13, 1880, a meeting was called at the Court House in Hart, the President of the Union, Dr. J. B. McPherson, occupying the chair, when the old organization was abandoned and a new one formed under the name of the "Oceana County Veteran Association." The object of this Association is to bring old soldiers and sailors together, thus creating a closer relation and more fraternal feeling among them. The first officers elected were: D. C. Wickham, President; J. B. McPherson, Vice President, with eight others; W. E. Thorp, Sec'y, and A. J. Underhill, Treasurer. At this first meeting one hundred and fifty-seven soldiers and sailors joined the Association. In August, 1880, another meeting was held, at which time G. W. Woodward was elected President, and H. J. Holmes, Vice President. At a meeting held Nov. 10, 1881, W. E. Thorp became the President, and E. F. Coon, Vice President. Aug. 16, 1882, a meeting was held at Camp Houk, which name, however, was not given to the grounds until the following year. At this meeting the same officers were elected. The next meeting occurred Aug. 31, 1883, at the place which was then named Camp Houk. The officers elected were: E. F. Coon, President, and Daniel Landon, Vice President. The annual meetings have since been held each time at

Camp Houk. Aug. 29, 1884, the same officers were elected. Aug. 28, 1885, T. G. Houk, President, and Nathan Adams, Vice President, were elected. Sept. 3, 1886, the same officers were elected. At this meeting it was decided to purchase the land upon which the Association had been meeting, and in pursuance of this resolution the Trustees purchased the northeast quarter of the northeast quarter of section thirty-two of the township of Elbridge, for a consideration of three hundred dollars. At the annual meeting, Sept. 3, 1887, Nathan Adams was elected President, and Alva Darling, Vice President. Aug. 31, 1888, W. H. Barry become President, and J. R. Thompson, Vice President. July 5, 1889, Geo. B. Dikeman, of Weare Township, was elected President; Geo. H. Eddy, of Shelby, Vice President; J. A. Collier, of Hart, Secretary and Treasurer; D. C. Wickham, Pentwater, W. R. Collier, Elbridge, W. H. Barry, Shelby, Trustees, they being the officers at the present time. The present membership is eighty-nine.

The meetings of the Association have been very successful and among the residents of the county, not only soldiers but civilians, the annual reunions have been very enjoyable affairs. The Association has laid out considerable money upon the grounds and they are fast becoming a favorite resort in the county.

PATRONS OF INDUSTRY

OF NORTH AMERICA,

Were organized by F. W. Vertican, in Port Huron, Mich., and the first Subordinate Association was organized in 1887, at Port Huron, Mich. Jan. 1, 1889, there were 270 Associations with a membership of 20,000. Jan. 1, 1890, there were 1,600 Associations with a membership of 100,000. The first Association in Oceana Co. was organized in Sept., 1889, and the last meeting of the County Association, held at Shelby, Jan. 29, 1890, there were 28 Subordinate Associations in the county, with a membership of 1545. The officers of the County Association are: President, W. F. Lewis; Secretary, J. R. Grant; Treasurer, L. L. Taylor.

The object of the P. of I. is the protection and education of the farmers and laboring men not included in trades unions, and the growth of the Society has no parallel in American history.

The Patrons' Mutual Fire Insurance Co. of Oceana, Newaygo and Muskegon Counties, was organized June 30, 1876, with headquarters at Fremont, Mich., and is commonly known as the Farmers' Insurance Company.

Years.	No. Losses.	No. Ass'ts.	No. Ass'ts. in Mills.	No. Members.	Capital or Amt. Insured.
1876	0	0	0	105	$ 136,860
1877	0	0	0	242	315,445
1878	0	0	0	421	531,401
1879	1	1	2	549	711,021
1880	7	1	1	640	856,841
1881	1	0	0	733	1,020,591
1882	2	0	0	837	1,214,296
1883	10	1	1	940	1,424,229
1884	10	2	4	1018	1,506,665
1885	6	0	0	1091	1,589,036
1886	15	2	3	1194	1,791,336
1887	9	1	1	1255	1,905,210
1888	7	1	2	1372	1,984,687
1889	10	1	1	1648	2,157,423

The President is John Barnhart, of Hesperia; Secretary, A. O. White, of Fremont; Directors for Oceana Co., C. A. Sessions, L. McCallum and R. E. Southwick.

The Company has been very successful in its business transactions, and has done business for fourteen years without litigation.

CHAPTER XIII.

—x—

REPRESENTATIVE AND JUDICIAL.

—x—

The territory of which Oceana County has formed a part has been represented in Congress since 1865 by four persons, three of whom secured national reputations. The first was the Hon. Thomas W. Ferry, son of the Rev. Wm. Ferry, the pioneer lumberman of the county. Mr. Ferry was always a leader, and on several occasions while occupying important positions he demonstrated his ability and statesmanship to the eminent satisfaction of his constituents and the people. He served as Congressional Representative for this territory from 1865 to 1871, when he was called to the U. S. Senate by vote of the State Legislature. Here he also served with marked ability from 1871 to 1883. His residence was Grand Haven, but he had many intimate personal friends in Oceana County who knew him in the trying pioneer days devoted to lumbering at Stony Creek. From 1871 to 1873 W. D. Foster, of Grand Rapids, was the Member. He was followed in Congress by the Hon. Jay A. Hubbell, who also commanded great influence from the outset of his Congressional career. His residence was the Upper Peninsula, but he made every section of his District the object of his attention, and to him and his influence is largely due the large appropriations received for Pentwater harbor improvements. He served from 1873 to 1883, and during this time was honored by being made a member of the National Republican Committee. He was forcible, active and shrewd, and to secure his support for a measure was considered a great advantage. He was unfortunate in being selected as the especial object of attack by the democrats and civil service reformers. After his retirement from Congress he served his District in the State Legislature, where he was a prominent figure.

Following Mr. Hubbell came General Byron M. Cutcheon, of Manistee, who is the present Member, and who has represented this District since 1883. General Cutcheon was born in Pembroke, N. H., in 1836. At the age of 13 he entered the Pembroke Academy, taught school at the age of 17, and shortly removed to Michigan, locating at Ypsilanti. Became principal of Birmingham Academy, in Oakland County, in 1857. Entered the University of Michigan and graduated as a member of the class of '61, when he accepted the position of Professor of Ancient Languages, etc., in the Ypsilanti High School. He entered the military service in 1862. Was Second Lieutenant 20th Michigan Infantry, July 15, 1862. Captain, July 29, 1862. Major, October 14, 1862. Lieutenant Colonel, November 16, 1863. Wounded in action at Spottsylvania Court House, Va., May 10, 1864. Brevet Colonel U. S. Volunteers, Aug. 18, '64, "for gallant service at the battle of the Wilderness, Va., and Spottsylvania, Va., and during the operations before Petersburg, Va." Colonel 27th Michigan Infantry, November 12, 1864. Resigned March 6, '65. Brevet Brigadier General U. S. Volunteers, March 13, '65, "for conspicuous gallantry at the battle of the Wilderness, Va." He commanded the 2nd brigade, 2nd division, 9th army corps, from October 16, '65, until the date of his resignation, having been compelled to leave the service on account of sickness in his family.

BYRON M. CUTCHEON, M. C.

At the close of the war he entered the law school of the University of Michigan, graduating in March, 66. Admitted to the bar at Ann Arbor in '66. Practiced law at Ionia in '66-7, when he removed to Manistee.

On March 20, '67, he was appointed a member of the Board of Control of Railroads. In '66 he was appointed President of the Michigan Soldiers' Home Commission by the Governor. In '68 he was a Presidential elector from this State. In '70 he was chosen City Attorney by a Democratic Council. City Attorney of Manistee in '71, and Prosecuting Attorney of that county in '73-4. In '75 he was elected Regent of the State University for the term of six years. He was elected to the 48th, 49th and 50th Congress, and again re-elected to the 51st Congress by a vote of 23,026 to 18,651 for Hiram B. Hudson, democrat, and 2,476 for Lathrop S. Ellis, prohibitionist.

STATE LEGISLATURE.

The following are the names and terms of service of Oceana's representatives in the State Legislature:

SENATE.

Nelson Green	Claybanks,	Mich	'61-2-3-4
James B. Walker	Benzonia,	"	'65-6
Israel E. Carleton	Muskegon,	"	'67-8-9-'70
Wales F. Storrs	Coopersville,	"	'71-2
Edgar L. Gray	Newaygo,	"	'73-4-5-6
Marsden C. Burch	Hersey,	"	'77-8
Wm. E. Ambler	Pentwater,	"	'79-'80-1-2
Shubal F. White	Ludington,	"	'83-4
Ed. E. Edwards	Fremont,	"	'85-6-7-8
Theron S. Gurney	Hart,	"	'89-'90

HOUSE OF REPRESENTATIVES.

Charles W. Deane	Pentwater,	Mich	'67-8
Israel E. Carleton	Muskegon,	"	'69-'70
Nelson Green	Claybanks,	"	'71-2
A. R. Wheeler	Benona,	"	'73-4-5-6
O. K. White	Grant,	"	'77-8
Amos Lewis	Shelby,	"	'79-'80
James E. White	Pentwater,	"	'81-2-3-4
T. G. Houk	Elbridge,	"	'85-6-7-8
Daniel G. Crosby	Elbridge,	"	'89-'90

PERSONAL.

Of the Senators above named Edgar L. Gray, who still lives in Newaygo, has always been a prominent figure in local politics. He is a lawyer by profession and a successful practitioner. In the Senate he was a leader and secured many concessions for his locality.

Marsden C. Burch, who followed Mr. Gray, appeared before the nominating convention as a candidate in opposition to R. M. Montgomery, who was an aspirant for the same position. Mr. Burch's residence was Hersey, Osceola Co. He was young and at this time unknown outside his county. In the nominating convention, however, he was victorious, defeating Mr. Montgomery by a very few votes. At the polls he was also successful, and served his term with credit to himself and to the satisfaction of his constituents.

His opponent in convention, Mr. Montgomery, became his steadfast friend, and after his return from Lansing engaged in the practice of law with him at Grand Rapids. Mr. Burch has since been U. S. District Attorney, and is now Circuit Judge at Grand Rapids.

William E. Ambler, of Pentwater, who followed Mr. Burch, was born at Medina, Ohio, Dec. 18, '45, and resided there until his parents removed to Hillsdale, Mich., in '59. He entered Hillsdale College but in '65 left that institution, going to Albion College where he graduated in the scientific course. In '66 he entered the law school at Albany, graduated, and was admitted to practice. In '67 he finished the classical course at Adrian College, graduating with the degree of A. B. The same fall he established himself as a lawyer at Minneapolis, Minn., but in '68 returned to Michigan and began the practice of law at Pentwater, where he continues to reside.

WM. E. AMBLER, 7th SENATOR.

He has been President of the village, and is a member of the firm of Nielsen & Co., bankers. In '70 Adrian College conferred on him the degree of A. M., and in '75 Hillsdale College did likewise. Mr. Ambler is now serving his second term as Trustee of the latter institution. He was elected a Senator in '78, and was re-elected in '80 by an increased majority. He was President *pro tem.* of the Senate during his last term and chairman of the important Committee on Ways and Means. At the time General Cutcheon was nominated for Congress at the Reed City convention in '82, Mr. Ambler, although not a candidate, was the choice of the entire Oceana County delegation, and would have been the second choice of the Muskegon delegation. By his declining to allow his name to be used and requesting the delegation to support General Cutcheon, it had the effect of making the General's nomination unanimous. Upon the death of Judge of Probate Landon, Governor Luce appointed him Judge of Probate for Oceana County. He is now actively engaged in the practice of his profession at Pentwater and is one of its most enterprising citizens nearly every manufactory and public improvment being largely indebted to his energy and financial support.

Shubal F. White, of Ludington, who followed Mr. Ambler, was a fine lawyer and regarded as a man of attainments. He gained for himself considerable notoriety throughout the State during the session of '83, by securing the passage of the village "local option clause" without the opponents to such action being aware of the fact until the bill became a law. Mr. White is now practicing law in Duluth.

Ed. E. Edwards, formerly a pioneer resident of Oceana County, but at the time of his nomination a resident of Fremont, Newaygo Co., was brought forward by the temperance element of the party and nominated in answer to its demands. In the Senate he fulfilled all the pledges made to his constituents and was found to be a ready, willing and effective worker for temperance legislation. He commanded influence and was successful in securing favorable legislation for his locality. He was returned with almost no opposition in his party and by an increased majority at the polls.

Theron S. Gurney, of Hart, present Senator, was born at Chester, Geauga County, Ohio, in '36. He finished his academic course at Willoughby, Ohio, University, and graduated from Ohio State and Union Law College at Cleveland, Ohio in '62. He was principal of Chardon, O., Union Schools from '63 to '65, and came to Hart, Oceana Co., in '66, and has followed the practice of law at that place ever since. Mr. Gurney has held the office of Supervisor one term, Town Clerk four terms, Village President one term, and Co. Clerk and Register of Deeds two terms. He was elected to the State Senate in '88.

THERON S. GURNEY, PRESENT SENATOR.

Charles W. Deane, the first Representative of Oceana County in the State Legislature, was *the* pioneer lawyer of the county, and as has appeared elsewhere in this work, was prominent in its early development. He is now a resident of Chicago where he practices his profession.

Nelson Green, the first State Senator and third Representative of this county in the House, was a typical pioneer. He was a man of more than ordinary ability and his advice was often sought. He served his people with credit. He has long since been gathered to his fathers.

Amos R. Wheeler was the fourth Representative elected in this county. He was born in Cavendish, Vt., Sept. 12, '15, of Scotch and English ancestry. In '53 he engaged in lumbering in Benona with a Mr. Campbell. Afterwards he became interested with Ira Minard and Sons, of St. Charles, Ill., and continued the management of this business until the day of his death. He married Jan. 15, '40, Phidelia Randall, by whom he had five children all of whom died except one daughter. He held many local offices and was very popular with the people. He served two terms in the State Legislature. He died at his home in Benona Feb. 7, '83, in the 68th year of his age. His wife followed him some five years thereafter.

Oliver K. White, Representative from Oceana County in '77, was born in Clinton County, N. Y., Feb. 13, '31, removing three months subsequently to Erie County, where he received a common school education. In '52 he removed to Cattaraugus county, where for two years he held the positions of Township Superintendent of Schools and Justice. In '57 he removed to Michigan and settled in Grant, where he still resides. He has been Supervisor six years, and was Sheriff of Oceana County during '75-6. In politics a republican.

O. K. WHITE, 5th REPRESENTATIVE.

AMOS LEWIS, 7th REPRESENTATIVE.

Amos Lewis, Representative from Oceana County in '79, was born March 6, '21, at Highland County, Ohio. He moved to Laporte County, Indiana, in '36, and to Oceana County, Michigan, in '66, where he is a farmer. Politics, national.

James White, republican, of Pentwater, engaged in shingle mill business, contested the election in the fall of '80 with Amos Lewis on the fusion ticket and defeated him by a small majority. He was a bright member, and was quite a prominent figure in the House. It was his vote that defeated Bagley for the U. S. Senate and elected O. D. Conger. Mr. White with his family now reside at Kalamazoo.

Theodore G. Houk, Representative from Oceana County in '85 and '87, was born in Seneca County, O., Aug. 2, '33. Removed to Kent County in '50. He has followed various occupations, farming, ship and house carpentering, brick making, and sailing. Enlisted as a private in Co. A, old third Michigan volunteer infantry, in the spring of '61; re-enlisted in the fall of '63; was promoted to the rank of Corporal; was wounded at Cold Harbor, Va., June, '64, and honorably discharged in August, '65. Returned to Kent Co. and engaged in farming. Re-

T. G. HOUK, 8th REPRESENTATIVE.

moved to Oceana County in the spring of '73. Has been elected Supervisor seven years in succession. Has held the office of Justice of the Peace and School Inspector. A republican.

Daniel W. Crosby, present Representative from Oceana County, was born at Barrington, Yates Co., N. Y., in '33. In earlier years he was a teacher, but is now a farmer. He has been a resident of Michigan twenty-eight years; has been Superintendent of Schools one term, Township Clerk eight years, Supervisor nine years County Clerk and Register of Deeds two years. He voted on crutches for John C. Fremont and Abraham Lincoln, and has voted for every republican nominee for President since that time.

D. W. CROSBY, PRESENT REP.

THE JUDICIARY.

BENCH AND BAR OF OCEANA COUNTY.

In Feb. 1855, the Legislature passed an act erecting a Judicial Circuit, embracing not only the counties of Oceana and Muskegon, the present Fourteenth Judicial Circuit, but also those of Ottawa and Kent and the territory north indefinitely. The history of the organization of a Circuit Court in Oceana County and its first term appears on page 36. The big Circuit, as it has until recently been known, has been divided from time to time until at last we find Oceana County with Muskegon County constituting the Fourteenth Judicial Circuit of Michigan. The Judges who have occupied the Bench in this county in regular line are as follows: Flavius J. Littlejohn, Moses B. Hopkins, Augustine H. Giddings, Michael Brown, Frederick J. Russell and Albert Dickerman.

Upon the inside of the cover of the first journal used, and dated

Sept. 21, 1858, appear the following names, constituting the first Bar of Oceana: W. T. Howells, Newaygo; J. H. Standish, Newaygo; Wm. H. Parks, Grand Haven.

The "Anderson House," Claybanks, used as the first Court House of the County.

The following are the attorneys that have become members of the Bar since:

Charles W. Deane			1859
Lyman D. Grove	April	10	1861
Frederick J. Russell	Sept.	20	1866
William Crosby	June	17	1868
Theron S. Gurney			
Daniel H. Sumner	June	26	1868
Nathan Crosby			
John M. Rice			
A. H. Dunlap	Sept.	24	1868
Amos Crosby			
William E. Ambler	Sept.	24	1868
Edward E. Edwards	March	8	1870
Robert M. Montgomery	July	12	1870

Marcus H. Brooks............................July	12	1870
Louis M. Hartwick..........................March		1872
Rollin Rice...................................		1872
David Rice....................................Sept.	27	1872
Alfred H. Nelson............................April		1873
Richard A. Montgomery.................		1873
John S. Reynolds............................Dec.	12	1874
William H. Hubbard, Jr..................Dec.	14	1875
William H. Tuller..........................June	6	1876
Willard B. McPherson....................March	15	1877
Charles P. Barker..........................July	29	1880
Charles A. Gurney.........................June	21	1881
James Brassington.........................June	6	1882
Cyrus B. Stevens...........................June	13	1882
Henry W. Harpster........................		1883
C. D. Bickford...............................Sept.		1885
John D. S. Hanson.........................Feb.	23	1886
Charles R. Johnson.......................Aug.	28	1886
Philip H. Travis............................Jan.		1887
Ned E. Whitney............................May	2	1887
William E. Osman.........................March	5	1887
William P. Sackrider.....................Oct.	31	1887
N. F. Burrows...............................Nov.	21	1887
J. P. Ackerson..............................Nov.	21	1887
Edward O'Brien............................Jan.	9	1888

Judge F. J. Russell, in a paper read before the Oceana County Pioneer Association, June 7, 1886, thus describes three of his predecessors upon the Bench:

"Judge Littlejohn has seen more of pioneer service than any Judge in the State. He made his pilgrimage north and south over his circuit, with a small flock of attorneys following him spring and fall, usually traveling on horseback and crossing the streams as best he could. Usually in his time after Court until late at night he might be seen in the Court Room, surrounded by the attorneys in attendance, telling stories to amuse themselves and a good crowd of spectators. He died at Allegan."

Judge Littlejohn's first term of Court was held Sept. 21, '58, and his last term Sept. 20, '66.

F. J. LITTLEJOHN, 1st JUDGE.

"Judge Hopkins, on account of sickness, was unable to hold many terms of Court, and died at Grand Haven before the expiration of his term."

Judge Hopkins' first term was June 18, '67, and last term June 8, '69.

A. H. GIDDINGS, 3rd JUDGE.

"Judge Giddings had a very pleasing address and was a polished gentleman. It is said that his first official act was to order the Prosecuting Attorney to dismiss the cause of The people against Augustine H. Giddings. He said he knew something of the facts of the cause, and he thought it but due to the respondent that the cause should be dismissed, and that a *nolle prosequi* should be entered accordingly. He died in Philadelphia while yet Judge."

L. G. Rutherford, in Page's History thus describes Judges Giddings, Brown and Russell:

"Judge Giddings was a graduate of Yale College, and had received a complete legal education. He was regarded by all who knew him as one of the ablest jurors in the State; but too great a love for strong drink partially destroyed his usefulness, and no doubt prevented him from rising to the highest judicial honors. He died in Philadelphia while attending the Centennial exhibition in 1876."

Judge Giddings' first term was held March 8, 1870, and his last term June 10, 1876.

"Hon. Michael Brown, of Big Rapids, was appointed to fill the vacancy occasioned by the death of Judge Giddings, and having served to the end of the term, he was re-elected without opposition. He made a good judge, and while he had his enemies, as have all public men, the writer, who was in active practice before him during all the time he was on the Bench, takes great pleasure in recording that Judge Brown was always a patient, honest and able judge. He resigned Jan. 1, 1881, for the reason that the mean salary of $1,500 per annum would not allow him to serve any longer."

Judge Brown's first term was held March, 1877, and his last term Dec., 1880.

"Hon. Frederick J. Russell, of Hart, was appointed to fill the unexpired term, and at an election ordered, he was, in April, 1881, elected by the people, the opposition not having nominated any one to oppose him. Judge Russell was born in Michigan, and has been a resident of Oceana County for twenty-two years. As a judge he is well liked by all. He is a man of strong sense, and a hard worker,—qualities which well become a judge."

Judge Russell's first term of Court was held March, 1881, and his last term in Dec., 1887, covering a period of nearly seven years' service, and during which some of the most vexed legal questions coming before the Court during its existence appeared and were disposed of. Judge Russell

F. J. RUSSELL, 5th JUDGE.

was of rugged, robust build, and was always promptly on hand to attend to the people's business. He developed as a judge rapidly while in office, and it has been truthfully remarked that he retired from the Bench just in the prime and vigor of his usefulness. At the close of his last session the Bar of Oceana gave a banquet at the Wigton in Hart, at which time a fine gold-headed cane was presented him in token of the esteem in which he was held by members of the Bar.

The Hon. Albert Dickerman 6th Judge, was born in Masonville, Delaware Co., N. Y., in 1840, and lived on a farm until seventeen years of age, going to district school in winter and

A. DICKERMAN, 6th JUDGE.

working on farm in summer. At the age of seventeen he removed with his family to the township of Newberg, near Cleveland, Ohio, and most of the time thenceforth until the war commenced, was either teaching or studying.

He was teaching in Missouri when the war commenced. Returned to Ohio where he continued his studies, teaching at the same time for another year. In July, 1862, he enlisted as a private in the 105 Ohio Infantry. In the spring of 1863 he was appointed Adjutant of the regiment and served in that capacity until the war closed. His reigiment belonged to the Fourteenth Army Corps, and was under Thomas, finally with Sherman.

At the close of the war he studied law at Cleveland, Ohio, and located at Hillsdale, in this State, in August. Held several minor offices there, was elected and served one term as Judge of Probate. 1880 was elected to the State Senate from Hillsdale county and served in the regular session of the Legislature in 1881, and in the special session of 1882. In the spring of 1883 he removed to Muskegon where he has since practiced his profession. Mr. Dickerman is a gentleman of pleasing appearance, dignified and courteous in his bearing. A good lawyer and makes a good judge."

Mr. Dickerman held his first term in Jan. 1888, and is still upon the Bench. He is clear-headed, cool, deliberate and courteous. He is conscientious in the performance of his duties.

To the members of the Bar of Oceana County we will refer briefly.

Charles W. Deane, undoubtedly the first resident attorney in the county, and was the first elected Prosecuting Attorney. He enlisted in the Union army and served with distinction during the war, coming out a Major. He was a good walker and a good story teller and was quite popular. He is now practicing in Chicago.

Lyman D. Grove was the next attorney on the list. In his early practice he was active and energetic. From 1862 to 1868 he held the offices of Circuit Court Commissioner and Prosecuting Attorney. He afterwards was a candidate for office many times, but defeated. He, too, was a good walker and during campaigns would travel the county on foot soliciting votes. He was regarded as well posted in law, but had an awkward delivery that prevented his acquiring a prominent position as a lawyer. He is now a resident of Poplar Bluffs, Mo.

Nathan Crosby is well remembered as a popular and efficient lawyer. He had a large practice and always maintained the confidence of his clients. He held the offices of County Clerk and Register of Deeds two terms. He died at Hart early in the seventies.

Amos Crosby, his brother, practiced with him and was a kind, courteous and pleasing gentleman. He held the office of Judge of

Probate from 1868 to 1872. After his brother's death he removed to Albion, Michigan, where a few years later he died.

John M. Rice is thus spoken of by Judge Russell in his paper before the Pioneer Society: "John M. Rice enjoyed an extensive practice and was closely identified with the legal proceedings of the county during his residence here. He was elected Prosecuting Attorney of Oceana County; is now a resident of Cadillac, where he was elected Circuit Judge, which office he resigned after a few months of official duty. While with us he enjoyed the confidence of a large circle of acquaintances and had the respect of all who knew him." He removed from Pentwater to Cadillac in the year 1881 and engaged in the practice of law there, after which he was made Circuit Judge and which position he filled for a time, finally resigning because of insufficient salary. He was also engaged in the banking business with his brother-in-law in Cadillac. Owing to circumstances beyond the firm's control he lost all his property. He is now a resident of Los Angeles, Cal.

R. M. Montgomery, studied with F. J. Russell and after his admission to the Bar opened an office at Pentwater under the firm name of Russell & Montgomery. He early displayed qualities of a good lawyer and rose rapidly in his profession until he stood at the head of the Oceana County Bar. He held the office of Prosecuting Attorney two terms and made a good record. He removed to Grand Rapids where he held the office of Deputy U. S. District Attorney. Afterwards Judge of Kent County, which last position he filled with great honor to himself. He is now enjoying a lucrative practice in the city of Grand Rapids, and is regarded as a leading member of the Bar.

R. A. Montgomery, a cousin of R. M., and a brother of M. V. Montgomery appointed by President Cleveland Commissioner of Patents, and later Judge of the District of Columbia, appeared in Oceana as a young attorney with a mind quick, active and well stored. He had a fine flow of language, and often in the trial of causes became eloquent. He remained in Oceana only a few years and then removed to Lansing, where he formed a copartnership with his brother, M. V. Here he soon acquired distinction and is regarded as one of the best lawyers in the capital city.

William E. Ambler of Pentwater, from his first advent to the county to the present time has held a prominent and leading position among the attorneys. He is full of energy and ambitious, yet careful, systematic and methodical. His practice has undoubtedly included as many important cases as that of any other attorney in the county. While he has a fine address and never loses by his appearance before Court or jury, he is as careful in arranging the details of his case and securing evidence as though everything depended upon this. He has been eminently successful, and now enjoys a leading practice. He was twice elected State Senator, to which reference has been made under another head.

T. S. Gurney, at present State Senator, has also enjoyed a fine practice. His early practice was general but of late years it has been largely on the Chancery Calendar. He is a fine penman and having been elected Clerk and Register for 1872-4 gave the records a fine appearance. He here laid the foundation of his subsequent great loaning business which has yielded him abundant returns. He is still engaged in the practice of law at Hart.

L. G. Rutherford is another prominent figure of the State of Michigan who developed himself in Oceana County. His career as a soldier, and in the Grand Army since the war is too well known to repeat here. The positions which he has held have brought him a widespread reputation, and given him a standing in the democratic party of Michigan near the front rank. As a lawyer he early displayed natural ability, especially in his examination of witnesses and presentation of facts to a jury, that developed with experience in the Courts and soon placed him at the head as an examiner and advocate. Of late years he commands a large practice in Oceana County. He removed to Grand Rapids in 1888, and now enjoys a large and growing practice in that city. He was elected and served the county as Prosecuting Attorney and as such bro't many criminals to justice.

E. E. Edwards, whom we have referred to under another head, was an attorney who, although not enjoying as large a practice as some mentioned, always commanded by his appearance the attention and respect of Court and jury. He removed from Pentwater to Allegan early in the seventies, from there to Fremont, Newaygo County, where he enjoyed a fine practice, and from there in 1889 to Minneapolis, Minn., where he formed a copartnership with Charles P. Barker for the practice of law.

M. H. Brooks is a lawyer possessing more of the qualities of a judge than an advocate. He has held the office of Justice of the Peace of Hart almost continuously since his admission to the Bar, and has probably tried more causes as Justice than any other Justice in Northern Michigan. He has also held the office of Circuit Court Commissioner several terms.

A. H. Nelson came to Oceana in 1873, and commenced the practice of law. He did not have a large practice, but was very popular with all the members of the Bar. He was twice elected Prosecuting Attorney, and once Circuit Court Commissioner. Several years ago he removed to Ogden, Utah, where he engaged in the abstract and real estate business and speedily accumulated a competence. He is at present President of the Board of Trade at Ogden, as well as one of its most popular citizens.

L. M. Hartwick, of Pentwater, practiced law before the Courts of Oceana from 1872. He held the office of Circuit Court Commissioner one term, was appointed Prosecuting Attorney upon the resignation of L. G. Rutherford, served the balance of his term, was elected and served another term. Has since March, 1880, published the Pentwater News, which he still owns and publishes.

R. Rice we have no record of, but he is thought to be practicing in the Eastern States.

David Rice did not practice in Oceana, but commenced practice in Cadillac where he was quite successful.

John S. Reynolds is now a resident of Chicago, being one of the proprietors and managers of a successful theater in that city.

W. H. Hubbard, Jr., was quite successful as a young lawyer, and was elected Prosecuting Attorney in 1873. He removed from the county before his term expired, and is now successfully managing a newspaper in Southern Michigan.

W. H. Tuller has not engaged in the practice of law since his admission, but for many years was F. Nielsen's Assistant in Nielsen & Co.'s bank. He has held many local offices and for several years has been Secretary and Treasurer of the State Fireman's Association.

W. B. McPherson is engaged in the practice of law at Manistee, Michigan.

Charles P. Barker has a fine practice in Minneapolis, Minn.

C. A. Gurney, who for two terms held the office of Circuit Court Commissioner, has abandoned the profession and is now engaged in the drug business at Hart, Mich.

James Brassington is one of the county seat's busy lawyers and is never disheartened at failure in the Court below. He is often found in the Supreme Court with his cases and quite often comes out with flying colors.

H. W. Harpster has been actively in practice in the County for several years. Is well read and successful. He has been for a year and over an assistant in the Hon. W. E. Ambler's office.

C. D. Bickford came here a young lawyer from Hillsdale. His pleasing ways and courteous practice soon won for him hosts of friends. He also was associated with Hon. T. S. Gurney, the firm name being Gurney, Bickford & Travis. Just in the promise of a fine career he was cut off by death and sincerely mourned.

Cyrus B. Stevens is a lawyer of careful, methodical habits that insures success when he once decides to commence proceedings. He is well informed and his counsel often sought. He filled the office of Prosecuting Attorney two terms, successfully performing its duties. It was his fortune to prosecute the first murder case that occurred in the county.

John D. S. Hanson is the son of one of Oceana's earliest pioneers. Was admitted to the Bar in Feb., 1886, and elected Prosecuting Attorney in 1888. He has secured many convictions and been remarkably successful in preparing his papers.

Charles R. Johnson is engaged in the express and insurance business at Pentwater. Still he occasionally appears in Courts.

Philip H. Travis, after his admission to the bar, entered into co partnership with T. S. Gurney. He soon acquired a prominent position, but with the idea of adding to his store of information he entered the Law Dept. of the University at Ann Arbor in Oct., 1889.

W. E. Osmun is located at Montague; is Village President and has a large Chancery and general practice.

Wm. P. Sackrider devotes the whole of his time to the performance of the duties of the office of County Clerk, to which he was elected in 1888. He is a fine penman, courteous and accommodating, and is popular alike with attorneys and patrons of the office.

N. E. Burrows went West to practice and after a short time was taken ill and died.

J. P. Ackerson is practicing at Hesperia.

MEMBERS OF OCEANA COUNTY PRESS ASSOCIATION.

H. M. ROYAL,
    Shelby Herald

F. VanVALKENBURG,
    Oceana Tribune.

S. EDSON,
    Hart Journal.

L. M. HARTWICK,
    Pentwater News.

E. S. PALMITER,
    The Argus.

CHAPTER XIV.

—x—

PICTORIAL GALLERY OF PIONEERS AND BUSINESS MEN OF TO-DAY.

—x—

Arranged According to Date of Settlement in the County.

—x—

MRS OLIVE BYRNE—1849.

MRS. OLIVE BYRNE.

Olive Byrne was born at Middlebury, Addison Co., Vt., in 1828. She is entitled to the honor of having been the first white woman that came to what is now Oceana Co. She was married in 1845 to Chauncey Clements, and came with him to this county about the middle of April, 1849. At that time there were no "neighbors" nearer than White River excepting the Indians. About six weeks after she came the families of Dr. Thos. Phillips and his father came, settling about two miles away, being her then nearest neighbors. She lived first upon the R. E. Cater place now owned by Mr. Joseph Lee. It was a lonesome time for all at that time, the great lake upon one side with the wilderness upon the other. The Indians were generally friendly and not difficult to get along with except when intoxicated. They would occasionally get possession of some firewater and then pandemonium was let loose. There were no roads through the woods excepting Indian trails. What provisions were needed that could not be raised were procured by boat, often from traders who made it a business to trade along the shore. One of the first of these traders was W. Chapin, afterwards for a number of years a resident of Pentwater. In the fall it was necessary to lay in enough provision to last until navigation of the lake was practicable in the spring. The long winters were especially lonesome times to these early pioneers, with the lake covered with floating ice; and often with the snow piled in mountain drifts around the cabin. Mrs. Byrne endured all these inconveniences as did many others who settled soon after she came, but she has braved them all and continued to reside to the present time near her first home. On June 15, 1850, she was married to Thomas Byrne. They live within sight of the lake in the township of Claybanks, being comfortably situated. The subject of this sketch has had two children, a son and a daughter. Mr. Byrne is also an early settler of the county, and as interesting a dinner hour as has ever been passed was one passed by the writer in the company of A. Brady, Mr. and Mrs. Byrne, listening to their reminders to each other of incidents of those early days when they first came to Oceana Co.

DR. THOS. PHILLIPS—1849.

DR. THOS. PHILLIPS.

Dr. Thomas Phillips was born in New Brunswick, Apr. 4, 1817. He is a son of Thos. and Elizabeth Phillips. At the age of seven years he, with his parents, moved to Canada where he remained until 1847, then coming to Ionia, Mich. After about a year he came to White Lake, near Whitehall. Having previously with John Hanson, Walter Duke and others explored the lake shore and interior of what is now Oceana County and finding lands that were in every way satisfactory, early in the summer of 1849 he came with his family to Claybanks. Mr. Phillips built the first saw mill in the county (a frame one) at Stony Creek for Rev. W. Ferry. After settling at Claybanks he divided his time between agriculture and the practice of medicine. The doctor was married July 13, 1845, to Emaline Bowman by whom he had seven children, six sons and one daughter. His first wife dying, in 1873 he was married to Mrs. Anna M. Haggerty, whose maiden name was Vandeventer, she being a daughter of Abram and Charry Vandeventer. She was born in New York State, Nov. 16, 1821. By a previous husband she is the mother of eight daughters. Mr. and Mrs. Phillips are passing their declining years on their farm on Sec. 21. Claybanks, loved and respected by all who know them. He has been offered many official positions but as a rule has refused to accept them. He has, however, served as Treasurer of his township, and as Deputy Sheriff of the county. To him and a very few others belong the honor of being the first settlers of the county. He has seen many days and nights of laborious toil but can now honestly exclaim "I have done my part in making the wilderness to blossom as the rose."

ANNA M. PHILLIPS.

ALEX. S. ANDERSON—1849.

Alex. S. Anderson, a man who exerted a positive influence in the early affairs of this county, was born, as nearly as can be ascertained, in the State of Maine, on the 23rd day of March, 1811. Of his early life nothing is known excepting that he resided for some time in his native State and spent considerable time in traveling about over the United States. In Dec., 1849, he came to Oceana County, and from that time his history can be traced. He began work for Dr. Phillips who was then building a mill at Stony Creek for Rev. W. Ferry. He worked for Mr. Phillips until the fall of 1850, when he went to lumbering for Mr. Ferry. A year later he took charge of the mill and continued to run it for two years. He then moved to Claybanks and commenced farming which he followed until his death, which occurred Dec. 29, 1879. He was buried in the Claybanks cemetery. Mr. Anderson was politically a democrat. He was known as a man of positive opinions and exerted an influence in all the affairs of the county, and more especially in his locality. In 1855 he was elected Supervisor of his township and held that office for eleven years almost continuously. Upon the Board of Supervisors he possessed an influence as great as any other member. He was Treasurer of his township for three years. In 1858 he was elected Clerk and Register of Deeds of the county; and it was his mistake while in that office that caused the people so much trouble and money in their title suit mentioned on page 88 of this book. In 1860 he was elected to the office of County Treasurer, holding that office one term.

ANDREW BRADY—1850.

Andrew Brady, the subject of this sketch was born near Drammen, in Norway, on the 4th day of Feb., 1836. His parents were Hans and Maren Brady. He continued to reside with his parents upon their farm until the age of 14 years, when the whole family came to this country and direct to Michigan, reaching Muskegon in Sept., 1850. The family there divided for a short time, the men and boys walking and the mother and one sister coming on by sail vessel to the mouth of White River. From there they all walked through the dense forest to the southeast corner of what is now Grant township, Oceana Co., arriving there on

ANDREW BRADY.

the 12th day of Sept., 1850. The members of his family coming in at that time were his father and mother, his brother Halvor now located on Sec. 2, Claybanks, having a farm of 80 acres, 70 acres improved, with good buildings; his brother Tollof now located on Sec. 2, Claybanks, having a farm of 70 acres, 60 improved, with good buildings; his sister Hanna, afterwards married to Ole Gordon but now dead. His brother Otto M. and sister Julia were left at Milwaukee where the sister still resides, being the widow of Captain Jack Saveland and in good circumstances. His brother Otto afterwards came to this county, was married to Janette Myers and was killed in the woods in 1870.

After reaching this county Mr. Brady commenced work for Harry Hulbert on what is known as big creek. Worked there one year, at which time the mill dam broke away, washing the foundation from under the mill. The result of this was that the firm was unable to pay the men, leaving the Bradys with nothing to live upon excepting a few potatoes that they had raised. Fever and ague set in, all the family being sick. After Andrew became better he went to work on White River. Coming back in about a month he found his father had died and been buried. The only provisions they had were potatoes and salt. Meeting an Indian in the woods, one day, having a deer he had just shot, Andrew traded his gun for the deer, thus furnishing meat for sometime. During the fall the boys succeeded in getting work at the mouth of White River, where the family went for the winter. In the spring Andrew came to Whisky Creek, to work for L. D. Eaton, with whom he staid until fall. At that time the family came back to Sec. 10, Claybanks, built a shanty and

MRS. A. BRADY.

during the winter, being over-persuaded by others, cut timber from government lands and made shingles. In the spring of 1853 the boys had about six hundred dollars' worth of bolts and shingles piled upon the beach, when along came the Deputy U. S. Marshal and took them all, with others. Andrew then went as a sailor upon the lake. Sailed that summer and the next. In the winter of 1854-5 resided in Milwaukee. Came here again in the spring of '55, worked making shingles that summer and in the following winter bought from the government one hundred and twenty acres on Sec. 1 and 3, Claybanks, and commenced making a farm. In July, 1859 he married Miss Julia Brady, who was born Dec. 21, 1839, near Drammen, in Norway, her parents being Anders H. and Hellen Brady. She came to America and to Oceana County in Aug., 1853. Her people had a sad experience in crossing the ocean, the mother and a brother dying of ship fever and being buried in Milwaukee.

Mr. and Mrs. Brady have had two children, a son who died while an infant, and a daughter born Jan. 23, 1862, now the wife of Nicholas Thorson.

Mr. Brady has been Highway Commissioner several times, Treasurer four years and is now Justice of the Peace in his Township.

He now owns one hundred and twenty acres of land on Sec. 3, Claybanks, and Sec. 34, Benona, in one farm. Has 76 acres under improvement; an orchard of 8 acres, a part being among the oldest orchards in the county. Principally apples. He has a commodious two-story frame house, the upright 20x28, with addition 14x24; a barn 46x58; a horse barn 22x33; besides henhouse, etc. Is engaged in general farming.

Mr. Brady is a man who by hard work and close attention to his affairs has illustrated the fact that honest endeavor will bring its just reward. He is generally looked up to and respected by all.

HARVEY TOWER—1850.

H. TOWER.

Harvey Tower was born in Rutland Co., Vt., March 3, 1817. He received his education at the common schools, Prof. Allen's school at Vergennes and the Troy Conference Academy at West Poultney, Vt. He came to Jackson Co., Mich., in Oct,, 1839, and made teaching his principal occupation for six years. He then moved to Barry Co. and engaged in mercantile business. In 1846 he was married to Miss Laura L. Mallette, of Woodland, Barry Co. In 1850 he came with his family to Oceana Co., where he has since been engaged in making shingles, shingle bolts, and in saw mill business. In 1865 he commenced his present occupation, farming.

To Mr. and Mrs. Tower eleven children have been born: Ru (deceased), Emma (Huston), Ada (Hanson), Lee, Don, Uri, Ward, Ina (deceased), Ellie, Emmor and Joseph.

Though seldom an aspirant for official honors, Mr. Tower has been elected to the offices of County Clerk (being the first County Clerk of the county), Judge of Probate, County Treasurer, and was declared elected to the office of County Surveyor by the Board of Canvassers but declined to qualify, not thinking himself legally elected. He has also held the offices of Supervisor of Benona, Claybanks and Grant townships; and was appointed and served as census enumerator of Grant and Otto in 1880, and of Grant in 1884. Mr. Tower has had an influence in the history of this county that will be felt as long as the county endures.

MRS. LAURA L. TOWER—1850.

Mrs. Laura L. Tower was born in Ypsilanti, Washtenaw County, Mich., Feb. 18, 1829. At that time Ypsilanti was a mere hamlet. When thirteen years of age she moved with her parents, to Woodland, Barry Co., Mich. When only fourteen years of age she commenced teaching, being the first teacher in Woodland. From that time until her marriage she followed that profession. She was married to Harvey Tower Dec. 16, 1846; and has since, like all true and loyal wives, followed the fortunes of her husband. Mrs. Tower has seen pioneer life, and experienced its discomforts and hardships in three different counties of our State, which is a rare occurrence for a lady of her age. It seems a waste of words for us to say that now she is widely known and universally loved and respected.

MRS. LAURA L. TOWER.

MRS. L. D. EATON—1850.

Mrs. Rebecca Eaton was born March 23, 1823, in the State of Vermont. She is the daughter of John F. and Betsey Bragg. She was married Nov. 24, 1842, to Lorenzo D. Eaton, and came with him to Oceana County in Nov., 1850. At that time there were very few residents of the territory now known as Oceana Co. and she had some thrilling experiences during those early years in our history. She is the mother of eight children, five sons and three daughters, of whom three sons and two daughters are still living.

She at present resides with her son, Wm. A. Eaton, on what is known as the Anderson place on Whisky Creek, in the township of Claybanks. Her son owns the place and is engaging quite extensively in fruit raising. To the apple orchard already on the place he has added during the past year 250 peach, 100 plum and 115 pear trees. The house in which they live has been of historical interest in the county, being the building in which was held the first Circuit Court for this county.

MRS. L. D. EATON.

LORENZO D. EATON—1850.

See page 66 for sketch.

RICHARD E. CATER—1850.

Richard E. Cater was born in Clarence, Erie Co., N. Y., March 6, 1832. Settled in Oceana County in 1850. In Oct., '55, he was married to Miss E. J. Stewart, of Rainham, Ont., from whom he was afterwards divorced. In 1877 he married Mrs. Esther J. Bezzo, of Claybanks. He was quite a prominent character in early times. He was a member of Co. F., Fifth Mich. Cav. during the war. His health has been very poor since. Is now almost helpless, and is cared for by another old pioneer of New Era, Mrs. Jane E. Rouse.

R. E. CATER.

ADAM HUSTON—1852.

Adam Huston, one of the earliest settlers of Oceana County, was born at Sanford, York Co., Maine, Dec. 1, 1816. He was one of a family of eight children, only one of whom is now living. Frances, widow of Benjamin Linscott, who now lives at Flower Creek, this county. Mr. Huston's early life was spent with his parents upon their farm. In 1852 he first came to Oceana County and located on Sec. 27, Claybanks. It is needless to call attention to the fact that at that time this county was an almost unbroken wilderness and that it fell to his lot to endure his share of the trials and privations of those pioneer

ADAM HUSTON.

days. He continued to reside there until his death, which occurred June 6, 1886, on the farm he located and cleared. He died of heart disease, from which he had suffered for several years. That old pioneer preacher, Rev. A. A. Darling, preached the funeral sermon from II Timothy, 4:7, and his remains now rest in Mount Hope cemetery, Claybanks. He was a member of the Methodist Church and a conscientious Christian. In politics he affiliated with the republicans. Mr. Huston cut and put in the first logs that were ever run down White River. He was known as a hard-working man, public spirited and enterprising. He took a great interest in the establishment and maintenance of good schools and similar concerns. Dec. 8, 1836, Mr. Huston was married to Miss Eliza A. Lord, at Boston, Mass. Mrs. Huston was born at Portland, Maine, Nov. 8, 1814. She came to this Co. with her husband and shared with him in making a home for themselves and family in the woods. Among the incidents of those times one is especially remembered, not because of the harm that came of it, but because of the fact that harm was escaped where dangers were all around. In 1854 while out berrying she became lost in the woods where now is the northeast corner of Grant, and remained out all night, the woods being full of wolves, bears, and even panthers. At the breaking out of the war the love of her country ruled her and she said to three brave boys, "go." Alas! only one returned. She still lives, at present residing with her daughter, Mrs. H. Myers, at Cranston. Mr. and Mrs. Huston were the parents of seven children, Lucy E., now Mrs. Buell, residing at Muskegon; William H., John, Phebe E., Orin E., Chas. F. and Julia O., now Mrs. Myers, residing at Cranston. Orin E. and Chas. F. reside at Flower Creek, and Wm. H. and John sleep on Southern battle fields. Such is a very brief sketch of the lives of two of Oceana County's pioneers. Though they never trod the halls of princes or tickled the ears of a vain world with fine speeches, yet their lives are eloquent. Eloquent with good works and good results of honest labor; and when we look around us and be-

MRS. A. HUSTON.

hold the material prosperity we enjoy, let us not forget that to such as these we owe it.

ORIN E. HUSTON—1852.

O. E. HUSTON.

Orin E. Huston was born at Cumberland, Me., Dec. 5, 1847. He is a son of two of Oceana County's earliest pioneers, Adam and Eliza A. Huston. He came with his parents to Oceana Co. in December, 1852, and lived with them upon the farm on Sec. 27, Claybanks, until the breaking out of the war when he enlisted as a private in Co. K. 23rd Mich. Vol. Inf., and served two years and three months. At the time of his enlistment he was but sixteen years of age and was the youngest soldier carrying a musket in his regiment. He participated in the battles of New Hope Church, Lost Mountain, Kennesaw Mountain, Ga., Columbia, Duck River, Spring Hill, Franklin, Nashville, Tenn., Fort Anderson, Town Creek and Wilmington, N. C. Returning home in June, 1866, he remained on the old homestead until 1870 when he made a start on Sec. 34, Claybanks, where he now has 240 acres, 100 acres under improvement, with an orchard of 400 apple and 150 pear and plum trees. That he is an energetic, pushing man his surroundings show. June 5, 1870, he married the daughter of two pioneers of the county, viz., Miss Emma Tower, daughter of Harvey

MRS. O. E. HUSTON.

and Laura Tower. She was born in this county Dec. 27, 1830. She lived with her parents in Benona, Pentwater and Claybanks until her marriage. She was among the first of Oceana's lady teachers, commencing to teach when 15 years of age, teaching in Ferry, Benona and Claybanks. Mr. and Mrs. Huston are the parents of 7 children, 3 sons and 4 daughters. They had in their earlier days no school advantages but those afforded by the common schools of the county, which in those times were none of the best. No people in their part of the county now take a greater interest in school affairs than they. They possess in a marked degree the esteem of their neighbors and acquaintances. Mr. Huston has been honored by his fellow townsmen with the offices of Township Clerk and Treasurer.

WILLIAM J. HAUGHEY—1852.

The following is the sketch of Wm. J. Haughey as told by himself:

WM. J. HAUGHEY, aged 30 yrs.

"Was born in the High St., Glasgow, Scotland, Sunday, Dec. 2, 1832. When about 4 years of age we moved to London, England. Came to New York in May, 1848. My father died in Memphis, Tenn. Came to Milwaukee in July, 1849, and to Oceana in the summer of 1852. Early in 1852 I kept a retail boot and shoe store in Wilmington, Delaware. When peaches were ripe hucksters would come to the store and sell them, half a peck for 5 cts. I then determined to try peaches in Oceana Co. When I came to the county I had a quantity of pits which I planted. Thus the first peach planting in the county by a white man was my work. Also in 1853 I sent for and planted the first flower seeds and I set out the first apple trees one of which is now living on the old O'Hanlon farm. There are one or two of the old peach trees still living. My mother has sold peaches from those at 25 cts. each that measured 9½ inches around, and with one or two exceptions they have borne every year. Some one will find this knowledge worth ten times the price of the book, viz.: That when your budded stock fails your seedlings will give you a crop.

When I came to Claybanks the settlers were all shingle and bolt makers or fishermen. Usually each man engaged in all three occupations. Every one, however, was willing to share with a neighbor his last potato or piece of pork, or for want of the above go fishing and divide the haul. We sent to Milwaukee and Chicago then for our supplies, including whisky; but little was raised here then. I have started and cleared three farms, and slept in the snow to make roads from LeRoy to Pentwater.

Have served the people as Constable, Justice, Treasurer, Highway Commissioner, School Inspector, School Director and Postmaster. Was married to Miss Catherine Anna Clark, at St. Louis, April 19, 1855, and with my wife came back to Michigan the same year.

Have been blessed with seven children, as follows: Maria Elizabeth, William James, Thomas Jefferson, Anna Jane, Lucy Clark, Lottie Margaret, Wilhelmina (deceased).

Was drafted in Nov., 1863, for Co. F, 2nd Mich. Cav. Served about ten days, furnished a substitute and was discharged.

Built two saw and shingle mills. Kept store since 1861. Of late years kept meat market and grocery store. My mill was burned in 1871; rebuilt and sold to E. D. Richmond & Co. in 1873. Moved to Pentwater and kept the Sherman House; was burned out in the M. E. Church fire and lost all but my grit. Was burned out again by a gambler in 1889, but am still hammering away. In 1873 signed the crusade pledge and have never tasted alcohol since. Same year quit using tobacco, which I had used from childhood.

I live in hopes of seeing Oceana County prosperous, fruitful and a prohibition county."

MRS. WM. J. HAUGHEY.

Mrs. Catherine Anna Haughey was born May 30, 1835, in Balmahan, County Longford, Ireland. Came to America in the fall of 1841. Settled in Pottsville, Schuylkill Co., Pa. In '52 removed to St. Louis, Mo., where both father and mother, Patrick and Mary Clark, died of cholera. She met Mr. Haughey there and was married to him by Rev. Father P. J. Ryan, at the Cathedral, April 19, 1855. They came to Michigan on their wedding trip to visit Mr. Haughey's mother.

MRS. W. J. HAUGHEY—aged 28.

then living in Oceana Co. She induced the young couple to settle near her, and Mr. Haughey bought land, settled down and commenced to clear. He planted corn, potatoes, squash, carrots, peas, beans, &c. He believed in trying to raise crops, and did. How nice it seemed to get a mess of sweet corn for dinner, or a mess of potatoes or squash. Mr. H. cleared about two acres by hand that she helped to log, and without a team. She helped him pile brush, roll logs, etc. They have partly cleared three farms, one on Sec. 6, Benona; one on Sec. 17, Golden, and one on Sec. 2, Hart. Seven children blessed the union, five girls and two boys, all living but the youngest, Wilhelmina, whom "God gave and whom God has taken away; blessed be the name of the Lord." She died Aug. 16, 1875, of scarlet fever.

Mr. and Mrs. Haughey have done their full share for Oceana Co., and while not enjoying in full measure the fruits of their labor, they have the satisfaction of knowing that through their work others find enjoyment. Both are residents of Pentwater at this time, pleasantly situated.

MARIA O'HANLON—1852.

MRS. J. O'HANLON—aged 46.

Maria Goldie was born in Dawn, Patrick County, Ireland, Mar. 10, 1816. Removed to Glasgow, in 1826. Was married to John Haughey, shoemaker, in Glascow, on the 8th day of Aug. 1831. There were two children born to them, one William J. Haughey, and one Maria, who died in Glascow. Her husband died in Memphis, Tenn., after their removal to America. Removed to America in 1848. She was married again in Milwaukee in the summer of 1852 to Jas. O'Hanlon, and shortly thereafter removed with her husband to Claybanks, Oceana Co. Mr. O'Hanlon was born in Lurigan, Ireland, and came to Claybanks in 1849, which after his marriage became his permanent home. He was prominently identified with the early history of the county and held many of the local offices. It is said that Mrs. O'Hanlon owned the first cow brought to the county, taught the first two terms of school in Claybanks, and was the person for whom the township of Golden was named. Mr. O'Hanlon died April 9, 1887, and Mrs. O'Hanlon March 14, 1888.

JOHN MUNSON—1854.

John Munson was born in Ulrika, Sweden, May 11, '29. He was the eldest child of Muns and Anna Hanson, and passed his childhood in his native place, with his brothers Nels and August, and his sister Anna. Following the national custom the sons became known as John, Nels and August Munson. Anna afterward married Swen Anderson, and now lives in the township of Claybanks, not far from her brothers, Nels and August, who also made for themselves homes in America, far from the graves of their parents, who are buried near the old home in Sweden.

JOHN MUNSON.

At an early age John Munson began to earn his way in the world, and as he grew older, the desire to seek his fortune in the New World grew stronger, and the summer of his twenty-fifth year marked an epoch in his life. He had now, by dint of hard labor and self-denial accumulated enough to pay his way to America, and in Aug., '54, he reached Chicago. Not meeting with success in the city he soon crossed over to Michigan, where he began work for Mr. Harvey Tower, of Claybanks, getting out shingle bolts. After a short time he left Mr. Tower and performed the same labor for Messrs. Holver and Tolef Brady. In 1855 he bought 40 acres of

MRS. JOHN MUNSON.

land in the township of Claybanks, and began getting out shingles and shingle bolts for himself. Disposing of this to his brother Nels he bought, in 1856, 160 acres in the township of Benona, where he passed the remainder of his life. He immediately began clearing and improving his new purchase. He first built a small log house in which he lived until the new and commodious frame structure now the home of the family was erected in 1864.

Nov. 9, 1861, Mr. Munson was married in Benona to Mrs. Frederika Lun Peterson, formerly of Lunberg, Sweden. Mrs. Munson was a daughter of Swen and Christina Lun, and came to Oceana Co. Aug. 30, 1861. Mr. and Mrs. Munson labored to improve their surroundings, and to build up a home founded upon mutual love and faith, which but grew the stronger as the years advanced.

In 1879 he bought 80 acres more, adjoining his original purchase on the north. Here Mr. Munson toiled away the months and years literally carving his home out of the primeval forest; and as acre after acre was cleared, he began to see the results and enjoy the fruits of his labors, and to gather about him some of the comforts of life. As the crops increased it became necessary to put up buildings in which to store the harvests, and granary, horse barn and hay barn, together with cattle sheds and outbuildings were erected in succession.

In the midst of his labors, at a time when the future seemed so full of the realization of his hopes, Mr. Munson was called home. While at work in oat-harvest he was prostrated by a sunstroke, and after but one week's illness, he died Sept. 4, 1883, in the 55th year of his age.

He left a wife, still living at the old homestead in Benona, and eight children to mourn his loss. He was buried from the Scandinavian Church, Claybanks, Sept. 6, 1883, Elder Chic, of Montague, and Rev. Hvid officiating. His children, in order of birth, are Frank A., John C., Sophia M., Nettie J., Oscar L., Oscar F., Herman O., Mary H. and Edward G. All are living except Oscar L., who died Aug. 15, 1873. Sophia M. was married to Rev. Charles Coors, Nov. 27, 1889.

Mr. Munson was a self-educated man, of sound judgment, honest, faithful and God-fearing. Quiet and somewhat diffident in manner, he was a man thoroughly liked and respected wherever known. For forty-six years he had been a member of the Lutheran Church, and taught its precepts by his daily walk. A member of no secret order he made his own way, winning all men for his friends. In politics he was a republican, although not given to much fruitless discussion. A kind, indulgent father, and tender, affectionate husband, Mr. Munson was deeply loved by his family, and in dying he not only left his family comfortably well off in this world's goods, but bequeathed them an inheritance of inestimable value, a good name, spotless and above reproach.

ENOCH T. MUGFORD—1854.

Enoch T. Mugford was born in Portland, Me., Jan. 14, 1829. He settled in Chicago in 1852, following the trade of carpenter and joiner. Settled in Oceana County in 1854, first locating at Pentwater, where he followed the occupations of fishing and lumbering. In 1858 he removed to Hart township, where he has since resided. March 1, 1851, he married Martha Jane Nutter, who was born in Wolfsboro, N. H., Sept., 1828. She came to Oceana County with her husband, and with him has endured the trials and enjoyed the pleasures of pioneer life. Ten children were born to them, only four of whom survive. Mr. Mugford is a man of positive convictions, and possessed of great mental force. Had he educated himself in one of the professions in early life he would have attained eminence. As it is, he has always been a prominent figure in his locality. In April, 1890, for the sixteenth time in succession was he elected Supervisor of Hart township. He is a prominent Mason, Odd Fellow, and a member of different farmer's organizations. Has been prominent in organizing and maintaining the Oceana Co. Pioneer Association. He owns a small farm

E. T. MUGFORD.

MRS. E. T. MUGFORD.

in Hart township, but is not engaged in farming. He was appointed Postmaster of Hart by President Cleveland, which office he held until recently. He is still in the enjoyment of health and has the promise of many years of usefulness.

CHARLES BLANCK—1854.

Charles Blanck was born in Germany, August 30, 1812. His parents' names were Carl and Maria. In early life he married Sophia Schumacker, by whom was born to him three sons and three daughters. His wife and children are all dead, he alone surviving. He came to Oceana County in August, 1854. Cleared a farm north of Pentwater, suffered and struggled with the other pioneers. He has held local township offices several times, and is now village ferryman for Pentwater. He lives by himself, is kindly disposed and ready to crack a joke with any one. He has one brother and one sister in the Old Country and one sister in this country, but has not seen or heard from any of them in many years.

CHARLES BLANCK.

WILLIAM A. OLINDER—1855.

William A. Olinder, son of Frederick and Doratha Olinder, was born in Sweden, June 19, 1835. He came to Oceana County July 14, 1855, and worked in saw mills summers and driving team winters until 1880, when he moved on to his farm in Benona township, where he now resides. He enlisted in Bat. B, 1st Mich. L. A. as a private, serving 18 months to the close of the war. He joined the Masonic order at Pentwater in 1867, and helped to organize Benona Lodge No. 289, at Stony Creek, of which he was a charter member. Since then the lodge moved to Shelby where it now meets. In June, 1889, he joined the Shelby Lodge No. 344, I. O. O. F. March 2, 1880, he married Mrs. Sarah L. Morse, who was born at Upton, Oxford Co., Maine, Feb. 15, 1845. She is a daughter of Samuel and Nancy C. Grover. Apr. 15, 1867, she was married to Y. N. Morse, and is the mother of three children, two sons and one daughter by him. Married in 1880 to Mr. Olinder, having been six years a widow. Mr. and Mrs. Olinder now have a fine home. The farm consists of 160 acres of which 120 are under good cultivation. He threshed in 1889 one thousand, three hundred and ninety bushels of grain. Their house is, upright 16x26, wing 16x24, both parts 18 feet high, containing twelve rooms, with cellar under the whole; woodhouse 14x28; cattle barn 46x60; horse barn 30x40; granary 16x24; corn crib 9x30; hog house 16x32; sheep shed 18x40; and well house 10x18 with windmill.

WM. OLINDER.

MRS. WM. OLINDER.

HIRAM E. RUSSELL.—1855.

Hiram E. Russell, son of Josiah Russell, and one of Oceana's earliest pioneers, was born in New York in 1830. He moved to Michigan when six years old. At the age of ten with his parents, moved to Otisco, Ionia Co., where they resided a short time, and, thence to Greenville, which they found but a vast wilderness. They spent several years here engaged in millwrighting and rafting lumber on the Flat and Grand Rivers, from Greenville to Grand Haven. In 1855 he came to Oceana Co. At this time not even the Indians had reached this fertile region, or but few whites. The place where Hart now stands was one solid growth of forest. He followed the section lines from Whisky Creek until he arrived at the

H. E. RUSSELL.

place he now occupies. He at once began the laborious task of clearing away the forest and converting the proud old wilderness into a home, where he lived a bachelor's life until 1865, when he was married to Betsey E. Polley, who was born in Lee Co., Iowa, in 1843. In 1845 she moved with her parents, Daniel and Hannah Polley, to Ashtabula Co., Ohio, where she resided until 1864, when she came to Oceana County and taught school until February, 1865, when she was married to Mr. Russell. They have two children, one son and one daughter.

MRS. H. E. RUSSELL.

Mr. Russell has a farm consisting of 240 acres of which 200 acres are cleared and 20 acres of this is set to fruit trees. He is engaged in fine stock raising as well as fruit growing. He has filled several places of public trust in the way of township and county offices.

ISAAC HAGGERTY—1856.

Isaac Haggerty, a son of Orra and Rebekah Haggerty, was born in Oneida Co., N. Y., Aug. 10, 1828. He left New York State in 1856 going to Chicago where he remained one summer, then coming to Oceana County in the fall of 1856. He immediately commenced clearing up a farm and continued upon the farm until '61, when he enlisted in Co. B, 5th Wisconsin Infantry and served three years. At the expiration of his term of enlistment he returned to his county to his farm. Since then his occupation has been farming. Mr. Haggerty is a man much respected by his neighbors, and has

ISAAC HAGGERTY.

MRS. I. HAGGERTY.

been two years Treasurer of Claybanks township. Oct. 10, 1852 he was married to Miss Elizabeth Salmon, a daughter of Heman and Betsey Salmon, who was born at Hamburg, Erie Co., N. Y., Jan. 13. 1830. They have one child, a son, who is now living at home and assisting his father with the farm work. Mr. Haggerty's present residence is on the SW¼ of the SW¼ of Sec. 23, Claybanks, which he has under fine improvement with a large, comfortable house and commodious barns and out buildings.

JAMES G. FARRELL.—1856.

James G. Farrell, an Oceana County production, was born in Claybanks, June 29, 1856. His parents were Owen and Catherine Farrell. The subject of our sketch was born and raised upon a farm and has always followed that business. He has been elected by his fellow townsmen to the position of Superintendent of Schools two terms and Treasurer two terms. As a public officer he has always given good satisfaction to all. He takes a great interest in educational matters and has taught school winters for the past nine years. He is a good writer, many of the racy articles in the different county papers being from his pen. He is a young man of whom the people of his section are justly proud.

DR. IRA JENKS—1856.

Dr. Ira Jenks was born Sept. 4, 1808, in the township of Homer, Cortland Co., N. Y. When he was nine years of age his parents removed to the township of Scipio, Cayuga Co., remaining there one year, then removing to the township of Sheldon, Genesee Co. From thence, after another year, removing to Middlebury, now Wyoming Co., remain there till the subject of this sketch was 24 years of age. At the age of 21 Ira took upon himself the entire responsibility of his father's family, consisting of three, besides his sister and her two children. At 20 he learned the shoemaker's trade. In the Patriot war in '38 he was in active service in the artillery as a fifer. At the age of 36 he received an injury in one hand and wrist that partially crippled him for life. At this time he began the study of medicine. At the age of 37 he was married to Miss Direna L. Davis, with whom he became acquainted while doctoring her mother, 40 miles from home. In 1846 they removed to the township of Portland, Ionia Co., Mich. Their experience there was a severe one as he was sick a whole year with ague and acute bronchitis, and his wife with ma-

DR. IRA JENKS.

arial fever over 4 months. This experience of sickness and want while at Portland was the most severe and trying of any in their lives.

In 1848 he removed to Roxland, Eaton County. At about this time he obtained a warrant for 160 acres of land for his services in the Patriot war.

In 1850 he removed to Greenville, Montcalm Co., remaining three years. From thence to North Oakfield, Kent County, in 1853, and from thence in May, 1866, he began his work as a "pathfinder" in the Oceana Co. wilds. He soon located his lands in Hart township on what is known as Prospect Hill, his nearest neighbor then being A. C. Randall, at Shelby Corners. The interesting vicissitudes concerning his experience in this county as a pioneer would fill a volume, and are better known to many of the citizens of this county than can be chronicled in the short space allotted in this volume. Physically Dr. Jenks was a "man of iron." Since the age of 21 he has been an active member of the Baptist Church, having been a deacon over 40 years.

The Dr. was in every sense of the word a self-made man. He was a conversationalist of great ability, instructive and entertaining. For the last few years his eyesight has been gradually failing till he is now nearly blind. At the age of 81 he is in the full possession of all the faculties of his mind, and he says he can walk a mile as quick as he ever could. Having been intimately acquainted with Elder Darling about 30 years, he has arranged with him to preach his funeral sermon, choosing for his text, Job 14:14: "If a man die shall he live again? All the days of my appointed time will I wait till my change come." He has his tombstone placed where his wife, who died eight years ago, is lying, and in faith and hope awaits the day of his coming rest from earth's tempestuous labor, care and sorrow.

JOHN D. HANSON—1856.

John D. Hanson, one of the early settlers of this county, and the very first to select and purchase land, was born in Christiana, Norway, in the year 1818, and sailed to America when but a young man, and first settled in Milwaukee and afterwards, in the year 1843, he located in Whitehall, Mich., going in the lumber business with Charles Mears, and for several years sailing and owning vessels himself. It was while sailing that he discovered the great Clay Banks country, and where he afterwards located what is now known as the "Hanson farm," the first land located and purchased in Oceana Co., and whereon he moved in the year 1856. He had improved and cleared up the farm previous to his moving on the same.

He moved his family from Whitehall to Claybanks in a yawl boat in the month of May. He sent to Ionia to be ground the first wheat ever grown in the county, and it took nine days to make the trip.

His farm house was always headquarters for the lawyers and judges, and many were the jokes and stories told and pleasant evenings spent at his house while the county seat was located at Whisky Creek. He was always prominent in the politics of the county and was a republican with strong convictions. He held the office of Deputy U. S. Marshal for several years, and was Consul to Norway and Sweden for a number of years.

MRS. BETSEY HANSON.

Mrs. Betsey Hanson was born at Kingsburg, Norway, in the year 1823. Her parents dying when she was but a small child she was left to the care of an uncle. At the age of about 16 she left Norway for America with her uncle and landed at Milwaukee, Wis. There she resided for a period of about 5 years, when she was married to her late husband, John D. Hanson, when she removed directly to Whitehall, Mich. This was about the year 1845, her husband having been in business there with Charles Mears for several years lumbering. She was the first white woman to see Whitehall, or White Lake as it was then called, and lived two months before any other white woman arrived, and her neighbors and visitors were found among the Indians, which language she could speak fluently after she had lived there a short time. She lived there until the year 1856, when she removed with her husband and family to Claybanks where she has since resided. She is the mother of nine children, seven of whom are still living: Mrs. G. C. Myers, Charles H., John D. S., Myron W., Winfield S., and Fremont M., all of this county, and Mrs. Lillie L. Peck, of Montague. Since childhood she has been a member of the "Lutheran Episcopal Church."

MRS. BETSEY HANSON.

JOHN D. S. HANSON—1856.

John D. S. Hanson was born Jan. 1, 1852, at Whitehall, Mich. He lived there until four years later, when he moved with his parents to Claybanks, this Co., on what is known as the "Hanson farm" on the banks of lake Michigan, and one of the most beautiful sites on the eastern shore of said lake. Here he lived and grew up to manhood, going to school, teaching school and working on the farm alternately, with two years at Hillsdale College, this State, until the year 1876, when he became proprietor of the old homestead through the sickness of his father, John D. Hanson. Here he had good success as a farmer, and held the offices of Constable, Supervisor and School Inspector until the year 1882, when he was elected to the office of Sheriff, and on Jan. 1st, he removed with his family to Hart, the county seat, where he still resides. In 1884 he was re-elected to the office of Sheriff by an increased majority. He also held the office of Deputy U. S. Marshal for several years. While holding the office of Sheriff he devoted all his spare time to the study of law, being encouraged thereto by Hon. F. J. Russell, then Circuit Judge, and in the year 1885, after a thorough examination by the Hon. W. E. Ambler, of Pentwater, Hon. F. W. Cook, of Muskegon, and Gen. L. G. Rutherford, of Hart, as committee, was admitted to the Bar of Oceana County as a full-fledged attorney and solicitor. In 1886 he was nominated for County Clerk, but was defeated by 31 votes. He was appointed Clerk of the Senate Committees on Cities and Villages and Counties and Townships, in the Michigan Legislature of 1887, which position he held during the session with ability. In Jan., 1888, he entered the law office of M. H. Brooks, Esq., to study and practice law, and at the convention of same year was nominated and afterwards elected to the office of Prosecuting Attorney, the duties of which he is now performing with success. In Jan., 1889, he was appointed Probate Clerk by the Hon. W. H. Churchill, Probate Judge for Oceana County, which

J. D. S. HANSON.

appointment he still holds. Is Village Attorney of Hart. Was census enumerator for Claybanks in 1880. In politics Mr. Hanson is and always has been a republican, and a firm believer in the American policy of protection. In habits he is strictly temperate in all things. Though not a member of any Church, he believes in the doctrines taught by the disciples of Christ, and the Sabbath will invariably find him in the Church. On the 22nd day of Oct., 1876, he was married to Miss Ada Tower, a neighbor and acquaintance from early childhood, and a most estimable and cultivated lady.

MRS. JOHN D. S. HANSON.

Mrs. Ada Hanson, daughter of Harvey and Laura Tower, of Grand View, Oceana Co., Mich., was born in the township of Benona, this county. She received her education in the district schools of Benona, Pentwater and Claybanks, and attended the union school of Hart, under the tutorship of Prof. S. Edson, and finished her education in the high school of Grand Rapids, Mich., under Prof. Milner. She began teaching school at the age of 16 years, and taught eighteen terms, nine of them being in one school house.

MRS. J. D. S. HANSON.

She was married to John D. S. Hanson Oct. 22, 1876, at Whitehall, Mich., by the Rev. D. M. Ward, pastor of the M. E. Church. The union has been blessed with six children, four of whom are now living: Laura B., Edith B., Vernie I. and J. Dwight Hanson.

AMOS C. RANDALL—1856.

Amos C. Randall was born in Yates County, New York, Feb. 8, 1818. He settled in Shelby township, Oceana County, May 1, '56. In 1869 he settled on section 14, Hart township, where he has since resided. Has been Town Clerk, Highway Commissioner and Justice of the Peace. The latter office he held three terms. Was married to Sophronia Anderson, Feb. 26, 1840. To them were born five sons and one daughter. One son, Lewis L., died in 1864 from disease contracted in the U. S. service during the rebellion. Mr. Randall is still living, although in feeble health.

EDGAR D. RICHMOND—1857.

Edgar D. Richmond was born to Edmund and Olive Richmond in Euclid, Cuyahoga Co., Ohio, May 5, 1837. His early life was spent upon his father's farm. In 1840 he entered the Shaw Academy in East Cleveland, and remained two years. After this he clerked in a dry goods store until the spring of 1857, when he came to Pentwater to work for Charles Mears. Mr. Richmond remained in charge of Mr. Mears' store until 1862, when he and Woodruff Chapin went into business at Pentwater. After two and one-half years they took in John Bean, Jr., as partner and together bought out Hart, Maxwell & Co. In 1862 they built a shingle mill and sawed the first shingles on the shore. They afterwards sold out to Phillips & Browne. He was also in 1872 in partnership with Mr. F. W. Ratzel in general merchandise, and still later with his brother-in-law, Mr. Dunwell. He removed to Hart in 1877 where he has continued to reside. He is now a large stockholder and cashier of the Oceana Co. Savings Bank at Hart. Also owner of some of the finest fruit and stock farms in the county.

Aug. 3, 1859, at Ionia he married Miss Josephine M. Rounds, by whom he had two sons, Eddie and Willie, both of whom are dead. Mrs. Richmond died July 6, 1866. Nov., 1869, he married Miss Lydia L. Dunwell,

E. D. RICHMOND.

of Allegan Co., by whom he has had four children, two of whom, a daughter, Olive, and a son, Jerome, are living, and two, a daughter Daisy, and a son, are dead.

Mr. Richmond has been Postmaster at Pentwater, held several township and village offices, been elected and served five terms as Clerk and Register of Deeds. His nomination upon the republican ticket always added strength to the ticket. He is popular with all classes. Is enterprising and one of the most sympathetic friends in case of sickness or distress.

CHRISTIAN MILLER JENSEN—1857.

Christian Miller Jensen was born in Denmark, March 26, 1826. His parents were Jens and Maren Miller Nelsen, and following the custom of that country his name became Jensen (Jens' son). His early years were spent in his native country where he became a sailor among a nation of sailors On Apr. 13, 1852, he was married in Denmark to Frederekke M. A. Halstibroe, who has proved a faithful wife to him during all these years, bearing him five children, two sons and three daughters. They moved upon the farm where they now live on April 10, 1858. He landed at Pentwater Oct. 13, 1857, with $80 in his pocket, without any experience in farming, having always been a sailor, but with a stout heart and determined purpose. The result of these qualities is a fine farm, in fact one that attracts universal attention from all who have occasion to pass over the main traveled road from Pentwater to Ludington thro' North Weare, composed of 300 acres, 125 improved, with a good bearing orchard to which he has recently added, a large well built house and other good buildings. Mr. Jensen has gone through the trying

C. M. JENSEN.

MRS. C. M. JENSEN.

experiences of pioneer life, in company with his faithful helpmeet, but, as he states, looking back along the track he has followed he has nothing to regret in coming to Oceana Co., and is well satisfied with the results of the labor and hardships of early settlement. It is needless for us to call attention to the fact that Mr. and Mrs. Jensen are respected by all who know them, as their wide circle of friends and acquaintances are well aware of it.

OLIVER K. WHITE—1857.

Oliver K. White was born in Peru, Clinton Co., N. Y., Feb. 15, 1831. He is a son of Hosea and Anna White. When but three months of age he removed with his parents to Erie Co., N. Y., where he remained until reaching his majority, in the mean time receiving a common school education. After coming of age he moved to Cattaraugus Co. where for two years he held the positions of Township Superintendent of Schools and Justice of the Peace. In 1857 he came to Oceana Co., locating in the then wilderness of Grant township, where he opened up a new farm where he has since continued to reside. He has cleared and improved his farm and now has a fine place with good buildings, including a large and commodious house. Mr. White has been honored by the residents of his township with the office of Supervisor six years, and by the Co. by the offices of Sheriff during 1875-6, and Representative in the State Legislature during 1877-8. He has also held the offices of School Inspector, Commissioner, and County Surveyor. He has always discharged the duties of his various positions with fidelity and strict honesty, thus winning his way from one position to another. Mr. White was married in 1852 to Miss Nancy Bartlett, who came with him to Oceana Co. and has proved a faithful and loving wife and mother. They now have six children, three sons and three daughters.

O. K. WHITE.

MRS. O. K. WHITE.

JASON CARPENTER—1857.

J. CARPENTER.

Jason Carpenter was born in the township of Ira, Rutland Co., Vt., near the foot of the Green Mountains, May 28, 1820. His father's name was Samuel Carpenter, and his mother's maiden name was Roxalana Newton. He graduated from what was known as the "Tower School House" at the age of ten years in the "A, B C and the multiplication table." He was compelled to walk two and one-half miles over a high range of mountains to school. In the fall of 1834 he, with his parents, moved to what was then the far West, Ohio, and settled near Sandusky City. There they lived until April, 1836, when they came to Michigan and located in Armada, Macomb Co., 40 miles north of Detroit. After helping his father to pay for his farm, upon which he lived until his death, Jason, at the age of nineteen years, left the paternal roof and embarked upon life's ocean for himself, his strong hope being his sails and his faithful ax serving as a rudder. For some years he drifted with the tide of circumstances until in 1847 he found himself in Grand Rapids where for the time being he cast anchor. Mr. Carpenter still remembers with what astonishment the natives witnessed his dexterity with his ax. In 1850 he was married to Miss Larissa A. Loomis, the faithful partner of his life to this time. She was born at Independence, Alleghany Co., N. Y., in 1825. Her parents were Andrew and Laura S. (Clark) Loomis. When she was yet a babe her parents moved to Exeter, Luzerne Co., Pa., where they remained until 1839, when they came to Walled Lake, Oakland Co., Mich. There they lived two and a half years, then removed to the town of Walker, Kent Co., about seven miles north of Grand Rapids. There she lived with her parents until her marriage with Mr. Carpenter in 1850, coming with him to Oceana Co. in 1857. Since then she has faithfully borne her share of the fatigues and difficulties of pioneer life.

MRS. J. CARPENTER.

In June, 1857, Mr. Carpenter with his wife, came to Oceana Co., locating in Claybanks. At that time the county was almost an unbroken wilderness, giving newcomers a prospect of plenty of hard work. That they have done their part in making the "wilderness to blossom as the rose" no one can doubt when he sees the proofs in their present surroundings. Mr. and Mrs. Carpenter have had a family of two sons and three daughters. Mr. Carpenter has followed farming as a rule, but was in mercantile business in Berlin, Ottawa Co., one year, and one year in this county. He has been honored by his fellow citizens with a number of offices, having been Township Clerk, Commissioner of Highways, and two years Supervisor of Claybanks. His home for the past twenty years has been on Sec. 20, Shelby township. His residence is one that attracts attention from all passers by.

JOSIAH RUSSELL—1858.

Josiah Russell was born at Newry, Oxford Co., Maine, April 25, 1804. In early life he settled where the city of Greenville now stands. He was elected County Judge of Ionia and Montcalm counties and opened the first Court of Record in the latter county. He served one term in the Michigan Senate, declining a renomination for that office. In 1856 he was induced by the report of a rich lead mine to come to this county, and being well pleased with its agricultural prospects he located on the west half of the section where the village of Hart now stands, but which owing to the sickness and death of his son George, was allowed to revert to the government. In March, 1858, he removed his family to this county. He was a pioneer in fact, held many of the local offices necessary to the organization of the different municipal departments of government. He held the office of Judge of Probate and County Surveyor. It was due to his influence as much as any one person that the county seat was removed to Hart. He died at Hart, April 25, 1874.

JOSIAH RUSSELL.

Harriet Russell, the wife of Josiah Russell, whose maiden name was Eggleston, was born at Colbrook, Litchfield County, Conn., Aug. 30, 1808. She was the faithful companion of her husband through

HARRIET RUSSELL.

all his pioneer experiences in Ionia, Montcalm and Oceana counties. She was the mother of ten children, of whom the Hon. Fred. J. Russell was one, and H. E. Russell, a prominent farmer and stock-raiser, of Hart, is another. She lived to a good old age loved and respected by all who knew her, and died at Hart, June 27, 1884.

HON. FREDERICK J. RUSSELL.

The Hon. Frederick J. Russell was born at Orion, Oakland County, Mich., Oct. 7, 1841. He was the sixth child and fourth son of Josiah and Harriet Russell. As a boy he had but few educational advantages. The country was new and school facilities entirely lacking. Later on the country improved, his father prospered and school advantages began to be realized. About this time his father lost his property, then for the first time young Frederick realized the importance of preparing himself for his manhood's career. He then attended school at Cook's Corners, Ionia County, where he had for a school companion the present Justice of the Supreme Court, Allen B. Morse. While attending this school he did chores for his board. Afterwards he taught school winters and attended the State Normal at Ypsilanti during the summers of 1861-2. He enlisted Aug. 8, 1862, in the 21st Mich. Inf., but was rejected by the examination board on account of the condition of his health. The following spring he was taken ill with consumption and pronounced by the physicians beyond hope of recovery. He however, in spite of all predictions, did recover and has since enjoyed good health. He borrowed law books from John Morse, father of Judge Morse, and commenced the study of law. Was admitted

HON. F. J. RUSSELL.

to the Bar Sept. 20, 1866, before Judge Littlejohn. He was first appointed, in January, 1867, Clerk of the Probate Court, and at the election in 1868 was nominated for the office of Circuit Court Commissioner, receiving, in the ensuing election, 1,060 votes to his opponent's three; and in 1870 he was re-elected by 930 votes, his opponent receiving 4. Soon after the expiration of his term in this office, in 1871, he was appointed Judge of Probate, and in the election in November, 1872, was elected to that office, and was again elected Judge of Probate, Nov. 7, 1876. He was on Jan. 5, 1881, appointed by Governor Jerome, Judge of the Fourteenth Judicial Circuit, which was then composed of Oceana, Muskegon, Newaygo and Mecosta Counties, to fill a vacancy caused by the resignation of Judge Michael Brown; and at the ensuing election he was nominated and elected to that position without opposition. He served in this capacity until January, 1888; then, at the expiration of his term, he retired to private life, again taking up the practice of the law, and, in addition, looking after his other interests. Since 1865 he has been engaged in farming at Hart and has been very successful. To him more than any other one person is due the introduction of Shorthorn cattle and Merino sheep into Oceana Co. He is also largely interested in various business enterprises, both at Hart and Muskegon. In 1875 he engaged in the banking business and is now one-third owner in the Citizens' Exchange Bank, at Hart, the pioneer banking institution of that place. In 1883 he assisted in organizing the Merchant's National Bank, of Muskegon, and is a member of its Board of Directors. He was one of the principal organizers and the first President of the Hart Improvement Company, a corporation organized to build a hotel and make other improvements in the town, which has successfully accomplished its objects. He was also one of the organizers of the Muskegon Electric Light Company, of which he is Vice President; and he was a liberal subscriber and active worker in inducing the Chicago and West Michigan Railway Company to extend its road to Hart, which was done in the summer of 1880. He assisted in organizing the Oceana County Agricultural Society, and was its President for a number of terms, finally declining a re-election. He joined the Masonic order November 25, 1868, and on April 8, 1879, became a Knight Templar. He was instrumental in securing, for the erection of the Congregational Church, large subscriptions, in addition to his own handsome donation, and actively aided in the work, of which the present beautiful church structure is the result. In politics he is a republican, and has been a delegate to many State Conventions. He has taken an active part in political matters, his voice being frequently heard on the stump in the interests of his party, and never without good effect.

MRS. CAROLINE WIGTON—1858.

Caroline H. Wigton, daughter of Josiah and Harriet Russell, was born in Otisco, Ionia County, Mich., Sept. 30, 1844. She lived with her parents and came to Oceana County with them in 1858. On the 1st day of Feb., 1864, she was married to Sergeant Wesley L. White, who had enlisted in the 8th Michigan Infantry in Sept., 1860, who was wounded at the battle of the Wilderness, May 7, 1864, and died at Campbell Hospital, Washington, Aug. 24, 1864, and is buried in the National Cemetery at Arlington Heights. On the 26th day of Jan., 1869, she was again married to William Wigton, son of Mahar Wigton, who died Sept. 24, 1872. She resides with her brother, F. J. Russell, and has for a number of years.

MRS. WM. WIGTON.

DAVID DILL—1858.

DAVID DILL.

David Dill, son of Clinton and Ann Dill, was born in Jackson Co., Pa., March 18, 1838. Ten years later he moved with his parents to Milwaukee, Wis., where he remained until 1853, when he started out for himself. In 1857 he came to Michigan locating at Muskegon, where he lived until 1858 when he came to Oceana Co., locating in Claybanks township. He at once went to work building him a home, being compelled to do all his work by hand as there were no roads over which to bring a team. He procured his provisions as others did and backed them from Stony Creek to his place.

MRS. DAVID DILL.

He continued improving his home until 1862, when he enlisted in Co. F. 5th Mich. Cav. and went to the front. He was assigned to the Army of the Potomac and took part in all its battles until the spring of 1864, when he was sent to the Shenandoah Valley with Sheridan. There he took part in the various battles and skirmishes until the surrender of Lee. He took part during his army life in 46 battles and twice that many skirmishes. At the close of the war he returned to this Co., where he left his family, and returned to farming which he has since continued. In 1871 he had the misfortune to lose by fire nearly all his buildings, etc., except the log house. In 1858 Mr. Dill was married to Miss Lucha L. Taylor, who was a daughter of Giles and Samantha Taylor, and was born Feb. 1, 1844, in the State of Ohio. With her parents she came to Ransom Center, Michigan, in 1849, and in 1856 to Muskegon, where she was living at the time of her marriage. She came with her husband to this county in 1858 and remained on the farm during his absence in the Army. Mr. and Mrs. Dill have raised a family of four daughters and three sons. They are now living in the enjoyment of the fruits of their early labors and hardships, and are respected by all who know them.

WM. MYRON GARDINER.

Wm. Myron Gardiner was born at Stony Creek, in Oceana County, Feb. 4, 1858, his parents being William and Rufena Gardiner, who still live in Benona. Mr. Gardiner is familiar with Oceana Co. history, having spent the greater portion of his life within its borders. He was for a time grain buyer in the Star mills, Grand Rapids. Was salesman for Wheeler Bros., at Shelby, for three and a half years, and for Paton & Andrus, at the same place, for four years. At present he is engaged in the grain, flour and feed business at Shelby. He is in every sense of the word a self-made man, who by industry and application to business has made for himself and family a pleasant and comfortable home. He is essentially an Oceana County production and the county may well be proud of such a son. He is a leader among the Masonic fraternity, being a member of Benona Lodge No. 289, F. & A. M., at Shelby; Oceana Chapter No. 56, R. A. M., at Pentwater, and Apollo Commandery No. 31, K. T., at Ludington. He is the present S. W. of Benona Lodge, and an active, earnest member. He enjoys the confidence and respect of all who know him. He is emphatically a domestic man, finding his greatest pleasure with wife and children in the pleasant home he has provided for them. In his efforts to make home happy he is ably seconded by his worthy wife. Mr. Gardiner was married April 27, 1880, to Miss Lilian Elliott, and three sons and one daughter now gather about his fireside.

WM. M. GARDINER.

FREDERICK W. POPKEY—1858.

Frederick W. Popkey was born in West Prussia, Feb. 2, 1851. His parents were Frederick William and Mary Louise Popkey. He came to Oceana Co. in 1858 with his parents, and at the age of eight years commenced helping his father to clear up the land where he now resides in Claybanks. When they came upon the land there was not a stick of timber cut. With his small ax the subject of our sketch began pioneer life by cutting small trees and trimming, and as he grew older and stronger gradually came to hold his own with the men. He has assisted in clearing every acre of the eighty acre farm he now lives upon. On April 1, 1870, he was married to Miss Adelaide Hill, and there have been born to them six children, two sons and four daughters.

ANDREW J. UNDERHILL—1858.

Andrew J. Underhill, son of Bartow and Eleanor Underhill, was born Sept. 27, 1832, at Brooklyn, N. Y. Resided at his birthplace until about six years of age, then moved to Suffolk Co., where he lived until coming to Detroit, Mich., in 1844. Resided at Detroit and other places with his parents until about 1857, when they came to Grand Haven, and from there to Muskegon. In 1858 the subject of our sketch came to Pentwater where he engaged in fishing, which he followed until 1863, when he enlisted in Co. A 26th Mich. Inf., as Orderly Sergeant. On March 13, 1863, he was brevetted 2nd Lieut., and resigned on Oct. 10, 1863, returning to Pentwater. He then engaged in mercantile business, was afterwards P. M. for a number of years. He has since, to the present time been engaged in general merchandise and lumbering, now having a store at Pentwater, and is the owner of two lumber and shingle mills. He was elected Supervisor of Pentwater township in 1860, and again in 1873, and was one year appointed by the Township Board. In 1877 he was elected Clerk of the township. In the village he has held the positions of Trustee six years, and President in 1878 and 1889. Mr. Underhill has always taken a strong interest in G. A. R. matters, having been Commander of the Pentwater Post in 1887. As a business man he is energetic and public spirited. Married Aug., 1864, to Miss Elizabeth Pringle, who died June 24, 1880. He has four children: Charles M., Grace, Herbert F. and Jessie.

A. J. UNDERHILL.

THOMAS COBLISTER—1858.

The subject of this sketch was born in the Isle of Man near the city of Pearl, on the 7th day of May, 1836, and died in Pentwater, Mich., Nov. 22, 1889, at the age of 53 years, 6 months and 15 days.

Of the early life of Mr. Collister but little is known. When only eleven years of age he was apprenticed on board a merchant sailing vessel and for some six years followed the life of a sailor. While the vessel lay at anchor at Quebec, Canada, he and a companion conceived the idea of running away, and watching a favorable opportunity made their escape, and remained concealed until after the vessel left port. Then he engaged his services to a stevedore for whom he worked a year or more. One day he was startled by the appearance of a vessel painted white, a sight he had never witnessed before, and on going aboard found it was a lake vessel. He shipped aboard of it and after a time landed at Port Huron. Here he fell in with Henry Webb, Sr., who was lumbering in that section, and engaged his services to him. He followed Mr. Webb to Oceana Co. He located at Pentwater in 1858, and engaged in fishing. In company with James Corlett he built the schooner Minnie Corlett. In 1866 he married Mrs. Jane Woolman, sister of Edwin Nickerson, which union was blessed with one child, a daughter. After only two years of married life Mr. Collister was left a widower, in which state he continued five years. On the 15th day of Oct., 1873, he was married to Miss Mary Tuttle, who for 16 years was a devoted wife and loving companion, and who during his long illness was untiring in her efforts to mitigate his sufferings.

In 1869 he formed a copartnership with his brother-in-law, E. Nickerson, and engaged in lumbering, manufacturing flour, etc. The firm, also, with Capt. Peterson, owned the schooner Winnie Wing, one of the most successful vessels on the lake. In business the firm was successful and ranked high in business circles.

THOS. COLLISTER.

He has held many of the village offices and was a member of the Common Council when he he died. He was also a prominent Odd Fellow, and for several years was Treasurer of Pentwater Lodge No. 378.

MOSES D. GIRARD—1858.

Moses D. Girard was born at Detroit, Michigan, Aug. 28, 1856. He is a son of Dominique and Rose Girard. In 1858 he first came to Oceana County with his parents, remaining at Pentwater about

two years, then going to Joliet, Ills. He remained there until 1868, when he returned to Pentwater, since which time he has worked in shingle mills and with his father until about three years ago, when he engaged as clerk in the store of C. Mears at Pentwater, where he has since remained. In the spring of 1889 he was elected without opposition to the office of Village Recorder. He is known as an enterprising young man who by energetic endeavor has made his own way in the world thus far.

M. D. GIRARD.

EDWIN L. BENTON—1858.

Edwin L. Benton was the only son of Orrin and Mary Benton, pioneer settlers of the township of Ferry in this county. He was born Aug. 20, 1847. He came with his parents to Michigan and settled at White River in 1855, and with them removed to Ferry in 1858. Sept. 12, 1886, he was married to Miss Nellie G. Devine, by whom he has one son. He is a successful farmer and business man. He has often been honored by his township with local offices, and was its Supervisor in 1889. In the spring of 1870 he was elected and is now serving as Justice of the Peace.

E. L. BENTON.

JANE E. ROUSE—1858.

Jane E. Rouse, the daughter of John and Sabia Moore, was born at Branchport, Yates Co., N. Y., June 5, 1829, and April 2, 1848, was married to Daniel Rouse. Her early life was uneventful and in many respects similar to that of many others. From the time of her marriage until the breaking out of the rebellion her life was happy and the family prosperous. With her husband she came to Oceana Co. in 1858. She endured the trials and privations of early days with a stout heart, and when the war broke out and her husband enlisted under Capt. Chas. Deane and went away she assumed the charge of their farm of 160 acres and the care of her eleven children. When the war was over her husband came back, but he had lost all inclination for farming and home life. He finally received a pension and then left his wife and companion of his early struggles alone with the family and a mortgage on the farm. She was obliged to give up the farm, and since 1883 has supported herself by nursing. Mrs. Rouse has considerable poetic talent and at the old settlers' reunions her poems are listened to with interest. She is the mother of eleven children, seven sons and four daughters. Her present home is at Montague.

JANE E. ROUSE.

WILLIAM WEBB—1859.

William Webb, son of Henry and Rose Webb, was born at Quebec, Can., on Aug. 2, 1831. He came to Oceana Co. in 1859, arriving at Pentwater on May 1st of that year. He came from Port Huron in a covered wagon in company with his father, mother, brother Frank, Asa Pringle and wife and William Pringle. Soon after reaching Pentwater he purchased lot 4 of block 6 in the village and built him a house and cooper shop. He made barrels for the fishermen and others for some time. In 1861 he was appointed a Deputy Sheriff of the county under J. J. Tapley, Sheriff. One of his first official acts of importance was the arrest of Orson A. Fuller, of Hart, for the killing of Andrew Rector (see page 45). Mr. Webb describes Fuller as one of the most hardened criminals he ever had under arrest during his official career. Another case was the arrest of a Southerner who robbed old Mr. Cheney of $550. He was living on what is known as the Cheney farm in the township of Hart where the robbery was committed. Mr. Webb was called in the night and before morning was at Cheney's home, found the robber's track at daylight and captured him at Carleton's mill on White River before night, getting all the money. The man was subsequently sent to Jackson by Judge Littlejohn. He was a cool fellow for when the Judge pronounced his sentence he arose and thanked him, saying the sentence would not expire before the war was over, hence he would not be compelled to be a target for either party. In 1862 Mr. Webb was elected Sheriff of Oceana County, and again in 1864. After being out one term he was again elected in 1868 and renominated in 1870 but was defeated at the polls by eight votes caused by a bogus ticket. In 1862 he was appointed a Deputy Provost Marshal for the Western District of Michigan, under Capt. Norman Bailey as Provost Marshal. He served in this capacity during the war and was in Milwaukee on his way to Beloit after a deserter when the news of Lee's surrender was received there. The joy manifested by the citizens of that city can only be appreciated by those who saw it. The wildest excitement prevailed. That night everything that would burn was used in making bonfires regardless of property rights of owners. Men took each other's hats and coats to feed the fires, and probably such a scene of excitement was never before witnessed. Mr. Webb found his man and delivered him at headquarters. He was immediately sent to Sylvania, Ohio, after another deserter who was also safely delivered at headquarters. These two arrests closed his services as Deputy Provost Marshal. Soon after the office was discontinued and upon parting with Capt. Bailey and the other members of the force, the Captain complimented him by saying

WM. WEBB.

to him: "Webb, you are one of my Deputies who never permitted a prisoner to escape." In 1868 he was appointed Deputy U. S. Marshal for the Western District of Michigan, under James Henry, U. S. Marshal, and served under him until Mar. 4, 1875. On the 3rd of the following April he was again appointed under John Parker, the new Marshal, and served under him until his death in 1880, thus serving in that capacity for twelve years. Mr. Webb was also census enumerator in 1870 for the counties of Mason and Oceana. During the years of 1860-1-2 he held the office of Treasurer of Pentwater township. In 1865 he started a store at Pentwater and continued that business for six years. In 1880 he commenced lumbering at Bass Lake where he continued for three years. In 1885 he entered the employ of Butters & Peters Salt & Lumber Co. at Ludington as foreman, and is still engaged with them. In 1851 Mr. Webb was married to Miss Esther Bemis, by which union two sons and four daughters were born to him. In 1885 he had the misfortune to lose his wife, an estimable lady. In 1888 he was again married. Looking back over the years he has passed in Oceana County, comparing the condition of the county when he first came, a dense primeval forest with only a trail through it for a wagon road, with what it is today, one of the most prosperous counties, of its age, in the State, he feels proud of the fact that he was one of its pioneers. As an officer Mr. Webb may also be proud of the fact that he never permitted a bondsman to suffer because of his neglect of duty, or a prisoner to escape by reason of his carelessness.

CHARLES DUMAW—1859.

Chas. Dumaw, a son of Julius Dumaw, was born Nov. 30, 1830, at Plattsburg, N. Y. He was raised upon a farm and has always made farming his business. In May 1859, he came to Oceana Co., locating on Sec. 8, Weare township, where he now has a farm of 320 acres, with 80 acres improved. He has a small house, a barn 40x50 feet and horse barn 22x32 feet. He has an orchard of 4 acres, principally apple. Mr. Dumaw has always been a hard-working, industrious man; and has held the offices of Highway Commissioner and Justice of the Peace, and is now a member of the School Board of his District. In 1854 Mr. Dumaw married Miss Julia A. Labough, and they have had nine children, seven sons and two daughters, in order as follows: Alice, now Mrs. Chas. Maynard, residing at Pentwater; William, Charles, Claude, Broomfield, Everett, Emmet, Bert and Lilian.

ASA M. PRINGLE—1859.

Asa M. Pringle was born in Fredericksburg, C. W., June 19, 1833. Was married to Caroline Webb, Dec. 8, 1858, who bore to him eight children, five sons and three daughters. Mr. Pringle moved to Oceana Co. May 1, 1859, and has been engaged in farming, lumbering and fruit raising. He now owns a fine farm in the township of Golden, where he still resides. His companion passed into the beyond a few years since. He has ever been an active factor in his locality. Has been Deputy Sheriff, Commissioner of Highways, Justice of the Peace, Township Treasurer and School Inspector. Concerning the county he thus speaks for himself: "I will say to the old pioneers of Oceana that if they are well situated here they had better be contented where they are. I have traveled about 8,000 miles through the Western countries. I have seen beautiful places but you consider everything, and it is hard to beat old Michigan very much. I have noticed that about nine out of ten who leave Oceana County come back as soon as they can get back, and it is not a very bad sign for this county. There are a great many chances yet to make money, and a good many ways to lose it. I like some of the Western countries very much, but a good many portions of it I do not like."

JOHN LEAK—1859.

John Leak, a son of William and Mary Leak, was born in Claybanks, Oceana Co., Mich., June 9, 1859. He was born upon a farm and has made farming his business except during the past six years, during which time he has been engaged in carpenter work and framing. He is looked upon as a good workman and has succeeded in obtaining considerable work in that line. A native of the township where he resides, he has done his fair proportion, for his age, in making the township what it is, and the good people, recognizing this fact, have honored him with the office of Treasurer of the township at the spring election of 1889. Through a mistake of the printer his name was omitted from the list of Treasurers on page 147 of this book. Mr. Leak married Miss Annie Brower on Nov. 13, 1883 and four children, one son and three daughters, have been born to them. Long may he live to assist in and witness the growth and prosperity of the county that claims him as a worthy son.

HERVEY S. SAYLES—1860.

Hervey S. Sayles, the subject of this sketch, was born at Stillwater, Saratoga Co., N. Y., June 27, 1827. He is a son of John and Catherine Sayles. He came to this State in 1848, and spent twelve years at Round Prairie, Kalamazoo Co., and on June 12, 1860, came to Oceana Co., locating in Crystal township. In 1861 he moved upon his present location in Elbridge township he being the first white settler in the township. He began trade with the Indians which he continued for some time. In 1874 he commenced farming which business he has followed to the present time. Mr. Sayles has always been much respected by all who knew him, and has been intrusted with the duties of various offices which he has conscientiously discharged. He was elected Treasurer of Elbridge in 1863 and four times thereafter. He was elected Supervisor in 1864 and for four consecutive years thereafter. In 1870 he was elected to the office of Sheriff of the county, and again in 1872, serving four years. On April 8, 1852 he was married to Miss Phebe H. Kinney, in Kalamazoo Co. She came with him to this county and has endured many hardships but thro' them all has assisted her husband with cheerfulness. They have three children, two sons and one daughter.

H. S. SAYLES.

WILLIAM N. SAYLES—1860.

William N. Sayles, known from one end of Oceana Co. to the other as Nila Sayles, was born at Prairie Ronde, Kalamazoo County,

Mich., Jan. 21, 1857. He is a pioneer and a son of pioneers, his parents being Hervey S. and Phebe H. Sayles, now residents of Elbridge. Nila came to this county in June, 1860, and has resided here since. His earlier years were spent in the backwoods of Elbridge where he was a pupil at the Indian Mission school; afterwards he attended school at Hart village. He has been engaged in various occupations from work at scaling and book-keeping to manager of lumber camps and stores. He has held the office of Treasurer of Elbridge and in 1886 was elected County Clerk, which office he filled with credit. Just previous to the expiration of his term of office as Clerk he became interested in the Oceana Co. Savings Bank at Hart, and when his term expired accepted the position of Asst. Cashier of that institution which he still fills. On Oct. 16, 1889, he married Miss Mary V. Booklass, of Coldwater.

W. N. SAYLES.

ANDREW JACKSON—1860.

Andrew Jackson, whose portrait is given herewith, was born Jan. 12, 1840, at North Shenango, Crawford Co., Pa. His parents were Alexander and Betsey Jackson. He is one of the pioneers of Oceana County, being familiar with the hardships and struggles of an early day having been a resident among us since Jan. 1, 1860. He has always followed farming as a business; and as a pioneer farmer has done his fair proportion of work in removing the heavy timber of this county and preparing the soil

A. JACKSON.

for agricultural uses. To such as he, the pioneer *farmers*, the county owes more of a debt of gratitude than to those men who have always resided at the villages making a living by furnishing supplies to workmen. The business men are a necessary factor in all countries, but it is the man who takes his ax into the woods that really makes the wilderness to blossom. On Jan. 12, 1861, he was married to Mary Jane Gray, and four children have blessed their union two sons and two daughters.

GEORGE C. MYERS—1861.

George C. Myers was born at Grand Haven, Ottawa Co., Mich., Jan. 21, 1848. His parents, Cornelius and Catherine Myers, now reside near him in Claybanks. He came to Oceana in the fall of '61 and since then has been engaged in farming and school teaching. On Oct. 7, 1874, he married Miss Lena S. Hanson, a sister of J. D. S. Hanson, now Prosecuting Attorney of the county. They have a family of four children, three sons and one daughter. Mr. Myers has held many positions of trust among them, Supervisor five years, Justice eight years, Superintendent of Schools four years, and has been a member of the County Board of School Examiners eight years, now holding that position. When such positions are repeatedly given a man it goes without saying that the duties have been faithfully performed. He now has a nice farm with good improvements, situated in the northeast corner of the township of Claybanks. His friends are as numerous as his acquaintances.

G. C. MYERS.

AHAZ A. DARLING—1862.

Ahaz Allen Darling, one of the pioneer preachers of Oceana county, was born in Washtenaw Co., Mich., Feb. 6, 1834. His parents were Simeon and Nesiah Darling. He came to this lake shore in the fall of 1861 as a Methodist Missionary to Manistee. Then on Oct. 21, 1862, he came to this county, making his home at Pentwater, and preaching at Lincoln and Claybanks in Mason Co., at Pentwater, two places in Weare, two in Hart, one in Ferry, four in Shelby, two in Benona, and two in Claybanks in Oceana Co. At that time there was no church building in the county. Mr. Darling preached at Ludington the first sermon by a Protestant minister. It was preached to a few fishermen and mill men. For the services that Mr. Darling rendered to the Pentwater mission he received the magnificent salary of $300 per annum. Leaving his wife at home alone he would start out upon his trips, fording rivers, lying in the woods over night when lost, and enduring hardships innumerable. He would ride a horse where possible and when not would make his way on foot, following Indian trails and the Government blaze on trees. There were no grist mills and when visiting a settler he would

A. A. DARLING.

take his turn at grinding wheat or corn in a hand mill. The people were universally kind and did what they could toward the support of the Gospel. Mr. Charles Mears, H. C. Flagg and wife and Mr. S. Moulton Mr. Darling especially remembers for their kindness to him. Many who were not noted for piety would put themselves out to do the missionary a favor. In those days the ministers at Conference shrank from such appointments as great calamities. Mr. Darling came to love the people and the woods and although twice sent to better charges, would at the end of a year ask to be returned to the sandy shore of

Lake Michigan and wilds of Oceana Co., now a land of fruits and plenty. We would be glad to fill many pages with accounts of his experiences, but space will not permit. Mr. Darling married March 25, 1860, Miss Catherine M. Wilcox, and six sons and two daughters have been born to them in Northern Michigan. Mr. Darling has held the position of Supervisor of Hart township and Superintendent of Schools for the county. For the past ten years he has spent part of his time at work at the carpenter trade. A man known throughout the county and loved and respected wherever known, is what can truthfully be said concerning him now. He says

"Wife and I are contented here," and what can a man have anywhere better than "sweet content?"

JOHN BAMFORD—1862.

John Bamford was born at Nottingham, Eng., Sept. 30, 1827. His parents were James and Hannah Bamford. He left England April 18, 1854, from Liverpool, and arrived at Chicago June 1, 1854. He at once opened a game and fruit store and continued in that business until 1862. On June 9th of that year he landed at Pentwater and went to work for Mr. C. Mears, with whom he continued until 1869 when he purchased forty acres of land on section 18, Weare township, and building a shanty among the timber moved upon it. His business previous to coming to America had been that of a designer and draughtsman of lace patterns, hence he went upon his farm in the woods with no knowledge of farming. After many years of hard labor he now has a farm with thirty acres improved and twenty acres free of stumps. He has made quite a business of market gardening, raising quantities of strawberries. He has a comfortable frame house 14x26 with wing 12x28, and considerable personal property. He has been School Director for three terms. June 11, 1848, he was married by Dr. Brookes, Vicar of St. Mary's Church, Nottingham, Eng., to Miss Emma Darker, a daughter of John and Mary Darker, who was born at Nottingham, England, Feb. 14, 1828. Mrs. Bamford came with

J. BAMFORD.

MRS. J. BAMFORD.

her husband to Oceana Co. and has been an efficient helpmeet to him during the years they have been here. They pride themselves today upon the fact that they do not owe one penny, believing with the poet that "an honest man's the noblest work of God."

STEPHEN SPELLMAN—1862.

Stephen Spellman, a son of John and Dorcas Spellman, was born at Wadsworth, Medina Co., O., in 1851. In 1862 he came to this county and lived on section 29, of Hart township. He followed farming until 1880 when he began horseshoeing which he still continues. In 1889 he became interested in a drug store at Shelby, where he now resides. Married Miss Matilda White, of Golden, and has three children, two sons and one daughter. Mr. Spellman has always been a hard-working man, and by hard labor has accumulated what he possesses. He has made many friends in Shelby since residing there.

S. SPELLMAN.

A. P. PETERSON—1862.

Andle P. Peterson was born Feb. 24, 1860, at Chicago, Ill. He is a son of Nels and Fredrike Peterson. He is one of the pioneers of Oceana County, having come here in 1862. He was raised upon a farm and is now engaged in farming in Claybanks township. June 12, 1887, he married Miss Anna B. Johnson, and they have no children. Mr. Peterson is an industrious young man and is fast making for himself and family a comfortable home.

ABRAHAM H. BEARSS—1863.

Abraham H. Bearss was born in the Province of Ontario, Can., July 17, 1841, his parents being Joseph and Susa Bearss. He came to this county in 1863 and began work in the lumber woods, which he continued for two years. In 1864 he purchased eighty acres of land on section 15, township of Shelby, which he cleared up and where he has since resided. The first seed sown on the place was procured by going fifty miles with an ox team. There is some difference between his first and last taxes. His first tax was $3.81; his last $155.40, and the improvements made by him can be estimated in the same ratio. He certainly has a fine place. In May, 1865, he returned to Canada, and was married at Dunville, Ont., to Phebe Ott, and among the pleasant reminiscences of those times was the housewarming the neighbors gave him and his bride upon the Christmas eve, after coming home. They have had five children, one son and four daughters. Mr. Bearss has held the offices of Highway Commissioner, Township Treasurer, Supervisor, and is now Co. Superintendent of the Poor.

A. H. BEARSS.

CHARLES P. RATHBONE—1863.

Charles P. Rathbone was born at Coneatville, Crawford Co., Pa., April 15, 1851. He is a son of Jerome R. and Elvira Rathbone. He came to Oceana County with his mother and family in May, 1863, settling in Ferry. Soon after coming here his two brothers, James H. and LeGrande, enlisted in the army, Jas. H. in Co. E 3rd Mich. Cav., and LeGrand in Co. D 10th Mich. Cav. James H. Rathbone died Mar. 17, '87, of an illness contracted while in the army. It was a hard struggle for the family to keep the wolf from the door, but the boys remaining at home work-

C. P. RATHBONE.

ed manfully and discharged their duty faithfully, supporting their widowed mother and four younger brothers and sisters. At that time they were compelled to back most of the necessaries of life from Whitehall. The subject of our sketch has lived through the "suffering times" of the county and now surrounded with the comforts of life remembers his early struggles and hardships as a "story that is told." He is an honored member of the Shelby Lodge No. 344 I. O. O. F., being one of its Past Grands. He has been fortunate in his marital relations, having married Jan. 4, 1874, Mary A. Dooley, of Kalamazoo, who has proved a loving, faithful wife. They have two children, daughters: Carrie, born Sept. 15, 1876, and Nellie, born Sept. 1, 1878. Both were born in Shelby. Mr. Rathbone was the first Marshal of Shelby village, and has been 8 years Constable of Shelby township.

BENJAMIN S. GARVER—1863.

Benjamin S. Garver was born on the 7th day of July, 1851, at Spencer, Medina Co., Ohio. He is a son of David L. and Nancy Garver, now residing near Hart. He came to Oceana Co. in July, 1863, and has since resided here, being engaged in school teaching, farming and fruit raising. On Dec. 25, 1874, he married Miss Pittinger, and they now have four children, three daughters and one son. In the spring of 1888 Mr. Garver became interested in the Oceana Canning and Evaporating Co. at Pentwater; and has been the manager of the business since, besides being one of the heaviest stockholders. His hobbies are the development of the fruit interests of the county and the improvement of our public roads. He takes a great interest in fruit raising and is considered an authority upon that subject. He has probably done more than any other man of his age and means in the county to build up our fruit interest and to urge the desirability of better country roads.

B. S. GARVER.

HIRAM BARRON—1863.

Hiram Barron was born in Stark County, Ohio, in the year 1831. He is a son of George and Charlotte (Carnes) Barron. In 1852 he was married to Miss Mary J. Porter, and three children have been born to them, one son and two daughters. On April 25, 1863, he arrived in Oceana Co., commencing at once to make him a home, at the same time making shingle bolts for a living. He was a hard worker, doing long days' work, much of his clearing being done by the light of log fires. Besides farming he does more or less lumbering. He has never sought public office. He is a man with numerous friends and acquaintances. His farm, which is located on Sec. 3 of Hart township and Sec. 34 of Weare, consists of 200 acres of which 120 are located in Hart and 80 in Weare. The 80 acres referred to he took up from Government and is the homestead. He has 140 acres improved, and the farm constitutes one of the finest stock farms in the county. "Hi," as Mr Barron is familiarly called, is a veritable pioneer. He bears his age well, and is still as fond of and can enjoy a pratical joke as well as thirty years ago.

H. BARRON.

WALTER H. CHURCHILL—1864.

Walter H. Churchill was born at Batavia, Genesee County, N. Y., April 27, 1838. His parents were Samuel and Eliza Churchill. His early life was spent upon his father's farm and the log school house was a feature of that life. He continued to reside upon the farm until arriving at the age of manhood, when he determined to start out in life for himself. Believing that the West offered advantages not possessed by the East, he decided that in the West he would seek his future home. He arrived in Oceana County on Feb. 14, 1864, locating at once in the township of Shelby. At that time the county was a wilderness and he became one of its earliest pioneers. After coming here he enlisted in Co. G 15th Mich. Inf., and took up his line of march for the front. At the close of the war he returned to his home in this county and has since resided in Shelby and vicinity. When the Shelby Postoffice was established in 1866 Mr. Churchill was appointed Postmaster, which position he continued to hold for nineteen years and nine months. He has held positions of trust in his township since its organization, among them being Township Clerk seven years, Treasurer one year, Justice twenty years, Supervisor two years, and in 1888 was elected Judge of Probate of the county, which position he now holds. He has also been Secretary and Treasurer of the Oceana Co. Veteran Association. In business matters Mr. Churchill has exercised great shrewdness and tact and from the small start made in 1864 he has become the possessor of considerable means. By an honorable, upright course he has won the respect and esteem not only of those associated with him, but also of those with whom he has had business transactions. His business relations have been varied. He was engaged in the hardware business in 1872 with Mr. A. Neff. He afterwards was engaged in the boot and shoe business. In 1883 the banking house of Churchill, Oakes and Co. was formed in which he became President and still holds the position. In 1886 the Benona Lumber Co. was formed with Mr. Churchill as its Secretary, and in 1888 he also became the Secretary of the Shelby Improvement Co. To dwell upon his social and personal qualities is useless in this connection as he is well known in all parts of the county. His residence and grounds are among the finest in the village, a view of which appears elsewhere in this book. Mr. Churchill has been three times married. In 1859 he married Miss Jane Green. In 1869 he was married to Lucada A. Carter, and in 1874 to Sarah A. Hamlin. He has had five children, three sons and two daughters, only one of whom is now living, Charles L. His present wife is a lady of refinement and exerts herself to make home pleasant and its occupants happy. They have an adopted daughter, Mamie, who is the pet of the household.

W. H. CHURCHILL.

CALVIN A. WOODWORTH—1864.

C. A. WOODWORTH.

Calvin A. Woodworth was born on the first day of July, 1848, in Ashtabula Co., O. He is a son of Calvin and Susan A. Woodworth, who were the second family to settle in the township of Colfax where they still reside. They settled in Colfax on Oct. 22, '64. The subject of our sketch thus early in life was made acquainted with the toils and privations of pioneer life. Amid the native forests his character was formed and Mother Nature was his teacher. He is now a man respected and trusted by his townsmen. Has been Treasurer and is now Supervisor of the township. On Dec. 22, 1875, he married Miss Jennie Robertson, and three children have blessed their union, two sons and one daughter. Since 1876 he has followed farming for a livelihood.

J. W. RUNNER—1864.

James Wallace Runner was born at Jerusalem, Yates Co. N. Y., May 5, 1852. His parents were James S. and Nancy A. Runner. He came to Oceana Co. with his parents in 1864, the coming of this family, which included seven children, occasioning the formation of a new school district (No. 2 of Shelby) which at this time has a school population of 489. The farm upon which the family settled is still known as the J. S. Runner farm, and is at present occupied by Mr. J. M. Runner, a brother of James W. The subject of our sketch followed farming and teaching until 1877, when he engaged in his present business, drugs and stationery, at Shelby village. By strict attention to business he has succeeded in establishing a good trade and has secured to himself a wide circle of intimate friends. He has held the position of Assessor of the school district, a position requiring good judgment and one usually conferred because of a reputation for honesty and integrity. On Nov. 6, 1875, Mr. Runner was married to Amelia E. Loomis, and two sons have been born to them.

JOHN M. RUNNER—1864.

John M. Runner was born at Cameron, Steuben Co., N. Y., July 13, 1856. He is another of the sons of James S. and Nancy A. Runner. He came with his parents and family to this county in 1864. He has always followed the business of farming and is now living upon and working the J. S. Runner farm. He is one of a family that has always borne a good name for honesty and industry wherever known, and is not behind the other members in this respect. On April 8, 1880, he was married to Miss Millie Carpp, of Van Buren Co. Two children, both boys, have blessed their union, coming to make glad the hearts of their parents who take great pride in them.

MYRON A. GILBERT—1864.

M. A. GILBERT.

Myron A. Gilbert was born Dec. 28, 1845, at Canaan, Wayne Co., Ohio. He is a son of J. W. and Rachel DeMoss Gilbert. In 1855, with his parents, he moved to Medina Co., Ohio, and in 1864 came to Oceana Co., arriving in Pentwater on April 18th. They lived one year on what is known as the Fuller farm in the township of Hart. In the spring of 1865 they moved into Benona (now Shelby) on the Geo. Piper farm. That summer Mr. J. W. Gilbert built one of the best log houses ever built in the county, and also a small blacksmith shop. In the early winter of 1866 he went back to Ohio to see "the girl I left behind me," and on Jan.

1, 1867, was married to Miss M. J. McConaughy. In Feb. of the same year he brought his bride to this county and has since resided here. In Feb., 1868, they moved upon the northeast quarter of section 31, Shelby, where they now live. His patent for this land was signed by President U. S. Grant. Mr. Gilbert is the father of four daughters and one son. Three daughters and the son are now living upon the old farm, which consists of ninety acres of land, seventy acres of which is well adapted for fruit raising. He has already twelve acres of peaches, pears, plums and o'her fruit. Mr. Gilbert is an enthusiastic member of Shelby Lodge No. 344 I. O. O. F., and is highly respected by all. He spends much of his time at Shelby village being engaged in well digging and putting in and repairing pumps.

HENRY ABSON —1864.

Henry Abson was born in Yorkshire, England, Aug. 26, 1844. His parents were Anthony and Mary Abson. He came to Oceana County in 1864 and settled in the then backwoods of Leavitt township. In the fall of 1864 he helped to cut the now well traveled road from Hazen Leavitt's to what is known as Sayles and Bean marsh. In Jan. 1865, he went to reside with Dr. J. J. Kittridge at Crystal, where he remained until Oct. of the same year, in the meantime chopping the first ten acres upon Mr. Kittridge's farm and assisting in building his house. After leaving Crystal in the fall of 1865 he returned to Pennsylvania where he remained until 1869, when he again came to this county and located in Leavitt where he still resides. He has held the offices of Township Clerk and Treasurer and is a man generally respected by all who know him. Mar. 18, 1865, he was married to Miss Ellen L. Gilbert and they have had born to them two sons and one daughter.

JESSE BEARSS—1865.

Jesse Bearss was born at Welland, Ont., in 1837. His parents' names were Joseph and Susan Bearss. He came to Oceana County in 1865. Bought his present home in Shelby township in 1867 and the following year commenced its improvement. In 1868 he married Miss Libbie Morningstar, of Welland, Ont., and there were born to them three children, two daughters and one son. On Dec. 18, 1876, his wife died. Dec. 29, 1879, he was again married. Miss Fannie Beam, of Welland, Ont., became his second wife and bore him two children, one son and one daughter. Feb. 11, 1883, he had the misfortune to again lose his wife. On March 2, 1886, he married his present wife, Miss Anna Lord, of Erie. N. Y., and one daughter has been born to them. Mr. Bearss chopped the timber on the land where the Shelby school house now stands. He became a citizen of the United States June 18, 1868. In 1870 he was elected Highway Commissioner and held the office eleven years. In 1879 elected School Inspector, holding that office three years. Elected Justice in 1881, held the office three years. In 1885 was elected Supervisor of Shelby, which office he still holds. Upon the Board of Supervisors he is an influential member. He has been a hard worker and many are the hunting and fishing expeditions that he has taken. He is of jovial disposition, inclined to look upon the bright side of life at all times.

JESSE BEARSS.

WILLIAM A. ROUNDS—1865.

William A. Rounds was born at Garrettsville, Portage Co., Ohio, Nov. 1, 1843. He is a son of William and Louisa Rounds. At the breaking out of the rebellion he enlisted in Co. C 16th U. S. Infand served to the close of the war. On July 6, 1865 he landed in Pentwater and has made his home here since then with the exception of a short time. He first commenced work at Pentwater for Richmond & Bean, and afterwards for Sands & Maxwell. He was also engaged for sometime in running a dray line at Pentwater and for six years had charge of Slocum's coal dock for the Engelmann line. In

W. A. ROUNDS.

the spring of 1888 he purchased a livery business and has since followed that business. He has the only livery and feed stable at Pentwater and also runs a stage line between Pentwater and Ludington during the winter season when the boats cannot run. He is a member of Oceana Lodge No. 200 F. & A. M., Oceana Chapter No. 56 R. A. M., and of Pentwater Lodge No. 378 I. O. O. F. May 29, 1867, he married Miss Emma Graham, and they have since had three children, two sons and one daughter. One of the sons has since died. Mr. Rounds has held the positions of Deputy Sheriff of the county, Treasurer and Constable of the township, and Village Marshal. As a police officer he is not excelled, having always been considered one of the best in the township.

CHARLES SERFLING—1865.

Charles Serfling, born in Germany; Dec. 31, 1850, is a son of Herman and Emma Serfling. He came to America at the age of thirteen years, and to Oceana Co. in the year 1865, in June. Mr. Serfling has been engaged in farming since coming to this county. At the annual election in 1879, he was elected Township Clerk of Greenwood and re-elected each year thereafter until '87 when he was elected to the office of Supervisor which office he still holds. On June 7, '75 he married Mary B. Devyer, and their family now consists of two sons. When an officer is re-elected term after term for twelve years, we can draw but one conclusion and that is that he has proven himself to be an efficient and faithful officer.

C. SERFLING.

JACOB WILLIAMSON—1865.

Jacob Williamson, the present Supervisor of Otto Township, was born Jan. 3, 1836, at Milna, Jeff. Co., N. Y. His parents were John and Margaret Williamson. He enlisted in the army in Co. C 94th N. Y. Vols., and was in the battles of Cedar Mountain, Chancellorville, Mine Run, Cold Harbor and before Petersburg. He is now a member of R. M. Johnson Post No. 138 of Ferry. He was one of the earlier settlers of Oceana Co., coming here in Oct., 1865. He has been honored in his township by nearly all the different offices, having been Supervisor fourteen years, Treasurer two years, Clerk one year, Supt. of Schools two years and Highway Commissioner. In all of the offices he has discharged his duties faithfully and with ability. His occupation is that of a farmer. Aug. 4, 1857, he married Tryphena Becker, and one son has blessed their union. As a member of the Board of Supervisors he has an influence that is acknowledged by all.

WILLIAM MCMILLAN—1865.

William McMillan, one of the early settlers of the township of Golden, was born in County Antrim, Ireland, on the 3rd day of Feb., 1835. His parents' names were David and Susan McMillan.

WM. MCMILLAN.

He came to America in 1863, and after spending some time in Lenawee Co., Mich., and in Indiana he came to Oceana Co. in Nov. 1865. He soon located in Golden township and commenced the erection of a log house and the clearing up of his land This log house he continued to occupy for fifteen years and then had things in such shape that he could afford a better one, building one of the most commodious frame houses in the township. He has always remained upon the same farm improving and adding to it, and now has 160 acres of land on section eight. On one three acre piece he has 500 peach trees, and on another three acres he has plums, apples, etc. He raises annually from 300 to 400 bushels of wheat and 200 to 300 bushels of oats. He is a man esteemed by all who know him, and the confidence of his neighbors has been manifested by making him Director of School District No. 2 for the past fifteen years. In 1867 he was married to Miss Mary White, and six children have been added to the family, two sons and four daughters.

SIDNEY S. BRANCH—1865.

Sidney S. Branch was born in York, Medina Co., Ohio, Feb. 20,

1842. His father, Levi H. Branch, was an old pioneer of the State having moved there at an early age, with his parents, from Genesee County, N. Y. His mother was from Massachusetts. On May 26, 1861, Mr. Branch enlisted in the 8th Ohio Vols., and served over 3 years. He was in the battles of Winchester, Antietam (where he was wounded in the head). Chancellorville, Gettysburg, Mine Run and the Wilderness, where he was wounded in the heel. He was mustered out July 13, 1864. He remained in Ohio about a year, and in 1865 settled on section 21, Golden township, Oceana County, Mich., where he has since lived. He married, Nov. 22, 1873, Miss Anna M. Hudson of LaPorte Co., Ind., by whom he has two children: Edna E.born Oct. 27, 1876, and Eda M., born April 23, 1879. Miss Hudson was born in Laporte County, Ind., Jan. 10, 1844. Her father was a farmer and carpenter, and in easy circumstances. Mr. Branch has a very fine farm, his specialty being fruit growing.

S. S. BRANCH.

DANIEL W. CROSBY--1864.

Dan'l W. Crosby was born at Barrington, Yates Co., N. Y., Oct. 1, 1833. He is a son of Selah and Frances Crosby. His early years were passed upon a farm until of age. He then taught school as his health would permit until 1866. He came to this county in April, '64, and has resided here and is identified with the prosperity of the county since that time. He came here as a teacher to the Indians and taught in the Cob-moo-sa school house. Has held various offices, and is now Representative in the State Legislature from this county. In 1880 was census enumerator, and represented this county on the last State Equalization Board. Married Oct. 6, 1863, Agnes Colestock, and has five children, three sons and two daughters. See page 221.

FREDERIK NIELSEN—1865.

Frederik Nielsen was born at Aaarhuus, Denmark, Europe, Nov. 16, 1844. His early training was of the strict character peculiar to European countries, but laid the foundation for business habits that has brought success to him in later years. He received a good education while at home and became proficient in different languages including the German and English. He came to Pentwater in 1865, which at that period contained many residents natives of Norway, Sweden and Denmark. These people selected Mr. Nielsen as their spokesman and adviser in all their intricate transactions arising under their new social and government relations. In 1871 he visited his old home in Denmark and returning became a member of the firm of C. Jensen & Co. The business of this firm was successful. It built the first brick store in Pentwater. It com-

FREDERIK NIELSEN.

manded a large trade and in 1877 was dissolved by mutual consent. The same year with Wm. E. Ambler he engaged in banking business under the firm name of Nielsen & Co. (see page 76). He acted as cashier and general manager for this institution, which has attained an enviable reputation and which he still manages.

In 1872 he married Nina M. Bacon, who has proved to him a loving and faithful helpmeet. Two daughters have been born to them who are now just entering womanhood. One, Cecil, is a graduate of Pentwater Union Schools, and at present attending the Rockford Ills., Seminary. The other, Viva is still with her parents.

In 1871 he joined Oceana Lodge No. 200 F. & A. M., and has since advanced to membership in the following branches: Chapter and Council, Pentwater; Muskegon Commandery; The DeWitt Clinton Consistory (32nd degree), Grand Rapids, and Saladin's Temple, Grand Rapids.

Politically he is a democrat, although not an active partisan. He is not an office seeker, but has many times been honored by office. He has served on the school Board from 1876 to the present time, except one year. Has been Village President five years, having been elected to that office each of the five years in succession and without opposition.

Mr. Nielsen is patriotic, charitable and enterprising. He is a loyal citizen of his adopted country and takes an active interest in its affairs. His charity is unostentatious, but of a character that is appreciated by its recipient. Every public enterprise in the village has found a ready backer in him, to which he has contributed not only in money but his active influence. He enjoys a large circle of friends who respect him not only for his social qualities, but his sound and practical views.

CHARLES M. UNDERHILL.—1865.

Charles M. Underhill, son of A. J. and Elizabeth Underhill, was born at Pentwater, on Dec. 25, 1865, where he has since resided. He received his education at the Pentwater High School, graduating in 1884, being the first male to graduate from that institution. attended the Michigan Agricultural College at Lansing one year, and the Metropolitan College at Chicago. one winter. In 1887-8 he was elected and served as Recorder of the village of Pentwater and is now Supervisor of the township. He is a member of the Masonic fraternity and a leading member of the I. O.

O. F. fraternity, being the present Noble Grand of Pentwater Lodge No. 378. He is an Oceana County production that the county need not be ashamed of, being a young man of good business ability and possessing many friends.

JONATHAN H. CRITCHETT—1866.

Jonathan H. Critchett was born in Ashland Co., Ohio, Dec. 3, 1843. His parents were Benjamin and Sarah Ann Critchett. When three years of age removed with his parents to Dekalb Co., Ind. He remained at home working on a farm until Aug., 1862, when he enlisted in Co. A 100th Ind. Vols. While in the army his parents died and the home was sold, the other members of the family being scattered to seven different States. He returned from the army to Dekalb Co. and took up his residence with a sister. Afterward he removed to Allen Co., where he made his home with relatives until his marriage on Feb. 13, 1866, to Mary Hurnie. Soon after his marriage he came to Oceana Co., homesteaded eighty acres of land, cleared some, planted spring crops and went to Indiana for his wife, arriving here again July 7th. Remained on homestead two years, sold out and in company with others went to Missouri. Returned here in Nov., 1868, purchased forty acres near his old home and moved on the place the same month, into a twelve by sixteen board shanty. His effects when he returned from Mo. were contained in two old trunks. Sold this place in spring of 1883 for $2,500, and soon after purchased the farm of E. O. Peck, in Ferry township, where he now lives. His wife died March 21, '87, leaving seven sons, five of whom continued to reside with their father until he was married again. Dec. 25, 1889, he was married to Miss Morr, of Hesperia. Mr. Critchett has been a member of the M. E. and U. B. Churches, in which he was Class Leader and Sunday School Superintendent. Has held various small offices of trust in his township. Was elected Township Treasurer in 1888-9.

J. H. CRITCHETT.

HARVEY J. CHADWICK—1866.

Harvey Jenner Chadwick, M. D., son of M. R. Chadwick, M. D., a son of R. M. Chadwick, recruiting officer in the British army, was born at Mt. Aetna Ind., Feb. 11, 1857; came to Hart in '66; began the study of medicine at 17 years of age; attended Rush Medical College, Chicago, at 19; graduated at the Michigan College of Medicine in Detroit at the age of 24 years. He was elected by his class Vice President of the Michigan College of Medicine Alumni Association; was made a member of the Michigan State Medical Society; later became a member of the Pere Marquette Medical Society. Passed the examination of the Michigan State Board of Pharmacy. Was elected by his township Health Officer and School Inspector, and has been President of the Village of Hart. He married Laura Estelle Teeple, Oct. 1, 1885. Their little daughter Eva, now three years of age, makes them happy.

H. J. CHADWICK.

WILLIAM VAUGHAN—1866.

William Vaughan was born in the State of New York, June 8, 1835. He is a son of Thomas W. and Elmina Vaughan. On Sept. 20, 1862, he married Elizabeth Washer and they have had a family of eight children, three sons and five daughters. Mr. Vaughan came to this county at a comparatively early day Aug. 3, 1866, and has done his portion towards reducing the wilderness to civilization. His business previous to coming here was lumbering and river-driving, but since he has confined himself to farming. The confidence of the people has been manifested by his election to the office of township Treasurer which he held for two terms. He is a man of firm convictions, a free thinker and considers free thought necessary to the preservation of a republican form of government.

CHARLES R. WHITTINGTON—1859.

The subject of this sketch was born in Hampshire, Isle of Wight, England, Jan. 12, 1835. His father was accidentally killed before our subject's birth. In 1845 his mother married again a man by the name of Dove, and the same year came to America, bringing Charles. He lived in Port Huron fourteen years and moved to Pentwater Sept. 6, 1859, and commenced work for Charles Mears at $20 per month. Out of his wages he had to board himself and family. On Sept. 27, 1856, he married Miss Jane Whittington, an estimable lady, who has shared with him the trials of pioneer life, and borne him three children one son and two daughters, all grown to man and womanhood and happily situated.

C. R. WHITTINGTON.

Mr. Whittington moved his family upon the land he now owns on Sec. 6, Hart township, in the winter when the snow was several feet deep and for six weeks his wife never saw a white person. He helped clear the Asa Pringle farm, the first clearing made in the vicinity of Mears. He helped put the first load of dirt on the old mill dam at Hart, and was a member of the noted Peck's logging crew which was never beaten in a fallow.

He is a good business man, is comfortably situated, has a pleasant home and is highly esteemed. He helped to organize the first Fire Department in Pentwater which he belonged to for ten years, and of which he was Foreman of Hose five years and Chief three years. Has been Township Treasurer two years, Village Treasurer three years, and member of the Common Council eight years.

EDWARD B. FLAGG—1860.

Edward B. Flagg, the son of Henry C. and Lucy H. Flagg, was born in Hartford, Conn., June 11, 1842. His ancestors were of the old puritan stock, one of them (Brewster) having come to America in the May Flower. The son of one of the most prominent of the county's pioneers, he also has figured largely in the social and municipal development of the county. He came to the county in 1860, and has since, with the exception of a few short intervals, resided here. June 21, 1862, in Chicago, he married Carrie Johnson. The union has been blessed with four children, two daughters and two sons. He has filled many of the local offices in the village; has served five terms as Village Recorder, and is at the present time a member of the Common Council. In 1888 he joined Oceana Lodge No. 200 F. & A. M., and has since passed the different chairs and is now serving as Master of the Lodge. Mr. Flagg has an active mind, a reliable memory, is a good penman, accurate and quick in figures. He is at present assistant to Mr. Nielsen in Nielsen & Co.'s bank.

E. B. FLAGG.

EDWIN NICKERSON—1865.

Edwin Nickerson, son of Elihu and Mary Nickerson, was born March 17, 1835, in Canada West. When three years of age moved with his parents to Cattaraugus County, New York, where they remained for about two years, then went to Lake Co., Ind., remaining there until 1848, when they came to Allegan Co., Mich. At the breaking out of the war he enlisted in Co. E 3rd Mich. Inf. and served two years and ten months as Sergeant. At the close of the war in June, 1865, he came to Pentwater where he has since resided. Mr. Nickerson's early life was spent upon farms; after coming to Pentwater he became interested in the planing mill which he continued for about five years, then formed a copartnership with Thos. Collister in the lumber business, which he has since continued. In 1876 the firm built a grist mill at Pentwater, which was burned in 1884, and a new and larger mill was immediately built upon same

site and roller process machinery put in. Mr. Nickerson has always been a public spirited man, energetic in his business affairs. He has been Supervisor of his township one term, and President of the village three terms. Has also served upon the School Board eight years. He was married Dec. 24, 1873, to Miss Maria A. Carmichael. They now have two children, Stella and Nettie.

E. NICKERSON.

JOHN M. CAHILL—1864.

John M. Cahill was born in Limerick Co., Ireland, June 21, 1842, to Daniel and Mary Cahill. He received a good common school education and emigrated to America in the summer of 1863. He went direct to Washington, D. C., and found employment in the Quarter Master's Dept., where he remained one year, then went to Chicago, staid a few months and moved to Pentwater, Oceana Co., arriving Dec. 31, 1864. In April, 1865, he enlisted in the Quarter Master's Dept. and was detailed for duty at Little Rock, Ark., where he was discharged for disability in Aug. of the same year. Afterwards he worked in the lumber woods, saw mills and on the river driving logs. In '73 he went to Chicago and was employed upon the regular police force until 1 '76, when he again returned to Pentwater, broken in health. He regained his health and has since resided here. Since his return he has kept saloon and for two years a barber shop. Aug. 27, 1868, he was married to Katie McAndrew, of Lower Canada, and after her decease, Feb. 27, 1881, he married Ellen McAndrew, of the same place. Seven children, three sons and four daughters, have been born to him. He is

J. M. CAHILL.

a democrat and quite a politician. Has held the positions of Harbor Master, Justice of the Peace, and is at present a member of the Common Council.

HENRY J. MARSH—1862.

Henry J. Marsh was born at Clarendon, Ruttana Co., Vt. and is a son of Henry and Sarah L. Marsh. He came to Oceana County in 1862, and since that time has spent more or less of his time in the county, and since 1880 has resided here permanently. He is a man who has made many friends and possesses much influence in his section. He resides and has a store at what is known as Marshville in Benona township, being also Postmaster of the office of that name. His wife is a lady of much refinement of person and manners. She was born in New

H. J. MARSH.

York City, and is a daughter of Theophilus L. and Anna Smith Houghton. She first came to this county in May, 1880. Mr. and Mrs. Marsh have a fine home, their house being large and commodious, a landmark in that section. Mr. Marsh owns a large tract of land in Benona.

MRS. H. J. MARSH.

T. S. GURNEY—1866.

See page 218.

A. L. CARR—1866.

A. L. Carr was born in St. Lawrence Co., N. Y., Feb. 6, 1841; settled in Weare, section 36, in 1866. He is quite an extensive farmer paying considerable attention to fruit culture, having some 20 acres of different varieties. Married, Feb. 8, 1865, Amelia L. Hazelton, who was born in St. Lawrence Co., N. Y., May 28, 1843, and died Feb. 1, 1875, leaving three children, Bower M., Etta P., Edgar A. Second marriage, March 1, 1876, to Naomi A. Ervin, who was born in Camden, Ont., Jan. 31, 1846. Mr. Carr is a Director and Vice President of the Oceana Co. Savings Bank. He is a prominent Mason, having been Master of Wigton Lodge No. 251, three years.

A. L. CARR.

WM. COOPER—1866.

William Cooper, son of Jas. K. and Eleanor Cooper, was born at Vienna, Ont., July 8, 1851. In Nov., 1866, he came to Oceana Co. and settled in Elbridge. He has always been an active, public spirited man and has been honored with various offices, now being Sheriff of the county, and has served as Under Sheriff. He owns one of the best forties in Elbridge and also ten acres within the limits of Hart village where he now makes his home. He is improving his land as fast as possible, and is setting out fruit trees of different varieties upon both places. His business now in connection with his duties as Sheriff is that of a contract-

WM. COOPER.

or and builder. On Jan. 1, 1873, he was married to Miss M. Hannum, and they now have two children, a son and a daughter. Mr. Cooper has given good satisfaction as Sheriff, and has made during his residence in the county many warm personal friends.

EDWARD B. GAYLORD—1866.

Edward B. Gaylord was born at Harpersfield, N. Y., June 9, 1845. His parents were Levi S. and Julia A. Gaylord. He came to this county in Oct., 1866 and engaged in farming. July 19, '80 he began the hardware business at Shelby village which he has since continued together with carrying on his farming operations. He has been twice Treasurer of the county in which office he gave the best of satisfaction. On March 17, 1870, he married Miss Miranda Jackson and four children, two sons and two daughters have been born to them: Truman P., Grace B., Gladys and E. Gardiner. Mar. 12, 1881, they had the misfortune to lose by death their daughter Grace B. As a straightforward business man Mr. Gaylord has always stood high in his community. As a gentleman all are pleased to make his acquaintance, and as a public spirited citizen he has exercised a positive influence on the history of the county.

E. B. GAYLORD.

JOEL D. LINSDAY—1866.

Joel D. Linsday, son of David and Anna Dayton Linsday, was born in Onondaga Co., N. Y., Oct. 5, 1822. He came to Michigan in 1836, settling in Branch Co., where he assisted in building the first log house in Butler township in that county. He remembers distinctly one incident that happened to him while living there by which he was frightened nearly out of his senses. While on his way to the shanty one day to prepare dinner, he espied an Indian with his gun leveled at him. He was not noted before that as a rapid runner, but thereafter his fame in that line was much increased. He considers it the greatest "running effort" of his life. He came to this county on Oct. 31, 1866, and located in the township of Claybanks, section 25, where he has since resided. He has always followed the business of farming. He now has a fine farm with good improvements, including one of the finest farm residences in the township. The voters of his township have made him at different times Supervisor, Clerk, Treasurer and Justice, the latter office being held by him for 24 years. On May 6, 1846, he married Polly H. Peabody, who died Aug. 25, 1856. On July 4, 1857, he married Eunice A. Draper. He has been the father of seven children, four sons and three daughters. He is now well along on the journey of life and in looking back can see many places where he has contributed his share to make the roses bloom.

JAMES E. PHILO—1866.

J. E. PHILO.

James E. Philo was born at Frankfort, Herkimer Co., N. Y., Mar. 3, 1843, being a son of Elisha R and Phebe Philo. At the age of ten years he commenced life upon a canal, continuing that occupation until he was twenty years of age. He then started West after putting in nearly a year in the quarter Master's Department in the army. He worked at any occupation that would yield him good wages, reaching Oceana Co. Nov. 1, 1866. Since coming here he has worked in lumber woods and taught school. May 3, 1868, he married Samantha Holcomb. They have had five children, two sons and three daughters. For the past 12 years Mr. Philo has been engaged in teaching and farming. He has held a number of offices in his township, among them Superintendent of Schools, Justice and Supervisor. He is now a member of the Board of Supervisors from the township of Newfield. Mr. Philo is in every respect a perfect gentleman and a man whose opinions being founded upon good sense, command attention.

FRANK O. GARDNER—1866.

Frank O. Gardner, today one of the leading business men of Pentwater, was born in Medina Co., Ohio, Feb. 28, 1844. He is a son of Henry and Elizabeth Gardner. He came to the township of Golden, Oceana Co., in Nov., 1866, and for two years was engaged in working in the lumber woods, clearing land and building houses. He then bought what was known as the "Dutch Boys" mill and has since that time been engaged in manufacturing lumber and shingles. Some time later the mill burned and he came to Pentwater and purchased the Bailey & Worden mill and opened a general merchandise store. He has since continued a resident of the village of Pentwater where he now owns considerable property and continues in the mill business also running a general store, at which he enjoys a good trade. Mr. Gardner has always been a public spirited man but has positively declined to accept political offices. He has since starting in business employed an average of thirty men continuously. He donated the land, hauled the lumber and logs for the second and third school houses built in the township of Golden. He also served his country in her time of need, being 1st Sergeant of Co. E. 10th Ohio Cav., and in Co. K, 84th Ohio Inf., serving in all 1,118 days. May 31, 1874, he was married to Miss Carrie A. Aubrey, at Pentwater, and four children have born to them, three sons and one daughter. Mr. and Mrs. Gardner are highly respected by all who know them.

F. O. GARDNER.

JOHN B. GEBHART—1866.

John B. Gebhart was born at Lebanon, Pa., Sept. 17, 1819. His parents were John and Barbara Gebhart. His father was a farmer and shoemaker, going about from house to house for the latter purpose. The family moved to Montgomery Co., Ohio, when our subject was six years of age. There he continued to live upon the farm until of age when he rented the farm and did business on his own account for six years. He then bought the farm and carried it on for another six years, then sold and moved to Huntington Co., Ind., where he lived four years, then sold and came to Oceana Co., arriving here Oct. 14, 1866. He came here because it was healthy here. At that time there were not to exceed a dozen houses in Hart village. After coming here he lived one season on the Ben Reed farm, one summer on the Whittington farm, and then on section 29, Hart, where he remained one year. He then bought tax title on forty acres on section 30, Hart, where he now lives. The second year thereafter he secured homestead papers on that and an adjoining forty. As soon as he had one and one-half acres cleared he commenced setting fruit trees plums, pears and peaches, and now has two peach trees of these first he set that have borne peaches since they were four years old and measure 11 and 12½ inches respectively in diameter. He has kept adding to the orchard and now has 23 acres of peaches, four acres of apples and peaches, and six acres of plums, all bearing. He is one of the men who have made a success of fruit raising, and now has a fine fruit farm with convenient and commodious buildings. In 1845 he married Angeline Philabaum, who died in 1889. They had nine children, seven sons and two daughters.

J. B. GEBHART.

JEPTHA WRIGHT—1866.

Jeptha Wright was born in Steuben Co., Ind., Dec. 7, 1847. His parents were Herman and Jemima Wright. At the breaking out of the war he enlisted in Co. B, 12th Ind. Cav., and served as a private nearly thirty-three months. During his service in the army he had the misfortune to lose his right eye, an honorable scar of which any one might be proud. At the time he was serving in the army of the Cumberland and was at the time engaged in a scouting expedition in the vicinity of Huntsville, Ala., at a place known as the

"Big Cone." The squad he was with was ambushed by "Bushwhackers." The fighting for a time was fast and furious, and in the melee Mr. Wright received a wound in the head which deprived him of his right eye, was wounded in the hip by a ball from a heavy rifle and his horse was killed and fell upon him. The rebels drew him out from under his horse and proceeded to divest him of spurs, boots and clothing, thinking he was dead. After forming their companies which had been scattered by the company to which Mr. Wright belonged cutting its way out of the ambush, the leader of the Bushwhackers discovered that he was alive and assisted him to a mud-puddle where he washed off the blood and entertained him with the news that the ball had penetrated his skull and that he could not live. He also in-

J. WRIGHT.

formed him that he wanted to send a message to the Union forces, and if he would like to undertake it he might do so. Mr. Wright consenting he informed him where he could find a horse at a plantation near by. After much difficulty and great suffering he succeeded in reaching the Union lines at Vienna, a small inland town twelve miles from Brownsborough, upon the railroad. He was well pleased to again get back with the boys in blue, but was compelled to lie at the stockades from July 8th until the middle of August, when he was taken to Huntsville, the ball extracted from his hip, and then sent to a hospital in Nashville. In Oct., 1864, he was able to return home upon a furlough, and remaining home but thirty days he returned to the front and was mustered out June 1, 1865. We insert this sketch of Mr. Wright's experiences because it gives an idea of the sufferings so many of our brave boys endured at the front. In March, 1866, Mr. Wright came to this county, locating in Shelby township. On Nov. 30, 1871, he married Miss Mary L. Vradenburg and they now have two children, a son and a daughter. They now reside on Sec. nine, having twenty-four acres of land all improved, and commodious house and other buildings. He also has about seven acres of orchard. The farm is within the limits of Shelby village and Mr. Wright is one of the present members of the Common Council. He is a member of Shields Post No. 68, G. A. R., Shelby.

SAMUEL E. LEWIS—1866.

Samuel E. Lewis, a son of Moses and Harriet Lewis, was born at Fredonia, Chautauqua Co., N. Y. He was for three years a soldier fighting in defense of his country's honor, being a member of Co. I, 112th N. Y. Inf. In April, 1866, when this county was in its infancy he came here and has since made his home among us, now residing upon a farm in the township of Benona. On March 18, 1867, he married Miss Adelle Wilson, and two sons have born to them. He is now well situated and possessed of many friends.

MRS. WILLIAM TUTTLE—1866.

MRS. WM. TUTTLE.

Mrs. William Tuttle was the daughter of John and Margaret (Williams) Hughes, her father an Englishman and her mother a native of North Wales. She was born in N. Wales, March 3, 1814, and came to America with her parents Oct. 25, 1832. They settled on a farm near Palmyra, Portage Co., Ohio, where she married William Tuttle. In 1854, with her husband she moved to Michigan and located on a large farm south of Ionia, where they lived until 1866, when they moved to Pentwater. Mr. Tuttle died in Pentwater shortly after their arrival. She has two daughters Mrs. T. Collister and Mrs. P. Hanifin, and one son, Andrew P. She is still in the enjoyment of good health and bids fair to comfort her children many years.

MRS. THOMAS COLLISTER—1866.

Mrs. Thomas Collister was born in Palmyra, Portage Co., O. She

is a daughter of Wm. (deceased) and Elizabeth Tuttle, now living with
her, and was born Feb. 4,
1852. She moved with her
parents to Michigan in 1854,
south of Ionia, where she
spent her youthful days. Her
father's health began to decline and he was advised to
make his residence near the
lake, and moved to Pentwater in 1866, she accompanying
her parents. He did not survive long, however. Mrs. Collister became a Christian in
early life. She lived with her
married sister, Mrs. Hanifin,
until her marriage. She was
married to Thomas Collister
Oct. 15, 1873, and remained
his faithful, loving companion until death called him,
which took place Nov. 22,
1889. Mr. Collister left his
widow in comfortable circumstances. She is still a resident of Pentwater and much esteemed.

MRS. T. COLLISTER.

JOHN W. ROBINSON—1866.

J. W. ROBINSON.

John W. Robinson was born at South Bend, Ind., April 1, 1856. He arrived with his parents in Oceana Co. on the 20th day of Oct., 1866. In 1870 he engaged in shingle manufacturing which business he followed until May, 1886, when he bought out the mercantile business of O. C. Stetson, at Walkerville, which he has continued up to the present time. His business has gradually increased from the time of his first taking possession of it. In 1886 he did over $12,000; 1887,

$20,000, and 1888, $25,000 business. He has been so long in the county that he is well acquainted with pioneer life. He was at the first town meeting of Leavitt, and in the fall of 1866 when ten years of age assisted in cutting a road a distance of seven miles to their homestead. In 1878, April 2nd, he married Miss Nellie E. Morris, a daughter of Rees T. Morris of Golden. They have one child, a son.

CALEB B. DAVIS—1866.

Caleb B. Davis, son of John and Betty Davis, was born on the 24th day of Feb., 1809, in Monongalia Co., Va. In his early manhood he became a minister of the gospel of our blessed Lord and has preached many sermons during his life. On Dec. 16, 1831, he was married to Sarah Wagner, and ten children, six sons and four daughters have been born to them. After his marriage he commenced farming, which he has continued to the present time. In 1866 he made this county his home and has seen much of the past struggles of its pioneers. He expresses himself as much pleased with the county on account of the good agricultural advantages, health and climate, and states that if he had another life to lead he would spend it all here. Full of years and the memory of pleasant days he still lives to enjoy the friendship and esteem of those who surround him.

C. B. DAVIS.

JOHN R. BUTLER—1866.

John R. Butler was born at Andover, Ohio, June 17, 1835, to Geo. and Ruth Butler. He acquired a good commercial education but chose farming for his occupation. He came to Oceana County in May, 1866, settling in the township of Hart. He improved and still owns a very fine farm situated about one mile from the village. Politcally he is a republican, but by reason of a pleasing address, frank and cordial ways he is very popular with all classes. He has held the office of County Treasurer thirteen years, and always performed the duties to the satisfaction of the people. After being re-elected treasurer several times he took up his residence permanently in the village, where he has built and with his wife enjoys one of the finest houses in the county. Since 1870 he has been engaged in the abstract of title business, he and T. S. Gurney owning the only set of abstract books in the county. Dec. 17, 1857, Mr. Butler was united in marriage to Delia M. Baker. The union was a happy one. One daughter was born to them, who is now the wife of a rising young attorney in Minneapolis, Minn. Socially Mr. Butler is one of the most agreeable of persons, and his presence always adds to the pleasure of any social gathering. He is quite gray although just in the prime of vigorous manhood.

J. R. BUTLER.

WILLIAM F. LEWIS—1866.

William F. Lewis was born in Chautauqua Co., N. Y., Dec. 12, 1829. Settled in Shelby. Sec. 31, 1866. Married, March 24, 1852, to Eliza Frazine, who was born Aug. 8, 1828, and died Mar. 3, 1882. Three children, Wm. F., born Sept. 15, 1853, died Feb. 11, 1869; George, born Sept. 26, 1855, died Aug. 21, 1876; Eugene, born March 17. 1860, and married, Apr. 20, '81 to Alzine Green, who was born in Noble Co., Ind., May 2, 1860. Has been Pres. of Oceana Co. Ag. Society, N. G. of I. O. O. F., and is now Pres. of the Co. Association of P. of I.

WILLIAM HILES—1867.

WM. HILES.

MRS. WM. HILES.

William Hiles was born at Dryden, Tompkins Co., N. Y., July 22, 1821. He is a son of John and Rosanna Allbright Hiles. On Jan. 23, '53, he was married to Miss Roxy A. Culver, a daughter of Rev. Simon B. and Betsey Vincent Culver, and was born at Hartford, Cortland Co., N. Y., July 4, 1836. The result of this union has been four children, two sons and two daughters. Mr. and Mrs. Hiles came to Oceana County in May, 1867 and he engaged in Lumbering which he continued until '80, when he retired from active business. That Mr. Hiles was an engeretic business man is evidenced by the fact that he has accumulated sufficient of this world's goods to maintain him during his declining years without the necessity of toil. He now resides at Shelby during the summer months and spends the winters South. It is no exaggeration to state that no persons in the county enjoy more fully the respect and esteem of their acquaintances than Mr. Hiles and the members of his family.

ARCHIE R. MCKINNON—1867.

Archie R. McKinnon was born at Masonville, Delaware Co. N. Y.,

A. R. McKINNON.

April 24, 1851. His parents were Archibald and Cordelia L. McKinnon. He came to Oceana County in the autumn of 1867, and commenced clearing up a farm on Sec. 26, Hart township. He afterwards took a position with the Chicago & West Michigan R. R. Co. and was for six years one of its most popular conductors. Later he purchased a hardware business at Shelby where he is now located. On Jan. 27, 1886, he was married to Miss Jessie McQuarrie, a lady who is now a great favorite in Shelby society and elsewhere where known. They have no children.

Mr. McKinnon is acquainted with pioneer life, having done his share towards driving back the forests, clearing fifty acres of land. He is acquainted with toil and is one of those who never hesitate to put their shoulders to the wheel when necessary. He is widely known, not as Mr. McKinnon, but as "Archie." Being the soul of honor, with frank and engaging manners, to know him is to be his friend. A good citizen, an honorable business man, and withal a self-made man, long may "Archie" live to enjoy the friendship of the numerous friends who surround him.

CLARK A. NOBLE—1867.

Clark A. Noble was born in the State of New York, July 21, 1839, being the son of Chauncey N. and Nancy Noble. He came to Oceana Co. in Jan., 1867, locating first at Pentwater and later at Crystal Valley. He married in May, 1869, Miss Linn Richards who was born in Pennsylvania, July 1, 1848. Her parents were Geo. W. and Mary B. Richards. Mr. Noble previous to 1875, was engaged in bookkeeping, clerking, insurance and patent right business. Since 1875 he followed the business of a scaler. He was for several years Postmaster at Crystal Valley. He has also been Superintendent of Schools, School Inspector and Township Clerk of Crystal township. Mr. Noble died from the effects of LaGrippe, April 12, 1890, leaving wife and three children, two sons and one daughter, to mourn his loss.

C. A. NOBLE.

W. D. ACKERSON—1867.

W. D. Ackerson is a Wolverine and a pioneer of this county. Born Jan. 22, 1849 in the township of Metamora, Lapeer Co., and residing with his parents, for different periods of time, in several places in the counties of Oakland, Wayne and Kent; Mar. 22, 1867, he arrived at Hart, having been four days on the road, driving two cows from Paris, Kent Co., his father (A. G. Ackerson) bringing the rest of the family and some goods through with the

team; having moved in most of the goods and a year's provisions the previous winter. Since Mr. Ackerson has been one of us he has spent the most of his time farming summers and teaching school winters until six years ago, when he engaged in his present occupation, photography. Many of the cuts in this book are copies of his work. On Dec. 1, 1883, he married Miss Mattie Davis, of Whitehall, Muskegon Co. He met with a clear loss of $450 in the great Hart fire of Jan. 13. 1889, which was a severe loss for him, but aside from the loss by fire, he has done what no other photographer ever did in Hart; he has made a living at his business, and has worked up so good a trade that it is now considered one of the best locations in the State.

DEWITT C. BENJAMIN—1867.

DeWitt C. Benjamin was born in Wayne Co., Ohio, Feb. 26, 1852. He is the eldest son of Ebenezer A. and Margaret Benjamin who reside in Weare township. He was raised upon a farm and has followed that vocation up to the present time. He came to Oceana Co. in April, 1867, and has resided here continuously since. On May 22, 1889, he was married to Miss Libbie Sage whose parents also reside in Weare. He has been School Inspector of his township. He now owns eighty acres of land on Section 17, Weare, upon which he has a comfortable house and a small barn. There is also upon his place an orchard of three hundred bearing trees, peach, apple, plum and pear.

D. C. BENJAMIN.

There is an improvement of forty-six acres altogether. He is known as a hard-working and honest man, having many friends among his neighbors and acquaintances.

JOHN WESTBROOK—1867.

John Westbrook was born in Castile, Wyoming Co., N. Y., Sept. 27, 1844. He is a son of S. K. and Mary Westbrook. He is also

J. WESTBROOK.

one of the old soldiers of our civil war, bearing an honorable wound which is noticeable to all who meet him. He was a member of Co. A, 104th N. Y. Vol. Inf. in which he served as a private about fifteen months. From Aug. 9th to Sept. 17th he was in seven battles and lost a leg at the battle of Antietam. In April, 1867, he came to Oceana Co., where he has since resided. On Sept. 26, 1868, he married Phebe A. Ballou, and they have one son and one daughter. Mr. Westbrook's business has been that of a glove-maker and farmer. At present he is engaged in the manufacture of broom handles. He has held several offices, such as Justice of the Peace, Township Treasurer, Highway Commissioner, Deputy Sheriff and Councilman. As an upright, honorable man his word is as good as his bond and no one hesitates to take either; hence it is not necessary for us to state that his friends are legion.

JOSEPH TYLER—1867.

Joseph Tyler was born at Sturgis, Mich., Dec. 24, 1835. He came to Oceana County in 1867, and commenced the clearing of a farm and cleared seventy acres half way between Hart and Shelby villages. In 1882 he sold his farm and engaged in the hardware business at Shelby where he continued for four years, then selling his business to Mr. A. R. McKinnon. He built and now owns the store building. He also owns a farm of 100 acres known as the old Peterson farm on the town line one and one-half

miles east of the State road in Shelby township. He lives in Shelby village, while his son Elmer conducts the farm. Mr. Tyler has been twice married. In 1859 to Roselia Blanchard, by whom he has one son and one daughter, the daughter now residing in California. His first wife dying in 1876, in 1877 he married his present wife, Janette Stevens, by whom he has one son. Mr. Tyler has always taken an interest in public affairs and in 1886 was elected Sheriff of the county. He has many friends in all parts of the Co.

CHARLES W. FISHER—1889.

Charles W. Fisher was born in Carbon Co., Pa., July 24, 1842. His parents were Jacob and Mary Fisher. At the the breaking out of the war he enlisted in Co. C, 3rd Penn. Cav. as a private and served three years and one month. In 1866, Dec. 19th, he married Miss Hannah J. Selser, and three children, one boy and two girls, now constitute their family. In June, 1867, he came to Oceana Co., spending about a year at Pentwater, then returning to Pennsylvania where he became Asst. Supt. of the Lehigh Valley Coal Co. He continued in that business for about ten years when he returned to this county, locating at Shelby and engaging in the hotel business, and for four years was known as landlord "Wes," being a popular landlord with all classes.

C. W. FISHER.

About a year ago Mr. Fisher quitted the hotel business to engage in the general mercantile business in which he still continues, and is meeting with fair success. He has been elected Constable of his township, and in March, 1890, was elected a Trustee of Shelby village. He is an ardent G. A. R. man, a warm-hearted citizen, and a kind husband and father. He enjoys as much as any man in Shelby the esteem and friendship of his neighbors.

JAMES H. SLATER—1867.

James H. Slater, the subject of this sketch, is a native Wolverine, having been born at Niles, Berrien Co., Mich., Nov. 12, 1832. He is a son of Henry J. and Lucy Slater. He came to Oceana Co. Aug. 15, 1867. He has followed different occupations, having been a grocer, hardware merchant and shoemaker. He is now engaged in the manufacture of artificial limbs, at which business he is kept busy, having more work in this line than one not acquainted with the business would suppose. Oct. 3, 1852, he was married to Miss Clarissa E. Wager, and one son and two daughters have blessed their union. Mr. Slater has done his part toward the maintenance of the Union of the States, having served as a private in Co. K, 83rd Ills. Inf. from Aug. 1, 1862, to July 5, 1865. He is at present prominent in G. A. R. affairs and is one of the Past Commanders of Joe Hooker Post, at Hart. As a civilian he has been called to various places of trust and honor, among them Township Clerk, Village Clerk and Village Marshal. He is a man who possesses in a marked degree the respect and esteem of all.

J. H. SLATER.

MARTIN BAKER—1867.

Martin Baker, the subject of this sketch, was born in Chautauqua Co., N. Y., March 20, 1829. He was one of five children of Thomas and Paulina Baker. His father died in Ripley, N. Y., April 14, '84, and his mother at Barcelona, N. Y., Sept. 10, 1889. Mr. Baker lived with his parents until he was twenty-two years of age, when the California gold excitement attracted him and he decided to try his fortune in the West. In 1852 he returned to his home and shortly afterward married Miss Azubah Graham. In 1854 he came to Michigan, settling in Hillsdale Co. where he engaged in photography remaining until 1859. In that year he removed to Ripley, Chautauqua Co., N. Y., and entered into the grocery and hardware business. He was successful in this business and continued it until '67, when he sold out and came to this county, locating in Claybanks, where he purchased a half interest in his brother Joseph's farm; also conducting a small tinshop. At this time he built the house where his family now reside. He resided upon the farm until the fall of 1880, when he removed to Montague, where on Aug. 26, 1881, he died. The remains were brought to Claybanks and buried in Mount Hope cemetery. The funeral sermon was preached by that old pioneer minister, Rev. A. A. Darling. Mr. Baker was honored and respected by all who knew him. He was for several years Supervisor of his township, and a leading member of the Grange. He left to mourn his death, a widow, one son, Frank L., three brothers, Levi, Joseph, and John W. Baker, and one sister, Mrs. John Barber, all now residents of Claybanks.

MARTIN BAKER.

EDWIN O. PECK, JR.—1867.

Edwin O. Peck, Jr., was born at Williamsfield, Ashtabula Co., O., Jan. 11, 1840. At the age of nine years he moved with his parents to Richmond, same county, where he remained upon a farm until 1860. On Oct. 14th of that year he was married to Miss Adelaide Landon, of Crawford Co., Pa. His effects at that time consisted of a horse and buggy, which were sold to purchase household goods. In Aug., 1863, he enlisted in Co. M, 2nd Ohio H. Art., leaving his wife and babe in the care of his and her parents. After 2 years of soldier life he was mustered out of the service

E. O. PECK.

at Nashville, Tenn. That same day, his babe, then three years old, died. In Sept., '75, he in company with his father, came to Oceana Co. There was at that time but one frame building, the old Court House, in Hart. He staid here about a week, then walked from Amos Putney's house in Ferry to Ferrysburg and took the train for home in Ohio. In Sept., 1867, he returned to Ferry where he has since resided. In April, 1873, his wife died leaving two little girls to his care, Maud E., aged six years and Laura J., aged four years. Mar. 29, 1874, he married Miss Matie Vanetten, and in Oct. 1877, their only child, Alida May, was born. His eldest child, Maud E., was married Feb. 20, 1887, to Henry Heim. Her health began to fail previous to her marriage, and on Dec. 23, 1889, after enduring with Christian fortitude much pain and suffering, she was called home where "the weary are at rest." Apr. 10, 1887, Laura J., his second daughter was married to Edwin D. Thomas, of Conneaut, Crawford Co., Pa. Mr. Peck has been an eye witness and an earnest helper of the development of Oceana Co., it being a wilderness when he came to it. He was a delegate to the County Convention that gave E. J. Reed the nomination for Sheriff, and since that time has taken an earnest interest in politics. His party owe him much for the work he has done in its behalf. He has held the offices of Supervisor, Highway Commissioner two terms, Justice two terms, Constable, and is now Deputy Sheriff. Most of his time in the county has been spent in the lumber woods and on river drives. He was Superintendent of the White River drives one year, making three drives in one season, something that he claims has never been accomplished before or since. This was during the summer of the Muskegon strikes and the strikers offered to work for him at reduced wages, but he refused to take them, continuing to keep the wages of his men up, thus securing the esteem of his men and good work.

EDWARD P. GREGORY—1867.

Edward P. Gregory was born at Guilford, Vt., Aug. 20, 1830. He is a son of Stephen and Hannah Gregory. He remained at the place of his birth until he was thirty-five years of age, then enlisted in Co. I, 8th Vt. Inf., and was mustered in as sergeant and served three years. He was at the battle of Port Hudson, La., which was an almost continuous fight for forty days. After the close of the war he went to Nebraska where he remained about one year, then coming to Oceana Co. in 1867, locating on Sec. 29, Weare township, where he has since resided. He now has eighty-four acres of land, fifty-four under improvement. On Sept. 23, 1868, he was married to Miss Fannie F. Smith, a sister of N. C. Smith, of Weare. Mr. Gregory has been Supervisor one term, Highway Commissioner one term, and five years a member of the School Board. He is known in his section as an honest, upright man, whose word is as good as his bond.

CHARLES LAMONT—1868.

Charles Lamont, familiarly known as Captain Lamont, was born near Montreal, Canada, Dec. 25, 1833. His parents were Lewis and Helen Lamont, both of whom are dead, the mother dying in 1874 and father in 1885, both at Goderich, Can. He had one brother, who is now located at Seattle, Wash., and is a man of means. No sisters. Mr. Lamont's early days were spent at his birthplace and in the city of Buffalo, N. Y., where in 1864 he was married to Miss Harriet Bates. In early life he commenced steamboating, and soon became master of a steamboat, which business he followed until his death. In 1868, in taking a tug around the lakes he ran in at Pentwater for fuel, and finding business good decided to remain, sending for his family. He continued in that business until March 14, 1880, when he was drowned. Mr. Lamont left a family consisting of a wife (now Mrs. H. Mohrdiek), three daughters and two sons, Ethia, now Mrs. Johnston, living at Seattle; Edith, now Mrs. Hutchinson, living at Pentwater, and Charles Guy, Rutherford and Hattie, living with their mother at Pentwater. Mr. Lamont was known as an open-handed, free-hearted man, and in consequence of these traits possessed many friends where known.

C. LAMONT.

FAYETTE WALKER—1868.

Fayette Walker was born at Warsaw, N. Y., Aug. 24, 183-; and is the son of Hiram F. and Almira A. Walker. He was married on Nov. 10, 1868, to Phebe I. Hoisington, on the same day started for the West, and on Nov. 20th, found himself in the Township of Leavitt, this county. Jan. 1, 1869, he commenced keeping house on the S. W. ¼ of Sec. 2, where he lived one year. Then moving to

Sec. 22, Colfax, he remained until the fall of 1880. He then removed to Sec. 8, Leavitt, buying a saw mill of Geo. Holt and A. C. Stetson, which he continued to own and run until the fall of 1882, then selling to Dunham Ross. In '83 he platted the now thriving town of Walkerville and in 1884 built the mill he now owns and runs, which consists of saw, shingle, planing and feed mill. In '78, Jan. 4, his wife died, and Nov. 30, 1882, he was again married, this time to Florence Munger. Both his wives were formerly of Warsaw, N. Y., his birthplace. He is the father of five children, four sons and one daughter. Mr. Walker has added materially to the prosperity of his section, and the town that bears his name bids fair to become one of the leading villages of the county.

F. WALKER.

RALPH F. AMES—1868.

Ralph F. Ames was born in Scio, Alleghany Co., N. Y., Aug. 28, '38, and was a son of Abner A. and Louisa Ames. He enlisted in Sept., 1862, in Co. F. 151 Pa. Vol. Inf., and served for twelve months. He says "served my government without squealing or kicking for $13 per month and took my pay in greenbacks." In '60 came to this county and has made his home here since. He began life as a farmer in 1856, and has followed that worthy occupation since. Oct. 29, 1856, he married Tirzah A. Chappell, and on

Dec. 2, 1863, he was again married, this time to Eunice M. Bigelow, and he is the father of twelve children, five sons and seven daughters. Mr. Ames prides himself upon his adherence to one political party through thick and thin. He has always been a republican.

JACOB FISHER—1868.

Jacob Fisher was born at Williamsport, Pa., Sept. 7, 1846. He is a son of Jacob and Mary Fisher. He lived with his parents until the age of 22 years, receiving a common school education. He came to Oceana Co. in May, 1868, and since that time has been engaged in various occupations. He was for some time the landlord of the Imus House at Pentwater, where he was very popular with the traveling public. For a number of years he has owned and run the steamer Wm. H. Browne between Pentwater and Ludington. Always a gentleman and considerate of the safety and comfort of his passengers, he has been enabled to do a good business in this line and rumor says has made money. He is a prominent member of the Masonic fraternity and the confidence of the citizens of Pentwater has been manifested by his election as Village Trustee. He was married in 1881 to Frances Amond, of Grand Rapids. They have no children.

J. FISHER.

GEORGE W. IMUS—1868.

George W. Imus was born in Bennington Co., Vt., July 14, 1840, and, like Stephen A. Douglas, emigrated young, coming to Michigan when only four years of age. He traces his ancestry back to revolutionary times, his grandfather, William Imus, having been a soldier in that war, and his father, Alonzo, a soldier of the war of 1812. Upon coming to Michigan Mr. Imus settled with his parents in Kent Co. near the now flourishing city of Grand Rapids, then a small village of about 1,500 population. He attended district school winters until fifteen years of age, then going to Albion College where he remained three years. After leaving college he engaged in teaching which he continued until 1865, when he was married. He then engaged in farming for three years at the expiration of which he sold his farm and came to Oceana Co., locating at Pentwater. He then engaged in the mercantile business until 1872, when he purchased the well known "Imus House" at Pentwater, which he still owns and which he has kept most of the time. Mr. Imus has held several offices of trust, among which are School Trustee, Village Trustee and Supervisor of Pentwater Township. His family consists of a wife and two daughters, Georgia F. and Alberta J. L. Mr. Imus is also a leading member of the Masonic fraternity and one of the Past Masters of Oceana Lodge No. 200 F. & A. M. He is also identified with the A. O. U. W. organization. He is a man of sound judgment and has given good satisfaction as a Supervisor.

G. W. IMUS.

EDWARD A. WRIGHT—1868.

Edward A. Wright, son of Austin and Lydia Wright, was born June 22, 1844, in Hillsdale Co., Mich. He resided with his parents on a farm until 1861, when he enlisted in Co. G, 18th Mich. Vol. Inf. and served as an Orderly under Gen. R. S. Granger for three years. After leaving the army he returned to Hillsdale Co., and shortly went to Eastman Business College, Poughkeepsie, N. Y. Leaving College he returned to Jonesville, Hillsdale Co., where he then accepted a position in the drug store of R. S. Varnum & Co., where he learned the drug business. After leaving

E. A. WRIGHT.

the drug store, in 1868 he came to Oceana Co., locating at Pentwater, where he soon engaged in the grocery and bakery business which he continued for four years, then formed a copartnership with C. W. Brown in the drug business. In 1876 he bought out his partner's interest and has since continued the business alone. Mr. Wright has been elected to various public offices, among them being Supervisor of Pentwater two terms, Recorder of the village six years and one year Trustee. He has always discharged the duties of his offices without fear or favor, and has been urged to accept others which he has declined. Married Oct. 4, 1868, to Miss Eva Tuller, and their family now consists of a daughter, Edna, born March 4, 1877, and son, Willie, born Jan. 6, 1883.

HENRY HURLEY—1868.

Henry Hurley was born at Belleville, Ont., Feb. 8, 1868. He was one of seven children of Dennis and Ann Hurley. Of the family there are still living his mother at Belleville, Ont., one brother, Jeremiah, and one sister, Mary. The subject of our sketch spent his early days at his birthplace with his parents upon a farm.

In the spring of 1862 he came to Michigan, living at Saginaw a short time and from there drifting about until in June, 1868, he came to this county, landing at Pentwater where he engaged at his trade that of a carpenter, for a few months, then as a foreman upon the government piers for Mr. C. Mears, and later receiving the appointment

H. HURLEY.

from the Government of Superintendent of the work. In June, '72, he accepted the position of Superintendent of Mr. Mears' lumber business at Silver Lake on Little Pt. Au Sable. Here he continued until 1884, when he returned to Pentwater to take charge of the Middlesex Brick & Tile Co. business, continuing as the manager of that business until his death. His death was very sudden and totally unexpected. For some time he had been subject to strange feelings, shortness of breath and weak spells. The night before he died he had severe chills and cold sweats, but was feeling better in the morning and in the evening seemed as well as usual. He retired to rest at his usual hour on Sunday evening, Apr. 28, 1889, his wife not retiring at the same time. He had been in bed about half an hour when she hearing unusual sounds from him ran into his sleeping room and found him in the agonizies of death, and in about five minutes his spirit had departed. Mr. Hurley was married May 24, '64, to Mary A. Donovan, who survives him, now residing at Mears. He was the father of three children, Thomas J., Henry J. and John F., who still survive. He was born and bred in the Catholic faith to which he clung during life. He was buried by that denomination Rev. Father Willigan officiating, May 1, 1889. In his lifetime Mr. Hurley affiliated politically with the democratic party, and an evidence of his popularity is to be found in the fact that he was elected Supervisor of Pentwater township which was at that time a republican township. Slow to anger, but withal strenuous in defense of his own and others' rights. Mr. Hurley possessed many warm personal friends to whom the announcement of his sudden death was a great shock.

JOHN H. MOORE—1868.

J. H. MOORE.

John H. Moore, a son of Benjamin and Hannah Moore, was born in Washtenaw Co., Mich. He came to this county in 1868, and has resided here since that time. In 1878 he started in the lumber business and was for six years manager of the lumber department for Wheeler & Bros. at Shelby. He with D. R. Watters built the Blooming Valley saw mill which was burned in 1881. Was also engaged for C. Rolph one year in the lumber business. He bought the Shelby grist mill in 1888, and the next year formed the Shelby Roller Mill Co. and together with Mr. McLeod built the Shelby roller mills, afterwards selling his interest to Mr. G. B. Getty. At present he is engaged in lumbering. Mr. Moore was married in 1876 to Miss Mary C. Cutler and now has two children, a son, Floyd, and daughter, Eda. Mr.

Moore has seen considerable of pioneer life, enduring its hardships and enjoying its sports. He has had many a pleasant time hunting bear by day and deer by night, and believes that pioneer life is not all hardship. He is now well satisfied with his surroundings and not inclined to grumble.

THOS. KELLY—1868.

Thomas Kelly was born in Chautauqua Co., N. Y., Jan. 31, '45. His parents were John and Betsey Kelly. At the commencement of our late civil war he enlisted in Co. I, 8th N. Y. Cav., and was mustered as 1st Corporal, serving three years and two months. Dec. 22, 1867, he was married to Miss Lucinda Prosser, who has borne him one daughter who has since died. Nov. 3, 1868, he came to Oceana Co., coming here at an early day in our history. Always incapable of fear, what he lacked in the advantages that money brings he made up in energy and pluck. Almost continually in office, having been Under Sheriff, Constable and Village Marshal for many years. No storm ever blew hard enough to deter "Tom" from the execution of a duty. He was the principal in ferreting out that great burglary case in which C. Mears' store at Mears, and later, A. G. Avery's store at Shelby were burglarized and a large quantity of goods stolen. Mr. Kelly's shrewdness and correct management of the case would have done credit to an experienced Pinkerton detective; nearly all the stolen goods being returned to their owners. "Tom" is a great lover of good horses and at present the happy possessor of Goldwin, registered in Wallace's Register 8979, and a very promising animal; having cost him about $1,000. J. I. C. and Phallos are half uncles to Goldwin who promises to equal the performances of his illustrious relatives. In the enjoyment of the fruits of hard labor he still resides in the county where he has made what property he possesses. Mr. Kelly is now living at Shelby where he has a wide circle of friends and acquaintances.

T. KELLY.

WESLEY AND BERTIE ROLPH—1868.

Wesley and Bertie Rolph, sons of Wm. and Hanna Rolph are now in partnership on the old home farm on the road between Shelby and Hart villages. They are both pioneers of the county. Wesley, born at Fullerton's Corners, Perth Co., Can., May 29, 1868, came with his parents to this county in the fall of 1868, and Bertie was born in this county in Shelby township, April 13, 1870. Their father was a carpenter and farmer, and since his death they have run the farm. It is now one of the best farms in the township. The boys have won the respect and confidence of their neighbors.

WM. E. AMBLER—1868.

See page 217.

MARK A. RICE—1869.

Mark A. Rice was born at Greensburg, Trumbull Co., Ohio, Mar. 1, 1846. He is a son of Allen and Sophia Rice. He resided with his parents at his birthplace until eight years of age, and at different places in Ohio and Penn. until about 1858, when they came to Hillsdale, Mich. Here he resided for eight or nine years during which time he was for a short time a student in Hillsdale College. While there he learned the jeweler's trade and later took up telegraphy, securing a position on the air line road. He continued this for a short time and then secured a situation with Mr. A. Gleason in the business of die sinking. This he was engaged at for four years after which he came to Pentwater, in June, 1869, on a visit and decided to remain, making his home here since. He commenced here as a watchman in the Moulton & Flagg mill one season, filed for two years and then went to work at the jewelry business with Mr. Jesse Root. When the railroad came he took the telegraph station up town and has held it ever since. Finally he took the express also, and Mr. Root leaving

M. A. RICE.

he after a time started a jewelry business of his own and has gradually added to it until at present he carries a good stock and does a good business. He was one of the sufferers by the fire of Sept. 20, 1889, losing his building and considerable of his stock. On Aug. 6, 1860, he married Mrs. Martha Craine, and one daughter, Margaret, has been born to them. Mr. Rice has held the positions of Village and Township Treasurers, and is now a member of the Common Council. A jovial, whole-hearted man he possesses many friends.

ORIN WISWELL.—1869.

Orin Wiswell was born in Windham Co., Vt., in 1833. His parents were James and Betsey Wiswell. He was raised upon a farm, enjoying only the usual school benefits enjoyed by farmer's sons. In 1859 he was married to Frances S. Freeman, and two sons have been born to them. He was one of those who answered to the call of his country in her time of peril; and went to the front in Co. D, 4th Regt. Mich. Cav. He served 22 months as a private of that Co. He came to Mich. in '56, located in Newaygo Co. moving into Oceana Co. Oct., 1869. He is familiar with pioneer life, although his first experience was not in this county, but over the line in Newaygo Co. He has all his life been engaged in farming, and is known as an honest and upright man. He has been honored by the electors of his township with the position of Superintendent of Schools. He now has a farm on section 34, Ferry, of forty acres with thirty improved. Mr. Wiswell is a member of R. M. Johnson Post No. 138, at Ferry, and has held the office of Commander therein.

O. WISWELL.

JOSEPH SCHANER—1869.

Joseph Schaner was born at Detroit, Mich., March 10, 1842. His parents, Nicholas and Catherine Schaner, were of German descent.

J. SCHANER.

On Oct. 6, 1864, he married Christina Wehren, who was born in Holland, Aug. 21, '47 her parents being Lorenz and Marie Wehren. Twenty days after they were married they arrived in Oceana Co. and located upon their present farm. At that time there were but eighteen acres cleared, but now there are 100 acres cleared and free from stumps. He may boast, without fear of contradiction of having one of the finest farms in the county. Where stumps abound so universally as they do in the county it is a pleasure to gaze upon his broad fields, smooth and clear of all obstructions. In addition to the broad acres of land Mr. Schaner has a fine brick residence, a view of which is given on page 147 of this book, three commodious barns, a steam thresher and feed mill. Mr. and Mrs. Schaner have always been known as hard-working, economical people, full of push and energy. As a business man Mr. S. is well known, his word being as good as his bond, and any man wanting work is lucky to secure it of him as it always means cash. They have had ten children, seven sons and three daughters.

MRS. J. SCHANER.

CHRISTIAN ANDREAS—1869.

Christian Andreas was born at Niederdunzebach, Prussia, July 14, 1830. His parents were Conrad and Annie Andreas. He came to America March 21, 1864, and settled in Ohio remaining there until he came to this county April 16, 1869. He purchased 80 acres of school land on Sec. 16, in Leavitt township, and sent for his wife after he had raised a small log house. At that time there were only sixteen settlers in the township. When he first came he worked in lumber woods to support his family until he could clear enough land on which to raise his living. His nearest point for trading was Pentwater, from which place he backed his provisions. The country was full of wild beasts. One incident he well remembers. One day his children were out gathering beech nuts and a bear came into their midst. The parents saw the affair and were thoroughly frightened. The children that they might not see the bear threw their clothing over their heads, and the bear went on without molesting them, to the great joy

C. ANDREAS.

MRS. C. ANDREAS.

of the parents. He worked four years at first without any team, and logged eight acres by hand. On June 18, 1853, he was married to Mary Schmidt, who was born in Prussia, Feb. 12, 1828, being a daughter of Henry and Christiana Schmidt. She came to this county in June, 1869, and from that time to the present has been a faithful helpmeet to her husband. Her father was a farmer, and at the age of sixteen years she commenced to work out and proved so faithful that in ten years she changed places but twice. When her husband has been sick she has taken the children with her and gone into the logging fallow. She suffered from fear of wild beasts and from loneliness considerable. She remembers a terrible thunder storm in the middle of one night when she was alone with the children, she gathered them in the middle of the room expecting each moment the house would be destroyed. They have six children, five sons and one daughter, who is now the wife of Levi Vaughan. Mr. Andreas and his present surroundings are illustrations of what pluck and energy will accomplish. When he reached this county he had eleven cents left in his pocket. Now he has 160 acres of land, 100 under improvement; a two-story house 18x26 with addition 16x16; woodhouse and shop 16x26; barns 32x72 and 32x40; granary 20x28; wagon shed 18x20; machine houses 18x30 and 18x24; hog house 16x20. Farm fenced with board fence. 21 head of cattle; 7 horses; 12 sheep; 10 hogs; 11 swarms of bees, and altogether one of the best appointed farms in the township. His father, 89 years old Nov., 1889, lives with him.

RANSOM SABIN—1869.

Ransom Sabin was born in New York, June 19, 1836, being a son of Ransom and Jane Sabin. He enlisted in Co. H, 2nd Missouri Cav. and for nearly two years cared for the sick and wounded soldiers in hospital at Benton Barracks, St. Louis, Mo. In May, 1869, he came to Oceana Co. and since coming here has followed his profession of physician and surgeon. He owned a drug store at Benona which was burned in 1870. For fifteen years he has resided at Shelby. The first fifteen years of his experience in this county were full of hardships and toils, riding day or night rain or shine, over new and poor roads. His health failing he spent part of two winters in the South, returning to Shelby summers. Besides attending to his professional duties he has found time to invent a folding pail, folding baths and a portable pantry. He is also author of a book entitled "Home Pleasures," published at Battle Creek, Mich. Mr. Sabin was married in 1859 to Ann E. Prine, who died in 1861. Again married in 1862 to Louisa M. Boll, who died in 1880. In 1886 he married Elvira S. Halleck, his present wife. He has three children, two sons and one daughter.

R. SABIN.

FRANKLIN M. MEYERS—1869.

Franklin M. Meyers, born at Independence, Iowa, Feb. 4, 1859, is a son of Peter and Betsey A. Meyers. He came to Oceana Co. on Aug. 20, 1869, and has since resided in Benona and Shelby. In 1883 he had the position of Assistant Postmaster, in 1887 was Clerk of Benona township and in 1888 was Clerk of Shelby township. May 11, 1885, he married Miss Emma Boughner, and their union has been blessed with one child, a son. Mr. Meyers is now connected with Messrs. I. E. Ilgenfritz and Sons as their agent for the sale of fruit trees and other nursery stock in this county. He has been a success in the business because of his push and energy. He is widely and favorably known and has many friends. He is a leading member of Shelby Lodge No. 344, I. O. O. F., having just finished a term of office as Secretary and commenced a term as Vice Grand of that lodge.

F. M. MEYERS.

BENJAMIN F. ARCHER—1869.

Benjamin F. Archer was born at Jamestown, Indiana. His parents were Benjamin and Sophronia Archer. When three years old he came with his parents to Branch Co., Mich., and lived there until 1861, assisting his father in clearing a farm summers and attending district school winters. Being in a new country and with limited means, his chances for an education were not good. On April 9, 1861, in response to his country's call, he enlisted in Co. C, 1st Mich. Inf. as private and served three months, the time for which he enlisted. Discharged in Aug., 1861, returned home. The following February, his father, then 57 years of age, enlisted in Co. A, 15th Mich. Inf. and was killed at the battle of Shiloh. In July, 1862, the subject of our sketch again enlisted, this time in Co. G, 4th Mich. Cav., for three years, as a private. He served the full time, being in 25 hard fought battles besides many skirmishes, having two horses killed under him, but being fortunate enough to escape without a scratch. He was discharged as Commissary Sergeant, July 8, 1865. It was his regiment that captured Jeff. Davis. Nov. 1, 1866, he was married to Miss Eunice J. Barber, of Quincy, Mich. They have had nine children, seven sons and two daughters. On Feb. 4, 1869, with all of his effects in one wagon, consisting of some bedding, a few dishes, and three months' provisions, he started for Oceana Co. arriving here on the eleventh of the same month. He first settled on Sec. 36, Ferry township, where he has cleared up a farm of fifty acres which he still owns and manages. That section was then covered with a very heavy growth of beech and maple timber. The farm is now well fenced, with good orchard and buildings. In 1886 he moved to Ferry village and engaged in the hardware business, being the first and only hardware in Ferry, which business he still follows. In 1887 he opened a tin shop in connection and manufactures nearly all the tin handled in the shop. His oldest son, Charles B., runs that part and is now one of the best tinners in the county. Mr. Archer has taught two successful terms of school. Has been Supervisor, Treasurer and Justice of the Peace in his township, and Notary Public. In 1887, was appointed Postmaster at Ferry.

MRS. EUNICE J. ARCHER.

Mrs. Eunice J. Archer was born in Branch Co., March 17, 1850. Her parents' names were Alson and Phebe Barber. Mrs. Archer was the youngest of nine children. Her mother died when she was but seven years of age, leaving the family much broken up. When nine years old she left home to live with an uncle with whom she lived two and a half years, then going back to keep house for her father, the older children being grown up and scattered. Five of her brothers responded to the call for troops and went into the army. After about another year and a half she left home and worked by the week in different places until the fall of 1866, when she met and married Mr. Archer. Since then the years have been spent in a wife's work and a mother's duty. For two years she owned a millinery shop, but her health failing she was compelled to sell out. She then went to Ann Arbor for treatment, spending four weeks there and having two operations performed. Since then her health has been slowly improving. She has suffered much from ill health, but has borne her sufferings with fortitude.

JAMES A. WEYANT—1869.

James A. Weyant was born Jan. 13, 1843, in Brutus, Cayuga Co. N. Y. His father, George Weyant, was born March 28, 1808, in Orange Co., N. Y. Moved to Cayuga Co. in 1834, where he purchased a farm of 100 acres. In May of the same year he married Amanda Mapes and they lived upon the same farm, where James A. Was born, over fifty years. The subject of our sketch was named after his grandfather, James Weyant, who was a Quartermaster in the U. S. army in the war of 1812, and lived to be over 80 years of age. James A. spent his early days on his father's farm attending district school until sixteen years of age when he went to an academy for two years. At this time the war broke out and he enlisted in the fall of '61, in the 19th N. Y. Inf., which afterwards became the 3rd N. Y. Light Art., and served in the campaign in Maryland, Virginia, North Carolina and South Carolina, participating in several sharp engagements. Received an honorable discharge at the expiration of his term, June 2, 1863. With health injured from exposure, and especially by the malaria of the swamps of North Carolina, being quartered in and about Newberne, N. C., for nearly a year, he returned to his home and remained with his father off and on until Jan. 1, 1867, when he was married to Miss Phebe V. Green, of Highland Mills, Orange Co., N. Y. In Dec., 1860, he came to Oceana Co., living in Weare until fall of '70, when he moved into Elbridge. Taught school in Hart township in 71-2, and in Elbridge in '72-3. In '72 he purchased 80

J. A. WEYANT.

acres of land on Sec. 24, Hart, where he now resides. Mr. Weyant was converted in early life uniting with the M. E. Church at Hart June 19, '70. In '74 he received a license and began to preach the gospel, preaching in Elbridge, Crystal, Leavitt, Colfax, Ferry and other localities until Sept., '76, when he was appointed pastor at Freesoil, Mason Co., where he remained one year. He was at Cadillac '77-8, Fyfe Lake '79, Spencer Creek '80-1, Bear Lake '82-3, Milbrook '84, Browne '85, Danley '86-7, Coral, '88, Saranac 89. In '78 he was ordained a Deacon and in '82 an Elder. He preached thirteen successive years, receiving during the time about three hundred members besides other tokens of acceptable work. Sept. '89, his health failing he returned to his home in Hart township, suffering from throat difficulties Mr. Weyant has three children, two sons and one daughter; Fred N., now a junior in Albion College, James E., residing at home, and Sarah A., also at home. Having shared somewhat largely the cares and hardships of pioneer life conserves to make him a friend to those struggling in new localities.

CHARLES R. JOHNSON—1870.

C. R. JOHNSON.

Charles R. Johnson is the eldest of four children, two boys and two girls, born to David and Lydia E. Johnson. He was born at Hastings, Mich., June 2, 1862. Moved with his parents to Olivet, Eaton Co., Mich., where he lived until eight years of age, when they moved to Hart, Mich., this occurring in 1870. His father engaged in the hardware business. He attended the high school at Hart and took a two years course in the Agricultural College at Lansing. In 1883, April 14th, he entered the Hon. W. E. Ambler's law office as a student, and was admitted to practice in 1887. He remained with Mr. Ambler until Jan., 1889. Nov. 1, 1889, he purchased the insurance business of J. W. Loomis, was also appointed express agent and is now engaged in the practice of the law, and managing the insurance and express business. In Jan., 1890, he married Miss Jennie Lewis, a daughter of one of Pentwater's first settlers, Mrs. I. N. Lewis.

CLARK B. GENUNG—1870.

Clark B. Genung, of Golden, Oceana Co., Mich., was born in Steuben Co., N. Y., March 20, '48. His parents' names were N. E. and Sophia Genung. He came to Michigan in 1869, and Dec. 18, 1870, to Oceana Co. March 18, 1868 he was married to Emma V. Folsom, who died Oct. 10, 1879, leaving three children, one daughter and two sons. Nov. 9, 1880, Mr. Genung married Jennie L. Baker, who was born in Erie Co., N. Y., Feb. 13, 1861, and the daughter of M. C. Baker, a pioneer of the Co. One son and one daughter have been born to them.

Mr. Genung is a hard-working, enterprising and energetic man. Since locating in this

C. B. GENUNG.

county he has been engaged in lumbering and farming. He owns a fine, well improved farm located next to the village of Mears. When he moved upon the place there was not a house in sight. He has an orchard of 1,500 fruit trees growing, and in 1890 sets 500 more. The popular breed of Poland China swine was first introduced into Golden by him, and it is an open question if he was not the first to bring pure bloods of this breed into the county. He has held the following official positions in his township, viz.: Treasurer two years; Supervisor three years, and Justice of the Peace four years.

MRS. C. B. GENUNG.

MARTIN S. PERKINS—1870.

Martin S. Perkins was born in East Penfield, now Webster, Monroe Co., N. Y., Nov. 15, 1832. He lived in that county until Sept. 1841, when with his parents he moved to Coldwater, Branch Co., Mich. As a boy M. S. was of a combative disposition, until July, 1848, when he met a lad from Ohio, by the name of Smith. After they had been together a few minutes Martin's father came along and assisted him home. His mother thought a good deal of him and plastered him up so that he was able to attend school the next winter. He remembered the event distinctly until about the year 1883, when he met another fellow by the name of Kilbeck. He weighed only 210 lbs. After this meeting H. C. Flagg led him home and he has since been a quiet citizen.

M. S. PERKINS.

Aug. 16, 1852, he married Maria J. Tibbits, who was born in the town of Plymouth, Wayne Co. Mich., on the 2nd day of Nov., 1832. Six children have been born to them, four of whom are still living. They also rejoice in having thirteen grandchildren. They lived in Southern Michigan until 1868, when they moved to Mason Co. and built a mill at Bass Lake. Lived there two years and then moved to Pentwater where they have since resided. Since living in Pentwater Mr. Perkins has worked for Moulton & Flagg two years, Underhill one year, run the ferry two years, was in the livery business two years, and now runs the 'bus, carries mail, handles baggage, etc., and insists that he is still young and happy. He has been a republican in politics since the birth of the party, and has held many local offices conferred by the same. During the war he enlisted in Co. M, 11th

MRS. M. S. PERKINS.

Mich. Cavalry at the formation of the regiment. Was promoted to 2nd Lieut. Feb 1, 1864, and again promoted to 1st Lieut on the 14th day of November, the same year, and resigned the 24th day of June, 1865, at the consolidation of the 11th with the 8th regiment.

L. E. JOHNSON—1870.

Louis E. Johnson was born in Barry Co., Mich., June 17, 1863, and is the second son of David and Lydia E. Johnson. His father will be long remembered in this county as one of its most efficient Judges of Probate. The subject of our sketch came to this county with his parents in July, 1870, and has resided here since. On Nov. 13, 1887, he married Miss Minnie L. Tilden. He held the position of Deputy Co. Clerk in 1887. His trade is that of a tinner, having spent a number of years in learning it and in clerking in a hardware store thus fitting himself for his present business. Nov. 29, 1889, he opened a hardware store at Walkerville where he still remains. It is his intention to always be on deck with a full line of heavy and shelf hardware, windows, sash, doors and blinds, glass, putty, oils, paints, etc., plows, harrows, mowers, reapers and binders and all kinds of agricultural implements, wagons, sleighs and cutters will be furnished of any make desired. A complete line of parlor and heating stoves always in stock.

L. E. JOHNSON.

He will make a specialty of tin and sheet iron work, eave troughs and general repairing. So far as style and quality of work and goods, prices, and in fact reasonable satisfaction are concerned he guarantees them. By strict attention to business, prompt dispatch of any work entrusted to him and one price to all he hopes to merit and receive the patronage of the residents in his vicinity. He extends a general invitation to all to call.

WILLIAM J. TENNANT—1869.

William James Tennant, the subject of this sketch, was born in the city of Glasgow, Scotland, on the 5th day of Feb., 1839. His parents were William and Rachel Tennant. He resided there until the month of Feb., 1848, when he emigrated, with his parents, to America. Was married Sept. 12, 1858, to Jane Coveney, oldest daughter of Joseph Coveney, of Buchanan, Berrien County, Mich. Came to Oceana Co. with his family on the 10th day of May, 1869, and settled in the township of Elbridge, where he now resides, it being then an almost unbroken wilderness. As a public servant he has held the office of Justice 12 years, Township Clerk one year, Supervisor three years. One year while Supervisor was chosen Chairman of the Board of Supervisors. In all of these offices has discharged his duties with a clear record. He has raised a family of seven children, three boys and four girls. Four of his children have been successful teachers in the public schools of the county. His son William, twenty-four years of age, was killed by the falling of a windmill tower at Mears on July 13, 1883. The rest of his children are living at this time. Sixteen years of his life were spent at carpenter and joiner work, and twelve years trying to clear up a farm. Seven years ago he commenced the business of putting down tubular wells and erecting windmills, at which he is engaged at the present time, having made a successful record. His work may be found all over this county, and part of Mason and Newaygo counties, and parties in need of that kind of work need never be afraid to employ him for they will be sure to get a good job.

EZEKIEL J. SHIRTS—1871.

Ezekiel J. Shirts was born at New Lisbon, Columbia Co., Ohio, March 15, 1825. His parents were Samuel and Eliza Shirts. He moved to Indiana in 1845, but returned in 1847. In 1853 he engaged in the grocery business which he continued for three years; then worked at his trade carpenter and joiner. In 1864 he located at Lansing, Mich, engaging in the mercantile business there until 1871, when he moved his stock to Shelby. He built the first store building on the village plat, putting in the first stock of goods. At that time only three families resided on the plat. He had to pay the freight upon his goods at Whitehall, there being no depot or agent at Shelby until later. He has since made Shelby

his home and is now engaged in buying wool, fruit, etc., for shipment. Mr. Shirts was Deputy Sheriff six years in Ohio and Ind. and has held the same position four years in this county. Married July 10, 1852, Miss Elizabeth Imhoff, who was born Jan. 26, 1835, in Wayne Co., Ohio. They have had four children, three sons and one daughter. Mr. Shirts had four brothers in the army and was himself active in recruiting, now holding three certificates as Captain. He has held the appointment of Notary Public for twenty-five years.

ALBERT G. AVERY—1871.

Albert G. Avery was born at Poquitamick, Conn., Feb. 2, '43. His parents were Erastus and Caroline Avery. In the fall of 1869 he went to work for C. Mears at Lincoln, Mason Co., and continued in his employ at different points for nearly six years. He has lived in various places in this county, Pentwater, Mears and Hesperia. Also resided for a time at Whitehall. He came to this county in the spring of '71 and in '81 located at Shelby, engaging in the gen'l merchandise business which he has since followed successfully, being able at this time to discount all purchases. In religion Mr. Avery is a Methodist, but in belief holds the doctrine of the universal salvation of the whole human race. In politics he was raised and lived a republican for years, but now holds the opinions of a reformer. He married at Pentwater, Dec. 25, 1871, Loranda T. Hills. As a business man he is exact and prompt. As a gentleman the peer of any, and as a citizen public-spirited and open-handed.

A. G. AVERY.

LEWIS L. TAYLOR—1871.

Lewis L. Taylor was born at Otego, Otsego Co., N. Y., April 8, 1829, his parents being John C. and Mercy Taylor. He remained on the farm with his parents at his birthplace until six years of age when they moved to Erie Co., Pa. Here he remained with his par-

L. L. TAYLOR.

ents until the age of seventeen years, when he branched out for himself, going to Clarion County and commencing work in the lumber woods. He remained at that work for about six years and then went into the square timber business in Warren County, which he continued for four years. Working at different things in different places for a short time, he then became a pilot upon the Tionesta Creek, piloting lumber and logs. He continued at this employment for about twelve years, then going from one business to another until 1871, when he came to Oceana Co., locating on Sec. 7, Leavitt, and has since been engaged in farming. He now has one of the best farms in the county, consisting of 240 acres, 200 acres improved, with a large and commodious house, two large barns, with various outbuildings. Mr. Taylor married Aug. 28, '57, Miss Emily J. Reddington, by whom he had two children, Frank W., who was injured in the woods Jan. 23 and died Feb. 1, 1884, and Mercy A., who is now the wife of Raymond Ross, living on Sec. 12, Elbridge. His wife died March 31, 1862, and he was again married Sept. 10, '69.

MRS. L. L. TAYLOR.

His second wife was Mrs. Lucy A. Poff (Hall) and they have had four children, Emily J., Lenora V., Charles L. and Frank W., all of whom are living at home. Mrs. Lucy A. Taylor was born in Erie Co., Pa., Jan. 5, 1845. She lived upon a farm with her parents until she was married in 1865 to Daniel W. Poff, by whom she has one child, Daniel W., now living in Perry Co., Miss. Her first husband died in Oct., 1868. Mrs. Taylor has always been a careful, frugal housewife, and has fully done her share in accumulating what they now possess. Mr. Taylor has always been a pushing man, what might be termed a "hustler." He has made several small fortunes during his life and now possesses sufficient to keep him the balance of his days in comfort. He has held the office of Justice and was for three years Superintendent of the Poor for Oceana Co. He has never sought public office, but when holding any has discharged its duties fearlessly.

THEODORE P. LANDON—1871.

Theodore P. Landon, now a resident of Ferry, was born in Conneaut township, Crawford Co., Pa., Aug. 9, 1839. His parents were

Daniel and Nancy Landon. Another son of this same couple was Daniel Landon, who died while filling the office of Judge of Probate of this county in 1887. Mr. Landon enlisted as a private in Co. J, 2nd Pa. Cav., in which he served fifteen months. In 1871 he came to Oceana Co. He has been Justice of the Peace eight years and township Clerk two years, of Ferry township. By trade he is a carpenter and joiner but his present business is Notary Public, real estate agent and clerk in store. Mr. Landon possesses many friends and acquaintances and is a man who is universally esteemed. He is a prominent member of the G. A. R. and has been honored with different offices in that organization and been offered more that he would not accept.

SAMUEL D. FOSTER—1871.

Samuel D. Foster, farmer and fruit grower in Benona township, first saw the light of day in the town of Greece, Monroe Co., N. Y., May 23, 1850. His parents' names were Ozias and Josephine. He acquired a good common school education and adopted farming as his occupation. He came to Oceana Co. in 1871 with C. A. Sessions. He married Lettie J. Easton, who has borne to him five children, four sons and one daughter. He has a fine fruit farm located on sections five and eight, being in all 160 acres, where he now lives. He has 1,850 trees growing, 1,500 peach and the rest apple, plum and cherry. In the spring of 1890 he set 1,100 more trees. Of the 120 acre farm he has 90 acres improved and 7½ of the 40 acres. Mr. Foster is a clever calculator, energetic and pushing. He has made a success of his business although still a young man.

EBENEZER B. CLARK—1863.

Ebenezer B. Clark was born in Lower Canada, near Montreal, in '31, March 9th. He comes of Welsh and Irish stock. He acquired a good education. In 1861 he came to White River, and in 1863 he moved to Pentwater and started the first photograph gallery in the county. Many of the daguerreotypes taken by Mr. Clark are still to be found in the homes of the old pioneers. In 1867 he was elected Justice of the Peace and has seen twenty-two years continuous service in that office. He has also been

Township Clerk several times, and Village Assessor. He is a gentleman of engaging appearance and is quite popular with the people. He is public-spirited and always lends a helping hand in developing the interests of Pentwater and vicinity. He has three sons who are living.

DEWITT C. WICKHAM—1872.

DeWitt C. Wickham is the name of one who from one end of the Co. to the other is popularly known as "Geo." Wickham. He was born Dec. 7, 1843, at Yates, Orleans Co., N. Y., to Samuel K. and Lucy A. Wickham. He received a good common school education and was preparing himself for one of the professions when the war broke out and upon call for volunteers he enlisted in the army, serving three years in the 129th Inf. and 8th N. Y. Art. He enlisted as a private and came out as 1st Lieut. of Co. A, of the latter regiment. In 1872, Oct 22, he came to Pentwater. Has been Supt. of U. S. Gov. Works since '74. In 1886 he was elected Register of Deeds for Oceana Co., and in 1888 re-elected by a largely increased majority. He has held the office of Trustee of the village of Pentwater six years, and been a member of the School Board for six years. In politics he is a republican of the stalwart kind.

D. C. WICKHAM.

Has an opinion upon political issues and is ready at all times to give it. He is a forcible and eloquent speaker, and his services upon the platform are in frequent demand. Dec. 8, 1873, he married Addie M. Connell, who has been to him a faithful, loving wife. The union has been blessed with four children, two of whom, one daughter and a son are living. Mr. Wickham has left the impress of his character and work upon the locality, nearly every public improvement having received his support and active services.

PETER HANSEN—1872.

Peter Hansen was born in Denmark, May 26, 1837. He is a son of Hans and Anna Marie Peterson. He came to Oceana Co. in '72,

P. HANSEN.

and in the following year commenced farming on section 7 of Weare township. Previous to that time he had been a laborer. He has held the office of Justice of the Peace in Weare and takes a strong interest in the schools of his township. Oct. 25, 1863, he married Anna Christine Nelson, who was born in Denmark March 23, 1838. She is a daughter of Nels and Anna Marie Mortensen. She has been a dressmaker. They have two children, a son and a daughter. Their farm on section seven, Weare, is in a fine state of cultivation and comprises 173 acres, 55 acres cleared. There is also an orchard of two acres containing various kinds of fruit trees. They have a one-story frame house, a frame barn 50x50 feet, and a granary 20x30 feet, besides other buildings. Mr. Hansen is considered as one of the substantial farmers of his section, and both he and his estimable wife are highly respected.

MRS. P. HANSEN.

LOUIS M. HARTWICK—1872.

Louis M. Hartwick is the son of William M. and Mary L. Hartwick. He was born at Mishawaka, Ind., Feb. 14, 1848, and lived there until eleven years of age, when he accompanied his parents to Kansas, then a new State and the scene of many a bloody struggle

L. M. HARTWICK.

between the contending factions of pro-slavery and free-state men. He came to Michigan in 1860 and settled in Pentwater, Oceana Co. in January, 1872. He acquired his education in the Mishawaka High Schools, Hillsdale College, and the Michigan University. He graduated from the law department of that institution March 30, 1870, the youngest member of his class. March 16, 1870, upon examination in open Court, conducted by Judge Joslin, Judge Beakes and Robert Fraser, he was granted a certificate of admission to the Washtenaw County Bar. He practiced law in Jonesville, Mich., two years, then removed to Pentwater where he has since resided.

Politically he is a republican, having never voted any other ticket. He has held the following official positions in Oceana Co., viz.: Justice four years, U. S. Dep. Coll. of Customs five years, Village Recorder one year, Village Attorney seven years, Village President one year, County Supt. of the Poor two years, Circuit Court Commissioner two years, Prosecuting Attorney three years. Mar. 1, 1880, he purchased and has since conducted the publication of the Pentwater NEWS. Dec. 17, 1871, he married Alice A. Tuller, of Jonesville, which union has been blessed with three children now living: Louis W., Royal T., and Lilian M. He has one brother, H. D. Hartwick, a resident of Weare, and two sisters, Mrs. S. Andrus, of

Hart, and Mrs. Rose Hartwick Thorpe, of San Diego, California, now living.

GEORGE WYCKOFF—1872.

George Wyckoff, of Golden, Michigan, is a native of Ohio, the son of Jacob and Hannah Wyckoff. He was born in Geauga Co., Dec. 3, 1832. He acquired a good common school education. For many years he engaged in lumbering and land looking. It was the latter occupation that bro't him to Oceana County in July, 1872. He owns a fine farm, picturesquely located upon the beautiful little lake known as Round Lake. He is of a jovial disposition and enjoys life as he goes along.

G. WYCKOFF.

Aug. 23, 1856, he married Sarah H. Tice, who still continues his loving and faithful helpmeet. Two children have been born to them, both sons now grown to manhood. Since locating in Oceana Co. his business has been farming in which he has been very successful. He has been Supervisor of his township four years and Treasurer of Oceana County four years.

GEORGE W. WOODWARD—1872.

George W. Woodward was born in Ellery, Chautauqua Co., N. Y., Feb. 17, 1825. His parents were Daniel and Margaret Woodward. He came to Michigan in 1843 and in 1845 moved to Ottawa County where he remained until 1872, when he came to Oceana Co. and located at Shelby. In 1845 he was married to Roana Nowlen who died soon afterwards, and in February, 1852 he married Martha Bullen, his present wife. He now has three children living, one son and two daughters. His daughter Ida has long been known in the county as an earnest and effective temperance worker. In 1861 Mr. Woodward enlisted as a private and served his country as one of her bravest soldiers for nearly four years. He was promoted from the ranks to Sergeant, Second Lieutenant, First Lieutenant, Captain and Major, each time for meritorious conduct on the field of battle. He is now a prominent member of the G. A. R. and has held the office of Commander of Shields Post. In civil life he has been honored with numerous offices, having been elected and held in Ottawa, Kent and Oceana Counties the following offices: Treasurer of Ottawa Co. one term; Supervisor, 11 terms; School Inspector, one term; Justice, three terms; Township Clerk, one term; Postmaster, three times in as many places; Deputy Sheriff and jailer three years; Township Treasurer three terms; Highway Com'r, one term; Village Assessor one term; Village Trustee, one term; and has held appointments as Notary Public nearly all the time for forty years. He now holds four of the above offices.

G. W. WOODWARD.

JOSIAH CLEVELAND.

J. CLEVELAND.

Josiah Cleveland, son of Jedediah and Phebe A. Cleveland, was born in Randolph, Cattaraugus Co., N. Y., Feb. 15, 1840. He came with his parents to Lenawee Co., Michigan, when quite young, and lived in this State until he was of age. He then went to Fullerton Co., O., where he carried on business for two years, then returning to this State and has resided here nearly all of the time since. In Jan., 1872, he came to this county and was for a long time engaged in the blacksmith and wagon-making business at Pentwater. In April, 1880, he started the same business at his farm on section 32 of Crystal township where he is doing a fair business. Mr. Cleveland has been identified with the Odd Fellows' Lodge at Crystal Valley since its organization, and is an active, enthusiastic member. He married July 4, 1863, Margaret M. Lepper and they have one son and an adopted daughter.

TIMOTHY T. JONES—1872.

Timothy T. Jones, Supervisor of Crystal township, was born in Portage Co., Ohio, in the year 1841. His parents were John and Margaret Jones. At the very commencement of the civil war he enlisted in Co. B, of the old 4th Mich. Inf., and served for four years, one month and six days. He was at the first battle of Bull Run and at the surrender of Gen. Lee. He was present for duty every day except when home on a furlough. This is a record of service that few can show. In the fall of '72 he came to this county and engaged in farming in Crystal. He is a prominent G. A. R. man, being a Past Commander of the Crystal Valley Post. He has always taken a great interest in public affairs and his suggestions in his township are usually followed. He has been Justice of the Peace ten years. Elected Coronor of the county but failed to qualify. He was elected Supervisor in 1878 and again in 1885-6-7-8-9. Married Miss Rowena Aldrich and has had six sons.

T. T. JONES.

EGBERT N. BRIGGS.

At Rochester, N. Y., July 1, 1844, Caleb C. and Hattie Briggs rejoiced over the birth of a son, the subject of our sketch. Of his early life but few events out of the usual channel occurred. He enjoyed about the same privileges as other children and improved them as other children of his time. He possessed a sunny disposition and was ever popular with his companions. He removed from Jackson County, Michigan, to Oceana County in 1872, and has since resided here. During the war he enlisted in Co. A, 9th Michigan Cavalry and served two years, seven months and one day, and was honorably discharged. Since coming to Oceana County he has been engaged in lumbering and farming at Crystal, and later running a dray line at Pentwater. He married Miss Emma Willets, a daughter of one of Crystal's pioneers, and one son still living has blessed the union. He is a member of the order of Odd Fellows and has held offices in that organization. He is also an enthusiastic member of the G. A. R. and with his amiable wife contributes largely to the social enjoyments of both orders.

E. N. BRIGGS.

THOMAS MORIN—1872.

Thomas Morin, mason and plasterer, of Pentwater, Mich., removed to Oceana Co., Nov. 26, 1872, and has made Pentwater his home since. He is a native of Quebec, Canada, having been born to Isaac and Martha Morin, June 6, 1852. He left Canada when but eleven years of age, went to Providence, R. I., and drifted about from one place to another until in 1870 he settled in Detroit. He resided there two years then came to Pentwater. He was first employed as a lumber sorter and afterwards apprenticed himself to P. Sheridan and learned the mason's trade, which occupation he has since followed, most of the buildings of Pentwater erected within the past ten years showing his skill

T. MORIN.

as mechanic. Nov. 26, 1874, he married Eunice S. Hill, of Pentwater, daughter of Mr. and Mrs. Orin Hill. He is an enthusiastic member of the order of Odd Fellows and has passed most of the chairs in each branch of the order. In the spring election of 1890 he was elected Village Trustee.

JOHN H. BOUTON—1872.

John H. Bouton, the subject of our sketch, was born Jan. 24, 1848, at Rensselaerville, Albany Co., N. Y. His parents were Harry and Betsey E. Bouton. He resided with his parents until twenty years of age, at which time his father died. He remained in New York State, living at various places until 1872, when he came to Oceana Co., locating at Pentwater where he has since resided. He secured a position as clerk in a dry goods store where he continued for about four years. Afterwards clerked for the Pentwater Lumber Co. three years, and was engaged in the same capacity for different firms and in carpenter work until 1884 when he became shipping clerk in the Furniture Factory where he still continues. As an employe he has always given satisfaction. Mr. Bouton has always taken a lively interest in public affairs and has been entrusted with a number of township offices, among them being Constable and Treasurer three terms and has been ten years a member of the republican Township Committee. Under the village government he has been Marshal, Trustee and Treasurer, the latter two terms. He is a member of the Masonic fraternity and has held the office of Secretary in Oceana Chapter No. 56 for thirteen years, Secretary of Oceana Council No. 27 for twelve years and Secretary of Oceana Lodge No. 200 two years. He is also an active member of Pentwater Lodge No. 378, I. O. O. F., and for fourteen years an active member of the Pentwater Fire Department. Married Sept. 2, 1875, to Miss Cynthia S. Tuller, and they now have three children: Raymond T., born Aug. 11, 1876; Florence A., born June 14, 1882; Gertrude S., born April 27, 1884.

J. H. BOUTON.

FRANCIS W. FINCHER—1872.

Francis W. Fincher entered upon this world's stage at Hudson, Lenawee Co., Mich., May 1, 1855. When but a child he went with his parents to live on a farm in New York State. Receiving there a limited education at the district school, with his family he came to Pentwater in April, 1872. Arriving at Montague they waited three days for the railroad to be repaired, and finally, after a very rough ride in a freight car from that place, reached Pentwater April 12th, about midnight. His first summer here was spent in a shingle mill. The following winter he attended the high school, at the close of which he entered the Oceana Co. Bank where he remained a few months and then entered the drug store of Page & Jesson as clerk. Here he remained until the fall of 1875, when he went to Chicago, attending during the winter of 1875-6 a course of lectures at the Chicago College of Pharmacy. The summer of 1876 was spent at Muskegon, clerking in a drug store. The following spring Mr. H. F. Hastings having purchased the stock of drugs from Page & Jesson, he took charge of the store until the fall of 1877, when in company with A. W. Newark he purchased the business and continued the same until September, 1880, when Mr. Newark retired. The drug business which Mr. Fincher now conducts is the oldest established house of its kind in Oceana Co., having been started by Mr. James G. Gray in 1866. He was married Feb. 20, 1884, to Miss Ida M. Whittington, of Pentwater. Although a young man, by personal attention, integrity and uprightness in all his dealings, Mr. Fincher stands today among the substantial business men of the county.

F. W. FINCHER.

CHARLES A. HAWLEY—1872.

Charles Andross Hawley, fruit grower, Shelby, was born in Bridgeport, Vt., May 22, 1831. He was the oldest of six children. His mother died when he was but twelve years of age. The five children died one after another until his oldest brother, Samuel F., and the last except himself, died April 20, 1876, aged 44 years and five months. While a lad of eleven he engaged himself with his father's consent to a farmer and lived with him three years working for his board, clothes and three months' schooling each year. At the age of fourteen years he hired out to the same man for $4 per month, worked summers and attended school winters until seventeen years of age. Then engaged himself to another farmer until 21 years of age for $100, board, clothing and three months' schooling each year. Lived with him four years and received the schooling and clothing, but not the $100. He continued working for farmers until March 21, 1855, when he married Miss Electa Edwards Weaver, a very intelligent, Christian young lady, highly esteemed as a successful teacher and worker. They have three sons living, Samuel F., Edward Wm. and Joseph. Mr. Hawley is a self-made man. He first started for himself by purchasing a farm, paying a portion down, and then because of the extreme hard times of 1857 was obliged to surrender it. He then worked in a lumber yard in Chicago,

C. A. HAWLEY.

first as laborer, then as clerk, lumber inspector, and finally dealer in hardwood lumber, when the great fire of 1871 came and swept away his lumber yards and employment, although his home in Park Ridge escaped. Sept. 28, 1872, he came to Shelby, made a contract with Malcolm & Williams to saw two million feet of hardwood logs, and during the winter advanced them $2,000 with which to build a mill. Aug. 27, 1873, he and Joseph Clark bought three-fourths' interest in the mill, and in December the other fourth. Afterwards he bought Mr. Clark's interest. After various unfortunate experiences with the mill and his former associates, April 16, 1879, the boiler exploded (see page 103). In seventy-one days from the time he commenced to remove the rubbish he was sawing again. Aug. 18, 1886, this mill burned, and with it a feed mill and many new machines added. Mr. Hawley and Alexander Pittenger did much to make Shelby a growing village. Mr. P. would sell lots on time, and Mr. H. would furnish the lumber to build with, taking work or logs in pay. Many a person coming to Shelby got his first start by Mr. Hawley furnishing him work. In 1881 he purchased eighty acres near the village, and afterwards forty acres more, and after manufacturing lime upon the place has transformed it into a model fruit farm. He now has 5,000 healthy trees living and expects to set out 2,000 more next year. He has fine buildings upon his place and although he has seen hard times everybody wishes him well.

ALBERT Z. MOORE—1872.

Albert Z. Moore, or as he is known to his friends, "Al" Moore, was born at China, Kennebec Co., Maine, being a son of Robert and Lorania Moore. He has followed several occupations, being for seven years engaged in the business of tanning leather, eleven years in the railroad business most of the time as station agent at Shelby, and at present being engaged in the hotel business at Shelby as landlord of the Moore Hotel. He is one of Oceana's most genial and hospitable citizens. His friends are limited only by his acquaintance, as every one with whom he comes in contact is impressed at once by the engaging manner he possesses. He is a gentleman of high and generous impulses, living among his friends, quiet and unassuming, he wins and holds their esteem by his true manliness of character. He came to Oceana County in 1872, and has since resided at Shelby. He has been two terms Treasurer of his township. He is the present W. M. of Benona Lodge No. 289, of Shelby, and there is no better posted Mason in Northern Michigan than he, nor any who takes more pride in the prosperity of the order. Married in 1877 to Miss Jennie Popejoy. No children.

MARCUS H. BROOKS—1867.

Marcus Harrison Brooks was born in Lansing, Tompkins Co., N. Y., in 1837. His parents were Mark Hargen and Elizabeth Brooks. His father was born in Conn. Our subject received his education at Grotten, Moravian and Homer Academies. At the latter institution Prof. Clark, celebrated as the author of Clark's grammar, was his preceptor. Mr. Brooks started in life as a teacher at seventeen years of age and followed this occupation until he was twenty-nine years of age. He read law while teaching, was examined and admitted to the bar July

12, 1870. April 14, 1859, he married Anna Richards, who was born and grew to womanhood in Tioga Co., Pa. The union was a happy one and three sons and one daughter are still living to comfort and bless them. Politically Mr. Brooks has always been a republican. He is now serving his fourth term as Circuit Court Commissioner. Has been Justice of the Peace in Hart since April, 1868, and served as Justice in Pennsylvania seven years. He has also been a member of the school Board at Hart since 1868, and Director except one term. Has been Township Clerk several times. Mr. Brooks has been a careful, methodical business man, is pleasantly and comfortably situated, enjoys a large Justice business and is often engaged as counsel and advisor in the settling of conflicting interests where the parties do not wish to engage in litigation.

THEODORE G. HOUK—1873.

See page 220.

GEORGE R. BATE—1873.

George R. Bate was born in Hudson, Hillsdale Co., Mich., June 16, 1850. His parents were George and Mary Bate. He lived with his parents until the age of fourteen years when he branched out for himself, securing a situation in a hardware store in Adrian, where he continued for one year. He then went into a hardware store at St. Joseph where he remained until 1873. At that time he came to Pentwater and went to work upon a tug with his brother-in-law, Chas. Lamont, where he learned engineering the first year and obtained a license the next. He continued upon the tug three years. After being in business at Petoskey several years he returned to Oceana County and purchased the hardware business of Mathews & Chappell at Hart; in which business he is now engaged, carrying a full line of heavy and shelf hardware and hardware notions. In 1879 he was married to Miss Estelle Moore, of Hart, a daughter of B. Moore. They have one child,

G. R. BATE.

a son. Mr. Bate is a quiet and unobtrusive gentleman, but withal has a wide circle of acquaintances and friends. As a business man he commands the respect and confidence of those with whom he comes in contact.

JOHN A. COLLIER—1873.

John A. Collier, born at St. Johnsville, N. Y., Oct. 3, 1840, is a son of John and Harriet P. Collier. He is one of those men who, when their country needed their strong arms, went to the front and did their duty without flinching. April 17, 1861, he enlisted in the 3rd Mass. Vol. Inf. for three months and served ten days over his time before being discharged. He then went to New York State and on July 11, 1862, enlisted as a private in the 115th N. Y. Vol. Inf. for the term of three years. In August, 1862, he was promoted to Corporal; in October to 3rd Sergeant; May, 1863, to 1st Sergeant; Nov., 1864, to 2nd Lieut., and June, 1865, to 1st Lieut. and Adjutant. He was engaged in thirty battles and skirmishes and was slightly wounded several times. He served the three years less one month and was honorably discharged. On Sept. 7, 1868, he was married to Miss Myra J. Hicks. They have two children, a son and a daughter. Mr. Collier came to Oceana Co. Nov. 4, 1873,

J. A. COLLIER.

and has since resided at Hart where the greater part of the time he has followed blacksmithing. He has held the offices of Constable, Justice and Treasurer in the township, and Village Marshal. Upon the recommendations of leading citizens of Hart, he has recently been appointed Postmaster of that village. He is present Secretary and Treasurer of Oceana County Veterans' Association.

JOHN F. WIDOE—1873.

In October, 1873, a young man of good address, with an air of business about him, came to this county and in 1877 opened a small clothing store in Hart. This was the first attempt made by

any one to run an exclusive clothing store, and many predicted failure. The predictions failed and our young clothier succeeded. His business grew, and he grew in favor with it until today it is recognized as one of the principal business institutions of Hart and he is enjoying his second term as Mayor of the village. The name of the person referred to is John F. Widoe, and he was born at Danville, Ohio, March 18, 1856. Sept. 4, 1886, he married Cora Eastman. They have one child, a daughter, Iva, to comfort them. Mr. Widoe has ever enjoyed the confidence and esteem of the people of Hart, and has held many local offices. He is public spirited and has contributed largely to the general prosperity of the village.

J. F. WIDOE.

WILLIAM WOODLAND—1873.

William Woodland, son of John and Margaret Woodland, was born at Perth, Canada, Dec. 31, 1842. He came to Grand Rapids, Mich., in Nov., 1865, where he worked in the construction of the G. R. & I. R. R. thro' Grand Rapids. Went to Lamont in 1867, where he remained two years, then going West and engaging in lumbering which he followed until August, 1872, when he returned to Michigan. He came to Oceana Co. in May, 1873, and engaged in farming which he has continued to follow to the present time. When he first came to Shelby, in 1873, there was but one hotel, one

WM. WOODLAND.

hardware and Postoffice, one mercantile establishment, a peanut stand, school house, depot and saw mill in the village. He furnished some of the timber and contributed money toward building the Congregational Church. He also helped to build the M. E. Church. At the time the church frame was raised the ladies furnished a dinner at Hedges' Hall and he pronounced it an excellent one. Mr. W. was Highway Commissioner two years and School Director six years. He married at Lamont, Aug. 23, 1872, Miss Mary Roberts, and they have had six children, but have lost by death their oldest son and youngest daughter, leaving them three sons and one daughter.

WILLIAM H. DUNN—1873.

William H. Dunn was born in Wayne Co., Mich., July 14, 1842. He was one of our Union soldiers in the war of 1861, having been a member of Co. K, 27th Mich. Inf. Since the institution of G. A. R. Posts in this county he has always taken a great interest in their growth and general advancement. He is one of the Past Commanders of Shield's Post at Shelby. By occupation he is a farmer owning a fine farm in Shelby township. He came to this county in April, 1873, and has since taken a prominent part in the affairs of the county, and more especially of his township. He is a leading member and Past Grand of the Shelby Lodge I. O. O. F. His political doctrine is 'home protection to labor as well as manufactures must be our national policy.' In the House of Representatives of the State in 1889, he was made Sergeant-at-Arms, in which capacity he acted until its adjournment. He now holds a position on the capitol police force at Washington, D. C. Married April 10, 1864, Dema L. Doolittle. One child, a son.

W. H. DUNN.

ELIAB S. HOUGHTALING—1873.

Eliab S. Houghtaling was born at Green Oak, Oakland Co., Mich.,

May 22, 1848. His parents were W. O. and P. E. Houghtaling. When three years of age he, with his parents, removed to a farm three miles northeast of Grand Rapids. Here he attended district school winters and worked upon the farm summers until sixteen years of age; after which time attended the Grand Rapids High School and the Grand Rapids Commercial College. Like many other young men he then engaged in teaching school. He taught in Kent Co. several winters; and in 1873, at the solicitation of friends he came to Crystal Valley, this county, for the purpose of teaching that school, which he taught two terms. While teaching at Crystal Valley he met Miss Sadie A. Sackrider and in October, 1874, he married her. They have had born to them one child, a son. After his marriage he returned to Grand Rapids where he engaged in farming for two years, then embarking in manufacturing business. This business not proving as remunerative as could be desired, he gave it up and again came to Oceana Co. in 1883, locating at Hart and establishing his present business. He is proprietor of what is known as the "Star Grocery," and deals in groceries and provisions, foreign and domestic fruits and all articles usually found in a first class establishment of this kind. Mr. Houghtaling is known as a shrewd, careful and conscientious business man. He is now a member of the Village Council and is a prominent member of the Odd Fellows' fraternity, having the titles of P. G. and P. C. P. in that order.

E. S. HOUGHTALING.

GEORGE E. DEWEY—1873.

George E. Dewey is a son of George and Harriet Dewey and was born in Penn Line, Crawford Co., Pa., July 31, 1854. He resided at his birthplace until thirteen years of age, when he moved to Kelloggsville, Ashtabula Co., Ohio, where he worked at cheesemaking summers and attended school winters until 1873, when he came to Oceana Co. He located first at Crystal Lake where he run the Crystal Lake mill for seven years; then came to Shelby village and formed a copartnership with Mr. M. C. White, under the name of

White & Dewey, in the general merchandise business. This he continued until 1884, when they dissolved partnership and he became a member of the firm of Rankin & Dewey in the same business which he has since followed. The subject of our sketch has been generally prosperous in his business affairs, accumulating considerable property. The firm is now located in the new Opera House Block and doing a business of $40,000 per annum, starting with a business of $10,000 per annum. Mr. Dewey was elected Treasurer of Shelby township in 1885, and again in 1886. In the village he has been a Trustee since its incorporation excepting 2 years, Village Treasurer 1 year, and was President in 1889. He is an active Mason, and a public spirited man; now Treasurer of the Shelby Improvement Association. Married in November, 1882, to Miss Kate Rankin and they have three children, two sons and one daughter.

G. E. DEWEY.

CHARLES E. McCLURE—1873.

Charles E. McClure was born in Edinboro, Erie Co., Pa., Aug. 2, 1861. His parents' names were William and Eliza McClure. He lived with his parents at the place of his birth until he was twelve years of age, when the family came to Oceana Co., landing at Pentwater and going by team to Elbridge township. After 1 year removed to Crystal Valley and during several years worked in shingle and saw mills there and at Hamlin and Manistee. He then decided to become a sailor and shipped aboard a Lake Michigan craft and sailed upon that lake several years. During this time he was twice shipwrecked, once at Pilot Island and again at Round Island in Green Bay. After leaving the lake he shipped aboard an ocean sailing craft at New York. While on salt water he visited France, England, Germany, Spain, New Zealand, West Indies and Mexico. He again met with shipwreck while in the Gulf of Mexico. Deciding to give up sailing he left his boat at New York and went to Dakota. After starving there thirteen months he returned to Michigan and in 1885 located in Leavitt and commenced farming. Dec. 22, 1886. he married Miss Anna Jensen and they now have one child, a daughter. He still owns forty acres of land on Sec. 7, Leavitt, of which twenty acres are improved. In 1889 he engaged in business at Walkerville where he is still located. For a young man he has had an eventful life; but is satisfied that in Oceana Co. he can do as well as anywhere.

DANIEL E. McCLURE—1873.

Daniel E. McClure was born at Gerrard, Pa., Oct. 25, 1853. His parents were William and Eliza McClure. While living in Pennsylvania he worked in the lumber woods and at farming for the purpose of paying his way at the Edinboro State Normal School which he attended two years, fitting himself for teaching. He came to Oceana Co. in Sept., 1873, and while "looking about him" supported himself by farm work. He then secured a situation and taught school for seven years in Newaygo and Oceana Counties, two years in country districts, four years as Principal of Shelby schools, and one year as principal of Hesperia schools.

D. E. McCLURE.

Having saved enough money to warrant his attending some institution of learning with the idea of improving his education, he went to Valparaiso, Ind., to attend the Normal School from which he graduated. In 1882 he accepted a position with Harper & Bros. as salesman of their series of school books, traveling in Michigan, Minnesota, Dakota, Kansas, Wisconsin and Illinois. He continued in this business until

1889, having been very successful, his success being evidenced by an increase of salary from year to year. In 1876, Aug. 16, he married Miss Julia E. Rathbone. Their family now consists of two daughters and one son. Mr. McClure has been Township Superintendent of Schools, and in 1889 was elected Secretary of the County Board of Examiners for Oceana Co., which position he now holds. The subject of our sketch is pre-eminently a self-made man, having from his early boyhood been compelled to depend upon his own resources for his education and support.

WILLIAM H. TULLER—1873.

William H. Tuller, only son of Wm. and Alvira Tuller, was born at Jonesville, Hillsdale Co., Mich., Feb. 12, 1855. When nine years of age his father died and he was sent away from home to live with relatives. When thirteen years of age he returned to Jonesville and began work in the woolen mills which he continued with slight inter-

W. H. TULLER.

mission until seventeen, when he became janitor in the union school. At this time he acquired what education he has, excepting a few months at a time in country schools while living with relatives. In the spring of 1873 he came to Pentwater where he began life as a teamster in the woods, later clerking in a drug store, and in the winter of 1873 commencing the study of law with Grove & Hartwick. Attended the Law Department of the State University at

Ann Arbor in the winter of 1874-5 and 1875-6, graduating in spring of 1876, and being admitted to the bar in this county soon after graduating. He then formed a partnership with L. M. Hartwick which continued but six months. Was one winter with R. M. Montgomery and in about 1879 entered the law office of W. E. Ambler where he continued about two years, gradually working into a knowledge of banking business, and finally about 1881 engaging with Nielsen & Co., Bankers, where he continued until July, 1889, with a break of only about a year in 1886-7. In the fall of 1876 he was appointed Deputy Collector of Customs for the port of Pentwater, which office he held until 1885. In 1878 he was elected Justice of the Peace, holding one term. In 1881 he was elected Clerk of the township, and again in 1885-6-7-8. He has also been School Inspector of the township and a member of the Common Council of the village. He has been identified with the Pentwater Fire Department for fifteen years, holding the office of Chief for five years; also being the present Secretary of the Michigan State Firemen's Association, this being his fifth term. Mr. Tuller was married in April, 1877, to Miss Ida A. Newark, from whom he parted by mutual consent in 1885. On May 17, 1888, married Miss Mary E. McClure and they have had one child, W. Mack, born March 24, 1889; died May 21, 1890.

THOMAS H. BAKER—1874.

Thomas H. Baker was born Aug. 13, 1858, at St. George, Brant Co., Ont. His parents were Thos R. and Elizabeth Baker. He learned the tinner's trade when quite young. In 1874 he came to Oceana Co. July 2, 1880, he was married to Miss Lottie M. Phelps, of Jefferson, Ohio. They have two children, a son and a daughter. Mr. Baker has always followed his trade working in Shelby four years for Joseph Tyler and four years for Archie R. McKinnon. By close application to business and strict economy he has accumulated some means and has recently purchased a fruit farm. He is a young man with many friends. Has twice been

T. H. BAKER.

elected Clerk of the village of Shelby, and in the Odd Fellows Lodge has held the position of Noble Grand.

WILLIE H. SHIRTS—1874.

Willie H. Shirts was born at Bryon, Ohio, April 15, 1860, and is a son of E. J. Shirts. He came to Oceana Co. May 1, 1874, and has made Shelby his home most of the time since. He was, however, a clerk in S. H. Lasley & Co.'s store at Montague for three years. On May 1, 1881, he began business at Shelby with his brother, J. D. M. Shirts, as grocers, which they still continue, doing a good business. The subject of our sketch is a young man of good address, well thought of in his locality. He was elected Village Treasurer in the spring of 1887, and re-elected to the same office in 1888. In 1889 he was elected a Trustee of the village, which office he now holds. Oct. 1, 1883, he was appointed local agent of the American Express Co. and still continues to discharge the duties of that position. He was married, at Montague, June 8, 1882, to Margaret M. Raby, and one child, a daughter, now contributes to the happiness of their fireside.

W. H. SHIRTS.

WILLIAM H. BARRY—1874.

William H. Barry was born in Orleans Co., N. Y., Feb. 8, 1845. His parents were John and Mary M. Barry. He was brought up upon a farm and has followed that occupation nearly all his life. He came with his parents to Girard, Branch Co., Mich., in 1852, where he continued to reside most of the time until 1874. He taught school one winter and cut and run logs two years in Allegan Co. He spent one summer in Manistee loading lumber vessels. During the war he served as a private in Bat. E, 1st Mich. L. Art. from Oct. 4, 1864, to July 30, 1865. He came to Oceana County in June, 1874, and began chopping on farm in Shelby township in August of the same year. Has since then worked some in the lumber woods and mills in this county. In 1882 he engaged in keeping

W. H. BARRY.

bees and now has 102 colonies. He owns and partly works a farm of forty acres in Shelby, and one of eighty acres in Golden. Mr. Barry was elected Constable in 1877; Supervisor in 1881 and 1883, and Trustee of his school district. He has always been a leader in whatever he undertakes. Among the Grangers of the county he is a man of influence; is a leading member of the Masonic Lodge at Shelby, and also of the G. A. R. Post.

WILLIAM. P. SACKRIDER—1874.

William P. Sackrider was born at Norwich, Can., Oct. 28, 1864. His parents were Charles and Catherine Sackrider. He moved with his parents to Grand Rapids, Mich., in 1871, and to Oceana Co., locating at Hart, in '74. In 1880 he graduated from the Hart Union School, and commenced teaching. In '82 he graduated from Valparaiso, Ind., in the teacher's course, and continued school teaching until Jan. 1, 1887, when he entered the law office of L. G. Rutherford, at Hart, and began the study of law. Was admitted to the bar Oct. 31, 1887, and at once entered into partnership with Mr. Rutherford in the practice of that profession. He was Deputy County Clerk in 1888, and at the fall election was elected Clerk of the county,

W. P. SACKRIDER.

which office he is now filling, discharging its duties to the abundant satisfaction of all who have business with the office. March 24, '87, he was married to Miss Nina Bailey, at Hart. Mr. and Mrs. Sackrider are possessed of many warm personal friends whom they have made by their courteous manners.

EDGAR H. HOTCHKISS—1874.

Edgar H. Hotchkiss, son of Cyrus and Asenath Hotchkiss, was born at Colebrook, Litchfield Co., Conn., June 12, 1830. He attended common schools until the age of twelve years, since which time he has only been to school three days. He came to Michigan the 15th day of Oct., 1868, locating at Fennville, Allegan Co., where he remained working at his trade, carpenter and joiner, until he came to Oceana Co. He arrived in this county April 15, 1874, located in Golden township where he has since resided, working at his trade until 1884, when he was appointed express agent at Mears, which position he still holds. In 1852 he voted for Franklin Pierce that being the only democratic vote he ever cast. In 1856 voted for John C. Fremont. In October, 1878 he was elected Township Clerk to fill vacancy, and was re-elected in 1879-'80-1-2-5-8. He has also held the office of Justice of Peace 7 years. He has taken a great interest in Odd Fellowship and is one of the Past Grands of Hart Lodge. As a temperance worker he is known over the county having always been prominent in that line of work. Married Oct. 13, 1850, Miss Susan Hotchkiss and they have had three children, one son and two daughters.

OTTO W. MARSH—1874.

Otto W. Marsh, son of Wm. M. and Cynthia Marsh, was born at Jackson, Wayne Co., Ohio, Dec. 18, 1851. He came to Oceana Co. in 1874, and lived with his uncle, Mr. E. A. Benjamin, in Weare for two years. In 1876 he moved to Pentwater where he has since resided, excepting two years in Kansas. He made up his mind that he did not like Kansas, and that Michigan was good enough for him. He has followed teaming for a number of years and has the record of drawing the largest load of lumber ever hauled from Crystal to the docks at Pentwater. It scaled five thousand feet at Crystal Valley. He is now proprietor of the Pentwater Transfer and Dray Line, and is doing a good business, making it a point to go to the depot every day. On Oct. 3, 1876, he was married to Miss Susanna Sage, a daughter of Henry Sage, of Weare. They have two children, a son and a daughter.

AZWELL E. BURGESS—1875.

Azwell E. Burgess was born in Canada, June 4, 1835. His par-

A. Z. BURGESS.

ents were William A. and Nancy A. Burgess. He has been a sailor for the past forty years. Was master of the "Spartan," that bro't supplies to Cobb & Rector at Pentwater in 1854. He has since been master in sailing vessels and steam barges, being for three years back, master of the barge Daisy Day. He came to this county Oct. 21, 1875, and has since resided here. He has held the offices of Overseer of Highways and Trustee of School District. He is a leading member of Pentwater Lodge No. 378, I. O. O. F., and one of its Past Grands. On Dec. 24, 1862, he was married at St. Joseph, Berrien Co., to Mary Eliza Reynolds, who was born May 16, 1843, at Lawrence, Van Buren Co., Mich. They have had seven children, three sons and four daughters, all living and three married.

CORNELIUS W. CRAMER—1875.

Cornelius W. Cramer was born at Sharon, Washtenaw Co., Mich., on the 19th day of April, 1848. He is a son of Peter and Artemisia Cramer. His father now resides in North Weare. The subject of our sketch removed with his parents to Woodland, Barry Co. in 1852, where he resided until 1864, when he removed to Hastings, Mich., where he attended the high school. He was married April 16, 1873, to Miss Phebe Kinckerbacor, of Rutland, Barry Co.

He taught school in Barry Co. during six winters, working at the carpenter's trade summers. He was one of the pioneer carpenters of Cadillac, helping to frame and build some of the first buildings there. When he went there in 1872 there was but one frame house there. He studied medicine with Mr. E. F. Brown at Hastings in 1874 and during the winter of '74-5 was a student at the medical department of the University. In March, 1875, he came to Pentwater and began the practice of medicine as a homeopath, which he has since continued, working up a good practice. In February, 1886, he graduated from the Hahnemann Medical College at Chicago.

C. W. CRAMER.

He has one son, Fred W., born Oct. 28, 1875.

ALFRED E. SOUTER—1875.

Alfred E. Souter was born at Wingfield Castle, Suffolk Co., Eng., March 23, 1851. He is a son of Thomas and Mary Souter and was raised upon a farm. In August, 1875, he came to Oceana County and located upon a farm near Carpenter's school house. In 1883 he began his present business at Shelby, viz.: insurance, real estate and collecting. Mr. Souter has been always energetic in business affairs and a leader among his associates in other matters. He is one of the Past Grands of Shelby Lodge No. 344, I. O. O. F. In the first I. O. G. T. Lodge organized at Shelby he was for six terms W. C. T. In the township he is now serving his second term as Justice. Has been Village Attorney and Trustee of the graded school. In religious matters he is an earnest worker and for eight years has been Trustee of the M. E. Church. Mr. Souter married July 2, 1875, Miss Susie A. McClentic, who was born near Port Dover, Ont., July 9th, 1885. Her father died when she was about one year of age, leaving the care and support of a family of five children to her mother, who proved equal to the occasion and succeeded in giving them a fair common school education. Mrs.

A. E. SOUTER.

Souter came to Michigan with her mother at the age of eleven years. At the age of sixteen she began teaching school and taught thirteen terms, nearly half of them in one district. She came with her husband to this county and settled with him upon their woods farm. She afterwards taught the Carpenter school three terms and the Piper school, district No. 1, one term, during which time she, with the help of Mr. S., did the housework at home. She was a charter member of and held the office of Treasurer in the first lodge of I. O. G. T. organized in Shelby. She has for ten years been a member and earnest worker in the M. E. Church and its auxiliary societies. She has also been an active member of the W. C. T. U., and the Rebekah Lodge at Shelby. Her greatest pride and most pleasant work is in the care and education of her little family of children, consisting of four sons and one daughter. Mrs. Souter appreciates, with just reason, her pleasant home which she has helped to build. Having known the privations and hardships of pioneer life she can more fully realize the blessings of her present surroundings. With "Mrs. Grundy" she has no acquaintance.

MRS. A. E. SOUTER.

FRANK W. NEWMAN—1869.

Frank W. Newman was born in Eaton County, Mich., Jan. 21,

1859. Ten years later his parents moved to Oceana Co., where for the most part Mr. N. has since resided. His education was obtained in a common school and on a farm. From 1878 to 1881 he assisted his father in a general store, located at first in Shelby and later in Coopersville. Returning to Shelby in Nov. 1881, he taught school during the winter, and the following year entered the employ of Judson Palmiter, then proprietor of the Shelby Independent, as "devil," local reporter and general manager of that sheet. Spent the winter of 1883-4 in Chicago at the case. Returning in February, 1884, he purchased the office of the Independent, and has since been its proprietor until his death, which occurred Mar. 2, 1890. In November, 1884, he was married to Miss Florence A. Grousbeck, of Ellington, Minn. He was elected to the office of Township Clerk three years on the republican ticket. Under Mr. Newman's management the Independent has been an aggressive republican paper, taking an active part in the campaigns of '84, '86 and '88. On the tariff an ardent protectionist, and supporting the submission of

F. W. NEWMAN.

a prohibitory amendment to the Constitution of the State, and working for its success when submitted in 1887. A hearty supporter of prohibition by counties when the amendment had failed, and to the last had an abiding faith that the republicans of the State will give the people some temperance legislation that will be satisfactory to the great masses of temperance people.

BENJAMIN MOORE—1868.

The subject of this sketch was by birthright a Quaker, having been born of Quaker parents, John and Mary Moore, in Sadsbury, then in Lancaster, but now in Chester County, Pa., on the 28th day of Oct., 1814. His education was limited, being acquired at the common schools, and his early life uneventful. On the 20th day of Nov., 1839, he took to wife Hannah Harlan, at the Quaker church in Sadsbury, according to the order, and until death parted

B. MOORE.

them they remained a true and devoted couple. His wife was born on the 22nd day of Jan., 1819, in Newportville, Pa. Mr. Moore remained a Quaker in belief until a few years before his death when he became a Spiritualist. He had four sons and one daughter. The eldest son died at the age of 22 years. The other children are still living. He was by trade a carpenter. He never was conspicuous in politics, but was a Garrisonian abolitionist, and always a friend to the slave and the oppressed wherever found. The first time he ever voted was for Harrison in 1840. He also voted for the loved Lincoln. He came to Oceana Co. in the fall of 1868, settled in Blooming Valley and for many years kept an accurate record of rain and snow fall, temperature. etc., a table of which appears elsewhere. He died at Shelby, July 22, 1886, greatly respected by all who knew him for his honesty and fair dealing. His wife is still living.

WILLIAM F. HILLYARD—1876.

William F. Hillyard was born at Troy, Ashland Co., Ohio, Feb. 14, 1847. He is a son of Martin and Johana Hillyard. He came to Oceana Co. in 1876, locating in Leavitt, where he has since resided, and where he now owns and works a farm of eighty acres. He has been Treasurer three terms and Supervisor one term. He is an industrious, persevering man and is gradually accumulating this world's goods. On Jan. 1, 1868, he married Miss Ellen Plumley, and four children, three sons and one daughter, have blessed the union. As a public officer Mr. Hillyard has always given good satisfaction and as a neighbor is agreeable and pleasant.

RICHARD E. SOUTHWICK—1876.

Richard E. Southwick, the son of Josiah and Huldah (Hawley) Southwick, was born in Erie Co., N. Y., April 27, 1852. He is the eighth generation from Lawrence and Cassandra Southwick, who came from England to America in 1636 and settled at Salem, Mass. The family were Quakers and nearly all farmers. Mr. S. came to Oceana County in 1876, and bought a farm on Sec. 22, Elbridge. In 1877 he was married to Miss Emma Rogers, daughter of Isaac and Eliza (Mills) Rogers, of Ottawa Co., Mich. They commenced pioneer life in a log house; their stock consisting of one cow and a yoke of oxen. He now has as good a stock and fruit farm as any in the county, comprising 120 acres. Both he and his wife taught school before and after marriage; and he was two years Superintendent of Schools in Elbridge. He is one of the Directors and Agent of the Farmers' Insurance Co. Mr. S. believes that education is essential to a farmer, and that to be successful one must learn the trade and use more judgment and brains than in any other occupation. His children are J. Rogers, Bertha Sopha, Lulu and Richard I.

R. E. SOUTHWICK.

WILLIAM ELMER THORP—1876.

W. E. Thorp, as he is known throughout the length and breadth of Oceana County, like many of those whose sketches have before appeared is a native of New York State. He was born at Sherman, N. Y., Jan. 14, 1841, to Alfred and Frances R. Thorp. He received the usual advantages of common school education and engaged in school teaching and clerking. When the war of the rebellion broke out he enlisted as a private in Co. D, 21st N. Y. Inf., and served 2 years. Was in the U. S. Navy as a landsman 9 months and was honorably discharged. Since the war he has taken an active interest in G. A. R. matters and has done as much as any one man in Oceana Co. to secure veteran organizations in the county. The G. A. R. record published elsewhere, shows what positions he has held in the order. Possessing a good commercial education he was especially competent to fill the position of Assist. Adjt. Gen'l of the Dept. of Mich. G. A. R., to which he was appointed by Comdr. Rutherford; owing to the successful conduct of that department has received many flattering testimonials from his comrades. He married Helen M. Sheldon, an estimable lady, Jan. 7, 1868, who is still his faithful companion. He came to Oceana Co., May 1, 1876, and in September of the same year engaged in the mercantile business at Hart, which he has since successfully conducted. Mr. Thorp is an ardent democrat and has often been honored with nominations by that party, the most notable being the nomination in 1886 for Representative in the State Legislature. He has held the office of Village Trustee of Hart one term. Mr. Thorp is a genial, whole-souled gentleman, who not only seeks to enjoy life himself, but contributes all in his power to the comfort and pleasure of others. He still resides at Hart.

W. E. THORP.

RAYMOND ROSS—1877.

Raymond Ross, son of Dunham and Savina Ross, was born in Bradford Co., Pa., June 30, 1852. He came to this county in June, 1877, and bought eighty acres of wild land on Sec. 12, Elbridge, which he has since been engaged in clearing and working, at the same time doing carpenter work when opportunity offered. He now has sixty acres improved with an orchard of 600 peach, 200 apple trees and 100 grapevines. He is a member of the Stetson Lodge I. O. O. F. and is one of the best posted of its members. Married Jan. 13, 1878, to Miss Myrtie A. Taylor, and they now have five children, three sons and two daughters.

MELVIN O. FISHER—1877.

Melvin O. Fisher was born at Mendon, St. Joseph County, Mich., June 2, 1856. He is a son of William G. and Sarah A. Fisher, now

M. O. FISHER.

residing in Crystal township. He came to Oceana County in March, 1877, and is now residing at Crystal township. He has held the office of School Inspector two terms and that of Highway Commissioner one term. He is an active member of the Odd Fellows' fraternity, having just finished his term as Noble Grand of Crystal Valley Lodge No. 386. Has also been Treasurer of that Lodge. He has followed farming generally for a livelihood, but has also learned the carpenter trade. "Mel," as he is familiarly called, has many friends and is accounted a good fellow by all his acquaintances.

JOHN V. CAHILL—1877.

John V. Cahill was born at Alden, Erie Co., N. Y., May 8, '40. He is the son of Patrick and Ellenor W. Cahill. June 6, 1867, he was married to Lydia E. Miers. Mr. Cahill has been a farmer and mechanic and is now a member of the firm of Griswold & Cahill, carrying a general line of hardware, at Hart. He has been a soldier, having enlisted as a private in Co. G, 10th Wis. Inf. and serving three years. He was wounded at the battle of Perrysville, Ky. As a G. A. R. man he stands high, having been Commander of Joe Hooker Post at Hart, also having held other offices in that organization. He has been a resident of this county since November, 1877, and probably no business man in the county has the confidence of the public to a greater extent than he.

J. V. CAHILL.

RICHARD V. WANMER—1877.

The subject of this sketch was born in Schenectady, N. Y., April 24, 1857, the son of Uriah and Elizabeth Wanmer. His boyhood days were spent upon a farm. He came to Oceana Co. Dec. 27, 1877, and worked out upon a farm until the spring of '82, when having purchased a forty acre farm near the celebrated Gebhart fruit farm, commenced the business of fruit raising, and today he owns one of the model fruit farms of the county. His peach and plum orchards cover a large portion of his farm. Although still a young man he has secured for himself a fine home and competence, and established a reputation as one of the most successful fruit raisers of the county. Feb. 20, '84, he married Miss Mate Stark, who has borne to him two children, one son and one daughter.

R. V. WANMER.

WILLIAM HENRY CORNELL—1877.

"Harry" Cornell, as he is familiarly known, was born at Hamilton, Ont., Feb. 2, '54, the son of William and Elizabeth Cornell. He visited Oceana Co. Dec. 15, 1877, while traveling from place to place as a dentist. The advantages offered by Hart for a resident dentist induced him to locate there. Oct. 9, 1879, he married Miss Minnie Palmiter, and together this happy couple occupy a fine home in Hart village, blessed by one child, a daughter. Mr. Cornell is one of the best dentists in Northern Michigan and is the only one located in the county. His main office is at Hart, but he visits both Pentwater and Shelby weekly. Had he adopted the theatrical profession he would have made a success, as he is a natural actor and possesses unusual dramatic talent. He is manager and proprietor of Palmiter's Opera Hall, and to him our people are indebted for the appearance in the county of many fine troupes. Mr. Cornell has made a success in business, and enjoys a wide circle of friends.

JOHN M. HEIM—1877.

John M. Heim was born at Wittemburg, Germany, his parents being Michael and Mary Heim. He was married in New York City to Mary Shelcup, who died in 1875. They had seven children, four sons and three daughters. In 1876 he married Agnes Whitcomb, whose parent's names were William and Mary Anderson; they have had no children. Mr. Heim, besides serving four years in the German army before coming to this country, has been a Union soldier serving as private twenty-eight months in the 72nd and 38th Ohio Inf. He is now a prominent and enthusiastic G. A. R. member, and has held the office of S. V. By trade he is a cabinet maker and joiner, serving an apprenticeship of fourteen years; and following his trade altogether for forty years. Before going into the army he had provided his family with a home; but coming home from the war sick, and his whole family being sick, he lost his home. He then decided to come to Oceana Co. in Aug. 1877, arriving here with nothing of value excepting an old team. Never having farmed and being no judge of land he located in the openings of Otto, where he soon starved out. He then homesteaded 160 acres one-half mile east of Ferry on the "flats," a large portion of the land being under water. Afterwards he drained the land into White River. He and the boys worked hard and saved and they soon had a good farm. He gave each of the boys who were with him 40 acres, gave his daughter $300, and

J. M. HEIM.

sold the forty on which the buildings were located for $1,500, and moved into Ferry. In 1884 he built the hotel building in which he is now located, known as the "Eagle Hotel." In 1888 he built a large store building with hall above known as "Heim's Hall." Mr. Heim has always been a public spirited man and an evidence of that fact is the Baptist Church, the only church building in Ferry, a large share of the expense of which has been borne by him.

CHARLES F. LEWIS—1878.

C. F. LEWIS.

Charles F. Lewis, son of Charles E. and Ann E. Lewis, was born at Lyons, Ionia Co., Mich., Nov. 11, 1876. He came to Pentwater in August, 1878, and was for three years thereafter a clerk in the Pentwater Lumber Company's stores. After leaving there he was appointed a route agent on the F. & P. M. R. R., which position he held but a short time when he received the appointment of Postmaster at Pentwater in '81. He continued in that position for six years, giving good satisfaction to all concerned. After leaving the P. O. he became a member of the firm of C. F. Lewis & Co., general hardware dealers, and has since managed the business for the firm. Mr. Lewis is a young man of good principles, capable, honest and energetic, and under his management the business has prospered. Married April 1, '81, to Lizzie L. Webb, and they now have two children, a son and a daughter.

GEORGE B. GETTY—1878.

George B. Getty, the subject of this sketch, was born in Jackson, Pa., Oct., 1847. He is a son of Henry and Anna O. Getty. At the age of seventeen years, in 1864, he enlisted in Co. D, 45th Pa. Vet. Vol. Inf., serving until the close of the war, being discharged with his regiment in July, '65. He then returned to Pennsylvania, engaging in the lumber business, which he continued until the spring of '78, when he came to Shelby, this county. He went, as engineer, with E. Remick to East Golden for that season, subsequently with C. A. Hawley until '83. In that year the Shelby Lumber Company was formed, composed of George B. Getty, E. H. Cutler and Charles Rolph. They purchased and rebuilt the Williams saw mill and about a year later Mr. Getty purchased the entire property, adding a planing mill and other improvements, and successfully operated the same until Aug. 3, '89, when the mill and entire stock of lumber was destroyed by fire. The entire loss was about $25,000 Mr. Getty losing about $14,000 with only $2,000 insurance. This was a severe loss to him, but in no wise discouraged he turned his attention to his farm, just north of the village, formerly known as the Randall farm, and proceeded to build thereon a comfortable farm house, warmed

G. B. GETTY.

throughout by steam, one of the best farm houses in the county. Here, surrounded by a loving family, consisting of a wife, three sons and a daughter, he expects to round up the journey of life. Mr. Getty is a part owner of the Shelby Roller Flouring Mills, and one of the stockholders of the Shelby Improvement Company, owner of the Opera House block. He was the first President of the village and has been twice re-elected to the same office. Was one of the first movers in organizing, and a charter member of, Shelby Lodge No. 344, I. O. O. F.; also of Shields Post No. 68, G. A. R., and Ritch Command No. 28, Union Veteran Union, besides holding membership in several other benevolent organizations. Mr. Getty is well and favorably known, enjoying the esteem and confidence of a host of friends in Shelby and throughout the county.

HENRY SAGE—1878.

One of Weare's successful farmers is Mr. Henry Sage, who was born in Nailsea, Somersetshire, England, to Samuel and Elizabeth Sage, Sept. 6, 1828. He emigrated to America in 1852, and for many years was engaged in mining in Pennsylvania. In October

H SAGE.

'54, he was married to Mrs. Mary L. Bainton, who was born at Bradford, Wiltshire, England, April 8, '22, her father's name being William Taylor. She was first married to Samuel Bainton, and after his decease to Mr. Sage, as above. On the 26th day of January, '62, Mr. Sage enlisted in the 107th Pa. Vols., served until Dec. 2, '62, when he was discharged on account of wounds received in battle. Sept. 25, '64, he again enlisted and served until July 8, '65 when he was discharged. He held the office of Corporal. Mr. Sage came to Oceana County and settled upon the place he now owns on the 4th day of June, '78, his wife following him a year later. They have six children, one son and five daughters, all living. This worthy couple have done their share of hard work and have made their farm one of the finest in Weare. They possess the confidence of the business community and the respect of their neighbors.

MRS. H. SAGE.

HORACE J. HOLMES—1878.

Horace J. Holmes, a son of Abner G. and Hepsey B. (Davis) Holmes, was born in Erie Co., Pa., Dec. 19, 1822. At the commencement of the civil war, April 19, '61, he enlisted in Co. G, 10th Wis. Vol. Inf., as a private and served for three years. Was appointed Second Lieut. by E. D. Townsend, Asst. A. Gen'l, U. S. A., Dec. 14, '64. As a soldier Mr. Holmes saw some severe service. He came to this county April 4, '78, and has since resided at Hart. By profession he is an architect and builder, and since March, '87, he has been engaged in book-keeping, also doing architectural work. In 1847 he joined the I. O. O. F. and afterwards became a charter member of Oceana Lodge No. 327, at Hart, and its first Noble Grand. In 1851 he joined the Masonic fraternity, in '71 became a Knight Templar, and in '74 received the Council degrees. In '67 he became a member of the G. A. R. and was in '88 Post Commander of Joe Hooker Post No. 26, at Hart. Mr. Holmes was married June 9, '61, to Catherine C. Cahill, who bore him six children, three sons and three daughters.

H. J. HOLMES.

EDWARD F. COON—1879.

Edward F. Coon was born at Spofford, Onondaga Co., N. Y., Aug. 6, 1842. He is a son of J. V. R. and Clarine Coon. At the commencement of the war he enlisted in Co. I, 99th N. Y., and served three years. He came to Oceana Co. in '79 and settled at Shelby, where he remained until about two years ago when he accepted a position as traveling salesman with the Capital Wagon Co., of Lansing, which position he still holds. On Sept. 13, '86, at LaGro, Ind., he was married to Mary M. Kellar, who makes her home at Shelby while her husband is upon the road. Mr. Coon is deservedly popular with all classes, being of a genial disposition and always ready with a pleasant word for any he may meet. In '81-2 Mr. Coon held the office of Vice President; and '83-4 of President of the Oceana County Veteran Association.

FRANK W. WILSON—1879.

F. W. WILSON.

Frank W. Wilson was born at Tilbury, East Canada, Feb. 9, 1855. He is a son of Andrew and Maria Wilson. His early life was spent in Canada. In 1876 he entered the regular department of medicine of the University of Michigan, at Ann Arbor, from which he graduated in the spring of '79. He then came to Shelby and opened an office for the practice of medicine and surgery, where he has since remained following his profession. On Mar. 26, 1884, he was married to Miss Jessie Rankin, a daughter of D. H. and Christine Rankin. She was born Feb. 3, '67, at Marquette, Mich., and came to Shelby, Aug. 4, '79. Mr. and Mrs. Wilson now have one daughter, Gracie, born Oct. 24, '88. Mr. Wilson is a well read and consequently successful physician. He and his wife enjoy the esteem of their numerous acquaintances.

MRS. F. W. WILSON.

JOHN F. CUMMING—1879.

John F. Cumming was born in Delaware Co., N. Y., March 11, 1853. He is a son of John and Sarah Cumming. Came to Oceana Co. April 3, '79, and has resided here. From April, '84, for one year was engaged in tending the Little Point Au Sable Lighthouse. He, with Geo. Crandall, started a democratic newspaper, and while he was engaged at other work to procure funds to keep the paper "booming," Mr. Crandall became discouraged and left the State, giving the paper a natural death. He is at present engaged in clearing a farm for fruit. Was Postmaster during the last six months of Cleveland's administration.

J. F. CUMMING.

MRS. J. F. CUMMING.

Was Justice of the Peace one term and Supervisor in 1889. Married July 4, 1873, to Clarenda James who was born at Birmingham, Eng., Dec. 25, '53, being a daughter of David and Jane James. She came to America when four years of age and lived with her parents at Brooklyn for ten years. Her father was an iron moulder by trade. She was several years a member of the Plymouth Church Sunday School.

GEORGE H. EDDY—1879.

G. H. EDDY.

George H. Eddy, son of Moses and Sarah Eddy, was born in Cattaraugus Co., N. Y., Oct. 9, 1837. He was for two years a soldier serving in Co. D, 33d N. Y. Inf. Since leaving the army he has taken a great interest in anything that concerned the soldiers. He was Post Commander of Shields Post No. 68, at Shelby, during 1889. Previous to 1879 he followed the business of a mechanic, but in that year he came to Oceana County and began farming for a living, which he has since followed. Married in 1863 to Emily A. Lang, and now has three children, two sons and a daughter.

CHARLES E. CONVERSE—1879.

C. E. CONVERSE.

Charles E. Converse was born in Monroe Co., N. Y., Oct. 14, 1841. His parents' names were Joseph E. and Sarah Converse. He came to Oceana Co. April 15, 1879, and located in Ferry township on Sec. 8. He has been a successful school teacher having taught in all thirty terms in N. Y. and Mich. On Nov. 15, 1865, he married Lucy McLouth, and they have had born to them eight children, seven sons and one daughter. Mr. Converse has held the positions of Justice of the Peace and Superintendent of Schools. He is a man well known in the county where he also has many friends. He is one of those who has added his brain and muscle to the development of the county, now possessing a good home showing signs of thrift and enterprise.

CHARLES A. GURNEY—1879.

Charles A. Gurney was born in Geauga Co., Ohio, June 6, 1853, his parents being A. D. and Mary Gurney. In 1854 he came with his parents to Tuscola Co., Mich. He attended the Tuscola High School, paying his way by teaching winters and graduating at the head of his class. In 1879 he came to Oceana Co. and taught school for his support while studying law. Was admitted to the bar June 26, 1881. He was elected Circuit Court Commissioner in 1882, and again 1884. Has also been Township Clerk. On Dec. 11, 1888, he was married to Carrie M. Wigton, and now rejoices in the title of *pater familias*, having recently been presented with a son. He is a leading member of the Masonic and Odd Fellows' orders and Sons of Veterans' Camp. Whatever he undertakes he puts his strength into and pushes to the front. At present he is proprietor of a drug store at Hart.

C. A. GURNEY.

DANIEL H. RANKIN—1879.

Daniel H. Rankin was born in Dundee, Province of Quebec, Canada, July 12, 1834, being a son of Hugh and Jennette Rankin. At an early age he moved with his parents to London, Ont., where he remained until 1865, at which time he came to Michigan, settling at Marquette. Here he engaged in the manufacture of charcoal, which business with others he has continued to follow to the present time. Mr. Rankin came to Shelby, Oceana Co., in 1879, where he still resides. Since living at Shelby he has been engaged in the business of making charcoal for the Spring Lake Iron Co., making an average of 90,000 bushels a month at the kilns at Shelby and Mears. He is also a member of the firm of Rankin & Dewey, at Shelby, doing a

general merchandise business. Mr. Rankin was married Sep. 22, 1867, to Christie Rankin, who was born in Montreal, Can., Oct. 21, 1838. They now have six children, Kittie, now Mrs. Geo. E. Dewey, Angus D., Daniel D., Jessie, now Mrs. F. W. Wilson, Burt J., and Mary, all of of whom are residing at Shelby. They have lost one child by death, Duncan, born Sept. 26, 1865, who died Oct. 12, 1867.

D. H. RANKIN.

OSCAR H. DEAN—1879.

Oscar H. Dean, son of Henry and Calystia Dean, was born in Detroit, Mich., Aug. 6, 1836. When two years of age he moved with his parents to Grand Rapids, Mich., where he made his home until 1858, when he moved to Ionia, where he was engaged for three years in running a dry goods store. Enlisted Aug. 1, 1861, as private in Co. A, 21st Mich. Inf.; was soon after transferred to Quartermaster's Dept. as Sergeant, and served until Dec. 31, 1861, when he was discharged for disability. He then returned to Grand Rapids and engaged in a Gents' furnishing establishment. Continued about one year in that business, then went to Ionia and was in business there until Sept., 1879, when he came to Pentwater, where he engaged in business for the Pentwater Lumber Co., afterwards buying the stock and running the business for himself until 1886, when he sold to F. O. Gardner. Mr.

O. H. DEAN.

Dean was Village Trustee of Ionia for four years. Has been Justice of the Peace and Village Trustee at Pentwater, and in July, 1887, was appointed Postmaster, which position he held until June 1, 1890. He is in all respects a perfect gentleman and has numerous friends in the county. Married, Dec. 23, 1861, to Miss Alice J. Johnson, of Ionia, a daughter of Ethan S. and Jane B. Johnson, he being a prominent man in that locality. Mr. and Mrs. Dean are prominently identified with the Episcopal Society and are known as active workers. Mr. Dean is also an active Mason, one of the Past Masters of Oceana Lodge No. 200.

CHARLES W. JAY—1871.

Charles W. Jay, whose portrait appears below, was a man of remarkable intellectual ability, and who during a residence in the Co. extending over a period of about twelve years, was a prominent character, although he did not achieve success in his chosen occupation, farming and fruit raising. He was born in New Jersey in 1815. He thus describes his early life: "'I was born of poor but respectable parents.' My father was a shoemaker, and waxed poorer and poorer with the yearly increase of his family, until he could hardly make both ends meet. His sole means of support was his trade, at which he hammered away day and night, in order to get the upper hand of the hard necessity that tacks'd all his energies. At last, by unrelieved confinement, he was assailed by a stitch in the side, the thread of life parted asunder, and my worthy progenitor paid the only debt that he could not elude by the statute of limitations—the debt of Nature.

C. W. JAY.

My father's semi-occasional treatment of myself affords a striking illustration of the law of cause and effect. The only positive recreation in which he indulged, was in treating me to 'black-*strap*,' that he might stirrup my naturally sluggish temperament. And behold the result, a'ter I arrived to man's estate, the only real freehold I ever held or inherited! Scarcely a month has passed, in all the years since, in which I have not found myself completely 'strapped.' At the age of ten years I commenced the battle of life, with feeble hands, and a rebellious heart. I became a 'bearer-off' in a brickyard, at four dollars per month, finding my own board! The work was hard, very hard, and the memory of those long and bitter days, in which my little hands were never without great, painful blisters, and my young heart became hourly more calloused in its sensibilities, is not a picture to look upon with pleasure, or even with that indifference to past suffering, which time so humanely softens down in the recollection of those who have passed through deep and troubled waters. All through the long summer months, from dawn of day to the evening twilight of the same, did I carry the tempered clay in the moulds, bending down to deposit the green bricks upon the smooth floor of the yard, without rest or intermission, save a little half hour for a cold dinner, until back and heart were alike broken, and the spirit of my young life drunken up with silent and unavailing sorrow."

Mr. Jay became an editor and a public speaker of note in the East. He was successful in both undertakings, but failing to realize his ambitious longings he was cast down and afterwards used his remarkable abilities more as a diversion than with any practical end in view. He came to Oceana County and settled in Benona near what is known as Sammons' Landing, and engaged in clearing up his land and farming, afterwards turning his attention to fruit raising, in which, from his own account, he was not successful. From his advent into the county, although living with his family miles distant from any settlement, he soon became a noted personage. Articles from his trenchant and humorous pen appeared in the local papers, and O. P. Dildock (his *nom de plume*) soon had a reputation as a humorist and critic extending far beyond the limits of the county. The writer of this was personally acquainted with him, and upon a visit to his home was royally entertained and enjoyed a rare intellectual treat. He was an eloquent speaker upon any subject, political or moral, and his services upon the platform were often in demand. His conversation and his writings, however, all indicate a disappointed ambition. In appearance he resembled greatly Horace Greeley, and many of his personal attributes reminded one of the great editor. He married in 1841. Mrs. C. A. Sessions, of Benona, Mrs. Alice J. Sundt, of Washington, and Chas. Jay, of Benona, are his children. On Sunday, Dec. 7, 1884, Mr. Jay passed over the silent river and his faithful wife and companion followed him within an hour's time on the same day.

DANIEL S. RANKIN—1880.

Daniel S. Rankin was born in Lower Canada, Dec. 13, 1853. His parents were Samuel and Jennette Rankin. He came to Oceana Co. in 1880, and located at New Era in general merchandise business. In '83 he removed to Shelby where he is now located. In July, '88, he married Miss Jennie Willson. Mr. Rankin is now interested in the livery business with his cousin Duncan J. Rankin under the firm name of D. J. Rankin & Co.; also in drug business, the firm being D. S. Rankin & Co. He is also interested in the old Elliott House, which has been recently repaired and generally renovated. He came to Oceana Co. a comparatively poor man and by hard labor, honesty and economy has accumulated a comfortable fortune. He is known as one of Shelby's most enterprising and energetic citizens.

D. S. RANKIN.

FRANK E. REAMER—1880.

Frank E. Reamer was born at Orwell, Oswego Co., N. Y., Nov. 26, 1852, being a son of William H. and Lucy P. Reamer. He came to Oceana Co. in Sep., '80, seven months after his parents, and settled in Shelby village where he still makes his home. He is engaged in general mason work and building, and is a very successful workman in that business, upright, honorable and possessed of the confidence of the public. He is a leading member of Shelby Lodge No. 344, I. O. O. F., one of its Past Grands, and Representative to the Grand Lodge. He is never weary of working for the growth and advancement of the order, which is gaining in influence and membership. "Frank," as his neighbors all call him, is by hard work and his genial treatment of those with whom he comes in contact building up a substantial business and creating a wide circle of friends. Has been Constable and Deputy Sheriff. Married, Feb. 18, '84, to Miss Ida L. Loomis, and now has three children, two sons and one daughter.

IRA A. RICHMOND—1880.

Ira A. Richmond was born in DeKalb Co., Ind., April 10, 1859. His parents' names were William and Marie Richmond. He came to this county in '80, and with his parents settled upon the farm he now owns on Sec. 13, township of Golden. This is one of the finest farms in the township, and since his father's decease, which occurred several years since, has been under the management and control of the subject of our sketch. Before going upon this farm, while in Indiana, Mr. Richmond was engaged in the mercantile business. He is a prominent Odd Fellow and held in high esteem by the order. Dec. 11, 1879, he married Ida L. Portner. The union was a happy one and one son and one daughter have been born to them. Mr. Richmond, while not a pioneer, has done much to improve the standard of farming in the county, and always takes a lively interest in those things that tend to improve the condition of farmers.

I. A. RICHMOND.

F. L. PECK—1880.

F. L. Peck was born at Lancaster, Erie Co., N. Y., Jan. 8, 1841. He is the second son and fourth child of Joseph and Mary A. Peck, the former a native of Vermont, the latter of New York State. His father was a carpenter and worked on the mill at Stony Creek for Minard & Conkling in '63; his family living in DeKalb Co., Ill., from

'54 to '64, when they removed to Grand Rapids, thence to New York 'State where he died Mar. 10, '71. The subject of our sketch was in the employ of C. C. Comstock at Grand Rapids three years, a member of the firm of Konkle & Peck, wooden ware and handles, at Caledonia, Kent Co., for ten years. On Dec. 31, '70, he was married to Esther C. Lane, who was born Aug. 27, '53, at Spring Lake, Ottawa Co. They have two children, Florence M., born Nov. 22, '71, and Claud F., born Dec. 4, '77. Mr. Peck is a leading member of the Odd Fellows and an energetic business man, being now a member of the firm of Cutler & Peck, handle manufacturers doing business at Shelby.

F. L. PECK.

DENNIS HINCHIN—1880.

Dennis Hinchin, son of John and Mary Hinchin, was born in the city of Quebec, Can. When five years of age he came to the United States. He is another of our old soldiers, having enlisted in Co. B, 97th N. Y. Inf., in Nov., '61, and serving until June 23, '65. He was wounded at Spottsylvania, Va., and taken prisoner May 8, '64, and remained in rebel prisons until exchanged March 4, '65. He came from Lewis Co., N. Y., to this county in 1880 and located upon a farm near New Era, where he still resides. He has held the offices of Constable and Highway Commissioner. Was married in Pittston, Penn., in '72, and has five children, sons. Mr. Hinchin is possessed of many friends and all speak of him in the highest terms.

MRS. CLARINA E. COON—1880.

Mrs. Clarina E. Coon was an Edwards, a descendant of Alex. Edwards, who emigrated from Wales in 1640 and settled in Springfield, Mass. His son Nathaniel, born June 25, 1657. His son, Nathaniel Jr., born July 26, 1694. His son, Ebenezer, born April, 1727. His son, Alanson, born Jan., 1766. Clarina, his daughter, born Feb. 23, 1810, in Skeneatles, N. Y. Her mother was Elizabeth McKay. Clarina was a twin, the youngest (but one) of eleven children. Married Artemas Weaver, Oct. 7, 1830, who died Feb. 23, 1836, by whom she had two daughters, Electa Edwards and Jane Eliza. Jane Eliza died when ten months old. She married J. V. R. Coon April 21, 1840, who died Sep. 11, 1874, by whom she had one son, Edward F. For many years she resided in the immediate vicinity of her birthplace, Skeneatles, N. Y. In after life she made her home with her daughter, Electa Edwards, wife of C. A. Hawley, in Chicago. Since about the year 1880, she has resided in Shelby, making her home with her daughter, and her son, E. F. Coon. Grandma Coon has the honor of making four generations in one family: herself, Mrs. C. A. Hawley, her daughter; E. W. Hawley, her grandson, and Frankie, her great-grandson. She was eighty years old the 23rd day of Feb., 1890. Has one sister three years her senior. Her brother, Thaddeus Edwards, died in Skeneatles, N. Y., May 8, 1890, aged 93 years and 5 months. From her youth she has been a very useful Christian woman. Almost a natural nurse, she has been with the sick night and day assisting to save the lives of many. Always interested in the reforms of the day. Once an assistant agent at a station on the underground R. R. to run slaves into Canada. Notwithstanding her advanced age she enjoys good

MRS. C. E. COON.

health. Very intelligent and interesting, is good company and has a host of friends.

HENRY HARTER—1880.

Henry Harter was born in Harmony, Chautauqua Co., N. Y., in 1845, and lived there until the age of ten years, when he moved with his parents to Crawford Co., Penn. Parents' names are Jared L. and Cynthia E. Harter. He is the eldest of seven children all of whom are living at present writing. Was married in 1869 to Elizabeth Turner, daughter of Leland and Sarah Turner. Has five children, one son and four daughters. Came to Oceana Co. in 1880; bought eighty acres of land on section one, township of Claybanks. Moved into the woods and had to chop and clear away a place to build a house. Began to build in April, 1881, and had to shovel away three feet of snow to set down blocks to set a house upon and moved in before windows or doors were hung; might almost be classed as a pioneer. He has now about fifty acres down, and 28 of it cleared. Has set out 125 apple and 75 peach trees.

HENRY L. HODGES—1880.

Henry L. Hodges was born at Watertown, N. Y., June 10, 1841, and is a son of Stephen and Mary Hodges. On April 7, 1880, he came to Oceana Co. and purchased a farm described as the north half of the southeast quarter of Sec. 30, of the township of Elbridge. Here he has continued to reside and has improved it until now he has 40 acres under cultivation with three acres of orchard and good comfortable farm buildings. He is an old soldier, having seen service in Co. H, 1st N. Y. Light Art. one year, and as Captain in Co. G, 14th N. Y. Heavy Art. two years and three months. He has been two years Highway Commissioner of his township. Married Nov. 29, 1859, to Lucy Campbell, by whom he had twelve children, nine sons and three daughters. He had the misfortune to lose his wife in June, 1882.

MARION L. FERRIS—1882.

Marion L. Ferris was born in Broome Co., N. Y., April 30, 1854, being a son of Albert G. and Betsey (Conklin) Ferris. In Nov., '80, he came to this county and purchased a farm in the township of Shelby, two and one-half miles from Shelby village. This he cleared up and resided on same until Oct., '88, when he came to Shelby and engaged in selling merchandise, where he has since continued. On Nov. 3, '80, was married to Miss Addie M. Kibbe, a daughter of David J. and Rachel B. (Cotton) Kibbe, who was born May 5, '60, in Potter Co., Penn. She has always been a faithful, loving wife and fond mother and is justly proud of her two boys, aged respectively eight and six years.

HENRY J. SERVIS—1881.

Henry J. Servis, son of Thomas and Mary Servis, was born in Lower Canada in 1840. He came to Oceana Co. in May, '81, and has since resided at Hart, where he has been engaged as a carpenter and builder. In former years he followed sailing and shipbuilding for a livelihood. At present he is engaged in the pump business. Mr. Servis has been noted for his great interest in Odd Fellowship, having joined Sacarisa Lodge No. 307, at Lewiston, N. Y., in 1874 and transferred by card to Oceana Lodge No. 327, at Hart in '83. Became a member of Hart Encampment No. 12, in '84. In both of these societies he has held numerous offices and is now a P. G. and P. C. P. Married in '61 to Matilda Russell and has four children, three sons and one daughter.

H. J. SERVIS.

HENRY W. HARPSTER—1881.

Henry W. Harpster was born at Delta, Eaton County, Mich., May 16, 1856, being the youngest child of Elizabeth and Daniel Harpster, is of German descent. Lived on his father's farm until he was 16 years of age. He received his education at the Charlotte Union School and Olivet College. Commenced the study of law in '79 with Hon. D. P. Sagendorph, of Charlotte, Mich. Finished his legal education at the law department of the Michigan

State University. Came to Oceana County in the summer of '81. Was married to Carrie M. Darling in Oct., '83. Went to Shelby and commenced the practice of law in the spring of '85. Continued to practice at Shelby until Jan., '89, when he moved to Pentwater and associated with W. E. Ambler, where he now lives. He has been successful, as a rule, in his cases, and may justly be considered as one of the best read lawyers of the county.

LELAND C. BREWSTER—1881.

Leland C. Brewster was born in Mansfield, Tioga Co., Pa., Aug. 15, '50. His parents were Luther H. and Olive P. Brewster. The subject of our sketch has followed farming the greater part of his life. July 20, '69, he married Victoria E. Watkins, in Tioga Co. They have had three daughters. Minnie E., one of them, is now the wife of Ervie Cleveland and resides at Crystal Valley. Nov. 3, '81, Mr. Brewster came to Oceana Co. to unite his fortunes with the other residents of this Co. For the past six years he has presided over the destinies of Crystal Valley's only hotel, the "Brewster House." He is much attached to the doctrines taught by Odd Fellowship and follows their precepts. He is a member of the Crystal Valley Lodge in which organization he has just completed a term of office as its Permanent Secretary.

L. C. BREWSTER.

A jovial, good-hearted, level-headed gentleman, long may he exist to cheer the weary and refresh the hungry.

CHARLES E. ABRAHAM—1881.

Charles E. Abraham, son of William H. and Elizabeth Abraham, was born at Edinboro, Pa., Jan. 11, 1861. He came to this county Sept. 15, '81, locating at Shelby, where he has since resided, engaged in carpenter work summers and teaching winters, excepting the winter of '66-7, spent in Kansas City, Mo. By hard and unceasing labor he has succeeded in making for himself and family as nice a home as any could wish, comprising an acre and a half on the main thoroughfare of Shelby, with a large comfortable house, and the grounds covered with fruit of all kinds. Since coming to

C. E. ABRAHAM.

Shelby he has had an unfortunate and sad experience in the death of both parents, who lie buried in the Shelby cemetery. Mr. Abraham is an active member of the M. E. Society. Also of Shelby Lodge No. 344, I. O. O. F., in which he takes great interest, and in which he has held all the important offices, being now Noble Grand. Married Nov. 2, '83, to Miss Ella Shirts. Two daughters have blessed their union.

FRANK E. YOUNG—1881.

Frank E. Young, one of the successful educators of Oceana County, was born to J. A. and E. E. Young, at Lodi, Columbia Co., Wis., Aug. 17, 1858. He received a good education and since Sept. 20, '81, has been engaged in school teaching. He has been principal of the Hart Union Schools for several years, giving the best of satisfaction. He came to this county in '81, and has held, in the county, the offices of School Inspector, and Chairman of the Co. Board of School Examiners. Sept. 24, '78, he was happily married to Miss Sarah E. Holcomb. Mr. Young is a gentleman of sterling principles, and in his daily life commands the respect of all who know him. He takes a lively interest in all matters pertaining to intel-

F. E. YOUNG.

lectual improvement. and is regarded as one of the first educators of the county.

WILLIAM E. MERRILL.—1879.

William E. Merrill was born in Springfield Co., Maine, Feb 14, 1853. Removed to Rock County, Wis., with his parents in '69, and in '79 came to Oceana Co., where he has since resided. The first five years of his life in Oceana Co. was spent in the employ of Sands & Maxwell as Night Watchman. Since that time he has been employed on a fruit farm of his own, and growing fruits of all kinds, for which occupation he has a natural aptitude, even while a boy growing strawberries which one year netted him $150. He was married in '81 to Mrs. Anna Messenger, who

W. E. MERRILL.

was born in Wood Co., Ohio, May 15, '52, removing to Oceana Co. in '79.

MRS. W. E. MERRILL.

EDWARD H. CUTLER—1881.

E. H. CUTLER.

Edward H. Cutler was born in Westminster, Canada, July 21, '50. His parents' names were David and Sarah Cutler. He settled in Shelby in '81, and engaged in the manufacture of lumber. In '87 he commenced manufacturing broom-handles in company with F. L. Peck, and has made a success of the business. He is regarded as a good, safe business man and a public spirited citizen. He has served four years as Village Trustee, is a prominent Odd Fellow and has held many offices in the order. To his energy is largely due the organizing and maintenance of an efficient Fire Department in Shelby. Jan. 1, '71, he was married to Miss Mary C. Knowlton, and two daughters have been born to them.

CYRUS B. STEVENS—1881.

Cyrus B. Stevens was born at Avon, Lorain Co., Ohio, Jan. 9, '50. He is a son of Ransom F. and Finetta M. Stevens. After attending common schools until the age of seventeen he attended school at Oberlin, Ohio, and Hillsdale, Mich., from '67 to '70. Like many other young men he then engaged in teaching, at the same time studying law. He continued this until '80, when he engaged in the practice of the law. On May 6, '81, he came to Oceana Co., locating at Hart, where in '82 he formed a copartnership with Hon. T. S. Gurney. He remained with Mr. Gurney until '85, when his health failing he went South where he remained until '86. In that year he returned to Hart and has since been engaged there in the law business. On Aug. 5, '75, he was married to Miss Addie Drinkall. They have no children. Mr. Stevens has won the esteem of those with whom he has come in contact. He has been Township Superintendent of Schools three years, Justice of the Peace three years and Prosecuting Attorney of this county four years. As Prosecutor he was always ready and prompt in the discharge of his duties. As a genial gentleman he has many friends and few enemies.

MARION FRANK HYDE—1881.

Marion Frank Hyde was born in Royalton township, Berrien Co., Mich., Nov. 21, 1858, his parents' names being John V. and Catherine M. Parmenter. His mother died Feb. 9, 1861, at Berrien Springs, and he was adopted by John W. and Rebecca L. Hyde, April 11, '61. In the fall of '62 he removed with his adopted parents to Valparaiso, Ind., where he attended school. In the fall of '71 the family removed to Muskegon and in 1876 to Leslie, Ingham Co. In Nov., '81, he came to Oceana Co., and Jan. 29, '82, entered the Pentwater NEWS' employ as a job printer. He soon came to be known as a first class pressman and was given charge of the press work of the office, which position he held with scarcely a day's loss of time until May 3, '90.

M. F. HYDE.

Mr. Hyde belongs to the Odd Fellows' order, Subordinate, Encampment and Rebekah lodges, and has passed all the chairs in both Encampment and Subordinate lodges. May 27, '83, he was married to Mary Isabel Grant, of Pentwater, who was a compositor in the NEWS office, and who had been a faithful employe of the office since May 26, '71, and who still continues as head compositor of the office. Two children, a daughter, Beatrice, and son, Harold Frank, have been born to them.

DAVID J. HILL—1882.

David J. Hill is the son of Graham and Deborah Hill, and was

D. J. HILL.

born in Canada, April 13, 1829. He came to this county March 25, '82, becoming a resident of Elbridge township, where he engaged in farming. He soon became quite prominent in the affairs of the township and has been elected and served the township acceptably as Treasurer and Supervisor. Nov. 29, '52, he married Mary J. Bolton, which union has been happily blessed with three sons and five daughters. Mr. Hill is a pleasant gentleman whom one delights to meet and to know. He is pleasantly situated and commands the esteem and respect of his neighbors.

W. H. FLEMING—1882.

W. H. Fleming was born at Romulus, Seneca Co., N. Y., July 3, 1837. Oct. 8, '44, he moved with his parents to North Adrian, Mich., where he resided the most of the time until '59. In that year he went to Ypsilanti, where a part of the time he attended school, expecting to fit himself for teaching, but the war breaking out he decided to offer his services to the Government. He enlisted in Co. K, 1st Mich. Inf., and at the first battle of Bull Run, July 21, '61, was taken prisoner. He was held as a prisoner of war by the Confederates, ten months when he was exchanged, mustered out and came home. On Dec. 30, '62, he was married to Emily H. Crane, of Ypsilanti. The following year, on Oct. 10, he again enlisted, this time in Co. H, 11th Mich. Vol. Cav., and was mustered in as first Sergeant. He was severely wounded

W. H. FLEMING.

at the battle of Saltville, Va., in Sept., '64, and again received a slight wound at Marion, Va., in Dec., '64. He was mustered out Aug. 10, '65, and returned home. He then for thirteen years resided in Bay Co., holding the office of Supervisor in that county seven years. Sept. 1, '82, he came to Oceana Co. and is now serving his fourth term as Supervisor of Benona, where he has resided since.

ALEXANDER PATON—1882.

A. PATON.

Alexander Paton was born at Galston, Scotland, Dec. 22, '48. He is a son of David and Christian (Woodburn) Paton. He first saw Oceana Co. in 1870, before the railroad was built, and purchased land near Shelby. He came permanently in '82 and located at Shelby. In business he followed farming until '75. After coming to Shelby engaged with H. L. Andrus in mercantile business which they continued for about six years, then going into their present business, saw and planing mill, under the firm name of Paton & Andrus, and doing a good business. Married Oct. 20, '70, Hattie M. Wilson. No children. Mr. Paton has many good qualities and a host of friends and has done his share toward the prosperity of Shelby.

GEORGE O. SWITZER—1882.

George O. Switzer, son of George H. and Mary J. Switzer, was born March 8, 1854, at North East, Erie Co., Pa. Lived there with his parents until '60, when the family came to Barry Co., Mich. There he resided with his parents upon a farm, attending high school at Hastings, until he reached man's estate, when he started out for himself. He taught school two winters in Barry and two winters in Lake County. Had some experience in pioneer life in Lake County, having done more or less work in the lumber woods. In '76 he began the study of medicine at Cedar Creek, Mich., and in '81 graduated from the Bennett Medical College, of Chicago. Located at Ludington in the spring of '81, and the following year removed to

Pentwater where he has since followed his profession, having a large practice. He is a prominent member of the I. O. O. F. fraternity and is a Past Grand of Pentwater Lodge No. 378. He has been Health Officer of Pentwater township and village for a number of years and is at present a member of the School Board. Married Aug. 25, '76, to Miss Addie Morthland. One daughter, Allie, comprises their family.

G. O. SWITZER.

ORSON F. WICKHAM—1882.

Orson F. Wickham, son of George and Susan A. Wickham, was born in Orleans Co., N. Y., Feb. 18, 1864. He came to this county in Sept., '82, and in October began work for Sands & Maxwell as book-keeper at Homer Lake, where he continued until Nov., '84, when he came to Pentwater. On Jan. 1, '85, he commenced as head book-keeper for the same firm in their Pentwater office, and is still engaged with them. The length of time spent with this firm shows the satisfaction given by Mr. Wickham in one of the, if not the most, busy office in the county. The duties are arduous and require constant attention. Mr. W. is always at his post; when absent it can always be presumed that he or his family are sick.

O. F. WICKHAM.

He was married Sept. 12, '86, to Miss Etta Webb, a daughter of William and Esther Webb, old residents of Pentwater. They now have one child, a daughter.

BENJAMIN F. STONE—1882.

Benjamin F. Stone was born in Canada, Feb. 22, 1848, his parents being Andrew and Ann Stone. He came to Michigan in 1865 and in May, 1867 was married to Alice Winegar, of Kent Co. In 1882 he came to this county and worked at his trade and at mill work at Pentwater and Crystal Valley, finally locating at Walkerville. He is now engaged in the furniture and undertaking business at that place. He is the father of five children, two sons and three daughters. Mr. Stone, while at Crystal Valley, was elected to the offices of Justice and Township Clerk, and at Walkerville has been a leader among the Odd Fellows. He is a charter member of the Stetson Lodge and was its first Noble Grand. He is deserving of and undoubtedly will secure a good trade in his new venture.

BENJAMIN C. KNAPP—1882.

Benjamin C. Knapp, a son of William Knapp, was born in New York, Sept. 25, 1828. He had been engaged in lumbering before coming to this county; but in June, 1882, came here and located in Golden near Mears Station, and at once began the culture of fruit. He now has a fine fruit orchard and each year gathers in the shekels from his peaches. Married Feb. 5, 1848, Elizabeth Harmer, and has had nine children, five sons and four daughters. Mr. Knapp has been Director of his school district and is a man possessing the confidence and respect of his neighbors.

FRANKLIN A. SCOTT—1883.

F. A. SCOTT.

Franklin A. Scott was born at Stockholm, St. Lawrence Co., N. Y., Dec. 29, 1832. His parents were Ozias and Lucinda Scott. Mr. Scott left the State of New York in '53 and came to Barry Co., Mich. First came to Oceana Co. in '63, but remained here only a short time when he returned to Barry Co. In '67 he came to Muskegon Co. and again to Oceana Co. in 1883, locating at Shelby where he has since resided. He was drafted into service in the rebellion, but was not assigned to any company or regiment, but did duty in commissary department until discharged. Previous to coming here he was engaged at different times in selling goods, and farming. Since residing at Shelby he has been manager for the Shelby Furniture Co., a furniture and undertaker's establishment. He has been twice married, first in St. Lawrence Co., N. Y., to Harriet M. White, by whom he had a son, and second at Shelby, to Emma Williams by whom he has one child. He has held the office of County Coroner, and is a member of Whitehall Lodge No. 138, D. of R., No. 58, Hart Encampment No. 12, and Canton Gurney No. 14, I. O. O. F., and Benona Lodge No. 289 F. & A. M. Mr. Scott is a man possessing a great many personal friends, a good business man and a leader in whatever he undertakes.

OTTO GRANT—1875.

Otto Grant was born in Sweden, Europe, Dec. 12, 1840, his parents' names being Niels and Caroline Grant. He early in life became a sailor and in 1855 went to South America as such. He has with the exception of a few short intervals, followed that occupation since. He has visited England, Germany, France, Denmark, Spain, Italy, China, East and West Indies, South America and California. Has been master of a vessel fourteen years and at the present time is master of the steamer Saugatuck, plying between Pentwater and Chicago. He is regarded as one of the best captains on the lakes. May 17, '69, he married Mary E. Koehler, and 8 children have been born to them, seven of whom are living. He is prominent in both the Masonic and Odd Fellow orders. In the latter he has passed the principal chairs and been Representative to the Grand Lodge. As a citizen he is highly regarded, his word being accepted without question. He has served the township as Treasurer one term and declined a second nomination.

OTTO GRANT.

GEORGE RHODES—1883.

George Rhodes was born in England in 1840. He came to Coldwater, Mich., when a boy; and at the breaking out of the war enlisted April, 1861, in Co. C, 1st Mich. Inf. He was at Alexandria, Va., with his regiment when Col. Ellsworth was shot for hauling down the rebel flag. He was in the first battle of Bull Run, July 21, '61, and while taking care of his wounded captain, upon the field, was taken prisoner. He was kept in Southern prisons until the following June when he was exchanged and returned to his home in Coldwater where he engaged in the boot and shoe business. In the spring of '83 he, with his family came to Hart, this county, where he engaged in his present business. He has been a member of the School Board of Hart for six years. He was also one of the first Trustees of the village of Hart. He is now engaged in the mercantile business and enjoys a good trade. He aims to please all customers and to give full value for all money invested at his counters.

GEO. RHODES.

CHARLES H. TULLAR—1883.

Charles H. Tullar, the son of Simeon and Sarah Tullar, was born Jan. 14, 1852, at Jordan, Onondaga Co., N. Y. He received an academic education in his native town. He was for two years assistant Postmaster there. Afterwards he moved to Nashville, Tenn., where he served as book-keeper for the Singer Sewing Machine Co. From there he went to Detroit, Mich., then to Chicago, Ill., finally came to Plainwell, Mich., where he engaged in the furniture and undertaking business with A. H. Hill. Came to Shelby, this county, July 2, 1883, and has since been engaged in and has successfully conducted a furniture and undertaking establishment at this place. He is married and has one daughter named Bernice. Has served two terms as Coroner.

WILLIAM M. HARTWICK—1878.

William M. Hartwick was born at Brockville, Canada, Oct. 12, 1824. His parents' names were Morris and Elinor Hartwick. He moved with his parents to Mishawaka, Ind., when about fourteen years of age. There he learned the tailor trade, and adopting the custom of young tailors at that time traveled from place to place working at his trade a few months in each place. It was while on one of these trips that he met Mary L. Wight, daughter of the first white settler in Jonesville, Thaddeus Wight, whom he married. He came back to Mishawaka and started in business. Was reasonably successful, but in '58 lost his property through signing with another. He then moved to Kansas, staid a couple of years, then moved to Litchfield, Mich., where he kept a shop and was for many years the village tailor. From this point in '78 he removed to Oceana Co., where he has since resided. For several years he has been proprietor of the Pentwater news agency, and his is a familiar face to every resident of the village. The children of William and Mary Hartwick are Louis M., at present a resident of Pentwater and editor of the Pentwater NEWS; Rose Hartwick Thorpe, of San Diego, Cal., widely known as the author of "Curfew Shall Not Ring To-night;" Herbert D., a successful farmer in Weare; Mrs. Ellen Andrus, wife of S. Andrus, farmer and fruit raiser, of Hart, and Lillie, who died at Pentwater, July, '87.

W. M. HARTWICK.

DUSTIN C. OAKES—1883.

Dustin C. Oakes was born in Sherman township, St. Joseph Co., Mich., June 19, 1853. He is a son of David, Jr., and Mercy S. Oakes. His early life up to the age of eighteen years was spent upon a farm. His education was obtained in the common schools and the Agricultural College at Lansing, where he attended four years. Afterwards taught school and "operated" a farm for five years and was seven years in a bank. In '83 he came to Shelby and engaged in the banking business as a member of the firm of Churchill Oakes & Co., acting as Cashier. He has held positions of trust, having been for two years Supervisor of Lyons township, Ionia Co., Deputy Clerk of Ionia Co. one term under R. D. Sessions, and is the present Village President of Shelby. As a business man Mr. Oakes is prompt and energetic and the banking business under his management has been successful, the firm possessing the entire confidence of the public. Socially Mr. Oakes is without blemish, a courteous gentleman. He was married in 1876 to Miss Nora Kelly, and one child, a daughter, has blessed the union.

EDMUND S. RANDALL—1884.

Edmund S. Randall was born at Morristown, St. Lawrence Co., N. Y., Oct., 16, 1845. He is a son of Silas and Sarah A. Randall. He moved with his parents to Kent Co., Mich., in '51, where he remained until the war broke out. Nov. 19, '61, he enlisted as a private in Co. C, 13th Mich. Vet. Vol. Inf., and served until July 25, '65. After having served his country for nearly four years he returned to his home in Kent Co. and resided there until '79, when he removed to Lawrence Co., Tenn. Remaining in Tennessee until '84, he again came to Mich., arriving in Oceana Co. in Sept. of that year. On Dec. 25, '67, he married Laura M. Lewis, and they have one son and three daughters. He

E. S. RANDALL.

has followed farming for a living and is now engaged in that occupation in the township of Grant. In the spring of '89 the electors of Grant manifested their confidence in him by electing him to the office of Supervisor, which office he now holds. He has made a good man upon the Board and the confidence of the people was in no wise misplaced.

JOHN A. HARRISON—1884.

John A. Harrison was born in London, Ont., Feb. 21, 1861; his parents' names being John and Hanna Harrison. He learned the blacksmith trade and has made that his business. On Oct. 2, '83,

J. A. HARRISON.

he was married to Miss Rosena Doak; and is now the father of one child, a son, Gordon L. On Apr. 7, '84, he came to Oceana Co. and started in business at Shelby in Dec., '85. He now has a blacksmith and wagon shop and deals in cutters, buggies, plows, etc. By close attention to business and fair dealing he has added to his business from to time, and has possessed himself of a nice home. The appreciation in which he is held by his fellow townsmen has been manifested by his election as a member of the Common Council of the village. He also stands well among his brother Odd Fellows, his term as Noble Grand of the Shelby Lodge expiring Dec. 31, '89. He is of the class of men we are pleased to welcome to our State and county.

A. L. THOMAS—1884.

A. L. Thomas was born in Oakland Co., Mich., June 29, 1859, being the son of Homer A. and Betsey Thomas. He resided in Oakland County and vicinity until the spring of '79, when with his parents he went to Davis Co., Kansas. There for two and a half years he followed farming, but tiring of that occupation he returned to Michigan. Shortly afterwards he secured a position with the C. & W. M. Ry. Co., with which he has remained since. He worked at various places as agent and telegraph operator until Sept. 24, '84, when he came to Pentwater to take charge of the station, which position he still holds. June 26, '83, he was married to Mollie E. Bissell, of Oakland Co. They have no children. The time he has spent in the employ of the one company shows him to be a diligent and faithful employe. He and his wife are known as a gentleman and lady of high character with whom it is a pleasure to meet, and no door is closed against them.

O. W. STONE—1885.

O. W. Stone, photographer, was born in Washtenaw Co., Mich.,

O. W. STONE.

Feb. 7, 1853. His parents' names were James and Elizabeth (Kelsey) Stone. March 22, 1885, Mr. Stone married Miss Ida Kenney, an estimable lady who has borne to him one child, a daughter, who was born Oct. 7, '88. He came to Oceana County Nov. 15, '85, and opened a photograph gallery. He is a member of the M. E. Church, an honest, upright citizen, commanding the respect of all. He has been very successful in his business and owns the building he occupies.

JOHN W. BAKER—1885.

John W. Baker, son of Thomas and Lucinda Baker, was born in Ripley, Chautauqua Co., N. Y., Sept. 29, '47. Previous to coming to this county he was engaged in the drug business. On June 15, '85, he came to this county and located in Claybanks, moving upon his present farm in the fall of that year. He has held the position of Justice of the Peace. He married, Sept. 27, '71, Miss Philinda Jones. They have no children of their own but have adopted a daughter.

GEORGE HENRY CLEVELAND—1885.

The subject of this sketch is a native of Michigan, having been born to Charles M. and Susan A. Cleveland, at Adrian, Mich., Feb. 13, 1862. He received his early education in his native city and afterward took a three year course in the medical department of the Michigan University, from which he graduated with the class of '82. After this he practiced at Coleman, Mich., one year, then in Lansing, from which place he removed to Pentwater in June, '85. Since coming to Pentwater he has held the position of School Inspector. Been Chairman of the Board of Div. Surgeons for the C. & W. M. Ry. Co., and for several years Secretary of the Pere Marquette Medical Society. Mr. Cleveland married Jennie A. Jolly, at Ann Arbor, Mich., May 18, '80, which union was a happy one and has been blessed with two bright sons. In religion Mr. Cleveland is a Protestant Episcopalian, and Lay Reader of St. James Mission Chapel.

FRED SMITH—1880.

F. SMITH.

Fred Smith, whose portrait appears herewith, was born at Hudson, Lenawee Co., Mich., June 19, 1860. His parents were Joseph L. and Margaret Smith. When about one year of age they moved to Clayton where our subject spent his boyhood days. In April, '80, he came to Pentwater, and for the past five years has been in the employ of Sands & Maxwell Lumber Co., a very popular clerk. He is an active member of the Pentwater Athletic Club, and has been one of the most efficient members of the Pentwater Fire Department. Is popular among the boys for his genial ways.

JOSEPH LEE—1886.

Joseph Lee, a son of John and Mary Ann Lee, was born in Beverly township, Wentworth Co., Ont., April 13, 1845. He engaged in the business of a general contractor in Hamilton, Canada, previous to coming to Oceana County. In '86 he settled in Claybanks upon the old R. E. Cater farm, where he is very pleasantly situated. He is an energetic, pushing man and in '87 in order to facilitate the shipment of his and others' lumber, bark and farm products, built a pier into Lake Michgian. He is a genial, hospitable gentleman, to which fact the writer can testify. Coming to his place during a pouring rain the writer was urged to "put out" and stay to dinner and after dinner was urged to stay longer until the afternoon was well spent, the time being enlivened with cheerful and instructive conversation with Mr. Lee and his estimable lady. Mr. Lee married Dec. 24, '67, Miss Rosanna Peregrine, and they have six children, four sons and two daughters.

JOS. LEE.

JOHN A. TILLOTSON—1887.

John A. Tillotson, son of James and Ellen Tillotson, was born in Quebec, Can., Jan. 5, '47. He came to this Co. Aug. 27, '87, and located in Shelby, carrying on his trade of barber and hair dresser. He is now located in the Rankin House, having a neat shop and is doing a good business. He has had many years' experience and been employed in some of the best shops and is now in a positian to guarantee satisfaction to his customers. He expresses himself as much pleased with the people there and has decided to make his permanent home there, to that end having purchased a house and three lots, which he is adorning. Married Nov. 3, '73, to Annie Leacok and has had four children, two sons and two daughters.

J. A. TILLOTSON.

ROBERT L. BUNTING—1887.

Robert L. Bunting was born Aug. 10, 1836, in Erie Co., Pa., being the son of William and Mary A. Bunting. On Dec. 2, 58, he was married, at Cherry Valley, Ashtabula County, Ohio, to Betsey L. Brown. The result of this union has been eight children, four sons and four daughters. On Aug. 7, '62, he enlisted in Co. I, 105th regiment Ohio Vol. Inf., and again on Aug. 28, '64, he enlisted in Co. B 1st U. S. V. Eng. Mr. Bunting is a mason by trade, and has succeeded in accumulating some property. In '87 he came to Oceana Co. and built the first hotel in Walkerville when that thriving burg was in its infancy. On May 13, '88, he entered the hotel as landlord and still conducts that business. He is a man who is respected by all who know him; and the traveling public may be sure of a warm welcome and good entertainment at his place of business.

WILLIAM R. MATTHEWS.

William R. Matthews was born Jan. 13, 1843, in Branch County, Mich. He is a son of Sidney S. and Susan Matthews. His parents came to Branch Co. in '34, about three years before the Indians were removed from there, coming from Ontario, N. Y. The subject of our sketch is an old soldier having been a private of Co. C, 11th Mich. Inf., and serving three years. He was in hospital in Chattanooga, Tenn., for five months after his term of service expired, and has been a constant sufferer since. He has held the offices of Commander, S. V. C., J. V. C., S. M. and Adjt. He has traveled considerably having been in nineteen different States, and now expresses himself as best pleased with his present surroundings. He came to this county May 8, '80, locating at Ferry, where he now has a

W. R. MATTHEWS.

real estate and loaning agency, also doing Notary Public work. He is contented with Ferry and is endeavoring to settle and build up the village and township. He is prepared to offer inducements to any who wish to locate in the southeastern portion of Oceana Co., and any business in his line will receive prompt and careful atten-

He solicits correspondence. Married Dec. 20, '68, to Miss Mary A. Coon, and they now have one child, a daughter, L. Estella Matthews.

LORENZO BRIGGS MITCHELL.—1888.

Lorenzo Briggs Mitchell, known as the 'farmer poet,' was born in Brookfield, Wis., March 13, 1849. He married Miss Sarah E. VanNess, of Geneva, Wisconsin, at the latter place. In one year from his marriage, to a day, they arrived at the home of Mr. Levi Powers, of Ferry township, who lived adjoining the then unbroken forest which is now their beautiful country home in Hart township. The first years of their pioneer life were fraught with many hardships and discouraging circumstances, as the total cash on hand upon arriving at their new home was $18. But perseverance, economy and an indomitable will on the part of each has surrounded them with many of the comforts, not to say luxuries of life.

L. B. MITCHELL.

Mr. Mitchell's love of literature, and especially poetry, he attributes largely to the influence of his grandmother, Mrs. Sarah Porter, who, in his youthful days read and repeated from memory, poetry to him for hours at a time. Mr. Mitchell's original readings have been the unique feature of many an Oceana Co. audience, notably at fairs, soldiers' reunions, old settlers' meetings, etc. In this connection it is not too much to say that his eulogistic poem on U. S. Grant is one of the finest productions of its kind in our language. Mr. Mitchell is also a writer of music, being represented in many of the S. S. song books of the day by pieces of his own, words and music. In these times, when musical MSS. are rejected by hundreds where one is accepted, it speaks of a musical and literary ability of a high order when nearly all his efforts in this direction are accepted and published. Mr. M. has now seven published sheet music songs, all his own words and music. It would seem that his ambition in this particular line was to outdo his rivals whose productions represent both literary and musical work.

Mr. M. has four children living: Ethel M., now the wife of Mr. Alfred Woodland, of Shelby; Edwin L., Neva L., and Winnie E. An infant son, aged two months, died Jan. 10, 1887. Mr. Mitchell's home, with his interesting children, and literary and musical surroundings is the delight of his friends and those of his much esteemed wife. Among such as have ever shared their hospitality, their joint ability to pleasantly entertain goes without saying.

Taken altogether, L. B., as his friends call him, is a man of whom our county may justly be proud. He is not a "strait jacket" in any sense of the term, and he is not bound nor influenced by sects, creeds, clans or societies. He thinks, acts and speaks for himself and is as free in all matters of thought and action as though no clans among men existed. He says that life is too short and he has too much to do to give them due attention. In his personal habits Mr. M. is a true representative of temperance, being a total abstainer from tobacco and all intoxicants.

AMOS DRESSER, JR.
Editor of Pentwater News from Jan., 1871, to Oct., 1879.

CHAPTER XV.

―x―

ANECDOTES AND INCIDENTS OF PIONEER LIFE IN OCEANA COUNTY.

―x―

"NAVEL HILL."—In December, 1857 or 1858, the Highway Commissioners employed Harvey Tower, now a resident of Grant township, to survey a highway from the present north line of Hart to the south line of Shelby townships, which with slight deviations was adopted by the State Road Survey. The party consisted of H. Tower, Geo. Light, Jas. McNutt, A. C. Randall and Henry Hoffman, the last named Township Clerk. They ran from north to south on the section line between sections 4 and 5. Nearly two miles north of Shelby village they came to a long steep hill at the foot of which they halted. While considering whether to change the course or not, McNutt called Randall's attention to a tree and said it was about as large as his (Randall's) body. Randall protested that the tree was not so large. They finally bet a dollar, put the stakes in Tower's hands and chose him as judge. Of course he had to determine by actual measurement. The snow was about twenty inches deep and very light, the day cold. When he asked Randall to strip to be measured he hesitated, but saw he must submit or lose his dollar. Tower wore a pair of mittens heavily fringed all over, and used a large string in the operation which unfortunately (for Randall) fell into the snow several times before the measurement was completed, and was as often recovered with the shaggy mitten laden with snow and reapplied to his "goose pimpled" body, causing a deep sigh and the injunction "Tower, be spry; it's mighty cold here." Tower, deeply moved with sympathy for the object of his care, in his great haste and clumsy mittens, dropped and recovered from the snow again and again the measuring-tape (with care to load it well with snow) and applied it to the bare body of the shivering and waiting sportsman. The measurement completed, our shivering friend hurriedly brought his pants, which had dropped to his ankles while his hands held up his shirt to facilitate the measurement, to their position, only to find that McNutt, careless of everybody's comfort but his own, swinging his feet to keep them warm had filled the seat of Esq. Randall's pants with snow. Then went up (or down) the imprecations of the Squire mingled with the pitiless shouts of the company.

Randall lost the bet, and the money was voted to Dr. Jenks who had entertained them gratuitously the night previous. By this time the needle had settled and while on their course up the hill, Hoffman broke out with "You'm funny devils; Tower what do ve name dis hill?" Tower, without halting, and keeping his eye steadily on his object at the top of the hill, quickly answered: "This is Navel Hill." Hoffman responded "O! yes, dot is it. I puts 'im on de book" (township record), and there it stands to this day.

VOTE-UM-CROSBY—In 1866 Nathan Crosby was nominated by the republicans to the office of Clerk and Register, and William Wigton by the Democrats. During the campaign there was great strife between the friends of both candidates to secure the Indian vote. The Wigtons then, as later, ran the grist mill at Hart and supplied the country 'round about with flour. It soon became noised about among republicans that the Indians were receiving unusual favors at the mill and it was whispered that it was a scheme to secure the Indian vote for Wigton. Whether this was true or not it had the effect of stirring to greater vigilance the friends of Crosby, and when some Indians came to town again they were approached and the inquiry made as to their trading their votes for flour. One brave spoke up for the rest and said: "We like um Wigton flour, but we vote-um-Crosby." And the result proved it to be true, as Crosby was elected by a good majority.

THE INDIAN IDEA.—Skin-esse was an Indian. He wanted to buy some red calico for his squaw but he had no money. O. W. Knox offered to sell him the goods and take his gun as security for the pay. This pleased him. He took the goods and agreed to pay in thirty days. Knox tried to impress upon his mind the importance of paying on time or the gun would be sold. "Me pay um," said Skin-esse. The time had nearly expired and Knox meeting the Indian called his attention to the fact that unless payment was made at the time the gun would be sold. "Me pay um goods. If me don't pay um goods when time up you begin to sell um gun. Me pay fore you get um sold."

SHORT AND SWEET.—The following is a *fac simile* copy of a warrant issued by one of Oceana County's pioneer Justices of the Peace for the arrest of a man charged with theft, and which the officer, actually carried with him for his protection in making the arrest and returned to the Court with defendant in custody. It read as follows:

"Fetch him, d—n him."

JOHN BEAN, JR., Justice of the Peace.

PIONEER SCRAP.—It is well known, to the pioneers of Claybanks, at least, that an Indian burying ground is situated on the farm formerly owned by John D. Hanson, deceased. When the writer's mother came to Claybanks in 1852, she observed two graves in the burying ground which from being covered with a canopy of bark and cloth she judged must be occupied by bodies that in life were regarded, by the Indians, at least, as of more than ordinary importance. On inquiry she was told that one was the grave of a Chief's squaw, the other that of a Catholic priest who had died while on a visit to the Indians. Being at Chicago the next summer, 1853, she spoke of the matter to Rev. Fr. Kinsella, who in turn told her that during the administration of Bishop Quarter, first Catholic Bishop of Chicago (about 1844 or 1845), two Indians, who had come from north of Muskegon, around Lake Michigan in a canoe, called at the Bishop's residence and said that a priest had died while ministering among them and asked what they should do with the body. They were told to go home and bury the body in their own cemetery. If this theory be correct, Catholic services were held among the Indians of Claybanks before the advent of the whites.

THE FIRST MULE.—In 1858 the pioneer mule of the county put in its appearance at Pentwater. His prominent features and musical voice at once captivated Mr. H. C. Flagg, Mr. Mears' foreman at Pentwater, who by adroit figuring and the exchange of his Indian pony secured from its owner absolute title in his muleship, and from that time to the present said mule has been a resident of the county, and we believe is still in the enjoyment of good health. At that time the Board of Supervisors was composed of four individuals representing the four big towns of the county, and held their deliberations at Whisky Creek, at which place the county seat was then located. Mr. Flagg was Supervisor of Pentwater, and thinking to add somewhat to his influence upon the Board by the exhibition of a little style, saddled and bridled his new purchase, booted and spurred, mounted it and started down the beach road to Whisky Creek to attend the annual meeting. Happy in the thought of possessing an animal the like of which had never been seen in these parts, he jogged along humming snatches of Indian love songs and maturing plans for the removal of the county seat to Pentwater.

Arriving at the hill near the place now owned by J. Bloore, he started down. It was quite steep and a long distance to the bottom and the mule stopped to deliberate. "Stop, will you?" said Flagg driving the spurs into his flanks. That mule, true to the characteristics of his race, instead of starting just elevated his posterior members and Flagg at the same time. Being on an inclined plane with its head pointing downwards, Flagg could not keep his seat, but went right out in the air, going down, down, down, his arms and legs trying to perform the offices of wings, and at last struck sand at the bottom considerably shaken up but no bones broken. Looking back he could just discern the mule disappearing over the brow of the hill. He finished the journey on foot, returned home on foot, and with a number of mill men scoured the country in search of the mule, but finally gave it up as lost. At the end of nine days, however, the mule without saddle or bridle, quietly walked into town and thenceforth was used for mill duty. The mule referred to in the above sketch is one of the mules which Mr. P. Rasmusson, of Weare, drove for a number of years.

PLAIN ENOUGH.—Lawyers are proverbially bad writers, and Grove was no exception. On one occasion, many years ago, he wrote a letter to Abijah Peck, of Hart, in relation to some matter of trifling importance and not receiving an answer at the time he expected, the circumstance passed entirely from his mind.

Peck received the letter, but was unable to decipher a single word of its contents, or discover the identity of its author. He took it home and each member of his family tried a hand at it, but failed to make out anything intelligible. Some of his neighbors hearing about it, called in and puzzled their brains over it with the same result. And as curiosity became excited, nearly every man in Hart called upon Peck and requested a perusal of the famous document, but nothing satisfactory resulted. Finally some one advised Peck to take it to a lawyer, pay him for translating it, and the mystery of its contents would be solved.

Acting upon this advice he took the letter to Grove but before giving it to him made the following inquiry:

"Mr. Grove, are you an expert at deciphering bad writing?"

"I can read anything that contains a single principle of penmanship," replied Grove.

"Then be kind enough to read that for me," said Peck, handing him the letter.

Grove took it, and after scrutinizing its contents carefully a few minutes, handed it back with the remark:

"I think I told you that I could read anything that contained a *single* principle of penmanship, but my dear sir, this letter does not contain an approximation towards a single principle of penmanship, and all that I am able to glean from its contents is that the writer is either a fool or was drunk at the time of writing it."

"Perhaps this envelope will aid you a little," said Peck despondingly.

Grove glanced at the envelope, turned red and pale by turns, and said excitedly, "Let me see the letter again. Ah! to be sure! Why, it is as plain as A B C. It is *good* writing. Any fool ought to be able to read that. That is a letter I wrote you last spring concerning the election."

TAKEN AT HIS WORD.—R. M. Montgomery, a prominent member of the Oceana County Bar in 1872, and a rising attorney, was seated in his office one day busily engaged in preparing a brief, in his great "Jarndyce vs. Jarndyce" suit, when his cogitations were interrupted by a rap at his door, and in answer to his "come in," the door opened and in stalked a fair representative of the "auld sod" who handed Montgomery a dirty paper possessing some of the essentials of a promissory note, with the inquiry:

"Air yees Misther Montgomery, the Liar?"

"If you mean Lawyer," gruffly responded Montgomery, "yes."

"Thin will ye be afther casting yir eye over this bit of paper and tell me when the intrist is due?"

"Certainly, sir," says Montgomery, "it is due on the 12th day of December next."

"And how the d—l is that, whin Misther Hartwick towld me it was due now?"

"If Mr. Hartwick told you it is due now, he was mistaken," replied Montgomery.

"And isn't Misther Hartwick a good Liar?"

"Oh yes," returned Montgomery, "he is a very good Lawyer."

"And sure and I thought so, and as ye say he is a good Liar, and as he didn't say you was one, I'll believe you and take his advice. The top of the morning to you, Misther Montgomery, good day!"

A MINISTERIAL INCIDENT.—In the early days of Pentwater's history when lumbering was the principal occupation of its residents, saloons flourished, but religious denominations had a hard struggle to even secure fair congregations on the Sabbath. The Rev. J. B. Prichard, well known to our people to-day, was one of the pioneer laborers in this behalf in Pentwater, and recognizing the difficulties determined upon a bold stroke to secure better congregations. He caused a number of handbills to be printed, stating that he would hold religious services at a place named, on certain days and requesting the people to "turn out." These handbills he posted himself in every business house in the place, and in order that none might be slighted he concluded to visit the saloons also. Stepping into a saloon which was conducted by Geo. Schmidt, he was surprised to see the number of people there gathered. Four tables with four men at each table engaged in playing a game which he "did not understand," and the bar tender busily engaged in supplying the players with drinks. Inquiring for the proprietor, Mr. Smith promptly presented himself, when he showing him one of his notices asked him if he could post it up in the room. "Yah; puts it up vare you vants it," says George. "But," says the minister, "I want it right up there," pointing to a place on the wall behind the bar, over the bottles, "and how am I going to get it there?" "Dot's right; I fix you," and Schmidt rolled out a keg of beer for him to stand on. "Dere; you shust get right up on dot. It *von't tip you over if you don't meddle mit vat is in it.*" The reverend gentleman passed through the ordeal of laboring behind the bar of a saloon on top of a beer keg, without being tipped over and was rewarded with good congregations thereafter.

A JUSTICE'S HIGH AUTHORITY—One of Hart's early business men was elected Justice of the Peace. He was a shrewd, careful business man, but had a vague conception of the law or his duties as an official. One day shortly after he had qualified, a prominent attorney with whom he was well acquainted and in whom he had the utmost confidence, appeared before him and stated to him that the duties of his office required that he should keep an open eye and whenever he detected any one violating the law should restrain or punish the party. The attorney then called his attention to a couple in the township of Ferry who were notoriously living in adultery, and asked him to issue an injunction restraining them. He finally concluded 'twas his duty to do so and the attorney made complaint setting forth the facts, and he finding a form actually issued a writ of injunction against the offending parties and insisted upon the officer serving it. The joke got out after a time, and it is said that ever after all matters of that nature were referred to M. H. Brooks, Esq., while he confined himself to the duties of his private business.

HOW THE THIEF OUTWITTED A PIONEER.—E. T. Mugford had lost an ox and vowed vengeance on the first cattle thief he caught. This was along in the sixties. Shortly after registering the above vow he attended a Good Templar's Lodge at Pentwater and returning late at night drove straight by D. L. Garver's place. The full moon shed its refulgent rays o'er hill and dale and his lonely ride caused him to ruminate on the depravity of the human race. As he arrived at the foot of the hill south of Garver's he cast his eyes to the crest and behold, the full moon as it shone through the tree tops disclosed a man leading a cow by a rope. "Ah, ha!" soliloquized Mugford, "there he comes. Not satisfied with stealing my ox he has returned and is leading away my cow. I will keep my promise and retribution I will have, providing I am the stouter." When they approached each other Mugford sprang from his buggy and with his left hand grabbed the rope while his right clutched the thief's throat. They clinched and fell to the ground with Mugford on top, and in a few seconds he had "winded" the thief. What are you leading off my cow for?" he inquired. "It is not your cow, nor never was," he replied. On taking a second look Mugford discovered his mistake. The sweat actually poured from him as he begged pardon. The victim of his onslaught explained that he lived in Riverton, Mason Co. Had a brother at Grand Haven who wrote to him that if he would come there he would give him a cow and he was driving it home. He said that when he arrived at Shelby he only had two shillings, that he purchased some crackers and cheese; some feed for his cow, rested a while, and had got this far on his road. The penitent Mugford importuned him to go home with him and have a good night's rest, but he declined, saying his wife and children would expect him. About four o'clock the next morning a man rapped on Mr. Mugford's door and on entering inquired if he had seen any one leading a cow by. He said he lived in Shelby, and some one had stolen his cow the night previous. Mr. Mugford then related his experience of a few hours previous, and the man followed on but never found his cow.

His First and Only Treat.—A. S. White, the gentlemanly and courteous manager of the Citizen's Exchange Bank at Hart, was in the early history of that village engaged in the dry goods business with Mr. O. W. Knox, under the firm name of White & Knox. Their store was on the then main street, still called Main Street, although deserted by business houses. Directly across the way Flood kept a drug store. Mr. White, although not orthodox, is a man of exemplary habits, and was never known to gamble, drink, "set 'em up," engage or take part in a questionable act. On one occasion early in the seventies Russell and Knox got the joke on White and insisted upon his treating. They bantered and bluffed until he finally relaxed and agreed to it. They went across the way to the drug store and the following took place:

White—"Jim, the boys have got it on to me and I want to treat them. Got anything good to drink?"

Flood—"No; since the crusade I hav'n't kept any liquor."

White—"Hav'n't you got some wine?"

Flood—"No, hav'n't a drop; but I'll tell you. I have something here," pointing to a row of vinegar bitters bottles, "you can see what it says on the label, 'no vile properties.' I think it is just what you want," and he winked.

White—"All right; let us have some."

A bottle was taken down, opened and Knox and Russell took a good drink and White appeared to, also. In a few minutes they were gagging and spewing the stuff and in the intervals wondering why White made no face over it. Then for the first time they realized that White had taken Flood into his confidence and put up a job on them by treating them to the vilest compound in the store.

COFFIN ENTERPRISE.—A number of years ago, before Mr. Whittington hung out his shingle as undertaker for this community, carpenters were frequently called upon to perform the duties of such, and on one occasion our old friend Pete Labonta was waited upon by a delegation of Indians, who wanted a coffin for one of their tribe who had just passed to the happy hunting grounds. Pete, nothing loth to the making of a few dollars, even out of poor Lo, took the job, and in a short time delivered to the delighted red men a beautiful black coffin ornamented with a red stripe about four inches wide around the center of the coffin. In a few days thereafter he had another order, then another and another, until they began to come in so fast, that thinking he had struck a bonanza, he abandoned all other enterprises and undoubtedly would have made his fortune out of it, had not grave suspicions been aroused about this time that there was something wrong on the reservation to occasion such a fearful mortality among the Indians. Investigation proved that the delighted red men were killing off the old and sickly merely for the purpose of burying them in style in a black coffin with a red stripe around it.

WARM MEALS.—Following close upon the removal of the county seat from Whisky Creek to Hart was the opening of the first restaurant in that place, by one Barnard Putney; which event was made public by the appearance of a modest home-made sign over the door, reading, "Warm Meals." Barnard was one of that peculiar class of individuals who seem to have been created on purpose for people to play jokes upon, and many were the "sells" the wiseacres about the Court chronicled against him, all of which he took good naturedly and apparently without any idea of retaliation.

Among those who delighted to run upon poor Barnard was L. D. Grove, one of the pioneer attorneys of the county, and who never seemed satisfied until he had played some joke upon Barnard before the visiting attorneys from Grand Rapids or Grand Haven.

One day an important suit was upon trial, and quite a delegation of outside attorneys were present. During an intermission Grove regaled them with stories of the tricks he had played upon the restaurant keeper, and finally when the hour of noon approached invited judge and attorneys over there to dine with him at his expense, promising rare sport. On entering, Grove said:

"Barney, I see you advertise 'warm meals;' bestir yourself and prepare warm meals for five."

"There's another notice you overlooked, Mr. Grove, probably," replied Barney; "I must have my pay in advance, $1.25 for five."

"All right," laughed Grove, winking to his companions, "here's your cash."

Barnard moved meekly about and seating them at the table placed before them five saucers and five bottles of pepper-sauce, saying "Help yourselves, gentlemen, you'll find these will make *warm meals.*"

It is needless to add that the attorneys enjoyed the "rare sport" and Grove never heard the last of it.

BARNEY A CANDIDATE.—After Barney's success in turning the joke upon Grove he became for a time quite a lion among the attorneys. They told him it never would do for a man of his ability and shrewdness to be engaged in such a menial occupation; that he had the natural qualifications for a first class lawyer and advised him to procure a copy of Tiffany's Justice Guide and study law. Thereafter he donned a legal air, studied Tiffany and attended all sessions of the Circuit Court with regularity. Finally in 1870, after the nominations for county offices had been made and a serious bolt in the republican party announced, some of the attorneys told Barney that if he would announce himself as an independent candidate for Sheriff in a proclamation and scatter it well throughout the county, he could be elected. Scarcely 48 hours had elapsed after receiving this information before the following proclamation appeared and was distributed by Barney in person:

"Pentwater 1870.
B. Putney for Sherif.

To the People of Oceana County:

You have read in the papers that I were going to run for Sherif, and the reason why I intended to have told you all personally. But on account of sickness in my familey I have Ben obliged to stay at home, Hoping that if this mesage should reach you that it might Explain the matter satisfactory, in april 1863 I abandoned my trade as gunsmith in ashtabula County Ohio an came to this state an Invalid tending to consumtion and after Being here three years I began to improve in health, as out door Employment and sporting in the Woods was all the medsin that I used or kneded. in 1869 I thought I wer Entirely Well and commenced Business again as gunsmith and at present I am forced to Believe that if I wer to continue the Business three Weeks Longer Without rest or out Door Employment my fate would result in a case of Confirmed Consumtion, therefore I am Forced to resort to some other Employment and having acted as constable one year has proved to me that the office ot Sherif would be the Most appropriate situation for me. I Consider my legal learning sufficient to carry me through. the Most of you know that I am capable of giving counsil and practising law you might suppose that I should resort to that practis for a Living But the question is here prematurely answered. on account of a severe chronic Dificulty of my throat Broncail tubes and organs of speech I am again cut off From Employment in that Direction. Now Friends and Strangers if I Wer a single man like I Wer one year ago and Nobody but Myself to Support I never Would ask any of you to lend a Vote to Enstall me in office. But Now the case Different I have a Wife and three Orphan children to feed, Clothe and School to which I have so far Done properly and Wish to Continue But my health having failed I have Began to have the Blews some and this is one of my ingenious tacts to Bring about Means.

Now Gentlemen Friends and Strangers as I am personaly acquainted With the most of you I feel assured that you will Believe the above Statement to be tru and worthy, and I will Further say if I was to ask you for a Bushel of Wheat you could with propriety say you had not got any to spare. But you can all spare me a Vote and not feel any loss of it, and it Will not pay your taxes.

N. B. you will be on Lection Day thronged with several influential Politicians Who will beg of you to vote for two stought able Bodied men who are now Merchants and able to do any kind of Business in any place, or live without work. But my familey Eats for supper what I Earn through the Day and Now I appeal to your Christians spirits and Consider a Word to the Wise is sufficient.

Barnard Putney."

Alas! for Barney's hopes. The great Indian trainer of Elbridge, Hervey S. Sayles, was elected.

A SLIP OF THE TONGUE.—Judge Giddings, although famed for the dignity with which he presided over the trial of cases, often destroyed the dignity of the attorneys by the flashes of wit that he sometimes indulged in.

During one of his terms of Court there was a case on trial which involved the construction of a certain statute. L. D. Grove represented the plaintiff and L. M. Hartwick the defendant. The discussion was quite animated on both sides, each party insisting with considerable warmth and volubility upon that construction most favorable to his client, when the Judge, with a comical twinkle in his eye, gave his decision, with his usual urbanity, as follows:

"Gentlemen, the issue in this case having by stipulation of the parties been narrowed to a construction of this statute, and the discussion having been quite exhausting-ive, it will take but a few minutes to dispose of the case. I shall, without any hesitancy, sustain the construction contended for by Mr. Hartwick, it appearing to me that the language employed by the Legislature to express its intention is very plain and unambiguous (with a comical glance towards Grove); *so plain that the way-faring man though a fool need not err therein.*"

The Bar were convulsed, and Grove, very red in the face, springing to his feet inquired:

"Do I understand your Honor to insinuate that *I* am a fool?"

"Oh, no," replied the Judge blandly. "By no means, Mr. Grove. That was *purely a lapsus linguæ.*"

SQUIRE WEATHERBEE—Squire Weatherbee will be remembered by the pioneers as *the Squire* of early days before whom they were wont to appear and adjust their little differences. He was a typical Yankee, tall, raw-boned, slow ot speech, methodical in his movements, and as they used to say, "terrible sot in his way." He was, however, strictly honest and detested anything like trickery or dishonesty in others. Shortly after his qualifying as Justice of the Peace he was called upon to issue a summons in trespass, which he did, giving it to the officer with minute instructions as to the manner of service. The document was duly served and returned, and on the return day L. D. Grove appeared for the Plaintiff and T. S. Gurney for the Defendant. Mr. Gurney, upon looking at the summons discovered that the damage claimed was $300 instead of $100, simply called Mr. Grove's attention to it. Mr. Grove, after examining it, stated to the Court that on account of a fatal error in the summons, he should ask to have the case discontinued. The J. P. straightened back, and putting on a severe, dignified expression, said: Mr. Grove, I want you to understand this Court drawed that ere summons, and he knows its right. Yer can't squash any suits on a summons that I drawed. We will go on with the trial, gentlemen." After considerable vigorous talk on the part of Grove coincided in by Gurney, the case was finally discontinued, but his Honor never could understand the reason.

SUPREME COURT OVER-RULED.—It was during the period of Squire

Weatherbee's reign that Charles W. Deane, the first Prosecuting Attorney of the county and who was said to be the owner of a volume of the Michigan Reports, was engaged in the trial of a case before his Honor which was hotly contested. Upon the question of the admission of a certain paper in evidence the attorneys differed as to the law and proceeded to argue the question to the Court. It was the critical point upon which Deane's case depended and after his opponent had finished he rose to his feet and delivered a speech that for forensic eloquence "capped the climax" of anything that had ever been heard in "these parts," winding up by a reference to his Mich. report and read a decision that sustained his position, and feeling that he had driven home a clincher, took his seat while a triumphant gleam from his eye shot across the table to his crestfallen antagonist. Imagine, then, his astonishment when the Squire, straightening himself back, said: "All very proper, my dear sir. The Supreme Court has a right to believe just as she d—n pleases, and I'll do the same. In this case I think the Supreme Court is wrong."

APOLOGIZED.—Many years ago two prominent attorneys of Pentwater, W. E. Ambler and R. M. Montgomery, engaged in the trial of a cause before his Honor, Ed. E. Edwards, Esq., became considerably excited over the discussion of a question of the admission of evidence, when getting pretty close together they abandoned the legitimate line of their argument and seizing one another by the shoulders, commenced waltzing about the room in a lively manner. The Court interfered at this point, and as soon as quiet was restored, intimated that an apology from each would be in order before the regular business of the Court would be resumed. Silence reigned for awhile when Montgomery, with the evidence of contrition upon his countenance, rising slowly from his seat stated that he was sorry for the part he had taken in the disgraceful scene; that upon reflection he could see where he was in the wrong, and trusted the Court would pardon him. The Court bowed serenely as Montgomery took his seat, and smiled encouragingly upon Ambler to arise and do likewise. After a few moments A. arose and said that he, too, was sorry for what had taken place, and that upon sober second thought he, too, could see where Mr. M. was in the wrong, and trusted that the Court would grant Mr. M.'s request and pardon him, as he had already done.

CHAPTER XVI.

—x—

STATISTICAL.

—x—

COUNTY OFFICERS SINCE 1855.

SHERIFF.—L. D. Eaton, '55-8; A. Rector, '56; J. Tapley, '60; Wm. Webb, '62-4-8; E. J. Reed, '66; H. S. Sayles, '70-2; O. K. White, '74; O. P. Fortner, '76; W. R. Collier, '78-'80; J. D. S. Hanson, '82-4; Jos. Tyler, '86; Wm. Cooper, '88.

CLERK AND REGISTER—H. Tower, '55; L. S. Anderson, '56; A. S. Anderson, '58; E. D. Richmond, '60-2-4-'76-8-'80-2-84; N. Crosby, '66-8; D. W. Crosby, '70; T. S. Gurney, '72-4; W. N. Sayles, Clerk, '86; W. P. Sackrider, Clerk, '88; D. C. Wickham, Register, '86-8.

TREASURER.—A. R. Wheeler, '55; H. Tower, '56; Estes Rich, '58; A. S. Anderson, '60; O. Swain, '62; W. H. Leach, '64-6; J. R. Butler, '68-'70-2-4-8-'80; H. Hoffman, '76; E. B. Gaylord, '82-4; G. Wyckoff, '86-8.

JUDGE OF PROBATE.—J. Russell, '60; C. Camp, '64; A. Crosby, '68; F. J. Russell, '72-6; D. Johnson, '80; D. Landon, '84; W. E. Ambler, '88, to fill Landon's term; W. H. Churchill, '88.

PROSECUTING ATTORNEY.—C. W. Deane, '60; L. D. Grove, '62-4-6; J. M. Rice, '68-'70; R. M. Montgomery, '72-4; A. H. Nelson, '76; W. H. Hubbard, '78; L. G. Rutherford, '80, resigned in '82; L. M. Hartwick, appointed to fill vacancy, and elected in '82; C. B. Stevens, '84-6; J. D. S. Hanson, '88.

CIRCUIT COURT COMMISSIONER.—C. W. Deane, '60; L. D. Grove, '62-'64-6; F. J. Russell, '68-'70; A. H. Nelson, '72-4; M. H. Brooks, '76-8; L. M. Hartwick, '80; C. A. Gurney, '82-4; M. H. Brooks, '86-8.

VITAL STATISTICS.

Births and deaths in Oceana County in the years 1887, 1888, 1889, from official reports by Supervisors:

1887..............Births..............283	Deaths..............104
1888.............. " 284	" 96
*1889.............. " 284	" 103
Total 3 years..............851	303

*14 towns. 2 not reported.

Births and deaths in 1889, reported:

	BIRTHS.			DEATHS.		
Pentwater...Male	17......Female	15	Male	6......Female	14
Hart............. "	12...... "	15	"	6...... "	7
Shelby.......... "	26...... "	14	"	4...... "	1
Golden.......... "	11...... "	6	"	4...... "	5
Claybanks... "	9...... "	9	"	6...... "	2
Benona.......... "	19...... "	13	"	3...... "	2
Elbridge....... "	11...... "	12	"	2...... "	1
Newfield....... "	10...... "	17	"	7...... "	6
Weare........... "	10...... "	7	"	2...... "	2
Ferry............ "	5...... "	7	"	7...... "	3
Grant .... "	7...... "	10	"	0...... "	2
Crystal........ "	11...... "	4	"	4...... "	4
Colfax.......... "	0...... "	3	"	1...... "	2
Otto .... "	3...... "	1	"	0...... "	0
Totals......151	133	52	51

POPULATION.

1850—	300	U. S. Census.
1860—	1,816	" "
1864—	2,373	" "
1870—	7,222	" "
1880—	11,699	" "
1884—	14,519	State "
1890—	18,500	Estimated from School Census.

POSTOFFICES.

Pentwater,	Shelby,	Hart,	Mears,
Grand View,	Allen Creek,	Benona,	Holstein,
Bird,	Houseman,	Claybanks,	Rothbury,
Cranston,	Stetson,	Crystal Val.,	Smith's Corners
Elbridge,	Woodburn,	Ferry,	Hesperia,
	Flower Creek.		

VOTE ON PRESIDENT AND GOVERNOR.

	President.			Governor.	
1856—	Fremont	Rep............... 82		Bingham............... 83
	Buchanan	Dem............... 21		Felch............... 21
1860—	Lincoln	Rep............... 192		Blair............... 191
	Douglass	Dem............... 158		Barry............... 159
1864—	Lincoln	Rep............... 356		Crapo............... 354
	McClellan	Dem............... 177		Fenton............... 179
1868—	Grant	Rep............... 1080		Baldwin............1079
	Seymour	Dem............... 405		Moore............... 412
1872—	Grant	Rep............... 1158		Bagley...............1159
	Greeley	D & L............... 196		Blair............... 225
	O'Connor	 51		
1876—	Hayes	Rep............... 1365		Croswell............1368
	Tilden	Dem............... 599		Webber............... 554
	Cooper	G B............... 29		
1880—	Garfield	Rep............... 1481		Jerome...............1401
	Hancock	Dem............... 482		Holloway............... 542
	Weaver	G B............... 501		Woodman............ 491
				McKeever Pro..... 25
1884—	Blaine	Rep............... 1637		Alger...............1597
	Cleveland	Dem............... 661		Begole...............1218
	Butler	G B............... 552		
	St. John	Pro............... 357		Preston............... 647
1888—	Harrison	Rep............... 1726		Luce...............1718
	Cleveland	Dem............... 1426		Burt...............1421
	Fisk	Pro............... 434		Cheney............... 443
	Streeter	U L............... 23		Mills............... 25

TEMPERATURE TABLE

showing extremes of cold and heat. Record made by B. Moore, Shelby. Table covers extreme years:

	1870				1872				1874				1876				1878			
	Coldest Day		Warmest Day		Coldest Day		Warmest Day		Coldest Day		Warmest Day		Coldest Day		Warmest Day		Coldest Day		Warmest Day	
	Date		Date		Date		Date		Date		Date		Date		Date		Date		Date	
	A	B	A	B	A	B	A	B	A	B	A	B	A	B	A	B	A	B	A	B
January......	24	2	12	34	31		5	11	31	31		11	3	52	26	2	8	42	7	8	20	33
February...	20		3	17	35	3	11	24	41	1	5	15	36	2	4	11	36	13	6	21	38
March......	3		2	30	39	5	18	25	32	14	3	3	38	19		6	6	52	24	29	7	52
April	4	21	15	59	1	15	30	58	8	9	30	31	1	10	14	49	4	29	25	37
May........	10	36	18	64	4	30	9	50	1	28	30	68	9	30	20	62	13	28	25	56
June........	8	42	29	71	5	13	30	71	2	44	28	73	5	14	11	72	9	38	24	66
July........	6	47	26	74	19	17	17	72	13	11	6	74	26	51	7	74	23	44	17	76
August.....	27	10	9	68	31	43	4	74	3	44	12	70	21	12	21	72	26	45	7	71
September..	12	10	5	68	30	10	5	71	21	36	26	66	15	37	21	61	28	35	8	72
October	29	30	27	62	23	22	21	56	19	31	31	21	27	27	30	55	28	12	16	64
November...	19	18	8	56	28	10	7	40	30	12	7	52	20	14	13	49	14	18	19	44
December....	28	0	5	36	24	9	6	42	29	6	3	34	10	12	18	34	21		9	10	32

RAIN FALL—INCHES.

	Jan.	Feb.	Mar.	Apr.	May	June	July	Aug.	Sep.	Oct.	Nov.	Dec.
1870—	1¾	0	1	3	5	6½	6	5½	6	8½	1½	1½
1871—		....	....	4	1	4½	4½	2¾	2¼	2¼	1¼	1½
1872—	....	½	....	1½	6½	4½	1¾	4½	13	1½	2¼	2¼
1873—	....	....	¾	½	3¾	9½	6	1¼	4½	2½	¼	2¾
1874—	1	¾	1¾	1	3½	3	3	1½	5	3	2¾	....
1875—		....	....	1¾	5	3	7¼	6½	3¾	5¼	¾	3¾
1876—	2½	2	¼	1½	4	6¾	6	1¾	3¾	2¾	4½	....
1877—	....	....	¾	3	3¼	6	1¾	5	3¼	9½	3	2¾
1878—	....	¾	3	5¾	4¾	4¾	2⅔	3⅔	4½	6⅔	1⅔	....

SNOW FALL—INCHES.

	Oct.	Nov.	Dec.	Jan.	Feb.	Mar.	Apr.
1870—	0	7	38	42	15	46	9
1871—	0	17	17½	41	18	4	3
1872—	2	34	34	22	17	25	34
1873—	14	51	8	23	6½	13½	4½
1874—	1	22	8	40	7	13	4
1875—	1	6	19	35	18½	14	7
1876—	1	17	28	10	21½	24½	0
1877—	0	27	64	28	0	27	1½
1878—	13	1½	5½	18	11	¾	0

A FEW ORCHARD REPORTS—1888-9.

R. V. Warner,	'88— 450	bu.	Peaches,	sold for	$ 225.00
	'89— 650	"	"	"	1300.00
B. C. Knapp,	'88— 130	"	Plums,	"	275.00
	'89— 101	"	"	"	202.00
J. B. Gebhart,	'88—2000	"	Peaches,	"	2500.00
	'89—2600	"	"	"	3000.00
C. A. Sessions,	'88— 350	"	"	"	725.00
	'89— 300	"	"	"	750.00
John Near,	'88— 500	"	"	"	565.00
	'89— 950	"	"	"	1200.00
C. A. Hawley,	'88— 650	"	"	"	900.00
	'89—1000	"	"	"	2000.00
H. S. Elliott,	'88— 197	"	"	"	397.50
	'89— 631	"	"	"	1631.24
N. B. Farnsw'th	'89— 360	"	"	"	1064.70
R. F. Ames,	'89— 500	"	"	"	1000.00
A. Tennant,	'89— 203	"	Plums,	"	400.00
S. S. Branch,	'88—1000	"	Peaches,	"	900.00
	'89—1158	"	"	"	1750.00
E. Stanhope,	'88— 683	"	"	"	785.00
	'89— 809	"	"	"	1267.35
C. F. Hale,	'88—1200	"	"	"	1800.45
	'89—1300	"	"	"	3200.00

GENERAL INDEX.

―――x―――

Anecdote	56
Agricultural Society	85
Apologized	424
Boundaries	21
Benona	24 62 148
Banks	77 95 120 121
Bull of the woods	105
Benona Lodge No. 289 F. & A. M.	164
Barney a Candidate	421
Crystal	24 158
Colfax	25 162
Claybanks	25 34 146
Circuit Court	36 38
Catholicism in Claybanks	48
Crystal Valley Lodge No. 386 I. O. O. F.	188
Coffin Enterprise	420
County Officers	425
Dog Tax	103
Deborah Lodge No. 93 D. of R.	191
Dan Landon Post No. 397	207
Early History	18
Elbridge	35 151
Ferry Township	25 156
First Settlers	26 30
Fourth of July	41
Fruit	61 95
First Mule, The	415
Few Orchard Reports, A	428
Golden	24 149
Game	29
Greenwood	35 159
Grant	161
Grand Army Posts	192
Gen'l Sill Post No. 299	203
Hart Township	39 54 140
Hart Village	63 141
Hayes, Mike	67
Hesperia	72 155
Hopkins, Judge	66
Hawley's Mill	103
Horse Thief Captured	105
Hart Improvement Company	144
" Atheonian Society	144
" Union School	144
" Chautauqua Circle	145
" Business Houses	145
Hesperia Lodge No. 346 F. & A. M.	170
" " " 334 I. O. O. F.	177
Hart Encampment No. 12 I. O. O. F.	190
How the Thief Outwitted a Pioneer	418
His First and Only Treat	419
Introductory	9
Indians	28 42 44 50
Indian Patriotism	45
Irons, A., Disappearance	109
Integrity Lodge No. 58 D. of R.	191
Indian Idea, The	414
Jail	37
Joe Hooker Post No. 26	193
John F. Reynolds Post No. 52	205
John A. Dix Post No. 9	209
Judicial	221
Justice's High Authority, A	418
Leroy	24
Lamont, Wreck of	107
Leavitt	152
Lakeside Encamp. No. 109 I. O. O. F.	190
Mud Hen	53
Minnie Corlett, Wreck of	77
Mills, Jennie, Disappearance	101
Mercury, Wreck of	106
McClure, Warren, Death of	115
Makin Murder	117
Middlesex Brick & Tile Co	127
Masonic	164
Mark Satterlee Camp No. 28 S. O. V.	208
Marvin Gibson Camp No. 60 S. O. V.	208
Ministerial Incident, A	417
Name	13
Newfield	24 154
Newspapers	40 67 103 109 121 122 125
Navel Hill	413
Otto	24 160
Organization	32
Oceana Times	40 73
Orders	73
Oceana Lodge No. 200 F. & A. M.	164
" Chapter No. 56 R. A. M.	171
" Council No. 27 R. & S. M.	172
Oddfellowship	172
Oceana Lodge No. 327 I. O. O. F.	173
Oceana Co. Veteran Association	211
Population 1890	11
Pentwater Township	31 123
Peaches	43
Pentwater Village	57 124
Pigeons	80
Peach Defalcation	85

Pentwater Titles........................ 88
"   Furniture Factory 113
"   Parks 129
"   Lodge No. 378 I. O. O. F......184
Patrons of Industry....................212
Pioneer Scrap..........................415
Plain Enough...........................416
Population.............................426
Postoffices............................426
Quinn, George P., Death of.............115
Reed................................... 25
Rector, Andrew, Shot................... 45
Removal of County Seat..............46 54
Rebellion.............................. 51
Railroad............................66 68
Ruby Lodge No. 109 D. of R.............109
R. M. Johnson Post.................138 201
Representative.........................214
Rain Fall..............................428
Surveyor General's Report.............. 19
Stony Creek............................ 34
Small Pox.............................. 75
Souvenir, Wreck of..................... 77
Scandinavian E. L. Church..............116
Shelby Township........................133

Shelby Village.........................134
"   Business Houses...............138
"   Lodge No. 344 I. O. O. F......178
Stetson Lodge No. 390 I. O. O. F.......189
Shields Post No. 68....................197
State Legislature......................216
Short and Sweet........................414
Slip of the Tongue, A..................422
Squire Weatherbee......................423
Supreme Court Over-ruled...............423
Snow Fall..............................428
Trotting Stock......................... 97
Taken at His Word......................417
Temperature Table......................427
Vote-um-Crosby.........................414
Vital Statistics.......................426
Vote on President and Governor.........427
Weare...............................39 147
Whisky................................. 42
Women's Crusade........................ 82
Wigton Lodge No. 251 F. & A. M.........166
White River Valley Lodge
        No. 86 D. of R.................192
Will B. Chandler Camp No. 114 S. O. V..210
Warm Meals.............................420

INDEX OF PORTRAITS AND SKETCHES.

——x——

Anderson, A. S.......................88 283
Ambler, W. E., Residence...............127
Abraham, C. E......................183 313
Archer, B. F.......................201 331
"   Mrs. B. F.....................332
Ambler, W. E...........................217
Abson, H...............................287
Ackerson, W. D.........................312
Ames, R. F............................ 320
Andreas, C.............................328
"   Mrs. C........................329
Avery, A. G........................... 330
Baker, T. H....................137 182 332
Benton, E. L.......................157 270
Barry, W. H....................168 199 363
Burgess, A. E......................184 365
Byrne, Olive...........................231
Brady, Andrew..........................234
"   Mrs. A........................235
Blanck, Charles........................248
Bamford, John..........................279
"   Mrs. J........................279
Bearss, A. H........................... 28
Barron, H..............................283
Bearss, J..............................287
Branch, S. S...........................291

Butler, J. R...........................308
Benjamin, D. C.........................313
Baker, M...............................316
Briggs, E. N...........................348
Bonton, J. H...........................350
Brooks, M. H...........................353
Bate, G. R.............................354
Brewster, L. C.........................393
Baker, J. W............................407
Court House.....................31 50 222
Clark, E. B....................45 128 342
Cogswell, I. H.........................103
Cahill, J. M.......................131 298
Cutler, E. H...................126 181 395
Chadwick, H. J.....................142 295
Collier, J. A..............143 173 194 375
Carr, A. L.................148 167 300
Cumming, J. F......................151 351
"   Mrs. J. F.....................381
Cater, R. E........................168 239
Cooper, Wm.........................176 300
Cramer, C. W.......................185 266
Cahill, J. V.......................143 373
Cutcheon, B. M.........................215
Crosby, D. W.......................221 291
Carpenter J............................260

Carpenter, Mrs. J 261	Haggerty, Mr. & Mrs. Isaac.............251
Collister, Thos............................269	Hanson, Mr. & Mrs. John D.......253 254
" Mrs. T......................307	" Mr. and Mrs. J. D. S.....255 256
Churchill, W. H..........................283	Hiles, Mr. & Mrs. Wm..................310
Critchett, J. H...........................294	Hurley, H.................................323
Cleveland, J..............................347	Hansen, Mr. & Mrs. Peter.........343 344
Cornell, W. H............................374	Hawley, C. A............................351
Coon E. F................................379	Houghtaling, E. S......................357
Converse, C. E..........................382	Hotchkiss, E. H.........................365
Coon, Mrs. C. E.........................390	Heim, J. M..............................375
Cleveland, G. H.........................407	Hinchen, D..............................389
Darling, Rev. A. A..................45 277	Harter, H................................391
Dean, O. H........................165 384	Hodges, H. L............................391
Dunn, W. H....................178 198 357	Harpster, H. W.........................392
Dickerman, A............................225	Hartwick, W. M.........................403
Dill, David...............................265	Imus, G. W...................131 164 321
" Mrs. D........................266	Jones T. T.....................156 204 348
Dunaw, Charles..........................273	Jenks, Ira...............................252
Davis, C. B...............................308	Jensen, Mr. & Mrs. C. M.............258
Dewey, G. E..............................358	Jackson, A..............................276
Dresser, A. Jr............................412	Johnson, C R...........................334
Eaton, L. D..........................96 238	" L. E......................337
" Mrs. L. D.....................237	Jay, C. W................................385
Eddy, G. H........................199 382	Kelly, Thos..............................325
Fleming, W. H....................149 398	Knapp, B. C.............................401
Flagg, E. B.......................165 297	Littlejohn, Judge F. J......36, 108 223
Fisher, M. O......................189 373	Lamont, Capt. Chas...............107 319
Farrell, J. G..............................252	Lewis, W. F.......................178 309
Fisher, C. W.............................315	Lewis, Amos............................220
" Jacob..........................321	Leak, John..............................274
Foster, S. D..............................342	Linsday, J. D............................301
Fincher, F. W............................351	Lewis, S. E..............................306
Ferris, M. L. and Wife..................391	Landon, T. P............................341
Giddings, Judge A. H......67 79 101 224	Lewis, C. F..............................376
Girard, M. D......................128 270	Lee, J....................................408
Gardiner, W. M...................169 267	Mugford, Mr. & Mrs. E. T..143 167 177 247
Gurney, T. S......................174 218	Myers, Geo. C....................146 277
Gurney, C. A.....................171 383	McKinnon, A. R........................169 311
Getty, G. B........................180 376	Myers, F. M......................184 331
Grant, Otto.......................186 402	Morin, Thomas.................187 349
Garver, B. S..............................282	Munson, Mr. & Mrs. John............245
Gilbert, M. A.............................286	McMillan, Wm..........................290
Gaylord, E. B............................301	Marsh, Mr. & Mrs. H. J.............299
Gardner, F. O...........................303	Moore, J. B.............................324
Gebhart, J. B............................203	Moore, A. Z.............................353
Gregory, E. P............................318	McClure, C. E..........................359
Genung, Mr. & Mrs. C. B..............335	" D. E......................360
Hoffman, H. G...........................101	Marsh, O. W............................365
Hill, D. J..........................152 398	Moore, B................................369
Hillyard, Wm. F..................154 370	Merrit, Mr. & Mrs. W. E..............395
Holmes, H. J.....................173 195 379	Matthews, W. R........................410
Harrison, J. A....................183 405	Mitchell, L. B...........................411
Hartwick, L. M...................185 345	Nielsen, Fred....................171 292
Hyde, M. F.......................197 307	Nickerson, E....................205 297
Houk, T. G..............................220	Noble, C. A.............................312
Huston, Mr. & Mrs. Adam........239 240	Newman, F. W.........................369
" Mr. & Mrs. O. E...........241	Oceana Co. Savings Bank............120
Haughey, Mr. & Mrs. W. H.....242 243	O'Hanlon, Mrs. J......................241

Olinder, Mr. & Mrs. W. A............248
Oakes, D. C.......................404
Pay-baw-me School House...........60
Palmiter, J. L....................66
Pentwater News Block..............126
Philo, J. E.......................155 302
Peck, E. O........................202 317
Phillips, Mr. & Mrs. Thos..........232 234
Popkey, F. W......................267
Pringle, A. M.....................274
Peterson, A. P....................280
Perkins, Mr. & Mrs. M. S..........336
Peck, F. L........................389
Paton, A..........................399
Ratzel, F. W......................125
Rice, Mark A......................130 326
Richards, Dave....................139
Randall, E. S.....................162 405
Richmond, E. D....................166 257
Rathbone, C. P....................179 281
Reamer, F. E......................182 387
Rutherford, L. G..................192
Russell, F. J.....................225 263
"   Mr. & Mrs. H. E...........249 250
Randall, A. C.....................256
Russell, Mr. & Mrs. Josiah........202
Rouse, Jane E.....................271
Runner, J. W......................285
"   J. M....................286
Rounds, W. A......................288
Robinson, J. W....................307
Rolph, W. and B...................326
Ross, Raymond.....................372
Rankin, D. H......................383
Rankin, D S.......................387
Richmond, Ira A...................488
Rhodes, George....................403
Sands & Maxwell's Store............91
Switzer, G. O.....................130 186 399
Shirts, W. H......................135 363
Schaner, Joseph, Residence........147
Serfling, C.......................160 289
Servis, H. J......................175 392
Stevens, C. B.....................175 396
Sackrider, W. P...................176 364
Souter, Mr. and Mrs. A. E.........181 367 368
Slater, J. H......................194 316
Sayles, H. S......................275

Sayles, W. N......................275
Spellman, S.......................230
Schaner, Mr. & Mrs. J.............327 328
Sabin, R..........................330
Shirts, E. J......................338
Southwick, R. E...................371
Sage, Mr. & Mrs. H................377 378
Stone, B. F.......................401
Scott, F. A.......................401
Stone, O. W.......................407
Smith, F..........................408
Thorp, W. E.......................142 166 193 371
Taylor, L. L., Residence..........153
Tower, Mr. & Mrs. H...............236 237
Tuttle, Mrs. W....................306
Tyler, J..........................314
Tennant, W. J.....................337
Taylor, Mr. & Mrs. L. L...........339 341
Tuller, W. H......................361
Tullar, C. H......................403
Thomas, A. L......................406
Tillotson, J. A...................409
Underhill, C. M...................188 293
Underhill, A. J...................205 268
Vaughan, Wm.......................295
Wright, J.........................135 304
Woodward, G. W....................137 198 347
Woodworth, C. A...................163 285
Wickham, D. C.....................171 195 343
White, O. K.......................179 219 259
"   Mrs. O. K....................260
Woodland, William.................180 356
Wiswell, O........................202 327
Wigton, Mrs. C....................265
Webb, William.....................271
Williamson, J.....................289
Whittington, C. R.................296
Westbrook, J......................314
Walker, F.........................319
Wright, E. A......................322
Weyant, J. A......................333
Wyckoff, G........................346
Widoe, J. F.......................355
Wanmer, R. V......................374
Wilson, Mr. & Mrs. F. W...........380
Wickham, O. F.....................400
Young, F. E.......................394

www.ingramcontent.com/pod-product-compliance
Lightning Source LLC
Chambersburg PA
CBHW020539300426
44111CB00008B/730